Uneven Social Policies

Recent decades have seen a breakthrough in the expansion of social policies in Latin America. Conditional cash transfers and health policies that are nondiscretionary, broadly targeted, and noncontributory can truly transform the lives of those excluded. Nonetheless, national policies are unevenly implemented across subnational units. Focusing on Argentina and Brazil, *Uneven Social Policies* explains why mayors and governors in decentralized countries have incentives to block national policies that have clear attribution of responsibility, like conditional cash transfers, but not policies where attribution is blurred, like health policies. Having strong state institutions that collaborate with civil society and having positive policy legacies also influence implementation patterns. The book shifts the focus of welfare state analysis away from policy development and toward the political and institutional conditions under which social policies are successfully implemented. It is based on fifteen months of field research in two provinces and four municipalities each in Argentina and Brazil, which involved over three hundred in-depth interviews with political elites and social policy recipients.

Sara Niedzwiecki is Assistant Professor of Politics at the University of California, Santa Cruz. Her research on the politics of social policy and on the territorial structure of government has been published in *Comparative Political Studies, Latin American Politics and Society, Studies in Comparative International Development, Electoral Studies, International Political Science Review*, and elsewhere. She is coauthor of *Measuring Regional Authority: A Postfunctionalist Theory of Governance* (2016).

T0381919

Uneven Social Policies

The Politics of Subnational Variation in Latin America

SARA NIEDZWIECKI

University of California, Santa Cruz

CAMBRIDGE
UNIVERSITY PRESS

University Printing House, Cambridge CB2 8BS, United Kingdom

One Liberty Plaza, 20th Floor, New York, NY 10006, USA

477 Williamstown Road, Port Melbourne, VIC 3207, Australia

314-321, 3rd Floor, Plot 3, Splendor Forum, Jasola District Centre, New Delhi - 110025, India

79 Anson Road, #06-04/06, Singapore 079906

Cambridge University Press is part of the University of Cambridge.

It furthers the University's mission by disseminating knowledge in the pursuit of education, learning and research at the highest international levels of excellence.

www.cambridge.org
Information on this title: www.cambridge.org/9781108454896
DOI: 10.1017/9781108588225

© Sara Niedzwiecki 2018

First published 2018
First paperback edition 2020

A catalogue record for this publication is available from the British Library

Library of Congress Cataloging in Publication data
NAMES: Niedzwiecki, Sara, author.
TITLE: Uneven social policies : the politics of subnational variation in Latin America / Sara Niedzwiecki, University of California, Santa Cruz.
DESCRIPTION: New York : Cambridge University Press, [2018] | Includes bibliographical references and index.
IDENTIFIERS: LCCN 2018007409 | ISBN 9781108472043 (alk. paper)
SUBJECTS: LCSH: Argentina – Social policy. | Central-local government relations – Brazil. | Latin America – Social policy. | Central-local government relations – Latin America.
CLASSIFICATION: LCC HN263.5 .N54 2018 | DDC 306.0982–dc23
LC record available at https://lccn.loc.gov/2018007409

ISBN 978-1-108-47204-3 Hardback
ISBN 978-1-108-45489-6 Paperback

Para Jeff y Uma

Contents

Figures

Tables

Acknowledgments

I started this project almost ten years ago and I have been fortunate to count on the support of many generous friends and colleagues along the way. They have enriched this work in more ways than I can express with words.

I would first like to acknowledge my graduate adviser at the University of North Carolina (UNC) at Chapel Hill, Evelyne Huber, who spent countless hours helping me improve this project. Evelyne's dedication to asking questions that matter, and questions we are passionate to know the answer to, has been a constant source of inspiration. She has provided detailed and constructive feedback on this work more times than I care to admit. I have also been privileged to find other wonderful mentors who share the same passion for understanding politics and who have provided exceptional feedback at multiple stages. Kent Eaton, Mala Htun, and Jennifer Pribble have inspired this work with their own and have provided detailed feedback to large portions of the manuscript (and multiple times).

I want to express my deepest gratitude for the intellectual support of UNC friends Santiago Anria, Juan Bogliaccini, Agustina Giraudy, Liesbet Hooghe, Gary Marks, John Stephens, and Ali Stoyan. They provided invaluable advice at key moments in this process. After graduating from UNC, I could not have asked for better colleagues at the University of New Mexico and at the University of California, Santa Cruz. The multidisciplinary writing groups at both institutions were crucial to bring this book to fruition. I have particularly benefitted from the insight provided by Eva Bertram, David Gordon, Melina Juárez, Sikina Jinnah, Kendra Koivu, Jami Nelson-Nuñez, Mark Peceny, Juan Diego Prieto, Ben Read, Roger Schoenman, Bill Stanley, and Richard Wood. In addition, senior colleagues at both institutions protected my time and provided much-needed research support for completing this book.

I also had the privilege of receiving excellent feedback on portions of this book from Kaitlin Alper, Camila Arza, Pablo Beramendi, Merike Blofield, Marissa Brookes, Ernesto Calvo, Thomas Carsey, Jennifer Cyr, Tulia Falleti,

Jonathan Hartlyn, Wendy Hunter, Robert Kaufman, Jonathan Kropko, Juan Pablo Luna, Stephan Leibfried, Germán Lodola, James Mahoney, Juliana Martinez-Franzoni, Cecilia Martinez-Gallardo, James McGuire, Alfred Montero, María Victoria Murillo, Thomas Mustillo, Rosario Queirolo, Maria Paula Saffon, David Samuels (and four anonymous reviewers of *Comparative Political Studies*), Lars Schoultz, Jim Stimson, Sondi Stachowski, Mariela Szwarcberg Daby, Milada Vachudova, and César Zucco. To all these people, I am deeply indebted.

Two anonymous reviewers at Cambridge University Press also provided detailed and constructive criticism, which has tremendously helped to improve this book. I am also grateful to Sara Doskow and to Cambridge University Press for trusting in this project. Jane Jones and Wesley Price provided helpful editorial suggestions.

Fieldwork in Argentina and Brazil would not have been possible if it had not been for the generosity of a number of people. In particular, I wish to express my humble thanks to the 148 social policy recipients who agreed to be interviewed. Their stories were a constant reminder of the importance of studying social policies. Too many politicians, officials, and academics facilitated my access to interviews and quantitative data to list them here. I would like to especially thank Alejandro Bonvecchi, André Borges, Soraya Cortés, Olivio Dutra, Sebastián Etchemendy, Carlos Gervasoni, Lucas González, Luciana Gutztat, Diego Leiva, Telassim Lewandowski, María Izabel Mallmann, Fernando Nuñez, Bruno Camara Pinto, Martín Sabignoso, Luciana Santos Servo, Catalina Smulovitz, Alberto Rodriguez Saá, Cristiani Vieira Machado, and professors at Universidad Torcuato di Tella and Pontifícia Universidade do Rio Grande do Sul, where I had institutional affiliation.

A number of outstanding research assistants provided much-needed support during and after field research: Nicoletta Lumaldo, David Nunnally, Sofía Elverdín, Fiorella Vera-Adrianzén, Carlos Contreras Vidal, Rizwan Asghar, Vladimir L'Ouverture, Facundo Ibarlucia, and Hernán Silva. Their hard work allowed me to collect quantitative data and conduct archival research. They made it possible for me to engage in a mixed methods strategy.

Extensive field research for this project was possible thanks to the generous funding from the European Research Council Advanced Grant #249543 "Causes and Consequences of Multilevel Governance." I also received financial support from UNC's Uhlman Summer Fellowship Award, the Pre-Dissertation Field Research Grant from the Institute for the Study of the Americas, and the Graduate School's Off-Campus Dissertation, Summer Research Fellowship, and Dissertation Completion Fellowship. The coding of political alignments in Argentina was possible thanks to funding from Fondo para la Investigación Científica y Tecnológica (FONCyT) PICT 2427–2012 from the Ministerio de Ciencia, Tecnología e Innovación Productiva, and the team of researchers I co-coordinated with Nicolás Cherny, Carlos Freytes, and Gerardo Scherlis. The Watson Institute for International and Public Affairs at

Brown University hosted me for a summer of intensive writing, and I would like to particularly acknowledge the generosity of Peter Evans, Patrick Heller, Dietrich Ruschmeyer, Richard Snyder, and Andrew Schrank.

Finally, I am particularly thankful to my family, who has filled our dinner tables with political discussions since as long as I can remember. My mother's support to my career has never waned, even when it took me away from home in Argentina. My father was the first to make me interested in politics and my brothers, Pablo and Fede, helped to keep me grounded. I would also like to thank the Erbig Family, and especially Karen, Jeff, Kerri, and Tony, for making the United States my other home.

As I was finishing this book, my daughter was born. Uma has illuminated every aspect of my life, and I thank her for making me into the happiest version of myself. Last, but certainly not least, I would like to thank my partner Jeff Erbig. Jeff has been my pillar and my home. He has helped me find coherence in my thoughts, challenged me to improve my work, and provided much-needed advice at key moments in this journey. The last couple of months, Jeff took care of Uma almost exclusively to make sure I could finally submit the manuscript. Without his emotional and intellectual support, this book would have never seen the light of day. For his generosity, love, and commitment to equality, I will always be thankful. To him and to Uma, I dedicate this book.

Acronyms

ACA	Patient Protection and Affordable Care Act
ANSES	Administración Nacional de la Seguridad Social (National Social Security Administration)
AUH	Asignación Universal por Hijo (Universal Child Allowance)
BF	Bolsa Família (Family Allowance)
CABA	Ciudad Autónoma de Buenos Aires (Autonomous City of Buenos Aires)
CAPS	Centro de Atención Primaria de la Salud (Primary Health Center)
CCT	Conditional Cash Transfer
CIC	Centro de Integración Comunitaria (Community Center)
CMAS	Conselho Municipal de Assistência Social (Municipal Council of Social Assistance)
CORAS	Conselho Regional de Assistência Social (Regional Councils of Social Assistance)
CRAS	Centro de Referência da Assistência Social (Reference Center of Social Assistance)
ESF	Estratégia Saúde da Família (Family Health Strategy)
EPH	Encuesta Permanente de Hogares (Permanent Household Survey)
FASC	Fundação de Assistência Social e Cidadanía (Social Assistance and Citizen Foundation)
FEDEM	Federación de Entidades No Gubernamentales de Niñez y Adolescencia (Federation of NGOs for Children and Teenagers)
FUNDEC	Fundação Municipal de Desenvolvimento Comunitário (Municipal Foundation for Community Development)
FPE	Fundo de Participação dos Estados (State Participation Fund)
FPV	Frente para la Victoria (Front for Victory)
GDP	Gross Domestic Product

ICMS	Imposto sobre Circulação de Mercadorias e Prestação de Serviços (Tax on Goods and Services)
IGD	Índice de Gestão Descentralizada (Index of Decentralized Management)
INDEC	Instituto Nacional de Estadísticas y Censos (National Statistics and Census Institute)
IPEA	Instituto de Pesquisa Econômica Aplicada (Institute for Applied Economic Research)
IPTU	Imposto Sobre a Propriedade Predial e Territorial Urbana (Real Estate Tax)
ISS	Imposto Sobre Serviços (Tax on Services)
MDS	Ministério do Desenvolvimento Social e Combate à Fome (Ministry of Social Development and the Fight Against Hunger)
PAN	Partido Acción Nacional (National Action Party)
PCSE	Panel-Corrected Standard Errors
PDT	Partido Democrático Trabalhista (Democratic Labor Party)
PETI	Programa de Erradicação do Trabalho Infantil (Child Labor Eradication Program)
PFL	Partido do Frente Liberal (Liberal Front Party)
PIS	Plan de Inclusión Social (Social Inclusion Program)
PJ	Partido Justicialista (Peronist Party)
PJJHD	Plan Jefes y Jefas de Hogar Desocupados (Unemployed Heads of Households Program)
PMAQ	Programa Nacional de Melhoria do Acesso e da Qualidade da Atenção Básica (National Program for the Improvement of Access to and Quality of Primary Health Care)
PMDB	Partido do Movimento Democrático Brasileiro (Brazilian Democratic Movement Party)
PN	Plan Nacer (Birth Plan)
PP	Partido Progresista (Progressive Party)
PPS	Partido Popular Socialista (Popular Socialist Party)
PRI	Partido Revolucionario Institucional (Institutional Revolutionary Party)
PRD	Partido de la Revolución Democrática (Party of the Democratic Revolution)
PROMIN	Programa Materno Infantil y Nutrición (Maternal and Child Nutrition Program)
PSDB	Partido da Social Democracia Brasileira (Brazilian Social Democratic Party)
PT	Partido dos Trabalhadores (Workers' Party)
PTB	Partido Trabalhista Brasileiro (Brazilian Workers' Party)
RAI	Regional Authority Index
RS	Rio Grande do Sul

SENARC	Secretaria Nacional de Renda de Cidadania (National Secretariat of Citizen Income)
SUAS	Sistema Único de Assistência Social (Unified Social Assistance System)
SUS	Sistema Único de Saúde (Unified Health System)
UBS	Unidades Básicas Tradicionais (Traditional Basic Health Units)
UCR	Unión Cívica Radical (Radical Party)
UMAS	Unidades Municipais de Assistência Social (Municipal Units for Social Assistance)
USF	Unidade Saúde da Família (Family Health Facility)

Politics of Social Policy in Decentralized Countries

In 2009, the Argentine government launched a conditional cash transfer (CCT) program for impoverished families named *Asignación Universal por Hijo* (Universal Child Allowance). Seeing the program as an unwelcome federal imposition, the governor of San Luis obstructed its implementation, executing his own provincial program to compete with the federal one. In the words of the province's then governor, "In the past we suffered the Washington Consensus, now we suffer the Buenos Aires Consensus, and San Luis does not follow it … We don't accept national policies because [the federal government uses] them politically" (Interview Alberto Rodríguez Saá).[1] Similarly, when the Brazilian government launched the CCT *Bolsa Família* (Family Allowance) in 2003, the state of Goiás hindered its implementation, promoting its own state cash transfer instead. Despite this obstructionism, San Luis and Goiás welcomed the federal government's health policies and even invested state resources in their success. Other states and provinces worked to support both federal CCTs *and* health policies, partly by developing complementary subnational policies.

Subnational governments react differently to national policies.[2] While some engage in activities to enhance the implementation of national policies, others actively hinder them. The same subnational government can react differently to different national policies. This poses the first puzzle of the book: Why do *some* subnational governments reject *some* (and not all) national policies that could benefit their inhabitants? In addition, the same policies encounter different contexts when implemented across the country. In particular, capabilities and

---

[1] Throughout the book, all direct quotations from personal interviews and secondary sources in Spanish and Portuguese have been translated by the author.

[2] "Subnational" refers to both intermediate and local territorial levels of government. I use the terms "provinces" to refer to intermediate levels of government and "municipalities" to refer to the local level, unless I am referring to the specific denomination in a country (for instance, "states" in Brazil or in the United States).

legacies vary within countries. What role do state capacity and previous policies play in understanding the uneven implementation of national policies? This book, *Uneven Social Policies: The Politics of Subnational Variation in Latin America*, seeks to uncover the conditions under which national policies are more successfully implemented across subnational units in decentralized countries.

In decentralized countries, individuals receive social protection from both national and subnational governments. Provinces in Australia, Austria, Belgium, Bolivia, Canada, Indonesia, Italy, Mexico, Spain, Switzerland, and the United States have the authority to affect the implementation of national policies.[3] The Federal District of Mexico City, for instance, has criticized the national CCT *Oportunidades* (Opportunities) program, advocating an alternative approach. To establish its own party's signature on social policy, Mexico City enacted the Law of Social Development in 2000 and dedicated nearly 20 percent of its municipal budget to the law's three main social programs. Partly as a result of these policies, coverage of the national CCT is low in Mexico City (Luccisano and Macdonald 2014). The Affordable Care Act in the United States is another clear example of the role of states in national policy implementation. On July 9, 2012, Texas Governor Rick Perry declared that his state would fight the federal health reform, commonly called Obamacare, by not expanding Medicaid or creating an insurance exchange. The governor called the health policy "brazen intrusions into the sovereignty of our state ... [that would] make Texas a mere appendage of the federal government when it comes to health care" (Fernandez, July 09, 2012). By 2016, twenty states had not expanded Medicaid and thirty-four had not developed health exchanges. In addition, nearly half of state legislatures had issued hundreds of bills and resolutions to hinder the health reform (Cauchi 2016).[4]

These examples show that multiple levels of authority mediate the process through which policies on paper become realities for citizens. This book examines the implementation of CCTs and health policies across Argentina and Brazil. I conducted 235 interviews with politicians and 148 with policy recipients in two provinces and four municipalities in each country. These initiatives are representative of recent social policy expansions in Latin America. Policies not associated with work contributions became more broadly targeted and their benefits more generous after a commodity boom in 2000 that allowed for a departure from retrenchment strategies. In addition, these policies follow strict rules for implementation as the receipt of the benefit is not contingent on political support. Those who receive the policy are not pressured to vote for the incumbent or participate in political rallies. These broadly targeted and patronage-free policies have the

---

[3] For a description of regional authority in these countries, see Hooghe et al. (2016).
[4] Medicaid.gov http://medicaid.gov/Medicaid-CHIP-Program-Information/By-State/By-State.html Accessed June 23, 2016.

potential to reduce poverty and inequality while improving human capital development. In order to promote the well-being of a given population, social policies need to reach it first. Yet in reality, national policies are only partially implemented in subnational units. As a result, their transformative potential has been limited.

While a considerable literature has focused on the development of welfare states and the challenges of decentralization, far fewer scholars have studied variation in the actual implementation of policies. This is paramount because it connects the design of policies to their socioeconomic outcomes. Existing approaches shed light on the reasons behind policy choices but are less equipped to explain why some policies are implemented better than others, why this variation is particularly relevant *within* countries, and why some policies deliver votes to incumbent governments while others do not. On the latter, while there are a number of studies on the role of clientelistic distribution of policies, it is crucial to analyze a less studied topic – the political determinants of nondiscretionary policy implementation.

The main contribution of *Uneven Social Policies* is to account for variation in social policy implementation through a combination of political motivations and capacities across multiple territorial levels within countries. It argues that successful policy implementation depends on having positive policy legacies and a competent state capable of delivering goods and services. At the same time, policy implementation also hinges on a political calculation about whether implementation serves politicians' electoral interests. For the latter, it makes an original connection between policies with clear national attribution of responsibility and the incentives facing opposition subnational governments to hinder such policies. The main implication is that to be successfully implemented, social policies should avoid clear attribution of responsibility. While claiming credit may increase the popularity of a leader and her party, it decreases the chances that the policy will succeed in opposition subnational units.

CCTs, HEALTH POLICIES, AND WHY THEY MATTER

This book identifies the principal factors that shape the successful implementation of national social policies by studying the main CCTs and primary health care policies in Argentina and Brazil. These policies are representative of the expansion of welfare states in much of Latin America. During the first decade of the twenty-first century, candidates from left parties were elected to the presidency throughout the region. Aided by the 2003–2007 commodity export boom, these governments were able to move away from retrenchment policies and govern on a redistributive platform (Levitsky and Roberts 2011, 2). This development has been particularly salient in the most advanced welfare states of Argentina, Brazil, Chile,

Costa Rica, and Uruguay, all of which introduced more broadly targeted social policies (Huber and Stephens 2012; Pribble 2013; Martínez-Franzoni and Sánchez-Ancochea 2016).

Perhaps the most visible, and internationally acclaimed, social policy innovation is the implementation of broadly targeted CCTs.[5] For the first time, CCTs in the region target a high percentage of the population living in poverty and, importantly, are implemented in a nondiscretionary manner. In other words, most of these programs have been free from political intermediaries and clientelistic machines, and therefore those who most need the transfers are those receiving it, independently of their political connections. A broker in a municipality in Argentina put it in the following terms: "With Plan Trabajar [discretionary national cash transfer in the 1990s] people were required to engage in politics ... But not now; now beneficiaries are required to go to school and have health check-ups" (Interview Argentina #51). This difference is key. There can be gaps in policy implementation due to the action of clientelistic machines. In these cases, policies are allocated discretionally, benefitting those affiliated with the party of the local broker, and recipients are asked to participate in political rallies in order to maintain their benefit. Additionally, subnational governments controlled by opposition parties receive fewer benefits from federal policies due to their party affiliation. These topics have been broadly studied (e.g., Shady 2000; Giraudy 2007; Kitschelt and Wilkinson 2007; Magaloni, Diaz-Cayeros, and Estévez 2007; Stokes et al. 2013; Calvo and Murillo 2014; Weitz-Shapiro 2014; and Szwarcberg 2015). However, nondiscretionary social policies can also be unevenly implemented as a result of politics in the territory. This topic has received much less attention. Given their potential for social transformation, the uneven implementation of nondiscretionary social policies deserves to be further studied.

Oportunidades in Mexico emerged as the pioneer patronage-free CCT in the early 1990s. Since then, these policies have spread to virtually every country in Latin America. In general, these cash transfers are conditioned upon the recipient's use of particular services aimed at reaching educational and/or health objectives. Bolsa Família in Brazil and Asignación Universal por Hijo in Argentina share similar characteristics to other CCTs. They are targeted at individuals or families living in poverty. Recipients withdraw funds monthly through an ATM card and after meeting a number of conditions aimed at human capital development. The conditions in health care include periodic check-ups and vaccinations for children and pregnant women. Education requirements generally include school enrollment and regular attendance. For these characteristics, CCTs improve the well-being and opportunities of those in need.

---

[5] I refer to CCTs as "broadly targeted" and not "universal" policies because they are means-tested and therefore not universal like their Scandinavian counterparts.

The most immediate effect of CCTs is the reduction in the levels of poverty and extreme poverty (Handa and Davis 2006, 518). In addition, the CCTs in Brazil and Mexico seem to be responsible for more than 20 percent of the inequality decline there, while the Chilean CCT accounts for 15 percent of the national reduction (Soares et al. 2009). These policies also increase school enrollment and attendance while decreasing child labor. This is partly achieved through relaxing income constraints by increasing households' monthly income, thus allowing families to send their children to school instead of work (Skoufias and Parker 2001; Behrman and Parker 2010; Filmer and Schady 2011; Ham 2014). CCTs have also increased the use of preventive health services, particularly for children, which has contributed to significant reductions in the access gap between rich and poor (Fiszbein and Schady 2009, 155). In addition, since most cash transfers are given to the mother rather than to the father, they have the potential to increase the bargaining power of women in the household (Cruces, Epele, and Guardia 2008).[6] They also have the potential to protect recipients from exploitative jobs. A poor farmer in the province of Mendoza in Argentina remembered that since the national CCT had been implemented, the landlord found it almost impossible to find people to work for him in exchange for a small percentage of the production of red peppers (Interview Argentina #13). This small transfer increases the bargaining power of recipients, giving them more ability to reject unpaid or low-quality jobs.

The main critics of CCTs argue that recipients become dependent on them and therefore have fewer incentives to look for a job in the formal labor market. Empirical research on the relationship between CCTs and labor demand has shown either inconclusive or insignificant results (Medeiros, Britto, and Soares 2008; Garganta 2011; Bertranou and Maurizio 2012, 5; Soares 2012, 23–25; Alzúa, Cruces, and Ripani 2013). CCTs have no (clear) effect on the beneficiary's decision to look for a job. I asked thirty-nine Bolsa Família recipients whether, if they had the option, they would choose to work in the formal labor market (*cartera assinada)* or to stay in the welfare policy – 87 percent (34) said they would choose the formal labor market. Some of the justifications for choosing the formal labor market over Bolsa Família were that "in the formal labor market you earn more money and you access all your rights, such as vacation and unemployment; it is also more stable" (Interview Brazil #27), "it would give me more security, I could get sick without fearing losing my job" (Interview Brazil #43), or "Bolsa Família is not enough for supporting four children, and I do not like being unemployed" (Interview Brazil #20). Contrary to the idea that social policy recipients are comfortable with social assistance and do not choose to seek a job in the formal labor

---

[6] CCTs have also been criticized for being based on, and furthering, maternalist assumptions and gender roles (Molyneux 2006).

market, these interviews suggest that policy recipients would work if offered a good quality job, with adequate salary and working conditions.

Latin American countries have also strengthened their public health systems, with emphasis on preventive rather than curative health care. Chile and Uruguay, in particular, have made significant progress in this area (Huber and Stephens 2012; Pribble 2013). In Brazil, the Worker's Party (*Partido dos Trabalhadores,* PT) increased the funding and the actual coverage of the primary health policy *Estratégia Saúde da Família* (Family Health Strategy). This policy is truly universal: it aims at covering the entire population through health teams in the territory that provide vaccines, general check-ups, and primary health assistance. The challenge has been to move from the goal of universality to actual universal access through building more primary health units across the territory and reaching out to those who cannot access health-care facilities. In Argentina, *Plan Nacer* (Birth Plan) also aims at increasing the actual take-up rate of health provision. The policy reimburses hospitals and clinics for services provided to uninsured women, children, and teenagers, increasing the resources received by primary health providers.

The emphasis on primary health care has produced significant results for human well-being both in Latin America and in other developing regions. Most importantly, good quality, affordable, and accessible primary health care decreases infant mortality rates. This is achieved through preventive actions such as early pregnancy, neonatal, and infant check-ups both at the health center and in the house of the patient (McGuire 2010b). Avoidance of early death, as McGuire (2010b) argues, is necessary for anything else we might want to achieve, and high levels of infant mortality tend to be associated with other sorts of deprivations. Good, free primary health care also promotes social equality by narrowing the gap between provision in the public and private sectors. The better the quality of provision in the public system, the higher the possibility that the middle class may choose to also attend public health clinics for preventive health care and, therefore, the higher the pressure to improve the service. Such improvement is seen not only in the quality of doctors and other professionals but also in the physical condition of the building, the waiting time, and the availability of medicine and medical records for everyone.

Although individual policies cannot counteract the effect of economic cycles, a battery of noncontributory policies can act as a safety net against social and economic risks and therefore have a more sustainable effect on the well-being of the population. By contrast, a failure to cover the most basic needs of the population can hinder a government's legitimacy and the full development of citizenship rights (Marshall 1950; Singh 2015, 14). By providing basic income and access to good quality social services, these policies contribute to developing a social protection floor (Bertranou 2010, 10). They have been referred to as "basic universal" policies. To reach this category, policies should guarantee basic welfare, and they should be of good quality, broadly targeted, and financially sustainable. Their administration should be transparent rather than discretionary

(Filgueira et al. 2005; Molina 2006; Huber and Stephens 2012; Pribble 2013). The more universal social assistance and services are, the more they can promote social inclusion and the development of human capital.

This is particularly important in Latin America, where the levels of poverty and inequality are high, in spite of recent improvements. Measured by the international poverty line of $2 a day, in 2011 there were 76.6 million people (13 percent) living in poverty in Latin America (World Bank 2015). In addition, Latin America is the most unequal region in the world. In the late 1990s, it exhibited a Gini coefficient of 0.53. By 2010, the Gini coefficient fell to 0.50, and this decline is higher than the increase in inequality in the 1990s. However, the levels of inequality are still higher than in the rest of the world. In the mid-2000s, Latin America was 65 percent more unequal than the OECD countries, 36 percent more unequal than East Asia and the Pacific, and 18 percent more unequal than Sub-Saharan Africa (Lustig 2009; Lustig, Lopez-Calva, and Ortiz-Juarez 2013). By 2010, Argentina, Venezuela, and Uruguay were among the least unequal countries in the region, with Gini coefficients of 0.39, 0.44, and 0.45, respectively. Bolivia and Honduras were among the most unequal countries with Gini coefficients of 0.56 and 0.67, respectively. Brazil reached worldwide records of inequality, when its Gini coefficient reached 0.63 in the 1970s and 1980s, and it has progressively decreased since 1998, reaching 0.54 in 2009 (Lustig, Lopez-Calva, and Ortiz-Juarez 2013). Finally, most jobs in Latin America are in the informal sector, meaning that most people do not have access to social benefits through work contributions (International Labour Organization 2016). In the context of these high levels of poverty, inequality, and informality, the study of noncontributory and nondiscretionary schemes is crucial for understanding and responding to the more pressing needs of the population.

SUBNATIONAL VARIATION IN SOCIAL POLICY IMPLEMENTATION

Noncontributory social policies fulfill one of the basic responsibilities of a democratic government as understood by most of the world – the provision of welfare to the most vulnerable segments of the population. In order to fulfill this basic responsibility, policies actually need to reach the targeted population. Yet in reality, policies are implemented unevenly across subnational units. To put it differently, national policies are implemented in some subnational units only partially. This partial implementation is not because they are distributed clientelistically through the targeting of some recipients over others for electoral gains. These policies are implemented following strict criteria. And yet they are unevenly implemented. As a result, the transformative potential of noncontributory social policies on the degree of poverty, inequality, and human capital development has been limited.

Figures 1.1–1.4 represent within-country variation in the implementation of the national social policies analyzed in this book. They show coverage of CCTs and health policies (i.e., actual number of people receiving the program) as

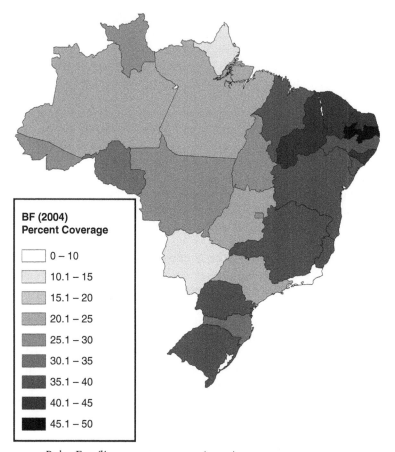

FIGURE 1.1 Bolsa Família percent coverage (2004)
Source: Brasil. Ministério do Desenvolvimento Social e Combate à Fome (2015).

a percentage of the targeted population in the first year of available data for all states and provinces.[7] The CCT Bolsa Família in Brazil (Figure 1.1) covered almost half of the targeted population in the Northeastern states of Piuaí, Ceará, Río Grande do Norte, Paraíba, and Alagoas in 2004, the first year of available data for all states. In the states of Río de Janiero, Amapá, and Mato Grosso do Sul the CCT reached less than 15 percent of the targeted population, and close to 20 percent in the states of Amazonas, Goiás, Pará, and São Paulo. Its coverage ranges from a minimum of 1 percent to a maximum of more than 90 percent from 2004 to 2015. The CCT Asignación Universal por Hijo in Argentina (Figure 1.3) reached all poor families the first year it was implemented in the provinces of Santa Cruz and La Pampa (the darkest two

---

[7] For a description of the dependent variable, targeted coverage across time, see Chapter 3.

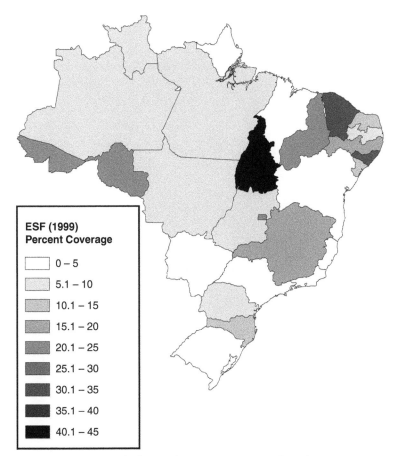

FIGURE 1.2 Estratégia Saúde da Família percent coverage (1999)
Source: Brasil. Ministério da Saúde Sistema de Informação de Atenção Básica (2015).

provinces in the map), while in the province of San Luis (the lightest in the middle of the country) it reached fewer than 10 percent. There is wide variation in the implementation of this CCT across provinces, ranging from fewer than 10 percent to more than 100 percent.[8] As a result, some citizens living in poverty in the low-coverage states and provinces are deprived of potentially transformative CCTs.

This variation in implementation levels is also present in health services. The primary health policy in Brazil, Estratégia Saúde da Família (Figure 1.2) had a particularly slow start. For the first year in which there is available data for all states, eight states had covered less than 5 percent of the targeted population. Alagoas, Ceará, and Tocantins, conversely, were among the most

---

[8] Percent coverage is higher than 100 because population living below the poverty line is under-estimated by official figures since 2007 and can therefore be lower than coverage.

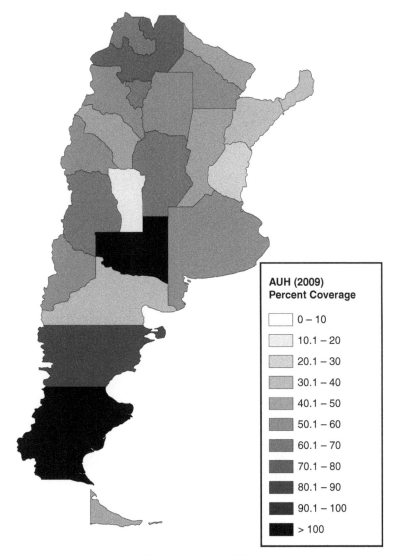

FIGURE 1.3 Argentina. Asignación universal por Hijo percent coverage (2009)
Sources: Anses (2015) and Argentina. Ministerio de Economía y Finanzas Públicas (2014).

successful with coverage between 30 and 40 percent of the population. The average standard deviation of this variable through 2015 is around 25 percent, and it covers almost the full possible range of values across time (0–98 percent). In Argentina, the implementation of health policy Plan Nacer (Figure 1.4) by 2010 had been more successful in the Northern provinces of Tucumán, Chaco, Jujuy, Corrientes, and Misiones (which started implementing

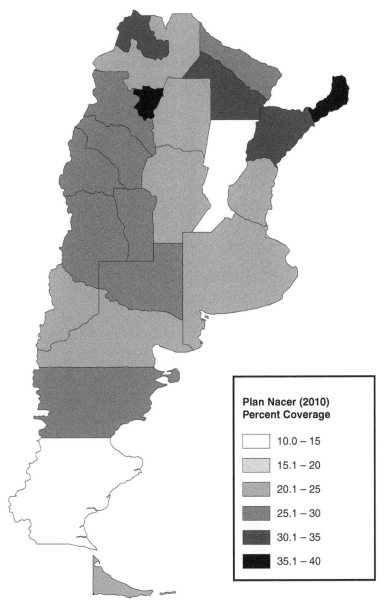

FIGURE 1.4 Argentina. Plan Nacer percent coverage (2010)
Source: Ministerio de Salud de la Nación (2015).

the policy years earlier) than in the provinces of Santa Cruz and Santa Fe (which are white in the map). The coverage of Plan Nacer has high variation, reaching a minimum value of close to 0 and a maximum value of 38 percent.

This high level of subnational variation in the implementation of national social policies is the focus of *Uneven Social Policies*. Simply put, access to national safety nets varies based on the place of residency. Uneven implementation is particularly acute in decentralized countries. Since their transitions to democracy in the 1980s, Argentina and Brazil have been among the most decentralized countries in the world, which means that subnational levels of government have fiscal, policy, and political authority in their own territory and in the country as a whole (Hooghe et al. 2016). This authority provides them with the tools to shape national policies in their implementation phase. While some provinces and municipalities engage in activities to enhance the implementation of national policies, others actively hinder their implementation. Besides their actions, policy implementation is shaped by structural factors, including institutional capacity and policy legacies.

THE ARGUMENT IN BRIEF

Attribution of Responsibility and Political Alignments

Politicians seek to maximize policies that increase their popularity and therefore their electoral chances. Which policies help them win elections? One of the main arguments of this book is that there are two kinds of social policies: those that clearly "belong" to the national government, meaning that attribution of responsibility is clear, and those in which attribution of responsibility is fuzzier.[9] Only the former can produce electoral dividends, because clear attribution of responsibility is necessary for voters to reward the national government. The potential for attribution of responsibility differentiates cash transfers from social services. Transfers are clearly palpable instruments for their beneficiaries: the provider either distributes the cash directly or its logo appears on the ATM card that recipients use to withdraw such funds. As a result, attribution of responsibility tends not to be disputed. For Bolsa Família, the Brazilian Electoral Panel Study project conducted around 4,600 interviews throughout 2010, an election year, and found that six months before the presidential election 76 percent of respondents identified the federal government as responsible for the program (Zucco 2013, 814). In Argentina, a survey of 2,200 respondents showed that almost 90 percent identified the National Social Security Administration (*Administración Nacional de la Seguridad Social* or Anses) as responsible for CCT Asignación Universal por Hijo (Deloitte and Anses 2010). For Mexico, a nationally representative survey of 3,767 respondents showed that almost 75 percent attributed the main CCT to the federal government or the president (Schober 2015, 21).

---

[9] Throughout this book, every time I use the term "attribution of responsibility," it refers to attribution of "national" responsibility unless otherwise stated.

In Latin America, CCTs with clear attribution of responsibility have provided electoral advantages to incumbent presidents. In the particular case of Mexico, the national CCT has been responsible for an estimated 10 percent increase in the votes of the presidential incumbent in the 2000 elections (De La O 2015, 135). Similar electoral effects have been found for CCTs in Uruguay (Queirolo 2010; Manacorda, Miguel, and Vigorito 2011) and Brazil (Hunter and Power 2007; Zucco 2008, 2013). In the latter, the importance of CCTs for electoral outcomes explains why former president Luiz Inácio Lula da Silva changed the name of his predecessor's flagship program (*Bolsa Escola*, School Grant) to Bolsa Família. This change in name made credit claiming easier (Melo 2008) and fueled not only his overwhelming reelection victory in 2006 but also the election of his chosen successor in 2010.

Attribution of responsibility is less clear for social services, especially when their provision is public and universal. A policy that aims at improving the quality of health and education, for instance, faces the problem of lack of visibility because the good called "quality" is not as tangible as cash. In particular, citizens have a hard time verifying whether the promises of better services have been met (Melo 2008, 182). In addition, providers (and not users) are the direct recipients of the funds, and therefore it is more challenging for voters to identify responsibility. As a result, attribution of responsibility tends to be blurred in social services so citizens do not know whom to reward in elections. In fact, the Argentine National Ministry of Health acknowledged the difficulty of measuring primary health policy Plan Nacer users' satisfaction because recipients do not identify receiving a policy at all. Recognizing that a desirable outcome (such as having access to better quality primary care) comes from a particular policy is necessary for attributing credit. The lack of visibility of Plan Nacer made the Ministry of Health measure users' satisfaction with the policy by observing changes in satisfaction with the overall public health system in the places where the policy has been implemented (Ministerio de Salud de la Nación 2013, 6).

In this book, I argue that for policies in which national attribution of responsibility is not clear, subnational leaders will be able to claim credit for policy success regardless of their alignment with the national government. At the very least, the opposition will not gain electorally, so all governors and mayors will want these to be implemented successfully.[10] In contrast, for policies with clear attribution of responsibility, both the national government and subnational leaders who are aligned with the president can potentially gain electorally from the successful implementation of these policies. For such policies, nonaligned governors will obstruct policy implementation, while aligned governors and mayors will facilitate it.

---

[10] I use the term "governor" and "mayor" to refer to the executives that head intermediate (e.g., provinces) and local (e.g., municipalities) subnational governments, respectively.

Table 1.1 shows all four possible combinations of attribution of responsibility and political alignments, their effect on policy implementation, and the cases included in this book. A "case" in this book is the combination between a state, province, or municipality and a social policy. By selecting policies with clear and blurred attribution of responsibility and subnational units aligned and in opposition to the national government, I include all possible combinations of one of the main arguments of this book.

One way to hinder national policies is through directly competing with them using subnational policies as tools. In many decentralized countries, subnational levels of government have the authority to design and implement policies of their own. These policies can be put at the service of the national policy or in direct competition against it. Subnational governments that lack the resources to enact policies that compete against national ones can instead affect the policy by omission, refusing to advance it in spite of their proximity to potential recipients. Opposition governors and mayors can also obstruct national policies through mounting bureaucratic obstacles. Refusing to share the list of beneficiaries of preexisting subnational policies is an example of such obstacles, since that makes it more challenging for the national government to reach a potential target population or to automatically check for incompatibilities, in the case that the two policies are not compatible by design.

This means that policy-makers face a dilemma: whether to design policies with clear attribution of responsibility or to promote even implementation of potentially transformative national policies. If the aim is the latter, and they want to implement CCTs, they can choose to blur attribution of responsibility. After almost a decade of implementation of Bolsa Família, this policy started losing its clear attribution of responsibility both due to the passing of time and an active strategy of the federal government. On the latter, the Brazilian federal government proposed including the logo of the state or municipality on the ATM card that recipients use every month to withdraw the funds. This blurred attribution of responsibility. In exchange for sharing the credit, subnational governments had to develop programs or use existing programs to complement Bolsa Família. These pacts have not been completely successful in terms of durability and scope; however, more states are slowly signing up. In mid-2012, eleven states had signed these agreements, many of which had opposition governors. By expanding attribution of responsibility, the federal government has enhanced the implementation of Bolsa Família. However, this smoother implementation of Bolsa Família is very recent and it is in part related to the fact that policies start losing attribution of responsibility the longer they have been in place. As time goes by, national and subnational governments change and recipients start forgetting where the policy came from in the first place. That is why subnational resistance to national policies is more evident when policies are first implemented.

It should be noted that Table 1.1 also exhibits two rows in which political alignments are irrelevant for predicting variation in policy implementation.

TABLE 1.1 *Combination of attribution of responsibility and political alignments*

Clear attribution of responsibility	Politically aligned	Effect of political alignments on implementation	Cases
Yes	Yes	Positive	**Argentina – Asignación Universal por Hijo** Province of Mendoza Municipality of Las Heras, Mendoza Municipality of San Luis, San Luis **Brazil – Bolsa Família** State of Rio Grande do Sul Municipality of Canoas, Rio Grande do Sul Municipality of Porto Alegre, Rio Grande do Sul Municipality of Goiânia, Goiás
Yes	No	Negative	**Argentina – Asignación Universal por Hijo** Province of San Luis Municipality of Villa Mercedes, San Luis Municipality of Godoy Cruz, Mendoza **Brazil – Bolsa Família** State of Goiás Municipality of Valparaíso de Goiás, Goiás
No	Yes	Irrelevant	**Argentina – Plan Nacer** Province of Mendoza Municipality of Las Heras, Mendoza Municipality of San Luis, San Luis **Brazil – Estratégia Saúde da Família** State of Rio Grande do Sul Municipality of Canoas, Rio Grande do Sul Municipality of Porto Alegre, Rio Grande do Sul Municipality of Goiânia, Goiás
No	No	Irrelevant	**Argentina – Plan Nacer** Province of San Luis Municipality of Villa Mercedes, San Luis Municipality of Godoy Cruz, Mendoza **Brazil – Estratégia Saúde da Família** State of Goiás Municipality of Valparaíso de Goiás, Goiás

These are my negative cases: in the *absence* of clear attribution of responsibility, political alignments do not matter for the implementation of national policies. In other words, attribution of responsibility is *necessary* for political alignments to affect implementation. At the same time, variation in policy implementation in cases in which attribution of responsibility is not clear points to the fact that political alignments do not explain everything. If they did, the implementation of health policies – with blurred attribution of responsibility – would be totally even across the territory. Yet Figures 1.2 and 1.4 show that primary health policies are also unevenly implemented. Institutional capacity and policy legacies also explain the uneven implementation of social policies.

Territorial Infrastructure and Policy Legacies

While political alignments only shape the implementation of policies with clear attribution of responsibility, institutional capacity and policy legacies matter for all policies.[11] There is great variation in state capacity across countries in the Global South, and such variation is exacerbated within countries that are decentralized. Countries that exhibit strong state capacity can deliver goods and services that citizens need. In places with weak capacity, the delivery of services is limited (Skocpol and Finegold 1982; Norris 2012).

I analyze a specific aspect of state capacity that is relevant for policy implementation: territorial infrastructure. It is associated with Michael Mann's definition of infrastructural power as the capacity to actually implement political decisions throughout the territory (Mann 1988, 5). The concept of territorial infrastructure captures two dimensions: the spatial reach of state institutions and their relationship with non-state actors (Soifer and Vom Hau 2008). First, strong territorial infrastructure can be achieved through subnational health, education, and social assistance institutions that deliver good quality services through trained personnel and in facilities in adequate condition. These subnational state institutions are accessible to the population, no matter how far away they live. Weak territorial infrastructure is manifested in facilities that are in poor condition and are staffed with personnel who are not adequately trained and earn low salaries. In addition, people who live in remote areas cannot reach these facilities.

Second, strong territorial infrastructure can also be achieved when civil society and the state work in close collaboration. In other words, there can be mutual reinforcement between a strong state and an autonomous civil society. In particular, civil society in collaboration with the state can generate channels of information through deliberative processes that allow for efficient delivery of social policies (Evans 1995; Evans and Heller 2015). The city of Porto Alegre in southern Brazil and the town of Las Heras in western central Argentina are examples of strong local government institutions collaborating with active civil

---

[11] I use the terms territorial infrastructure and institutional capacity interchangeably.

society organizations. In Porto Alegre, councils and participatory budgeting processes, in which state and civil society representatives participate, monitor the implementation of national policies by making sure that funds are used nondiscretionarily and that the quality of service provision is adequate. Effective territorial infrastructure similar to the one found in Porto Alegre decreases exclusion.

Besides territorial infrastructure, policy legacies also shape the implementation of all national policies. Previous policies empower institutions and actors that facilitate or challenge the implementation of current national policies. These legacies exhibit variation both across policy sectors and the territory. Previous policies generate institutional dynamics and select, empower, and weaken actors (Pierson 2004, 152; Pribble 2013, 3). In other words, policies produce politics (Schattschneider 1935; Pierson 1993, 595). The longer a given policy has been in place, the more supporters it will create and thus the harder it will be to change its direction. Even previously plausible reforms become prohibitively costly if the institution in question has been in place for some time and thus has generated deep and interrelated investments (Huber and Stephens 2001; Pierson 2004, 152).

When previous policies created processes and interests that are contrary to the new policy, the implementation of the new policy will be delayed. The primary health policy in Brazil, Estratégia Saúde da Família, faces organized opposition from doctors who support the previous primary health policy (called *unidades básicas tradicionais* or traditional basic health units) either for salary concerns or because their entire careers were organized in line with the previous policy. In addition, those who support a hospital-centered health provision lobby to avoid a flow of resources from hospitals to primary health centers. As a result, in the places that exhibit a strong presence of hospitals and traditional basic health units, the implementation of Estratégia Saúde da Família is more challenging. This is the main explanation for the low coverage of this policy when it was first launched, exhibited in Figure 1.2.

Conversely, when previous policies generated processes and actors' interests that are similar to the current policy, the implementation of the current policy will be enhanced. For instance, previous CCTs automatically transferred recipients to Bolsa Família, thus facilitating the implementation of the new CCT. Before Bolsa Família, there were 4.2 million people receiving transfers from other programs, many of which were transferred to the new policy (Soares and Sátyro 2010, 43). These previous programs had also started training local schools and health centers on the provision of education and health conditionalities. These previous CCTs left fertile ground for the implementation of Bolsa Família. At the same time, the level of implementation of these previous policies varied throughout the territory, demonstrating that policy legacies also exhibit variation across subnational units.

Overall, territorial infrastructure, policy legacies, and political alignments each have an independent effect on policy implementation and none of them can

18 Uneven Social Policies

override another one. The best context for the implementation of national social policies is aligned subnational units, with strong territorial infrastructure and positive policy legacies. By contrast, in opposition subnational units, with weak territorial infrastructure and negative policy legacies, the implementation of national policies is more challenging.

ALTERNATIVE EXPLANATIONS AND CONTRIBUTIONS TO THE LITERATURE

Welfare States

Uneven Social Policies brings together theories on welfare states and multilevel governance in order to construct a theoretical framework that helps to explain variation in policy implementation in decentralized countries. The literature on welfare states has analyzed the design and outcomes of social policies, but has excluded variation in the actual implementation of policies. This matters because policy choices and outcomes are linked through the process of implementation. Better implementation of policies will produce more positive socioeconomic outcomes. This book incorporates crucial variables for understanding variation in national social policy implementation in countries with multiple levels of governance. It also accounts for why variation across policy areas matters for implementation.

The main alternative explanation of variation in social protection at the national level is economic performance. After all, it is true that, in general, advanced industrial democracies fare better than developing countries in terms of social policy outcomes.[12] However, country differences show the significant effect of politics. Not all countries with the same level of economic development advance the same type of social policies. This is true both for high-income countries (Esping-Andersen 1990; Huber and Stephens 2001) and for middle-income Latin American countries (Huber and Stephens 2012; Pribble 2013; Garay 2017).

The literature on welfare states therefore incorporates the role of policy legacies, which shape the kinds of reforms that are both needed and possible. Previous policies generate problems that shape the reforms that are *needed*. If previous reforms expanded education coverage at the expense of quality, for instance, a necessary reform would be to design and implement policies that aim at improving the quality of the service (Pribble 2013). At the same time, previous policies shape the reforms that are *possible* by empowering some actors and weakening others (Esping-Andersen 1990; Pierson 1994; Huber and Stephens 2001; Haggard and Kaufman 2008; Niedzwiecki and Pribble 2017). Designing and implementing policies that face opposition from strong actors empowered by

---

[12] See Skocpol and Amenta (1986) for a literature review of the effect of economic development on welfare state development.

previous policies is a challenging aim to accomplish (Niedzwiecki 2014a). Given that previous policies and the ways in which they were implemented vary across and within countries, this book shows the mechanisms through which the legacies of previous policies exhibit variation not only across countries and policies but also *within* countries.

When welfare state theories are tested in non-OECD contexts, democracy and state capacity cannot be taken for granted. The record and quality of democracy matter for social policy development when it appears in tandem with a capable state that can deliver things that citizens need. Previous studies have found that democratic states make more efforts toward social policy than authoritarian ones. More democratic countries not only spend more on social development but their spending is also more egalitarian (Brown and Hunter 1999; Haggard and Kaufman 2008; Huber, Mustillo, and Stephens 2008; Huber and Stephens 2012; Niedzwiecki 2015).

Recent literature on the existence of different levels of democracy within countries (Gervasoni 2010b; Gibson 2012; Giraudy 2014) compels us to think about the connection between welfare and subnational political regime (McGuire 2010a; Giraudy and Pribble 2018). I find that subnational regime type does not affect the level of implementation of national policies directly, but it affects the way in which policies are implemented. National policies can be implemented with similar rates of success in subnational authoritarian and democratic units, as long as they are politically aligned and exhibit positive legacies and strong capacity. However, subnational regime type does affect the type of territorial infrastructure: in more democratic regions, civil society actively engages with the state in the implementation of social policies, thus potentially enhancing the infrastructure in the territory. This kind of synergy between state and non-state actors is absent in nondemocratic or hybrid provinces.

The state needs to have the capacity to implement political decisions throughout its territory (Mann 1988, 5). Michael Mann's "infrastructural power" can be conceptualized as the ability of the central state to reach the territory, throughout its subnational units, to provide services (Soifer 2008, 235). The even exercise of the state's infrastructural power is especially significant in decentralized countries, which tend to be larger and thus harder to control. This uneven state control was already noted by O'Donnell (1993, 1359), who argued that there are places with low or nil state presence for guaranteeing the rule of law, dubbed "brown areas." Although the welfare state faces the challenge of implementing social policies in remote areas that lack institutional capacity, I consider there to be no "brown areas" for the welfare state in the cases analyzed here. The CCTs and health policies analyzed in this book are implemented even in places where the police cannot enter. As numerous key informants in Brazil confirmed, even drug dealers respect the work of health professionals and social assistant workers in the territory, and there is a "peaceful coexistence" between the two (Interviews Antunes, J. Mallman, Mardemattos, M. Medeiros, Pereira, L. Souza). Therefore, a main challenge for the implementation of social policies is not reaching areas controlled by non-state actors but evenly reaching, through its radiating institutions, areas that are far apart and isolated due to socioeconomic and geographic conditions. Civil society can collaborate with state institutions to reach these remote areas. This book incorporates the collaboration of state and civil society as a central factor to achieve state capacity.

Left partisanship has also been a central variable for explaining variation in welfare states in advanced industrial democracies (Korpi 1989; Esping-Andersen 1990; Huber and Stephens 2001) and Latin America (Huber and Stephens 2012; Pribble 2013; Huber and Niedzwiecki 2015). In fact, most of the policies analyzed in these pages are examples of the expansion of the welfare state in contexts of commodity booms and left turns in this region (Levitsky and Roberts 2011; Huber and Stephens 2012; Pribble 2013).[13] Ideology is therefore the main alternative explanation to account for variation in policy implementation. However, I argue that when moving away from the design of policies to observe their implementation, it is not the ideology of national and subnational governments that shapes the implementation of policies, but rather the interaction of political alignments across the multiple levels of decentralized governance. This is particularly true for countries in which parties are ill-defined ideologically, and thus their linkages to citizens may not respond to programmatic demands. This is the traditional way in which the literature has analyzed Latin American party systems, with wide variations across countries (Mainwaring and Scully 1995; Coppedge 1998; Roberts 2002; Mainwaring and Torcal 2005; Kitschelt et al. 2010; Roberts 2013; Cyr 2017). In addition, the trend toward decentralization has exacerbated a denationalization of party competition in which left and right parties can join widely different coalitions at the different territorial levels (Jones and Mainwaring 2003; Krause, Dantas, and Miguel 2010; Wilson 2012).

Multilevel Governance

The articulation of politics across different territories is a characteristic of multilevel systems (Hooghe and Marks 2003). Subnational provision of public goods, in particular, can be positive because lower levels of government are closer to their constituents and thus have more information about the preferences of local residents (Tiebout 1956). However, decentralized social provision introduces potential challenges for cooperation (Derthick 1972; Huber 1995; Amenta 1998; Leibfried, Castles, and Obinger 2005, 340; Schneider 2006; Fenwick 2009; Eaton 2017). The formal characteristics of decentralization provide an alternative explanation to variation in policy

---

[13] However, right-wing parties in Latin America have also implemented CCTs (De La O 2013) and the expansion of some social policies started before the left turn (Garay 2017).

implementation. While some countries have rules that encourage cooperation between national and subnational levels of government, others have rules that encourage conflict. However, similar national rules cannot account for variation *within* countries and across policy areas. I argue that the type of federalism is the framework that shapes possible strategic interactions. The question in this book is not *who* has the authority to do *what* (i.e., the design of federal institutions), but *when* and *how* do subnational units enhance or hinder nationally designed policies in contexts of high levels of subnational authority. In doing so, a central contribution of this book is to develop a truly multilevel theory, in which national and subnational variables mutually interact.[14]

Multilevel political alignments are key for shaping fiscal and macroeconomic policy-making. Riker and Schaps (1957) argue that lack of partisan alignments between the federal and subnational governments endangers intergovernmental cooperation; and others have added that if national leaders are able to discipline subnational co-partisans, then cooperation across territorial levels is more easily attained (Jones, Sanguinetti, and Tommasi 1999; Garman, Haggard, and Willis 2001; Diaz-Cayeros 2004; Filippov, Ordeshook, and Shvetsova 2004; Wibbels 2005; Larcinese, Rizzo, and Testa 2006; Rodden 2006). This book moves away from fiscal and macroeconomic policy-making and tests the role of multilevel alignments in the implementation of social policies.

The literature on clientelism in Latin America also finds that partisanship produces unequal distribution of policies. This is a result of presidents' strategies to favor subnational co-partisans, convince swing voters, or punish political enemies with the aim of enhancing their electoral chances (Shady 2000; Magaloni, Diaz-Cayeros, and Estévez 2007; Stokes et al. 2013; Calvo and Murillo 2014). At the same time, governors and party candidates can mediate the central government's discretionary distribution of policies to core constituents (Albertus 2015; Szwarcberg 2015). This book shows that policies that are not distributed discretionally (i.e., for which the government cannot target recipients for electoral purposes) can still be unevenly implemented as a result of opposition parties at different territorial levels. In particular, I incorporate the possibility of subnational governments resisting national policies, in part through their own social policies. Subnational policies that openly compete with or complement national policies are a crucial variable in accounting for the level of implementation of national policies. A recent study by Eaton (2017) is the first to conceptualize subnational policy challenges in Bolivia, Ecuador, and Peru. According to the author, subnational commitments to policy regimes ("subnational neoliberalism" or "subnational statism") can deviate from national policy regimes and succeed in these efforts if they have economic leverage, institutional capacity, and coalitions with other subnational actors.

[14] See Giraudy, Moncada, and Snyder (forthcoming) for an analysis of subnational research strategies.

To explain subnational resistance to individual federal policies, an established literature on the United States gives us important insight. States tend to resist national policies in contexts of opposition advocacy groups and constituencies (Palazzolo et al. 2007), state control by opposition parties (Palazzolo et al. 2007; Regan and Deering 2009; Miller and Blanding 2012; Nicholson-Crotty 2012; Rigby 2012; Rigby and Haselswerdt 2013), and federal (unfunded) mandates (Grogan 1999; Derthick 2001; Gormley 2006; Krane 2007; Posner 2007; Regan and Deering 2009). On the latter, while transferring money alongside policy responsibility is key for explaining the success of a given policy, federal money cannot alone buy subnational cooperation in policy implementation (Nicholson-Crotty 2012). Opposition governors will block policies that harm their electoral prospects. Most of the US-based studies include individual analyses of federal policy areas such as the Affordable Care Act (Rigby 2012; Haeder and Weimer 2013; Rigby and Haselswerdt 2013; Barrilleaux and Rainey 2014), ID requirements (Regan and Deering 2009), No Child Left Behind (Shelly 2008), Medicaid (Grogan 1999), the economic stimulus package (Miller and Blanding 2012), and election administration (Palazzolo et al. 2007). My proposal is to also incorporate negative cases (in which there is no subnational resistance to national policies) to account for the fact that the *same* subnational unit sometimes *challenges* and sometimes *enhances* different national policies.[15] This book incorporates both types of cases, thus disaggregating the welfare state by arguing that a key difference between policies is whether attribution of responsibility is clear or fuzzy. To my understanding, previous literature has not made a connection between credit claiming and political alignments.

METHODOLOGY, RESEARCH DESIGN, AND SELECTION OF CASES

Combining multiple methodologies in a single research design has advanced our understanding of the welfare state (Niedzwiecki and Nunnally 2017). The theoretical framework in this book is tested through the combination of statistical analysis and case studies, connected by a nested research design. While the statistical analysis enhances generalizability and aids the assessment of alternative explanations (King, Keohane, and Verba 1994), the case studies corroborate the findings of the quantitative analysis, improve the measurement of the variables, and, most importantly, identify the causal mechanisms that lead to such results (Ragin 1989; Lieberman 2005).

The case studies of health policies and CCTs across two states, two provinces, and eight municipalities are nested within a statistical analysis of twenty-four provinces in Argentina and twenty-seven states in Brazil. I use

---

[15] Gormley (2006) does analyze environmental, health, and education policies. The author argues that the difference in the level of conflict among these areas depends on federal mandates and federal funding.

pooled time series analysis to measure the average effect of political alignments, policy legacies, and territorial infrastructure on the successful implementation of social policies across provinces and states from the time that there is data for the first policy that was implemented in each country (1998 in Brazil and 2008 in Argentina) until 2015. Regression analysis assesses the degree to which effects always follow causes, or the constant conjunction view of causality (Hume 1975 [1777]). Case studies, in turn, allow me to analyze social policy implementation in the selected subnational units in Argentina and Brazil. The incorporation of policies that have both clear and blurred attribution of responsibility, as well as subnational units aligned and in opposition to the federal government, incorporates the counterfactual view of causation – "if the first object had not been, the second never would have existed" (Hume 1975 [1777]).

The relationship between attribution of responsibility and political alignments is deterministic: attribution of responsibility is *necessary* for political alignments to have an effect on policy implementation. This type of causality is better tested in a qualitative context. At the same time, the relationship between political alignments, territorial infrastructure, and policy legacies and the dependent variable is probabilistic and additive in form. As a result, the statistical models have the form of ordinary least squares and its derivatives, and process tracing is conducted with an additive approach of causality. I explore whether these factors of interest contributed to the outcome in particular case studies, without making any assumptions regarding whether the factors are necessary for the outcome (Goertz and Mahoney 2012, 109).

Both research strategies employ the same dependent variable, social policy implementation, which is defined as the degree to which policies effectively provide social protection to the targeted population. To measure the dependent variable, I observe levels of coverage (i.e., actual receipt) of the policy as a percentage of the targeted population. The targeted population ranges from the entire population in the country (in the case of the health policy in Brazil) to families in poverty (in the case of the CCTs), and people without health insurance (in the case of the health policy in Argentina). These policies exhibit variation in coverage across provinces and municipalities, as well as across time.

I select cases across countries, provinces, and municipalities. National cases include Argentina and Brazil, which are the two most decentralized countries in Latin America, meaning that subnational governments enjoy significant regional authority in their own territory (self-rule) as well as a say in national matters (shared rule) (Hooghe et al. 2016). In addition, these two countries share similar trajectories in terms of welfare state development. They find their origin in the 1930s and 1940s, with employment-based social insurance and stratification of welfare state programs, particularly along occupational lines. They have undergone neoliberal reforms during the 1980s and 1990s, and have expanded their social protection systems since the 2000s (Huber and Stephens 2012). In spite of these similarities, these countries exhibit important differences in the variables of interest. In particular, the effect of political alignments is stronger in Argentina than in Brazil because the Brazilian party system is more fragmented and undisciplined. On the other hand, policy legacies in Brazil are stronger than in Argentina, because previous policies have been around for longer, have targeted a broader segment of the population, and have developed experience with the provision of conditionalities. Finally, the inclusion of these two countries responds to differences in collaboration between civil society and the subnational state for the implementation of national policies. State and civil society collaboration is more consistently relevant in Brazil than in Argentina.

At the subnational level, I select cases that show average values on the main control variables and show variation in political alignments; that is, states, provinces, and municipalities with similar levels of GDP per capita and population density but with different alignments to the national government.[16] The cases are Mendoza (and the municipalities of Godoy Cruz and Las Heras) and San Luis (and the municipalities of San Luis City and Villa Mercedes) in Argentina; and Rio Grande do Sul (plus Porto Alegre and Canoas) and Goiás (with Goiânia and Valparaíso de Goiás as the local cases) in Brazil.

The case studies build on fifteen months of field research in Argentina and Brazil, where I conducted more than 200 interviews with elected officials, high-level technocrats, street level bureaucrats, community leaders, and policy experts. In these provinces and municipalities, I participated in councils, forums, and meetings that tackled social protection issues. In addition to elite-interviewing and participant observation, I conducted 148 structured interviews with social policy recipients. Finally, I also conducted archival research of newspaper articles. On one hand, archival research in the opposition province in Argentina and opposition state in Brazil allowed me to trace the trajectory of the subnational cash transfers that have existed for more than a decade in each unit. On the other hand, the coding of political alignments across all provinces and time in Argentina also relies on archival research, in particular of two national and forty-four provincial newspapers.

BOOK OVERVIEW

This book is divided into seven chapters. After this introduction, Chapter 2 lays out the theoretical framework. I argue that attribution of responsibility, political alignments, policy legacies, and territorial infrastructure shape social policy implementation in decentralized countries. This chapter details the mechanisms through which these four variables affect policy provision. In particular, opposition subnational governments hinder some, but not all, national policies. They obstruct only those policies that enjoy clear attribution of responsibility, a characteristic that differentiates CCTs from social services. In addition, this chapter analyzes how variation in

---

[16] In the case of municipalities, I also select cases with different alignments to the provincial government.

territorial infrastructure and policy legacies shape the uneven implementation of national policies across subnational units.

Chapter 3 examines the dependent variable and research design. It first describes the measurement and variation of the dependent variable across policies, provinces, and time in Argentina and Brazil. Then it discusses why a mixed methods research design is an apt choice for unraveling the factors that shape social policy implementation. Finally, the chapter proceeds to explain the multilevel case selection strategy; I select cases at the country, intermediate, and local levels.

Chapters 4–6 provide empirical evidence for the theoretical framework that guides this book. Chapter 4 shows the relationship between political alignments, territorial infrastructure, policy legacies, and policy coverage across all provinces in Argentina and all states in Brazil from the 1990s to 2015. It uses Prais–Winsten panel-corrected standard errors regression to analyze an original dataset of the dependent and independent variables, as well as a number of control variables, including GDP per capita, ideology, population density, and distance to the capital, among others.

The following chapters test the theoretical framework through case studies. Chapter 5 studies the impact of political alignments on policies that enjoy clear attribution of responsibility in Argentina and Brazil. This is the case of CCTs Asignación Universal por Hijo and Bolsa Família. I study the process of implementation of these policies across two states and four municipalities in each country. The opposition province of San Luis in Argentina and the opposition state of Goiás in Brazil hold off the implementation of these national cash transfers by engaging in direct policy competition and mounting bureaucratic obstacles. Conversely, provincial and local governments that are politically aligned with the national government enhance these CCTs by designing complementary subnational policies and investing their own resources in the improvement of these national policies. This differentiated reaction in opposition and aligned subnational governments responds to the fact that the national government successfully takes credit for these CCTs. At the same time, the legacies of previous national and subnational policies enhance the implementation of these policies. Brazil's Bolsa Família builds upon other programs, which already covered 4.2 million families when the CCT was launched, and which trained health centers and schools for fulfilling the conditionalities of this policy. Argentina's CCT also builds on previous CCTs, although its legacies are weaker than in Brazil. Strong territorial infrastructure in the form of subnational state institutions, sometimes in collaboration with civil society, also enhances the implementation of these CCTs. In particular, social assistance institutions that are of good quality in terms of facilities and trained personnel are crucial for the implementation of these policies in both countries. In Brazil, the role of councils in which state and non-state actors participate is central for explaining national policy success.

Chapter 6 shows that when attribution of responsibility is blurred, political alignments are irrelevant for shaping the implementation of national social policies. This is the case of primary health policies in Brazil (Estratégia Saúde da Família) and Argentina (Plan Nacer). This chapter focuses on the sources of such fuzzy attribution of responsibility. In addition, it details the role of policy legacies and territorial infrastructure for the successful implementation of these policies across four states and eight municipalities. In terms of policy legacies, while Brazil's primary health policy competes against a previous primary health strategy and high-complexity health provision, there are no comparable negative legacies in Argentina's Plan Nacer because the policy funds public providers of both primary and high-complexity health care. In addition, policy implementation is enhanced by the presence of good quality primary health centers staffed with trained professionals and distributed evenly throughout the territory. In Brazil, civil society actors working alongside strong subnational states monitor the implementation of the primary health policy and thus improve its implementation.

The concluding chapter summarizes the main findings and discusses the implications of this book for policy and theory. In particular, nondiscretionary policies can also be subject to territorially uneven logics, politicians should blur attribution of responsibility to produce more evenly implemented policies, and building stronger state institutions can be achieved through incorporating civil society. The chapter also reflects on the generalizability of the argument on political alignments and attribution of responsibility to any country in which subnational governments have a role in the implementation of national policies and in which policies have clear or fuzzy attribution of responsibility. I demonstrate the applicability of this framework to the varied implementation of the Affordable Care Act in the United States – commonly called Obamacare. Finally, the conclusions discuss possible topics for future research.

2

Explaining Social Policy Implementation

Multiple government levels shape the success of national policies in reaching the targeted population. This is particularly true for noncontributory social assistance and social services, since subnational governments can directly shape national policies when they are in charge of implementation. Provinces and municipalities can also affect national policies even when they do not have the legal responsibility to implement them. Subnational governments can facilitate implementation through bureaucratic and political cooperation or they can hinder national policies by omission, policy competition, or bureaucratic obstacles. By recognizing and analyzing the crucial role of multilevel dynamics, this book studies the conditions under which national noncontributory social policies are more successfully implemented in decentralized countries.

In this chapter, I present a theory to account for the successful implementation of national social policies. I identify the importance of four variables – attribution of responsibility, political alignments, territorial infrastructure, and policy legacies – to social policy implementation. As a first step I disaggregate social policies into two types: those in which *attribution of responsibility* is blurred and those in which attribution of responsibility is clear. For the latter, the national government can potentially gain electorally, and therefore multilevel *political alignments* matter. Governors and mayors of subnational units that are not aligned with the national government have incentives to obstruct the implementation of this type of policies.

Finally, I address the ways that *policy legacies* and *territorial infrastructure* affect the implementation of national social policies. Policy legacies enhance the implementation of social policies when previous processes and empowered actors' interests at the different subnational levels are compatible with the new policy. Conversely, entrenched interests in previous policies that are contrary to the current one will obstruct its implementation. In addition, having capable institutions facilitates policy implementation. Territorial infrastructure includes subnational state institutions and their relationship to civil society.

THEORETICAL FRAMEWORK

The existence of strong territorial infrastructure and positive policy legacies enhances the implementation of all policies across all subnational units. Having weak infrastructure and entrenched (and contrary) interests in previous policies, in turn, challenges the implementation of all national social policies. Political alignments only matter when popular policies have clear attribution of responsibility and, therefore, the opposition faces electoral risks. Overall, in aligned subnational units with strong territorial infrastructure and positive policy legacies, there is better implementation of national social policies. In opposition subnational units with weak infrastructure and negative legacies from previous policies, implementation is more challenging.

Political alignments, territorial infrastructure, and policy legacies contribute to the successful implementation of national policies in an additive way: no single variable is necessary or sufficient for the outcome. Additionally, no independent variable can completely override another. The relative importance of the independent variables for the outcome varies across policies and countries. While negative policy legacies are key for explaining variation in the coverage of Brazil's primary health policy, in Argentina having strong territorial infrastructure takes the lead in health policy. Comparison across CCTs in both countries shows that political alignments are more relevant in Argentina than in Brazil, due to the characteristics of the party system, while policy legacies are more relevant in Brazil because CCTs have been around for longer and have targeted more people.

One of the main contributions of *Uneven Social Policies* is to construct a multilevel theory in which both national and subnational variables matter. Political alignments between presidents, governors, and mayors affect policy implementation, and this variable goes from the local to the national level and back. The same is true for policy legacies, a variable that combines previous national policies with variations throughout the territory. In the case of territorial infrastructure, the focus is on subnational dynamics – the strength of subnational state institutions and their collaboration with local civil society for the implementation of national policies.

ATTRIBUTION OF RESPONSIBILITY OR "WHOM SHOULD I THANK?"

The assumption is that politicians are motivated first and foremost by getting themselves or their parties reelected, in order to continue their careers in (particularly subnational) government (Mayhew 1974; Samuels 2003). To achieve these aims, they go through parties (Aldrich 2011, 5, 15). In federal countries, presidents or prime ministers shape the electoral success of subnational politicians (Campbell 1986; Carsey and Wright 1998; Wibbels 2005). The more positive a voter assesses the chief executive, the greater the likelihood that this voter will support subnational candidates affiliated with the chief executive's party (Piereson 1975; Holbrook-Provow 1987; Gélineau and Remmer 2006, 137). At the same time, voters evaluate the government's performance across a wide range of policy areas to decide whom to vote for (Marsh and Tilley 2010, 134). Politicians therefore want to claim credit for successful policies.[1] However, not all policies have clear attribution of responsibility that can generate direct electoral returns.

There are two kinds of social policies: those for which attribution of responsibility is clear and those for which attribution of responsibility is ambiguous. By clear attribution of responsibility I mean policies that clearly "belong" to a party or government level, and therefore policies that recipients can easily thank someone for. A recipient who gets an ATM card with the logo of the national government knows she can thank this particular government level every time she withdraws cash. If a basket of food is handed out by a city councilor, the recipient recognizes that politician as the source of that nights' meal. When attribution of responsibility is unclear, a voter cannot identify the party or government level that gave them the good or service. A user of the local clinic can be thankful that the doctor saved the life of his daughter, but does not know whether the facility and the money for medicine came from the mayor, the governor, the president, an international organization, or a private donor.

Policy recipients can *only* reward a party or government level with their votes when they can establish that a particular government is responsible for such policies.[2] Attribution of responsibility is therefore a necessary condition to reward or punish elected politicians: it determines who is responsible for a particular outcome and it leverages these judgments to hold leaders accountable (Atkeson and Maestas 2012, 105). If the president is considered responsible for a given outcome, then her party is likely to be rewarded (or punished) in the elections. Conversely, when she is not considered to be responsible for that particular outcome, then citizens' votes will not be shaped by that outcome (Abramowitz, Lanoue, and Ramesh 1988; Rudolph and Grant 2002; Marsh and Tilley 2010).

I argue that attribution of responsibility can be an inherent characteristic of the policy, and that one of the most important but understudied ways that different types of policies vary is in their ease of attribution.[3] Cash transfers are

---

[1] Contrary to macroeconomic adjustment policies in which politicians potentially fear the negative electoral consequences of these policies, cash transfers and social services are examples of policies for which politicians generally want to claim credit.

[2] This does not mean that policy recipients will automatically vote for the government responsible for a given policy, since there are other issues that shape voting behavior.

[3] I only focus on aggregate attribution of responsibility and not on the individual ability or disposition to attribute credit. For individual-level characteristics to explain differences in attribution of blame and credit, see the literature based on psychological attribution (e.g., Lau and Sears 1981; Tyler 1982; Abramowitz, Lanoue, and Ramesh 1988).

tangible and attributable instruments that can aid reelection when delivered at key moments before the election (Tufte 1978). In cash transfers credit claiming is "easier" because policy recipients are the direct beneficiaries. In addition, the provider's logo appears in the ATM card or the provider directly distributes the cash transfer. Finally, cash transfers are "particularized" benefits in that they are targeted to specific groups (families or individuals in poverty) and they can sometimes be viewed by voters as being distributed in an ad hoc way (Mayhew 1974, 54). For these types of policies, attribution of responsibility tends not to be disputed.

For social services, especially when provision is public and universal, providers such as health clinics or schools (and not users) are the direct recipients of the funds, and therefore it is "harder" for voters to identify who is responsible. In addition, policies that aim at improving the quality of social services are less visible: people do not generally identify having access to better quality of health or education with the actions of a particular policy. The visibility of a policy (or the recognition that a given benefit comes from a particular policy) is a first necessary step for being able to attribute responsibility.[4] Only if recipients recognize the existence of a policy will they give credit to a particular government. This lower visibility partly responds to the fact that people have a harder time observing whether the promises of better quality services have been met (Melo 2008, 182). Keefer and Khemani (2005, 2) also explain that citizens have a hard time evaluating the quality of services such as health and education, and "[e]ven when they can, they cannot easily determine whether service providers, higher-level ministry officials, or politicians are responsible." In particular, given the lower visibility of health policies, which partly responds to their complexity, attribution of responsibility tends to be blurred (Mani and Mukand 2007).[5] Carmines and Stimson (1980) argue that while "easy" issues do not require sophistication in voting decisions, "hard" issues call for voters with high conceptual skills. In other words, in order to shape a voter's decision, "hard" issues require more information and deeper analysis on the side of the voter.

Conditional cash transfers (CCTs) in Latin America enjoy clear attribution of *national* responsibility because they are centralized at the federal government. The money goes from the capital city directly to the individual, in a nondiscretionary manner, without intermediaries in the territory. In other

---

[4] See Murillo (2009) on the sources of the salience or visibility of public utility policies.

[5] Not all aspects of social provision have blurred attribution of responsibility. Building a new school or hospital has clearer attribution of responsibility than improving the quality of provision (Keefer and Khemani 2005, 6). But these opportunities are more expensive and less common than receiving funds for quality improvement or coverage expansion. Additionally, in contexts of high politicization over the passing and/or implementation of a social service, we should expect clear attribution of responsibility. This is the case of the Affordable Care Act ("Obamacare") in the United States. In this case, the incumbent claims credit for it and the opposition rejects it, in a context of a polarized debate over this issue.

words, "[b]ecause the president is directly responsible for the policy's design and implementation, he is more likely to claim credit for it" (De La O 2015, 50). Provinces and municipalities may be in charge of checking for compliance with conditions, but the ultimate word in terms of who receives the CCT and who does not is in the hands of the central government. This is important because the literature on attribution of responsibility agrees that as the number of actors increases, clarity of responsibility decreases, making it more challenging for voters to determine which party or government level they should reward (Anderson 2006; Maestas et al. 2008; Atkeson and Maestas 2012, 112). In general, in more decentralized countries attribution of responsibility is less clear than in centralized countries. In particular, the decentralization of social services contributes to blurring attribution of responsibility because power is shared among multiple levels of government as opposed to just one level of government. As a result, voters may confuse who is responsible and will not shape their voting decisions based on the performance of these services.[6]

Politicians adopt a distinctive set of strategies for maximizing credit-claiming opportunities. Mayhew (1974, 52–53) defined credit claiming as "acting so as to generate a belief in a relevant political actor (or actors) that one is personally responsible for causing the government, or some unit thereof, to do something that the actor (or actors) considers desirable." Parties have incentives to increase policy ownership, especially during election campaigns, and especially on issues for which they have an advantage over their opponents. In the context of the United States, for instance, Petrocik (1996) finds that Democrats are seen by the electorate as better able at handling welfare issues while social order issues are better handled by the Republican Party. Along similar lines, Lowry, Alt, and Ferree (1998) find that Democrats are rewarded for moderate increases in spending while Republicans are not. Therefore, during campaigns candidates will emphasize the particular issues owned by their parties.

One strategy to enhance attribution of responsibility is to emphasize CCTs over social services. CCTs have provided electoral advantages to incumbent presidents in Latin America (Hunter and Power 2007; Baez et al. 2012; De La O 2013; Zucco 2013). In the particular case of Brazil, competing parties at the national and subnational levels recognized that CCTs had the potential to yield electoral benefits. Thus, they developed and claimed credit for programs that preceded *Bolsa Família* (Sugiyama 2011, 30–31). Former President Luiz Inácio Lula da Silva even changed the name of Fernando Henrique Cardoso's flagship program (*Bolsa Escola*, School Grant) to Bolsa Família. The same happened with Mexico's CCT *Progresa*, first enacted by the *Partido Revolucionario*

---

[6] Besides decentralization, majority governments with cohesive one-party rule enhance clarity of responsibility, while minority, divided, and coalition governments diffuse responsibility (Powell and Whitten 1993; Leyden and Borrelli 1995; Lowry, Alt, and Ferree 1998).

Institucional (PRI), then rebranded as *Oportunidades* by the *Partido Acción Nacional* in 2002, and *Prospera* when the PRI won the presidency in 2012. Changing the name of these programs made it easier to claim credit (Melo 2008). Renaming CCTs to make it look like a brand new idea is a smart strategy because attribution of responsibility is clearer when policies are initially implemented. The longer a policy has been in place, thus surviving different government administrations, the more citizens take it for granted and the more its attribution of responsibility is blurred. As a result, electoral returns for a given policy decay over time (Bechtel and Hainmueller 2011). This is arguably the case of Bolsa Família, which was first implemented more than a decade ago. As a result, the identification of this CCT with the presidency is slowly decreasing, as Chapter 5 discusses.

Decreasing attribution of responsibility can also be the product of a government strategy to enhance territorially even implementation: in Brazil, the federal government proposed to include the logo of the state on the ATM card recipients use to withdraw funds in exchange for developing subnational programs that complement Bolsa Família. In addition to adding the state logo, the federal government proposed to provide a document to each beneficiary family, showing the separate contributions from the federal and state governments. The strategy of sharing responsibility with subnational units has slowly but surely enhanced the coordination across territorial levels and therefore improved the implementation of the policy. Another possible strategy to decrease attribution of responsibility is automatic indexation. When the amount of transfers is automatically adjusted, following changes in inflation for instance, the chances for future credit claiming decrease because they are independent of politics (Weaver 1988).

National governments can also choose to share ownership of a policy by implicating multiple levels in the decision-making process from the initial stage. When subnational governments are allowed to co-determine national policy-making through shared rule mechanisms, such as a territorially representative second chamber or routine (bilateral or multilateral) meetings with the central government, this may facilitate the implementation of these decisions. The German Länder, for instance, has more leverage defining policy than US states, and this promotes a more cooperative policy-making process (Campbell and Morgan 2005). This may be one of the reasons why international policy organizations such as the OECD are so keen on shared rule multilevel governance mechanisms that incorporate subnational governments in the decision-making and implementation processes (Charbit 2011).

Overall, *Uneven Social Policies* argues that while CCTs carry clearer attribution of responsibility than social services, attribution of responsibility is not fixed. Politicians can modify it at the design and/or implementation stages. This matters because attribution of responsibility is necessary to shape voters' behavior.

Attribution of Responsibility and Voting

Weyland (1999, 392) observes that targeted social programs with the aim of reducing poverty are designed to solidify the mass support of leaders both in Latin America and in Eastern Europe. De La O (2015) systematically tests this intuition by taking advantage of Mexico's CCT randomized design. The author explains that "assignment to early program enrollment led to a 7 percent increase in voter turnout and a 9 percent increase in incumbent vote share in the 2000 presidential election. The experiment also reveals that exposure to program benefits had no influence on support for opposition parties. Together, these findings lend evidence to Progresa's [Mexico's CCT] pro-incumbent mobilizing effects" (De La O 2015, 135). Bolsa Família in Brazil has also been associated with an increased number of votes for the incumbent presidential candidate. Lula's reelection in 2006 is partly explained by the vote of poor Brazilians who had benefitted from Bolsa Família (Hunter and Power 2007; Zucco 2008). The incumbent party presidential candidate also benefitted from the national CCT in 2002 and 2010 elections (Zucco 2013).

For the case of Uruguay, Manacorda, Miguel, and Vigorito (2011) find that individuals who received the national CCT were 11–13 percent more likely to support the president than those who barely failed to qualify for the program. At the same time, recipients do not express significantly higher levels of support for other institutions, such as congress or local councils. Also for Uruguay, Queirolo (2010) finds that receiving the government's flagship CCT translated into higher levels of electoral support and thus partly explains the incumbent party's reelection in 2009. Aggregate analysis of Latin America also shows that social assistance makes recipients more likely to vote for the incumbent, independently of the president's ideology. In other words, citizens reward both right and left incumbents for the provision of CCTs (Layton and Smith 2015).[7] Taken together, academic evidence across countries and research designs consistently shows that in elections, CCT recipients have been rewarding national incumbents who provide cash transfers.

There is also widespread media speculation about the electoral returns of CCTs. Bolsa Família has been credited with Lula's success in 2006 presidential elections, particularly in the poorest regions of the country. Media outlets also predicted that CCTs in Mexico and Colombia would favor the incumbent party in the elections in 2006. In Guatemala, CCT *Mi Familia Progresa* (My Family Makes Progress) was credited with the high levels of popularity of the first lady

---

[7] Corrêa and Cheibub (2016) find that recipients of CCTs in Latin America are more likely to support incumbents; however, they also find that the implementation of large CCT programs can cost the incumbents votes from non-beneficiaries who oppose income redistribution. This group represents an electoral minority that belongs to the richer and better-educated strata of the population.

and presidential candidate (De La O 2015, 16). Besides presidents benefitting from these policy instruments, there is evidence that co-partisan governors have also benefitted electorally from the implementation of national CCTs (Borges 2007, 129–30; Souza 2015).

The potential positive electoral outcomes motivate both national politicians' emphasis on CCTs and potential conflict with opposition subnational governments. In Pierson's (1995, 455) words: "The building of direct links with the electorate, through which government authorities could claim credit for assuring a certain degree of economic security, has had broad political appeal. In a federal system, the popularity of social provision becomes a source of potential conflict among competing centers of political authority." I now turn to the potential political conflicts that arise in the implementation of noncontributory social policies that enjoy clear attribution of responsibility.

POLITICAL ALIGNMENTS

Political alignments refer to the electoral support that mayors and governors provide to the president. One way to show alignment is to use the president's party tag in elections. In addition, subnational executives may express their support to the national administration in electoral campaign speeches and in conversations with the media. They can even appear with the president in television campaign spots or printed advertisements. Opposition subnational executives may do the exact opposite, including refraining from using the president's party tag and criticizing the national government in media outlets and campaign speeches. The president needs aligned subnational executives to win elections but also to be able to govern effectively. In particular, political alignments matter for the implementation of national policies when national attribution of responsibility is clear (Cherny et al. 2015; Niedzwiecki 2016; Freytes and Niedzwiecki 2016).

Politically aligned subnational units are interested in enhancing national-level policies. This is because the electoral fates of national executives influence the electoral chances of subnational politicians (Campbell 1986; Carsey and Wright 1998; Wibbels 2005). Voters tend to support subnational candidates affiliated with the president's party if they positively evaluate the president's performance (Piereson 1975; Holbrook-Provow 1987; Gélineau and Remmer 2006, 137). As Rodden (2006, 125) put it, voters focus retrospectively on the party label of the federal executive to reward subnational leaders in elections. Therefore, co-partisan subnational executives have incentives to boost the implementation of national-level policies in which recipients identify the federal government as the main provider.

Opposition subnational units will only enhance national policy implementation when attribution of responsibility is fuzzy and therefore they will be able to claim credit regardless of their alignment with the national government, or at least the opposition will not gain electorally. Conversely, when attribution of national responsibility is clear, opposition governors and mayors have incentives to hinder these policies. This is because, on the one hand, their own opposition at the subnational level may be aligned with the national government, and therefore their main incentive is preventing their local opposition from winning votes through the national policy. On the other hand, governors may also be playing in the national arena, because they or their allies will be competing for national elected offices. In this case, their membership in the national opposition explains their incentives to obstruct policies that can benefit the national executive.

It should be noted that this is an argument about politicians' expectations rather than actual voters' behavior. In other words, it is only when recipients can attribute policy responsibility to the national government and recognize multilevel alliances that they *might* reward that party or government level in the elections. This is because attribution of responsibility can have an independent effect on public opinion (Iyengar 1989). However, this book does not test whether policy recipients automatically vote for the incumbent and acknowledges that there are other issues that shape voting behavior, including the performance of subnational incumbents (Gélineau and Remmer 2006). In other words, as long as subnational politicians *think* that CCTs will benefit or hurt them electorally, they will adjust their behavior accordingly. Interviews with politicians show that – indeed – the main reason for the opposition to block the implementation of national policies lies in the expectation that it will benefit the opposing party in the elections. And they have good reasons to think this way, as the previous section on the effect of CCTs for presidents in Latin America showed.

Contrary to welfare state theories that focus on social policy design and outcomes (e.g., Esping-Andersen 1990; Huber and Stephens 2001) and to the studies of social policy implementation in OECD countries (Battaglini and Giraud 2003; Turner 2011; Rigby and Haselswerdt 2013; Sager, Rüefli, and Thomann 2014), I argue that political considerations do not depend on ideology. They depend on political alignments instead. This is particularly true in contexts where parties are ill-defined ideologically, and thus their linkages to citizens may not respond to programmatic demands. That is the traditional image of Latin American party systems, with profound variation across countries (Mainwaring and Scully 1995; Coppedge 1998; Roberts 2002; Mainwaring and Torcal 2005; Kitschelt et al. 2010; Roberts 2013; Cyr 2017). In the words of Kitschelt et al., "[t]he overall substantive content of the left-right semantics is relatively low in Latin America when compared to other regions in the world. This is true for comparisons not only in Western Europe … but also with Eastern Europe" (Kitschelt et al. 2010, 111).

This image fairly represents the particular cases of Argentina and Brazil. In Argentina, the connection between left–right labels and party lines is among the weakest in the region (Kitschelt et al. 2010). The major party, the Peronist Party, has changed its traditionally labor-based ideology during market-reforms in the 1990s. It has been defined as a "populist machine," a party with flexible ideology and policy orientation that allows for the replacement of weak union-based linkages with clientelistic networks (Levitsky 2003; Levitsky and Roberts 2011, 14). Experts and voters disagree on where to place the Peronist Party along a left–right dimension.[8] In addition, the Peronist Party presents high levels of intraparty competition that results in different factions with different ideological affiliations. Finally, electoral dynamics and coalitions vary throughout the provinces, thus promoting different party systems and a denationalization of party competition (Jones and Mainwaring 2003, 150; Calvo and Escolar 2005; Leiras 2007).[9] The trend toward incongruence between national and subnational party systems has been increasing since the left-turn in 2003 (Suarez-Cao and Gibson 2010, 28).

For Brazil, Mainwaring (1995) and Ames (2001) argue that the only ideologically motivated parties are those on the left, while center and right parties are motivated by the distribution of resources. Center and right parties in Brazil are pragmatic; they will not oppose the implementation of social policies if it benefits themselves or their parties. If they oppose the implementation of social policies, it is for a logic of political competition, to maintain their base, but not for ideological considerations. At the same time, party elites and party supporters have low correspondence across issue and ideological divides and the ideological cohesion of individual parties is also very low (Kitschelt et al. 2010).[10] In addition, there are higher levels of convergence across parties since 1995, when former President Fernando Henrique Cardoso inaugurated a mode of "coalitional presidentialism" for the implementation of a broad neoliberal reform agenda. On that occasion, two parties that were on opposite sides of the 1964 coup, *Partido da Social Democracia Brasileira* (PSDB) and *Partido do Frente Liberal* (PFL), united behind this agenda. From that moment onward, parties have converged to the center (Power 2008). Lucas and Samuels (2010, 50) define this convergence as "the PT vs. the rest" with a diminishing difference between the PT and "the rest."

---

[8] Coppedge (1997), for example, finds no expert agreement on the classification of the Peronist Party, and therefore codes it as "other." The 1997 Parliamentary Elites of Latin America Expert Survey places the party at the center (Kitschelt et al. 2010, 102). Calvo and Murillo conducted a nationally representative survey with 2,800 respondents and confirmed "the difficulty of Argentine voters for the ideological placement of the two main Argentine political parties" (Calvo and Murillo 2012, 860). The two traditional parties are the Peronist (*Partido Justicialista*, PJ) and Radical (*Unión Cívica Radical*, UCR) parties.

[9] A party system has low nationalization when the votes of major parties differ between national and subnational levels, and among provinces (Chhibber and Kollman 2004, 4).

[10] Although recent works on Brazil show a tendency toward increasing party strength and pro-grammatic politics (Lyne 2005; Hagopian, Gervasoni, and Moraes 2008; Roberts 2014, 233–35), such tendency has been disputed (Lucas and Samuels 2010) and has not become evident at the gubernatorial or mayoral levels.

Ideological convergence partly responds to the fact that coalitions are necessary in Brazil to win elections and govern because of its highly fragmented party system. At the same time, the increase in coalition politics deepens convergence. In other words, parties need minimal agreement to join in a coalition, and once they form that coalition their ideological distance diminishes (Power 2008, 102). The number of coalitions between right and left parties has increased since the 1986 elections, reaching more than 60 percent of all coalitions for gubernatorial elections (Krause and Alves Godoi 2010, 43, 55; Borges 2016). Moreover, the same party can join widely different coalitions at the three territorial levels: national, state, and local (Krause and Alves Godoi 2010; Peixoto 2010; Ribeiro 2010). Even the PT has made a strategic move since 2003, forming alliances with parties far from its ideological positioning (Power 2008, 82; Hunter 2010; Miguel and Machado 2010; Handlin and R. Collier 2011, 158). The regional differences in the coalitions of the PT are also significant. In the state of Rio Grande do Sul the PT mostly makes alliances with the left, and in Goiás the PT is mostly aligned with right parties (Miguel and Machado 2010, 356–57).

While Brazil exhibits high levels of party fragmentation and low discipline (with the exception of the PT), the Peronist Party in Argentina tends to be more centralized and disciplined (Powell and Whitten 1993). Nomination and electoral rules shape these differences. In the closed list PR system in Argentina, provincial governors/party bosses control the rank order of the party list, and national party leaders can also intervene. In Brazil, the open list electoral system encourages candidates to employ personal vote strategies through making political alliances with subnational executives (Garman, Haggard, and Willis 2001, 214; Jones et al. 2002). Given these differences we would expect the effect of political alignments to be larger in Argentina than in Brazil, but significant in both cases.

Mechanism for Hindrance or Enhancement of National Policies

Subnational executives have a number of tools at hand to promote or resist national policies. Allied governors and mayors can enhance the implementation of national policies by putting their own policies, institutions, and personnel at the service of national policies. On the contrary, resistance to national policies due to political opposition can range from direct policy competition, to bureaucratic obstacles, to indifference. In the words of a former governor and former national vice president of Argentina: "social programs function much better when the national, provincial, and municipal governments are all of the same political color" (Personal Interview Cobos).

The decision to fund subnational policies that complement or compete with national ones is one mechanism through which subnational units can enhance or hinder the implementation of national policies. For this to be an option, provinces and municipalities need to have access to sources of funding, and have discretion over policy innovation. As a result, only relatively wealthy regions have the option to provide subnational policies. The nationally aligned state of Rio Grande do Sul in Brazil, for instance, complements the national CCT Bolsa Família through its subnational program, *RS Mais Renda Mais Igual* (More and Fairer Income). This program provides a higher transfer to recipients of the national policy between the ages of fourteen and seventeen with the aim of promoting high school completion. Conversely, the subnational program *Renda Cidadã* (Citizen Income) in the Brazilian state of Goiás directly competes with Bolsa Família. This competition is manifested through offering a higher transfer than the federal policy and through requesting that recipients not be included in the federal government's Unified Registry (*Cadastro Único*). This excludes recipients from any policy that comes from the federal government, Bolsa Família being one of them.[11] In the cases in which the subnational unit provides an alternative to the national policy, voters actually benefit from choosing the more convenient of the two policies. In the words of a recipient of a provincial program in Argentina, when asked whether she would change to the national program: "It is not in my best interest to change, here [with the provincial program] I earn 855 pesos and there [with the national program] I would earn 200 pesos" (Personal Interview Argentina #44).

This hindrance is partly why, having learned from previous failed experiences with CCTs, Lula originally tried to circumvent potential governors' reluctance to implement Bolsa Família by giving municipalities the central responsibility in implementation (Fenwick 2009; Montero 2010, 118). As a result, the legislation declares that states are merely in charge of coordinating and training municipalities, thus giving them a secondary role. This strategy works only to a certain extent because states also have the legal authority to design and implement their own social policies (Brasil. Congreso Nacional 1993, 27); therefore their cooperation is still relevant. Whether states decide to use these subnational policies to present direct policy competition or complement the national policy is a political decision.

While some provinces and municipalities have the option to provide policy alternatives, many cannot realistically compete with the federal government.

---

[11] It should be noted that in addition to the potential electoral benefits that opposition governors receive from hindering the implementation of national policies, there could also be economic and political costs associated with this behavior. Theoretically, the main cost for the subnational unit is economic: if they resist a national policy, they will have to fund a subnational alternative. This would be avoided if the subnational unit fully implemented the national policy. The political costs, in turn, depend on the national government's and recipients' reaction. The national government could potentially retaliate through denouncing these actions in the mass media or through withholding funds to the subnational unit. Recipients can change their electoral preference if they consider that their subnational government is depriving them of a national policy that could provide them welfare. Empirically, I have only encountered the economic cost of funding a competing subnational policy.

A second way through which subnational governments react to national social policies is through the decision to (not) sign agreements with the national administration. Signing agreements that allow for sharing databases that include beneficiaries of provincial social policies enhances the implementation of national policies because the federal government does not need to find every new recipient and can automatically check for incompatibilities. Nevertheless, subnational governments can undermine the implementation of a policy by refusing to sign such agreements and thus imposing additional bureaucratic obstacles onto recipients. This behavior increases the compliance cost and can strongly hinder the implementation of social policies (Moynihan, Herd, and Harvey 2014). The implementation of the CCT Asignación Universal por Hijo in the Argentine province of San Luis exhibits this mechanism. The Secretary of Social Development in the province justified the decision to not share the list of beneficiaries of provincial policies: "this is our *Plan de Inclusión* [Social Inclusion provincial program], our database, our people, and this is very sensitive data" (Personal Interview Tula Barale). This imposes a challenge to the implementation of the national CCT, since the national government determined that this policy is incompatible with the provincial workfare program yet cannot automatically cross-reference with the provincial database. Given the incompatibility between the two policies, people living in the province of San Luis and recipients of the national policy have to deal with an extra formality: every six months they have to present a certificate of negativity, a piece of paper signed by both the national and provincial social assistance agencies, that shows they are not beneficiaries of the provincial program. This means that every six months, the national policy is canceled and it can only be reactivated after each recipient provides this piece of paper. Many people forget to present this certificate or may decide it is not worth collecting the certificate to receive the stipend, and so coverage of the national CCT decreases.

Another way opposition subnational governments can hinder national social policies is through obstructing the functioning of federal institutions in the territory. In general, federal institutions function more efficiently in subnational units aligned with the federal government. This is particularly salient when the responsibility to staff and fund these institutions is shared between different territorial levels. The functioning of federal social assistance and employment institutions in provinces and municipalities in Argentina is a clear picture of this mechanism. In 2012, in the opposition province of San Luis, there were no *Oficinas de Empleo* (Municipal Employment Offices), while in the allied province of Mendoza there were at least fifteen. An employment training policy such as *Plan Jóvenes con Más y Mejor Trabajo* (More and Better Jobs for Young People) that works through employment offices is, as one would expect, more successful in Mendoza's municipalities than in San Luis'. At the same time, the representative of the

National Ministry of Social Development in the provinces, *Centro de Referencia* (Reference Centers), is active throughout the province in Mendoza, while in San Luis it only coordinates with municipalities governed by allies of the national government. A policy that lands in the territory through Centros de Referencia, such as *Argentina Trabaja* (Work Argentina), is therefore more successful in allied territories than it is in opposition units. Institutional coordination among different territorial levels can also allow subnational governments to engage in campaigns for the distribution of national IDs, which is a prerequisite for receiving most social benefits. Provincial and municipal governments in Argentina and Brazil, for instance, have conducted documentation campaigns to help people meet the eligibility requirement of the national CCT as a way to aid the implementation of this policy (Mazzola 2012, 121–23; Hunter and Brill 2016).

Subnational governments can also act by omission, by not putting the personnel under their control at the service of the national policy. This is the most common strategy chosen by municipalities. In a poor opposition municipality in Argentina, the Secretary of Social Development explained that the municipality saw no role for itself in the implementation of the national CCT: "Anses [the national social security administration] does everything, the municipality has no role … I do not even know how we could complement this national policy" (Personal Interview Fernandez). Conversely, in an aligned neighboring municipality, the official occupying this very same position explained their active role in the implementation of this policy: "we went neighborhood by neighborhood informing everybody" (Personal Interview Serú). The municipality coordinated with Anses and with municipal and civil society institutions to organize sign-up campaigns and inform the population about the new national policy. While the national CCT gives no legal role to municipalities, they can choose to contribute (or not) to its implementation.

By being closer to people, subnational governments are in an exceptionally advantageous position. They can shape social policy implementation from the initial provision of information (where to go, what to bring to sign up) to the identification of those who should be included but are excluded. Subnational officials in the executive branch are particularly relevant; they control human and material resources and service delivery systems that are essential for policy-making and implementation (Wilson et al. 2008, 262). In the words of Eaton (2017, 30), subnational chief executives "are best positioned to articulate and coordinate subnational policy challenges." At the same time, aligned executives will tend to provide better information on national policies and be more prone to identify potential recipients. Albertus (2015, 1676) notes that governors in Venezuela are well equipped to target individuals who are deserving of a national policy and can publicize the program in speeches and ceremonies. Their political affiliation, in turn, facilitates or inhibits the targeting and publicizing. Receiving accurate information on a given social policy, in turn, can increase the actual take-up rate of that policy (Moynihan, Herd, and Harvey 2014).

POLICY LEGACIES

While political alignments only matter for policies with clear attribution of responsibility, having positive policy legacies is always crucial for the implementation of policies. Numerous scholars have noted the ways in which the legacies of previous policies shape the formation of current ones (e.g., Pierson 1994; Huber and Stephens 2001; Haggard and Kaufman 2008; Pribble 2013). Moving away from the design of policies to their implementation, I also argue that previous policies matter because of their impact on institutional dynamics and actors' interests. How previous policies impact implementation varies across policies and territories in decentralized countries. Policy legacies can hinder or enhance the implementation of new policies, and they can be strong in some places and for some policies and weak in others.

Actors adapt to institutional environments by adopting new strategies, and those who do not adapt may be less likely to survive. In this way, policies select, empower, and weaken actors. Empowered actors range from individuals to organizations that either receive or provide services and transfers, who then, in turn, will support the status quo against changes that affect them negatively. Exactly *who* challenges a given policy will depend on each policy and the nature of the reform. As a result, policy feedback from previous choices influences current policy dynamics (Pierson 1993, 1994, 2004; Pribble 2013). At the same time, empowered actors from previous policies who oppose the implementation of new ones need to be organized to have a real effect. In other words, it is not enough to have the desire to oppose a particular policy; only organized groups affected by new policies will have the resources to oppose their implementation (Pierson 1994; Niedzwiecki 2014a). In the words of Haggard and Kaufman (2008, 198):

Institutional reform typically requires the cooperation of groups that may be adversely affected by the reforms in question: middle-level bureaucrats; state and local politicians and health and education authorities; teachers, doctors, and nurses. Such actors sometimes have limited influence on legislation, but when implementation begins, they can use a variety of organizational resources to effectively block or modify the reform agenda or simply 'wait out' the reformers.

The longer the policy has been in place, the more it empowers actors and the more entrenched their interests. The passing of time makes it more difficult to reverse the implementation of a given policy due to "accumulated investments" that make "the adoption of previously plausible alternatives prohibitively costly (Pierson 2004, 152). The cost of switching policies increases over time in a path dependent way, because once a particular course is initiated, it is hard to reverse. This is partly because individual and institutional adaptations to previous arrangements make changes unattractive (Pierson 2001, 415). Individuals make commitments responding to government actions and these commitments may "lock in" previous decisions, thereby making institutional reforms prohibitively costly (Pierson 1993, 1994, 2001).

The challenges faced by the primary health policy in Brazil, *Estratégia Saúde da Família* (Family Health Strategy, ESF), are a clear example of such commitments. This policy faces organized opposition from actors invested in the previous system of *unidades básicas tradicionais* (traditional basic health units, UBS) or in hospital care. Doctors, mostly for salary concerns and because their training is in line with the old system, prefer to stay in the previous basic provision model or in hospital care, instead of being incorporated into Estratégia Saúde da Família. Generations of doctors have been trained for the previous system and are, understandably, hesitant to change their training to adapt to the new circumstances. Organized interests who support a hospital-centered health provision also lobby to avoid a flow of resources from hospitals to primary health centers. The result is that in contexts of a strong previous presence of hospitals and traditional basic health units the implementation of Estratégia Saúde da Família is more challenging than in contexts that never introduced the previous primary health system and that do not provide hospital-centered health care. The implementation of these previous policies produced a network of organized stakeholders resisting changes to the status quo.

The effect of policy legacies is not always negative. Policy legacies can also enhance the implementation of new policies. Skocpol (1992, 58) argues that old policies change the institutional possibilities for future policies by transforming or expanding the capacities of the state. In that way, feedback effects facilitate the use of existing administrative arrangements for the implementation of new policies. Previous policies that target the same population, for instance, can extend the reach of the current policy by automatically transferring its recipients from the previous to the current policy, or by generating institutional learning that facilitates the implementation of the new policy. More broadly targeted policies, compared to narrowly targeted policies, leave stronger legacies because they tend to be backed by a bureaucratic system that allows for keeping track of recipients and that prepares institutions for the provision of services. These legacies can facilitate the implementation of current policies that use this same infrastructure as their base. More narrowly targeted policies are generally more unstable in terms of personnel and time horizon, and therefore do not develop the kind of institutional structure found in more broadly targeted and stable policies.

The implementation of Bolsa Família, for instance, did not start from scratch; there were 4.2 million families receiving other programs, such as *Bolsa Escola* (3,601,217), *Bolsa Alimentação* (327,321), *Cartão Alimentação* (346,300), and *Peti* (1,000) (Soares and Sátyro 2010, 43).

Some of these families were to be incorporated into Bolsa Família through the unification of databases. The first recipients included in Bolsa Família were generally those that were receiving other programs. In addition, these programs were present in the great majority of the municipalities (Da Silva e Silva and Santos de Almada Lima 2010, 113). Therefore, many of these municipalities had already developed institutions for the provision of social assistance, health, and education conditionalities that enhanced Bolsa Família when it was launched. A similar process is found in Asignación Universal por Hijo in Argentina, yet the legacies were weaker there partly because previous policies had been around for a shorter period of time, were more narrowly targeted, and health and education conditionalities were not systematically checked. Some recipients of the previous noncontributory CCTs, *Plan Jefes y Jefas de Hogar Desocupados* (Unemployed Heads of Households) and *Plan Familias* (Families Plan), were automatically transferred to Asignación Universal por Hijo. Immunization and school enrollment conditionalities of the previous policies had also started training schools and health centers in the territory on the practice of complying with conditionalities, yet they were not systematically enforced. Although CCTs in Argentina and Brazil are relatively new policies, there was fertile ground left by previous cash transfers for the implementation of new ones.

The cases incorporated in this book provide variation in the possible values of the policy legacy variable: positive and negative legacies with varying strength. CCTs in both countries benefit from positive legacies and the health policy in Brazil encounters negative legacies from previous policies. Overall, Brazil's policy legacies tend to be stronger than those in Argentina. This is because previous policies have been around for longer in Brazil and covered a broader percentage of the population. These positive or negative, strong or weak, policy legacies also exhibit variation across subnational units in decentralized countries. Previous national policies were unevenly implemented throughout the territory, and therefore the extent of their effect on the current policy is also uneven. Subnational policies also play a role: they can either enhance or hinder the success of new policies. The differences between the provincial CCTs in Mendoza and San Luis, in Argentina, illustrate this process. The scholarship program in Mendoza (*De la Esquina a la Escuela*, From the Corner to School) provides school tutors to assist recipients of the national Asignación Universal por Hijo. In this way, it contributes with one of the main aims of the national CCT, which is promoting school completion. Conversely, San Luis' employment program directly competes against the national CCT, in part through refusing to share databases of beneficiaries. This hinders full coverage of the national policy. The decision to put subnational policies at the service of national ones, or in direct competition against them, is a political one.

TERRITORIAL INFRASTRUCTURE

Countries with strong state capacity can provide adequate goods and services to their citizens, while in countries with weak capacity, the delivery of services is limited (Skocpol and Finegold 1982; Norris 2012). State capacity exhibits large variation across countries in the Global South. This national variation is exacerbated in decentralized countries, where some subnational units enjoy higher levels of capacity than others. Decentralization of responsibilities can take place overnight, "but the capacity necessary to make use of newly devolved authorities is another matter" (Eaton 2017, 39). As a result, the implementation of policies is uneven across subnational units as a consequence of this structural factor.

One aspect of state capacity – infrastructural power – is the capacity of the state to implement political decisions throughout the territory (Mann 1988, 5). Overall, territorial infrastructure refers to the institutional capacity to get things done. This means good quality institutions that are accessible throughout the territory, no matter how remote the location.

Two dimensions of territorial infrastructure are central for the implementation of policies. On the one hand, the concept captures the spatial reach of state institutions and therefore their subnational variation (Soifer and Vom Hau 2008). For the implementation of social policies in decentralized countries, territorial infrastructure includes subnational state facilities and professionals in areas such as health, education, and social assistance. These areas tend to be decentralized in federal countries, and this justifies a subnational approach.[12]

Strong subnational state institutions are capable of delivering services through facilities that meet basic requirements and are staffed by trained personnel. Facilities should be in adequate condition, such as having basic supplies (medicine, stretchers, wheelchairs, etc.), heating in the winter, ramps for people with disabilities, phones, and computers, just to mention a few. These facilities should be easily accessible to the population; they are evenly distributed throughout the territory so that people do not need to travel long distances to access services. Alternatively, these institutions might offer a car to transport those living in faraway places or mobile medical teams if they provide primary health care (McGuire 2010b, 82). Facilities located throughout provinces and municipalities are staffed with trained personnel, such as social assistants, doctors, nurses, and health agents. Having adequate training allows the staff to successfully perform their job, which can include activities such as administering vaccines, updating registries, and signing up new potential recipients. These professionals are hired following meritocratic rules and have

---

[12] For an analysis of local infrastructural power in the provision of health care in German cities, see Ziblatt (2008). Harbers (2015) also incorporates subnational state capacity.

good salaries. Good salaries and meritocratic hiring processes attract trained professionals who will have incentives to develop long career paths in the subnational state bureaucracy.[13]

States with weak territorial infrastructure are simply unable to implement social policies. In these contexts, facilities are in poor condition – they do not meet basic requirements for people with disabilities or lack basic supplies. Users of the system cannot access services because they live far away. In addition, these institutions are understaffed because salaries are low and therefore trained personnel only stay temporarily or choose other places to work. Those who work at these facilities are generally hired through non-meritocratic processes and lack the necessary training to successfully do their jobs. Overall, high levels of territorial infrastructure can be achieved by accessible subnational state institutions that include adequate facilities staffed with trained personnel, while low levels of territorial infrastructure include inaccessible institutions in inadequate condition staffed by personnel that have not been adequately trained for the job.

On the other hand, the second dimension of territorial infrastructure highlights the relational nature of state capacity by incorporating ties between state and non-state actors (Soifer and Vom Hau 2008). Strong territorial infrastructure can be achieved through the collaboration between a capable state and an autonomous civil society.[14] This connects with Evans' (1995, 1996) "embeddedness" of the autonomous state: social ties that provide institutionalized channels for the negotiation of goals and policies. If there is a synergistic relationship between the state and an autonomous civil society, they can boost each other's efforts. Ostrom (1996) used the concept of co-production to also highlight the relevance of state–society relations for achieving desired outputs: the active engagement of individuals and communities in the delivery of services ensures that such investments produce desired effects. According to Ostrom, the synergy between government agencies and citizens is crucial for achieving higher levels of welfare (also Putnam 1999). Building upon this idea, Evans, Huber, and Stephens (2017) argue that the concept of state effectiveness needs to incorporate state–society relations: "Without deliberative processes that enable the state to accurately identify

---

[13] This resembles a Weberian bureaucracy (Weber 1978). However, while Weber focuses on higher level bureaucrats, my focus is on street level bureaucrats in charge of implementing policy (Soifer and Vom Hau 2008, 223; Ziblatt 2008).

[14] Note that it is the relational component – the mutual reinforcement between a strong state and an autonomous civil society – that lies at the core of the state's success. Civil society needs to be autonomous to produce synergy with state institutions for the production of public goods. Non-state actors that are co-opted by the state do not generate quality exchange of information for the successful implementation of policies. I follow Evans and Heller's definition of civil society as "the full range of voluntary associations and movements that operate outside the market, state, and primary affiliations and that specifically orient themselves to shaping the public sphere. This would include social movements, unions, advocacy groups, and autonomous nongovernmental organizations (NGOs) and community-based organizations (CBOs)" (Evans and Heller 2015, 696–97).

community preferences, state efforts will be misdirected. Without the ability to engage the populace in the 'co-production' of capability expanding services, state investments will be ineffectual" (2017, 380). Participatory institutions promote channels of accurate information and continuous feedback loops that allow for policy corrections and thus efficient investment of public resources (Wampler 2015). In the words of Evans and Heller (2015, 695):

The centrality of accurate information makes deliberative institutions key contributors to development ... [E]ffective mechanisms of deliberation that include a broad cross-section of society are the foundation of effective public policy ... The continuous monitoring and feedback of civil society sensors can radically reduce leakage and improve both the quality and quantity of delivery ... Active participation by citizens is in fact a key ingredient for many social policies.

The state can build these "deliberative institutions" in order to enhance the synergy between state and non-state actors. Civil society participates more actively in Brazil than in Argentina in the implementation of social policies partly because Brazil requires by law the organization of councils for monitoring implementation. In other words, the relationship between state and civil society is formalized in Brazil. Councils incorporate representatives from the state, civil society, and private providers at the local, state, and national levels. In addition, the participation of a relatively autonomous civil society in health policies has a long tradition, through the *Movimento Sanitarista* or Health Workers' Movement (Falleti 2010b; Niedzwiecki 2014; Niedzwiecki and Anria Forthcoming). Even social assistance has incorporated participatory institutions (Mayka 2019). In Argentina, state–society collaboration takes place on an ad hoc basis and there is no movement compared to the Sanitaristas and no participatory institutions compared to mandatory councils.

Having a capable state is a precondition for developing synergistic relationships between state and civil society. Robust state structures are necessary for transcending the individual interests of non-state actors and solving collective action problems (Evans 1995, 12).[15] The combination of a competent bureaucratic apparatus and high levels of peasants' and workers' organization partly accounts for Kerala's successful welfare performance. In Kerala, subnational solidarity spread through sociopolitical movements and organizations and raised the chances that social expenditures actually translated into better public services (Singh 2015). The same is true for Austria's coherent state apparatus working in conjunction with a strong organized working class (Evans 1995). The redistributive success of Nordic European welfare states has also been attributed to the role of organized civil society with strong ties to a capable state (Esping-Andersen 1990; Huber and Stephens 2001).

---

[15] Cammett and MacLean (2014, 51) also show that only in the presence of high state capacity (and high capacity of non-state actors) co-production relations can develop.

TABLE 2.1 *Two dimensions of territorial infrastructure*

Subnational state institutions	State–society relations	
	Strong	Weak
Strong	Rio Grande do Sul (Brazil)	San Luis (Argentina)
	Porto Alegre, Rio Grande do Sul (Brazil)	
	Mendoza (Argentina)	
	Las Heras, Mendoza (Argentina)	
Weak		Canoas, Rio Grande do Sul (Brazil)
		Goiás (Brazil)
		Goiânia, Goiás (Brazil)
		Valparaíso de Goiás, Goiás (Brazil)
		San Luis City, San Luis (Argentina)
		Villa Mercedes, San Luis (Argentina)
		Godoy Cruz, Mendoza (Argentina)

Note: Coding of strength of subnational state institutions and state–society relations is based on fieldwork exclusively on social assistance and health sectors.

The cases included in this book also show that having strong state institutions is necessary for developing synergy with civil society. Table 2.1 shows where the subnational cases fall in the two dimensions of territorial infrastructure. Most cases fall in the strong–strong and weak–weak cells – strong state institutions are enhanced by strong relations with civil society, and weak state institutions exhibit weak collaboration with non-state actors. The weak–strong cell is empty – subnational states with weak institutions tend not to develop successful collaborations with non-state actors. Finally, subnational governments with strong institutions can have strong territorial infrastructure even in the absence of linkages with civil society – as shown by the case of San Luis in the strong–weak quadrant. This province is highly successful at implementing the health policy *Plan Nacer* because it has capable provincial institutions, though not embedded in civil society.

The City of Porto Alegre, in the strong–strong cell in Table 2.1, is an example of active participation of civil society that works in coordination with capable state institutions toward the enhancement of policies benefitting everyday citizens (Baiocchi 2005). Councils and participatory budgeting processes – in which state and civil society representatives participate – monitor the implementation of national policies by making sure that funds are used nondiscretionarily and that the quality of service provision is adequate. Conversely, in the weak–weak cell, the implementation of policies lags behind due to the combination of weak social assistance institutions in weak collaboration with civil society. In Porto Alegre's neighboring city of Canoas, social assistance facilities receive limited investment because most of them are rented, the amount of personnel is insufficient, and there is no systematic update of social policy recipients. In addition, my interviews in the municipality confirmed that civil society is not a not partner of the municipality in the implementation of social policies. Similarly, the state of Goiás, compared with the state of Rio Grande do Sul, faces the challenge of a relatively weak territorial infrastructure, coupled with fragile linkages to civil society. Goiás' state government does not enhance the development of independent civil society organizations that can effectively monitor the implementation of social policies.

To summarize, high levels of territorial infrastructure can be achieved through strong subnational institutions in the territory and the collaboration between a strong state and a robust and autonomous civil society. In the presence of both capable subnational state institutions and strong collaboration between state and non-state actors, territorial infrastructure will be strong. Strong territorial infrastructure can also be achieved through strong subnational state institutions without linkages to civil society. When both state institutions and their collaboration with non-state actors are weak, territorial infrastructure will be weak. The relationship between state and civil society, in turn, can be formalized like in Brazil (through legally mandated councils) or ad hoc like in Argentina.

THE INDIRECT ROLE OF SUBNATIONAL REGIME TYPE

In large federations, one can find different levels of democracy across provinces. In undemocratic places, political elites distort electoral rules and practices, interfere with the judiciary, and suppress opposition voices (Cornelius 1999; Snyder 1999; Borges 2007; Montero 2007; Gervasoni 2010b; Behrend 2011; Gibson 2012; Giraudy 2014).[16] Given the crucial role that national democracy plays for welfare development (Haggard and Kaufman 2008; Huber and Stephens 2012), it is natural to inquire about the effect of subnational regime type on the implementation of national policies. I argue that having a democratic or authoritarian subnational regime does not *directly* affect the implementation of national policies. National policies can be successfully implemented in politically aligned authoritarian *or* democratic states with strong territorial infrastructure and positive legacies. Subnational regime type shapes policy implementation *indirectly*.

On the one hand, it affects the unit of analysis (provincial or municipal) of political alignments. In other words, it could be a governor and/or a mayor whose alignment toward the president matters for national policy

[16] For a review of this literature, see Giraudy, Moncada, and Snyder (forthcoming).

implementation. In less democratic provinces, access to the territory is more centralized in that unit and only few responsibilities are decentralized to municipalities. In this context, political alignments of the provincial governor are crucial to understand the success of national social policies. In more democratic contexts, conversely, power is more decentralized to the local level, and therefore municipal mayors become more relevant in the implementation of national policies. In this context, political alignments of *both* governors and mayors matter.[17] This is because although democracy and decentralization have a complex relationship (not all democratic national governments decentralize nor do all authoritarian regimes centralize),[18] regime type and decentralization tend to move in tandem. Democratization is generally associated with decentralization (Niedzwiecki et al. 2018).

On the other hand, subnational regime type affects the relational dimension of territorial infrastructure described in the previous section – the degree to which civil society participates with the subnational state in the successful implementation of social policies. Positive collaboration between state and civil society can improve the capacity of the state for the implementation of policies. The active engagement of individuals in the delivery of goods and services can ensure more positive outcomes (Ostrom 1996). These types of collaboration between a strong state and an autonomous civil society can only develop in a subnational democratic context. Subnational undemocratic or hybrid regimes silence autonomous civil society and do not develop close collaboration with independent non-state actors. However, this does not mean that all democratic provinces have strong infrastructure while authoritarian states are doomed to be weak. Regime type is conceptually different from state strength. Some democratic subnational governments have weak institutions. Likewise, authoritarian states can achieve strong infrastructure without the assistance of non-state actors, through their own institutions in the territory.

CONCLUSIONS

The theory developed in this chapter guides the rest of the book. Its main contribution is to explain within-country variation in national social policy implementation as a combination of political strategy, policy legacies, and capacity. Incongruity of partisanship across territorial levels has consequences for social policy provision when there is clear attribution of policy

---

[17] It should be noted that the authority of governors versus mayors also depends on formal rules of decentralization (Brazilian municipalities are constitutionally stronger than Argentine ones) and on the specific policy design (some policies empower provinces and others municipalities). See Chapter 3 for a discussion of formal rules of decentralization and the characteristics of policy design.

[18] On the complexity of this relationship, see Eaton (2004) and Samuels (2004b).

responsibility. In the simplest model, this theory is about a decentralized polity, with policies that enjoy either clear or blurred attribution of responsibility, and subnational executives that are either aligned with or opposed to the president. Subnational governments opposed to the president's party are not interested in enhancing upper-level policies when recipients of the policy can identify where the policy is coming from and thus reward that party or government level in elections. These units will hinder the implementation of such policies by mounting bureaucratic obstacles, by open policy competition, or by being indifferent. When the policy does not have a clear electoral winner, because recipients cannot identify where the policy is coming from, cooperation between levels will be more easily attained and the policy will be more evenly implemented throughout the territory.

At the same time, agency is bounded by policy legacies and territorial infrastructure that shape the implementation of all national policies, independently of their attribution of responsibility. Legacies of previous policies create institutional dynamics and actors' interests that not only vary across policies but also across the territory. Positive policy legacies enhance the implementation of current policies. Negative policy legacies, in turn, will make the implementation of current policies more challenging. Finally, strong territorial infrastructure can be achieved through strong subnational state institutions or through the collaboration between state and non-state actors. The more developed the infrastructure in the territory, the more successfully policies are implemented.

3

Mixed Methods and Multilevel Research Design

Noncontributory social policies are not associated with wages. They are targeted at people who would not be able to make sufficient contributions if these benefits were insurance-based and who do not have enough income to purchase these services in the market. In addition, these policies are implemented following strict rules and are therefore nondiscretionary. The successful implementation of these national social policies depends in part on whether subnational executives are allied with the president (and therefore have no wish to block national initiatives) or voters are unable to credibly attribute the policy to national policy-makers (and thus there is no clear electoral risk for opposition governors and mayors supporting the national policy). Positive legacies from previous policies and strong territorial infrastructure also contribute to successful social policy implementation.

I test the theoretical framework through the use of mixed methods: case studies are nested within statistical analysis. This strategy aims at achieving detailed causal mechanisms and generalizability at the same time. The case study includes three levels: country, provincial, and municipal. The multilevel case selection strategy is represented in the first column of Table 3.1. At the national level, I select the two most decentralized countries in Latin America, Argentina and Brazil, which share similar historical patterns of welfare state development but differences in the types of political alignments, policy legacies, and territorial infrastructure. At the subnational level, I select provinces and municipalities with similar levels of GDP per capita – to rule out explanations based on wealth – but with different political alignments to the central government and different strategies for developing territorial infrastructure. Finally, I choose policies in health and social assistance sectors that exhibit variation in attribution of responsibility and policy legacies.

I collected original qualitative data through field research from September 2011 to December 2012 in the two provinces and four municipalities in Argentina, and the two states and four municipalities in

TABLE 3.1 *Interviews of political elites and social policy recipients by place*

Place	Public officials and experts	Social policy recipients[a]
Argentina – Autonomous City of Buenos Aires	13	36
Province of Mendoza	28	22
Municipality of Las Heras	17	
Municipality of Godoy Cruz	16	
Province of San Luis	20	34
Municipality of San Luis City	7	
Municipality of Villa Mercedes	4	
Brazil – Federal District of Brasília	20	
State of Rio Grande do Sul	27	26
Municipality of Porto Alegre	34	
Municipality of Canoas	15	
State of Goiás	15	30
Municipality of Goiânia	13	
Municipality of Valparaíso de Goiás	6	
Total	235	148

[a] To preserve their anonymity, I provide no further details on the characteristics of social policy recipients that were interviewed for this study.

Brazil, shown in Table 3.1.[1] During these fifteen months of field research, I conducted in-depth interviews with elected officials, high-level technocrats, street-level bureaucrats, community leaders, and policy experts at the three levels of government. The interviews lasted on average an hour and a half, during which interviewees reflected on the trajectory of a given policy in that place. Table 3.1 summarizes these interviews by locale (in the column "Public officials and experts"), and a list of all interviews is included at the end of the book.[2] In addition, I conducted almost 150 structured interviews with social policy recipients on their personal experience as users of the analyzed policies. Their geographic distribution is described in the last column of Table 3.1. These interviews were carried out in recipients' homes, social assistance centers, health centers, and hospitals.

[1] For a discussion of the benefits of field research, see Kapiszewski, MacLean, and Read (2015).

[2] In three municipalities (San Luis City, Villa Mercedes, and Valparaíso de Goiás) the number of elite interviews is lower than in the rest of the places. The first two municipalities are located in the Province of San Luis; this province has not decentralized authority to municipalities and therefore municipalities have a diminished role for the implementation of national policies (see Chapters 5 and 6). Valparaíso de Goiás only needed six interviews because it is a relatively small town with overall less people working in relevant bureaucratic positions.

I also conducted archival research at the main regional newspapers in the opposition province of San Luis (Argentina) and the opposition state of Goiás (Brazil). The aim of the archival research was to trace the trajectory of the main subnational cash transfers in these provinces, given that – contrary to the more current subnational policies in the aligned units – they have existed for over a decade. As a result, current bureaucrats had a fuzzy memory of the launching and implementation of these programs. In addition, a team of researchers co-coordinated by myself conducted archival research of national and provincial newspapers with the aim of coding the alignment of governors toward the president in all Argentine provinces from 2007 to 2015.[3] Finally, I participated as an observer in activities in Brazil and Argentina organized by provincial and municipal governments, NGOs, and universities to discuss issues related to social protection.[4]

For the statistical analysis, I constructed an original dataset at the provincial level and across time that includes indicators of social policy implementation, territorial infrastructure, policy legacies, and political alignments, as well as a number of control variables. These data is studied through pooled time series analysis of twenty-four provinces in Argentina and twenty-seven states in Brazil from when the first analyzed social policy was implemented in each country (1998 in Brazil and 2008 in Argentina) until 2015.

This chapter proceeds as follows. I first define and measure the dependent variable, social policy implementation. I then explain why the choice of a mixed methods research strategy is appropriate for unraveling the factors that shape social policy implementation. In this section, I also set the scope of this research as decentralized countries. I close the chapter by describing the multilevel case selection strategy.

---

[3] The coding of political alignments in Brazilian states did not require archival research because there are no subnational party labels in Brazil, compared with Argentina. See Chapter 4 for a description of the measurement of this variable.

[4] In the state of Rio Grande do Sul in Brazil I participated in meetings of the municipal health councils in Porto Alegre and Canoas, the regional health council in Bom Fim, the social assistance council in Porto Alegre, the *Centro de Referência da Assistência Social* (Reference Center of Social Assistance, CRAS) Extremo Sul, the municipal forum for the rights of children, and the network of social protection institutions in Porto Alegre. In addition, I observed meetings between CRAS and recipients for updating Bolsa Família's registry. In the state of Goiás, I participated in meetings at the social assistance council in Goiânia and the state health council, and in activities at the health center in Vila Pedroso. In the province of Mendoza in Argentina, I participated in meetings between the NGO Fedem and the provincial office for the right to food, a *Centro de Integración Comunitaria* (Community Center, CIC-Borbollón) meeting for the implementation of *Argentina Trabaja* (Argentina Works) program, and visits to vulnerable households with CIC-Borbollón and the secretary of health in Godoy Cruz. In the province of San Luis, I observed the Ministry of Social Inclusion's visits to recipients of the subnational workfare programs. In addition, I participated in territorial campaigns organized by Anses and the City of San Luis that took place at a catholic church and at the house of a community leader in San Luis City.

DEFINITION AND MEASUREMENT OF THE DEPENDENT VARIABLE

One of the main criticisms that Latin American welfare states have received is that they are unable to provide adequate social protection to a majority of their populations. When a large percentage of the population works outside of the formal labor market, contributory social insurance is exclusionary. Workers in the informal sector do not pay payroll taxes and therefore they do not have access to contributory-based benefits such as family allowances, health insurance, and pension benefits. Those who work in these precarious jobs or have no job, and are therefore the poorest, are excluded from much-needed transfers and services (Sen 1999; Pribble 2013, 4). As a result, studying noncontributory social policies is crucial in Latin America. The policies analyzed in this book have an additional characteristic besides being noncontributory: they are not implemented in a clientelistic way. The distribution of the policy does not depend on the recipient's political affiliation or participation in rallies, and in that sense the policies follow strict criteria for their delivery.

This book studies noncontributory and nondiscretionary conditional cash transfers and primary health care that have been particularly transformative. Almost every country in Latin America has implemented CCTs due to their immediate effect on reducing extreme poverty and their potential long-term investment on human capital development (Handa and Davis 2006). Investment in primary health care – particularly improving the quality and accessibility of services – reduces infant mortality and improves the general well-being of the population (McGuire 2010b). Positive outcomes aside, I choose to study health and CCTs because of their differences in attribution of responsibility (it is more challenging to claim credit for health services) and therefore the different role of political alignments for their implementation.

The dependent variable, social policy implementation, is defined as the degree to which policies effectively provide social protection to the targeted population. The concept of social policy implementation is continuous in nature; policies are implemented to a certain extent throughout the territory. In addition, there is no substantive reason to think that social policy implementation could be translated into typologies, as there is no clear threshold to differentiate successful from unsuccessful social policy implementation.

The operationalization of social policy implementation is also continuous through levels of coverage of national policies as a percentage of the targeted population. Coverage has been one of the main indicators of the success of social protection systems. It shows who receives the benefits and who is excluded from them (Pribble 2013). In that sense, it is a more specific indicator than the widely used and criticized "expenditure levels" (Esping-Andersen 1990). While levels of spending measure overall "effort" of welfare states, coverage taps into the actual output of social policies. The denominator (the targeted population), in turn, measures the aim of the policy in its design. It would be unfair to evaluate the implementation of a health policy that targets only uninsured citizens by whether it covers the entire population. At the same time, relative levels of coverage would be overestimated if the denominator included only families in poverty when the policy aims at covering everyone. The denominator in these policies varies from the entire population (such as in Brazil's health policy) to families and individuals in poverty (CCTs). Coverage as a percentage of the targeted population is measured on a yearly basis, from the moment the policy is first implemented (or from the moment there is available data) to the most updated data (2015) at the time of writing. A description of the four national policies analyzed in this book will clarify this operationalization.[5]

Estratégia Saúde da Família (Family Health Strategy, ESF) has been the main primary health policy in Brazil since 1994, aimed at covering the entire Brazilian population. The federal government defines the guidelines and regulations of ESF, which are enforced through federal transfers to states and municipalities with strings attached to them; states coordinate with municipalities, and municipalities are in charge of implementing it.[6] The aim of this policy is to strengthen preventive and basic curative health care. This includes immunization, nutritional controls, and basic medical and dental assistance to children; prenatal care, cancer prevention, and dental controls to women; and health check-ups to populations at risk, such as people with high blood pressure, diabetes, or tuberculosis.[7] The policy is implemented through *Unidade Saúde da Família* (Family Health Units, USF), which include, at a minimum, a team with a primary care physician, a nurse, a nurse auxiliary, and four health agents (*Agentes Comunitários de Saúde*).[8] This team is responsible for the health of no more than 4,000 people in a defined territory. ESF is characterized by reaching out to those who cannot access the health unit

---

[5] The decision to include social policies and not social sectors (such as health care or social assistance) makes the process of zooming in on political processes more feasible. At the same time, these national policies make a direct intervention in the overall sectors, such as Plan Nacer and Estratégia Saúde da Família in primary health care, and Asignación Universal por Hijo and Bolsa Família in social assistance.

[6] The health system in Brazil is divided into two tiers: private and public. The public system, *Sistema Único de Saúde* (Unified Health System, SUS), is free and universal. In simplified terms, the municipal level is in charge of primary health care, the state is in charge of medium complexity procedures, and the federal level deals with high-complexity procedures. Nevertheless, this division is not always clear, and the largest cities have also taken on responsibilities for medium- and high-complexity services.

[7] It should be noted that not being covered by ESF does not imply that the person does not have access to these services, since they could be covered through the alternative primary system, called *unidades básicas tradicionais* (UBS).

[8] Some USF also include a dental team (*Equipe de Saúde Bucal*) composed of a dentist, an assistant, and a dental hygiene technician.

(called an active search, or *busca ativa*), an activity for which the health agent in the community is responsible.

There is available coverage data for ESF from 1998 to 2015. The policy targets the entire population and therefore its coverage is calculated as a percentage of total population.[9] The standard deviation of this variable for the entire period is over 25 percentage points, and it covers almost the full possible range of the values (0.7–99 percent). Figure 3.1 shows the trajectory of this policy in each of the twenty-seven states in Brazil and across time.[10] The graph shows variation across time within states, as well as between more and less successful states. While twenty-four states had comfortably reached more than half of the population in 2015, three states were still below 50 percent of coverage. Distrito Federal, Rio de Janeiro, and São Paulo were among the worst performers. In addition, ESF implementation sometimes exhibits drastic changes in certain years and states. Roraima in 2014 is an example of sharp decline in a particular year. The sharp changes in the ESF coverage indicator can be attributed to various factors, including that the state did not report to the federal government the amount of coverage in that particular year, that the ESF health units did not meet minimum standards, or that a number of ESF units closed down, thus affecting the coverage of thousands of patients.

When the targeted population is narrower, such as in Brazil's *Bolsa Família* (Family Allowance) and Argentina's *Asignación Universal por Hijo* (Universal Child Allowance), the denominator is also narrower. Bolsa Família is a conditional cash transfer broadly targeted at poor families that was implemented by a provisional measure in 2003, and Law 10,836 in January 2004 established specific guidelines for its implementation (Brasil. Presidência da República, Casa Civil 2004). The amount of transfer depends upon the economic situation of the family. The Basic Benefit *(Benefício Básico)* of US$35 per month is for families who live in extreme poverty.[11] Besides this basic income, pregnant women and families with children up to fifteen years old receive US$16 per child up to a maximum of five children. Families with children of ages sixteen and seventeen receive US$19 up to a maximum of two teenagers (Brasil. Ministério do Desenvolvimento Social e Combate à Fome 2012a). Bolsa Família is inscribed within the legislation of the *Sistema Único de Assistência Social* (Unified Social Assistance System, SUAS) by which all levels of government (national, intermediate, and local) are responsible for social provision. The federal government funds and designs national policies,

---

[9] If an ESF opens in a given territory, wealthy people in that place cannot opt out of it. They may not use the services, but they would still be counted as covered.

[10] The original data in all the graphs is not transformed (by standardizing it, for example) to keep its substantive meaning.

[11] All monetary convertions are made at the exchange rate as of January 24, 2013. US$1=BR$2. Salaries and transfers are taken close to the year in which field research was conducted in 2012.

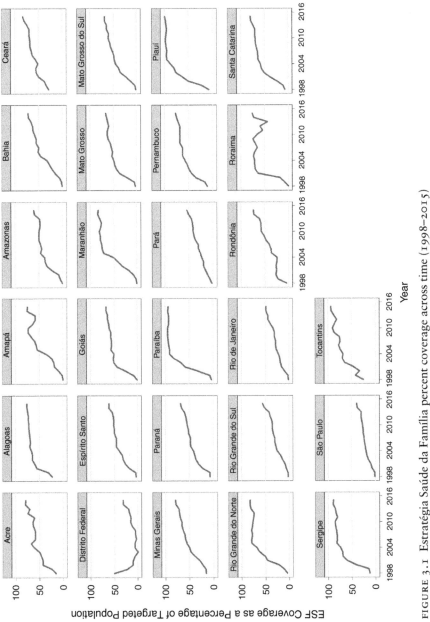

FIGURE 3.1 Estratégia Saúde da Família percent coverage across time (1998–2015)
Source: Brasil. Departamento de Atenção Básica da Secretaria de Atenção à Saúde (2015).

states support and coordinate with municipalities and provide social services where they are needed, and municipalities are in charge of implementation (Brasil. Presidência da República, Casa Civil 1993, 12–15).[12] For the implementation of Bolsa Família, the national *Ministério do Desenvolvimento Social* (Ministry of Social Development, MDS) is in charge of administering the policy, and municipalities are in charge of monitoring the conditionalities of health check-ups, school attendance, and updating of registration in the *Cadastro Único* (Unified Registry).

The Cadastro Único is updated by social assistants, who actively search for registrants who show socioeconomic deprivation and therefore are a potential target of Bolsa Família.[13] Successful implementation is measured as a percentage of this population in 2010, when the data was collected.[14] Figure 3.2 depicts the level of implementation of this conditional cash transfer across Brazilian states from 2004 to 2015. The trajectory of this variable exhibits variation both across time and states. While the general tendency is to increase coverage across time, with differences in each trajectory, some cases also remain at a standstill. In addition, Distrito Federal, Espírito Santo, Goiás, Minas Gerais, Paraná, Rio Grande do Sul, Santa Catarina, and São Paulo lag behind and show slower increases in coverage across time. The standard deviation of this variable is around 17 percent and it ranges from a minimum of 1 percent to a maximum of 92 percent.

The Argentine conditional cash transfer Asignación Universal por Hijo also targets economically deprived people. It is measured as a percentage of people living in poverty.[15] This policy, enacted by a decree in 2009, is a conditional cash transfer that targets pregnant women and families with children under the age of eighteen who are currently unemployed or underemployed and who earn less than the minimum monthly salary (roughly US$480) in 2012.[16] The monthly

---

[12] The federal government enforces these regulations through transferring specific funds with strings attached to them. The 1988 Constitution gave social assistance the status of public policy, the same status as health and social security. The 1993 Organic Law of Social Assistance (*Lei Orgânica da Assistência Social*, Law 8742) regulates this constitutional provision. Finally, in 2005 the SUAS aimed to further homogenize social assistance throughout the country to comply with social rights. SUAS divides social provision into basic and special. Basic social provision is in charge of the CRAS. Special social provision is offered to children and adults at social risk though a network of emergency institutions (Brasil. Ministério do Desenvolvimento Social e Combate à Fome, Secretaria Nacional de Assistência Social 2005, 3).

[13] To be included in the Unified Registry, the income per capita of a family is self-declared by the registrant.

[14] There is available data of this percentage since 2009. For 2004–2008, I develop own calculations based on Cadastro Único figures.

[15] The share of the population in poverty in Argentina is calculated from a survey (Permanent Household Survey – *Encuesta Permanente de Hogares*, EPH) that covers only the 31 largest metropolitan areas in the country, which together include about 80 percent of the population. The 20 percent of the population living in rural areas is not covered by the survey.

[16] Official exchange rate US$1=$6, as of November 20, 2013. All salaries and transfers are taken close to the year in which field research was conducted in 2012.

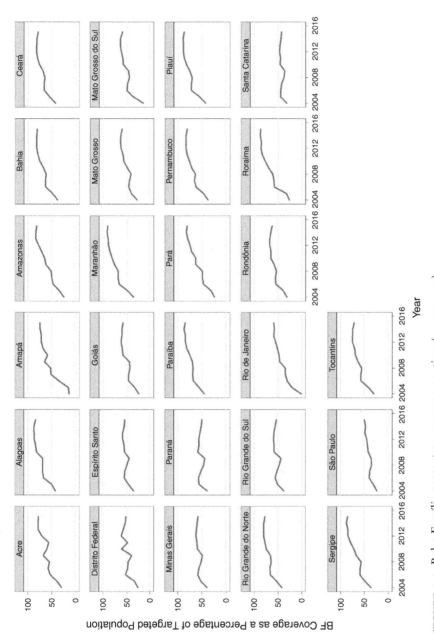

FIGURE 3.2 Bolsa Família percent coverage across time (2004–2015)
Source: Brasil. Secretaria de Avaliação e Gestão da Informação do Ministerio do Desenvolvimento Social e Combate á Fome (2015).

cash transfer is over US$75 per child per month up to a maximum of three children per family and pregnant women from the twelfth week of pregnancy. This amount of transfer equals the highest amount of family allowance received by those children of workers in the formal labor market that receive a contributory family allowance.[17] According to CEPAL, the level of the monthly transfer positions this policy as one of the most relevant CCTs in the region (CEPAL 2013). While 80 percent of the total sum is paid through an ATM card, the other 20 percent is in a bank account and is contingent upon health check-ups and school attendance.

Figure 3.3 represents the variation across provinces and time in the implementation of this policy. Percentage covered is higher than 100 because official figures for population below the poverty line (estimated targeted population) are known to be underestimated in Argentina. Moreover, this figure excludes those in poverty who live in rural areas that may be covered by the CCT. An additional source of overestimation responds to the fact that those covered include workers in the informal sector and unemployed workers who may not be included among those living in poverty. As a result, the targeted population (i.e., the denominator) can actually be smaller than that which is covered.[18] The most successful provinces for the implementation of this CCT are La Rioja, Mendoza, Salta, San Juan, La Pampa, and Santa Cruz (the final two are excluded from the graph for presentation purposes). The rest of the provinces lag behind, with the Autonomous City of Buenos Aires (CABA) being among the most unsuccessful. The standard deviation of this variable reaches 127 percent and it varies from a minimum of 16 percent to a maximum of 694 percent.

Plan Nacer (Birth Plan), also in Argentina, directly intervenes in the provision of public health by affecting resources received by primary health care providers.[19] It was first implemented in 2004 in nine provinces and progressively expanded to all provinces. The health policy entails transfers from the federal government to provinces and municipalities and then to health providers with the aim of guaranteeing basic health care to people without insurance. The services include delivering pregnancy, birth, and neonatal health coverage to pregnant women and immunizations and general health coverage for

---

[17] Those who work in the informal market or are outside the labor market altogether receive Asignación Universal por Hijo.

[18] Official poverty figures are biased equally throughout the country, so as to not affect the comparison across provinces and time. The Argentine government calculates percentage coverage as a percentage of people between ages 0 and 17 (Anses 2011). However, not everyone between those ages should be part of the targeted population, only those that are in poverty, unemployed, or in the informal sector.

[19] Argentina's health system includes three components: a publicly financed sector (administered by provinces and big municipalities), social insurance funds (*obras sociales*, mainly administered by unions), and a private sector. Health policies in Argentina are designed and mostly funded by the federal government and implemented by provinces and some large municipalities. Not being part of Plan Nacer does not mean a lack of health care coverage, since a person can receive care in the public system independently of being part of Plan Nacer, in the private system, or through *obras sociales*.

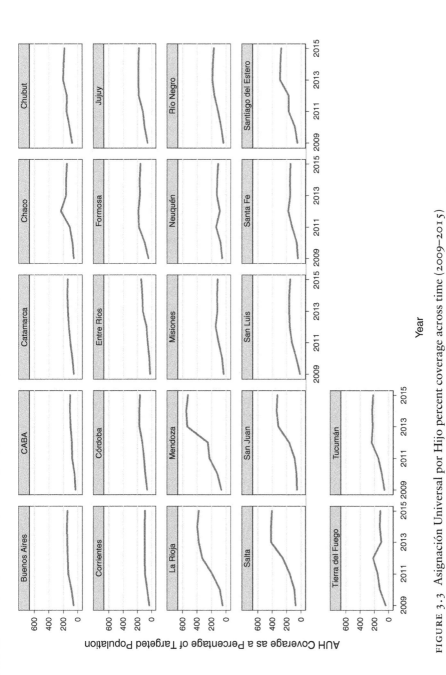

FIGURE 3.3 Asignación Universal por Hijo percent coverage across time (2009–2015)
Note: For clarity purposes, the provinces of La Pampa and Santa Cruz have been excluded.
Source: Argentina. Administración Nacional de la Seguridad Social (2015) and Argentina. Instituto Nacional de Estadísticas y Censos
(2014). I thank James McGuire for making the latter data available.

children under the age of six. In 2012, the federal government extended coverage to uninsured men and women up to the age of sixty-four (Argentina. Ministerio de Salud de la Nación 2012).[20] The World Bank funds most of Plan Nacer. Normatively, 60 percent of the funds are transferred after a province qualifies and the other 40 percent is conditional upon expected results. Subsequently, the province transfers the resources to health providers based on quantity and type of medical services actually offered the previous month.

The targeted coverage of Plan Nacer is broad (uninsured population) and the policy is distributed to all those who meet the eligibility criteria and sign up for it. The measurement of the implementation of this health policy has been constructed by the Argentine Health Ministry. The Ministry measures it as the average of the percentages of coverage (previously agreed with each province) of ten medical interventions. The following ten percentages are averaged: pregnant women with the first prenatal check-up before the twentieth week of gestation, newborns' health check-ups, newborn babies with normal weight, vaccine coverage of pregnant women (including tetanus and tests for sexually transmitted diseases), evaluation of cases of maternal and infant mortality, vaccine coverage in babies under eighteen months (measles, mumps, rubella), sexual and reproductive counseling to puerperal women within 45 days after giving birth, children's complete health check-ups (this counts as two percentages – for children under age one and between one and six in age), and personnel trained in indigenous medicine. After the expansion in 2012, the Health Ministry added regular check-ups for teenagers and uterine and breast cancer prevention.

Figure 3.4 shows that the trajectory of each province varies and some provinces perform better than others. The provinces of Chaco, Corrientes, Jujuy, Misiones, and Tucumán started their implementation earlier and reached peaks that surpassed 30 percent of coverage. Conversely, CABA and the provinces of Buenos Aires, Catamarca, and Rio Negro have never reached 30 percent of coverage. This figure also exhibits an overall decrease in coverage in 2013 as a result of the expansion of the target population, from pregnant women and children to women, men, children, and teenagers. In 2015, the most successful provinces in implementing Plan Nacer were San Luis and Tucumán. The standard deviation of this variable is almost 9 percentage points, which is relatively high considering that it reaches a minimum value of 0 percent and a maximum value of 38 percent.

MIXED METHODS RESEARCH DESIGN

The case studies of two states, two provinces, and eight municipalities is nested within a statistical analysis of Argentina's twenty-four provinces and Brazil's

---

[20] The policy covers women and children until nineteen years old, and men and women from nineteen to sixty-four years old. The elderly in Argentina are covered by a different health scheme.

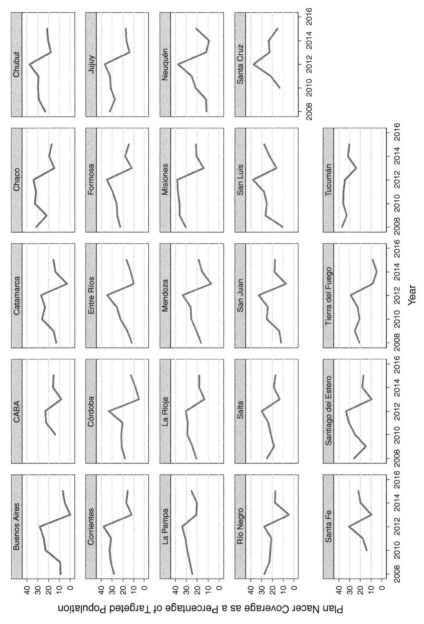

FIGURE 3.4 Plan Nacer percent coverage across time (2008–2015).
Source: Argentina. Ministerio de Salud de la Nación, Plan Nacer (2015).

twenty-seven states. This allows for the combination of two different types of questions: (1) What is the average effect of political alignments, territorial infrastructure, and policy legacies on social policy implementation in Argentina and Brazil? (2) Do attribution of responsibility, political alignments, territorial infrastructure, and policy legacies explain successful social policy implementation in the selected provinces and municipalities in Argentina and Brazil? While quantitative analysis tackles the first type of question, qualitative methodology addresses the second (Goertz and Mahoney 2012, 43).

A mixed methods research design allows for combining two views of causation: the constant conjunction between cause and effect, with affinities to quantitative research, and the counterfactual, prevalent in qualitative analysis (Goertz and Mahoney 2012, 6). For the first view of causation, regression analysis assesses the degree to which effects always follow causes. Specifically, "we may define a cause to be an object followed by another, and where all the objects, similar to the first, are followed by objects similar to the second" (Hume 1975 [1777]; Goertz and Mahoney 2012, 75). The relationship between the independent variables (political alignments, territorial infrastructure, and policy legacies) and social policy implementation is probabilistic and additive. This has two important consequences for the research design. First, the statistical models have the form of ordinary least squares and its derivatives. Second, process tracing is conducted with an additive approach of causality. I explore whether the factors of interest contributed to the outcome in particular case studies, without making any assumptions regarding whether the factors are necessary for the outcome (Goertz and Mahoney 2012, 109).

The counterfactual view of causation, in turn, represents the relationship between attribution of responsibility and political alignments. As was explained in Chapters 1 and 2, attribution of responsibility is *necessary* for political alignments to have an effect on policy implementation. I assess the counterfactual view of causation related to necessary conditions through including policies that are clearly attributed to the national government, and others for which recipients cannot identify the responsible entity.[21] Goertz (2016, 84) explains that necessary conditions are most useful for explaining the *nonoccurrence* of events. In general, "if the first object had not been, the second never would have existed" (Hume 1975 [1777]; Goertz and Mahoney 2012, 75). In policies with blurred attribution of responsibility, the effect of political alignments is irrelevant for the outcome. As a result, the relationship between these two independent variables is deterministic rather than probabilistic.

The presence of both probabilistic and deterministic views of causation calls for a mixed methods research design. I begin with a regression analysis of

---

[21] For a discussion of the relationship between necessary causes and counterfactuals, see Koivu (2016).

Argentina's twenty-four provinces and Brazil's twenty-seven states across time. The statistical analysis guides and complements the case studies, allows for enhancing external validity, and aids the discussion of alternative explanations (King, Keohane, and Verba 1994; Lieberman 2005, 2015). The aim of the regression analysis is not to attain the highest R-squared but to test which variables statistically significantly predict changes in the dependent variable. If the theory is accurate, significant correlations should be found in regressions. To respect the unit homogeneity assumption of statistical analysis, I run the regressions for each country separately. It is reasonable to assume that the relationship between the independent variables and social policy implementation is the same across Brazil and Argentina, when the regressions of each country are run separately and exhibit similar results. When pooling cases across time, the choice of model matters. I run a Hausman test to decide whether fixed or random effects models are more appropriate and, based on its result and the fact that the model includes a number of non-changing variables across units within time, I select a random effects model.[22] The models are Prais–Winsten regressions (panel-corrected standard errors and first-order autoregressive corrections), which adjust standard errors to compensate for heteroscedasticity, first-order autocorrelation, and cross-sectional correlation of the error term (Beck and Katz 1995). The models also include a number of robustness checks to rule out multicollinearity and influential outliers driving the overall results.

The statistical analysis is conducted at the provincial or state level. Two reasons motivate this decision. First, intermediate units in both Brazil and Argentina have more overall capacity than local units to hinder the implementation of national-level policies. They can do so by implementing provincial policies in direct competition with the national ones or by mounting bureaucratic obstacles. The opposite is also true: provinces have higher capacity to enhance national-level policies. Therefore, political alignments and territorial infrastructure are particularly relevant at the intermediate territorial level. Second, data availability makes the analysis at the local level an unfeasible endeavor in Argentina, where local-level data is scarce at best. In addition, there are around 1,922 municipalities in Argentina (Falleti 2004, 69) and around 5,500 in Brazil (Montero and Samuels 2004, 6), so measuring the variables across all municipalities across time would be challenging in both countries. The decision to choose the provincial level as the unit of analysis for the statistical analysis comes with a problem of aggregation, since it obviates significant variation at the local level.[23] To deal with this challenge, the case studies include both the intermediate and local levels, thus studying mechanisms at all levels of government. The qualitative analysis therefore

---

[22] Fixed effect models only account for variation within states throughout time, and therefore they do not allow for the inclusion of invariant variables within units across time, such as population density.

[23] This problem is exemplified by Rodrigues-Silveira (2013, 7–8) for urbanization figures in Brazil.

assesses the degree to which the conclusions in the statistical analysis are valid in spite of the higher level of aggregation.

Case studies included after the regression analysis corroborate the findings of the quantitative analysis, improve the measurement of the variables, and, most importantly, assess the causal mechanisms that lead to such results (Ragin 1989; George and Bennett 2005; Lieberman 2005, 2015). One of the main goals of case studies is to identify and explain causal mechanisms by combining within-case causal inference with analyses of causal mechanisms (Goertz 2017). Goertz and Mahoney (2012, 8) explain how process tracing is particularly adequate for observing causal mechanisms that lead to causation. To enhance the validity of casual inference, I develop comparisons both between countries across subnational units, as well as within countries and subnational units, and across time. Across time variation is particularly relevant in Brazil, where the primary health policy has been implemented since the mid-1990s and the CCT since the early 2000s. This time span allows for tracing the effect of alignments, legacies, and infrastructure on implementation across time in a single subnational unit. In Argentina, both the CCT and health policy have been around for less than ten years and, as such, there is less variation across time. In addition to including within subnational unit comparisons, I also include controlled comparisons across subnational units (aligned and nonaligned with the national government, with higher and lower levels of infrastructure) and policies (with clear and fuzzy attribution of responsibility and with different policy legacies) that allow for generalizing not only the relationship between the independent and dependent variables but also the causal mechanisms through which they are connected (Brookes 2015).

This research design includes variables at multiple territorial levels. This is *Uneven Social Policies'* main methodological contribution. The implementation of national policies exhibit within-country variation due to both subnational-level factors (such as political alignments and territorial infrastructure) as well as national-level variables (such as national attribution of responsibility and policy legacies). At the same time, political alignments and policy legacies matter at the three territorial levels, from the local to the national and from the national to the local. This multilevel framework explains within-country variation in national policy implementation. In other words, unevenly implemented social policies require the inclusion of factors at multiple territorial levels. Looking below the national level makes for a more nuanced analysis of social policy implementation, the role of structural variables that vary across the territory, and the effect of strategic interactions between the national and subnational levels.[24]

---

[24] Recent cutting-edge studies on social and labor policies have chosen subnational research designs for some of these reasons (Tsai 2007; Sugiyama 2013; Alves 2015; Pribble 2015; Singh 2015; Amengual 2016; Wampler et al. 2017). Earlier subnational studies on welfare politics include Kohli (1987) and Tendler (1997).

Finally, while I follow the traditional "nested" design (Lieberman 2005, 2015) in which case studies are conducted *after* the statistical analysis, the order of the different research methodologies could be reversed without altering the product. Flipping the order of the chapters by discussing first case studies and then regression analysis would achieve an initial discussion of causal mechanisms to then move onto the generalizability of such mechanisms (Goertz 2017). The order of the chapters follows a practical aim: simplicity of the regression analysis before complexity of the case studies. However, it does not assume a hierarchy between the pooled-time series analysis and the case studies. The actual research process is not a one-way street but a conversation between each research strategy characterized by feedback loops (Wolf 2010, 153).

MULTILEVEL CASE SELECTION

The scope of this research is narrowed to decentralized countries. This means that the causal mechanisms proposed in this book are generalizable to countries in which subnational levels of government enjoy high levels of authority. I do not expect subnational politics in territorially centralized countries to have a significant effect on the implementation of national social policies. Decentralized countries transfer authority to subnational levels of governments, thus making them relevant actors in the policy implementation process. In particular, only decentralized countries provide the opportunity for subnational governments to design and implement their own social policies (Bonvecchi 2008), a crucial aspect for the implementation of national policies. Territorial infrastructure also exhibits greater variation in decentralized countries compared to territorially centralized ones.

I select two decentralized countries, Argentina and Brazil. Decentralization includes devolution of authority to subnational units in administrative (social services), fiscal (revenues), and political (representation) realms (Falleti 2010a, 17). The Regional Authority Index (RAI) uses two dimensions to define subnational authority (Hooghe, Marks, and Schakel 2010). Self-rule taps into the power that subnational governments have to determine their own rules and institutions – for instance, through the election of governors. Shared rule is the authority that subnational governments have in defining national laws and policies, such as in the senate. This distinction has been widely used in the literature on decentralization and federalism (Elazar 1987). Besides being highly decentralized, Argentina and Brazil also share similar welfare state trajectories from insurance-based to neoliberal reforms to more broadly targeted policies (Huber and Stephens 2012).

One of the goals of the subnational case selection strategy, given that case studies are carried out after the statistical analysis, is to show variation in the variables of interest and be representative of a broader population (Lieberman 2005). Therefore, I select cases that are average in the main control variables and show variation in the independent variables. As a result, subnational case selection follows a "most similar" design, in which cases are similar in background variables, but different in the independent variables with the aim of testing hypothesized relationships and unraveling causal mechanisms (Gerring 2007; Seawright and Gerring 2008). Subnational governments have different alignments with the president. In addition, subnational cases show variation in the capability of the state and their relations with non-state actors. Policy legacies also vary across cases. The selection of cases based on the values of independent variables follows the characteristics of the causal model. Since the aim of case selection is to demonstrate the robustness of causality from cause to effect (Lieberman 2005, 444), selecting the values of the independent variables avoids "cherry-picking" cases that support the causal argument. The next section presents the case selection strategy across multiple territorial levels, as introduced in the first column of Figure 3.1.

Case Selection at the National Level

Argentina and Brazil are two highly decentralized countries with similar trajectories in terms of welfare state development.[25] Argentina and Brazil score consistently high in the RAI. This means that in these countries subnational governments between the national and local levels enjoy significant regional authority both in their own territory (self-rule) and in the country as a whole (shared rule) (Hooghe et al. 2016).

While both Argentina and Brazil are federal and decentralized countries, municipalities are constitutionally stronger in the latter, so one does not find the kind of power concentration in Brazilian states as the one that exists in Argentine provinces. As a result, it is expected that in general Brazilian municipalities will have a stronger role than Argentine municipalities in the implementation of national policies, and provincial governments in Argentina will be in general more crucial than Brazilian states. Brazil is gradually implementing the unified health and social assistance systems (*Sistema Único de Assistência Social* – SUAS and *Sistema Único de Saúde* – SUS) that give municipalities the main role in basic health care and welfare provision. In Argentina, social policies have varied the level of government in charge of implementation. For example, since 2009 Asignación Universal por Hijo has been directly implemented by the federal government, while the previous *Plan Jefes y Jefas de Hogar Desocupados* (Unemployed Heads of Households Program, PJJHD) in 2002 was implemented by provinces. As a result, Brazilian municipalities will generally have a stronger role in the implementation of health and social assistance policies, while the role of subnational units will vary

---

[25] The analysis of decentralization is partly taken from the country profiles in Hooghe et al. (2016). The analysis of Argentina's and Brazil's social policy trajectories is partly taken from Niedzwiecki and Huber (2013) and Huber and Niedzwiecki (2015).

across policies in Argentina, with a general prevalence of provinces over municipalities. However, and in spite of their weaker constitutional standing, Argentine municipalities can challenge implementation patterns if they decide against putting their institutions, personnel, and knowledge of the territory at the service of the national policy.

Argentina is divided into twenty-three provinces, which are further divided into municipalities, and the CABA or Autonomous City of Buenos Aires. Provinces have authority over institutional setup, residual powers, the judicial system, primary and secondary education, health, housing and sanitation, social assistance and food programs, and some other major responsibilities such as environmental and industrial development. The CABA has shared similar competencies as the rest of the provinces since 1996, though it was not given control over the police until 2010 and does not have residual powers. Municipalities have more limited competencies. Although municipalities were defined as autonomous by the 1994 Constitution (Art. 123) and all municipalities elect assemblies and mayors, the extent of their autonomy is decided by each province (Smulovitz and Clemente 2004, 42; Fenwick 2016, 43). Therefore, there is wide variation in terms of municipal autonomy across provinces. In terms of resources, municipalities collect a minor cleaning and sewage tax and depend on transfers from the provinces. A portion of the taxes collected by the federal government are transferred to provinces. These federal transfers finance more than half of all provincial budgets (except from the province of Buenos Aires) and a large majority of such transfers are automatic and unconditional, called *coparticipación* (Tommasi 2002; Gervasoni 2010a, 311; González 2016). Provinces also co-determine legislation and policies through the directly elected senate with ample and symmetric powers and diverse councils that discuss national policies, such as *Consejo Federal de Educación* for education policies and *Consejo Federal de Salud* for health policies. These are examples of shared rule mechanisms.

Brazil is divided into twenty-six states, which are further divided into municipalities, and the Federal District of Brasília. States, municipalities, and the federal government have equal juridical status since the 1988 Constitution. The three levels have concurrent competencies in social policy, which means that they can all legislate but none have specific obligations, and health care, education, and pensions have been decentralized. Brasília has competencies more similar to states than municipalities, but while states have their own constitution, Brasília is regulated by a national organic law. A good amount of revenue comes from state and local taxes, as well as national transfers. States control the rate of state value added tax (*Imposto sobre Circulação de Mercadorias e Prestação de Serviços*, ICMS) and municipalities control the rate of a tax on services (*Imposto Sobre Serviços*, ISS) and real estate (*Imposto Sobre a Propriedade Predial e Territorial Urbana*, IPTU). Federal transfers to states and municipalities include the constitutionally mandated sharing of tax revenue, as well as nonconstitutional specific-purpose taxes.

While some of the wealthier states fund most of their expenditures through their own revenues, poorer states are highly dependent on federal transfers (Rodden 2006, 193–194).[26] States co-determine legislation through the directly elected national senate with broad authority. Both municipalities and states also co-determine national policy though councils in health, education, social assistance, transportation, and justice, among others. Councils are generally composed of representatives of the government, citizens, and providers.

Argentina and Brazil also share similar trajectories in terms of welfare state development. Together with Chile, Uruguay, and Costa Rica, they have built the most advanced welfare states in the region (Mesa-Lago 1978, 1989; Huber and Stephens 2010, 2012). These social states find their origin in the 1930s and 1940s, with employment-based social insurance and stratification of welfare state programs, particularly along occupational lines. In addition, they underwent retrenchment during the 1980s and 1990s, and have expanded their social protection systems since the 2000s.

Import Substitution Industrialization strategies initially financed social security systems through a combination of employer, employee, and state contributions. During the 1930s and 1940s, Argentina and Brazil expanded their social states through the co-optation of labor (Huber 1996). Powerful leaders (Juan Perón and Getúlio Vargas) mobilized and co-opted the newly organized urban working classes (Collier and Collier 1991). The Peronist Party in Argentina established a major social protection system that included pensions and the expansion of the union-run mutual health insurance (*obras sociales*) and of public hospitals (Rock 1985; Lloyd-Sherlock 2000). Vargas' regime in Brazil set the foundation for urban sector incorporation into the social security system and the military's bureaucratic-authoritarian regime expanded coverage to the rural sector in 1971 (Malloy 1979). Nevertheless, in neither of these two countries was this a citizenship right, and the informal and rural sectors were generally excluded or received low quantity of cash and poor quality health care.[27] The results were stratified and fragmented social protection systems. In addition, these systems proved to be financially unsustainable, due to a declining ratio of workers to pensioners and the low levels of contribution (Cruz Saco and Mesa-Lago 1998, 7–8; Kay 1999, 406). The crisis of social security systems, together with high levels of debt and decreases in the price of primary commodities, incentivized the retrenchment of social policies in the 1980s and 1990s.

International financial institutions prescribed a reduction of government expenditure, privatization, deregulation, and liberalization of trade and

---

[26] The main federal transfer to states is the *Fundo de Participação dos Estados* (State Participation Fund, FPE), funded with 21.5 percent of the net revenues of the main national taxes, namely personal, corporate, income, and VAT taxes. The distribution of this fund follows redistributive criteria among states (Rodden 2006, 193).

[27] Argentina's 1954 introduction of pensions for rural workers and the self-employed, and Brazil's 1971 expansion of noncontributory pensions were noticeable exceptions.

financial markets. In social policy, the blueprint was to narrowly target the provision of social assistance, partially or fully privatize social security, and increase the participation of private providers in health care and education. These prescriptions influenced policies mostly through conditionality of funds, but the receptivity varied in Argentina and Brazil. While Argentina partly privatized its pension system, Brazil did not engage in any major reform (Niedzwiecki 2014a). Social assistance remained narrowly targeted to the poor in both countries. As a result of neoliberal reforms, including deregulation of the labor market, the number of workers in the informal sector increased, and therefore contributory-based systems came to exclude even larger portions of the population. Poverty and inequality levels also increased. ECLAC's figures show that in the early 1990s, more than 40 percent of Brazil's population and 16 percent of the Argentine population lived below the poverty line. Inequality similarly rose to a Gini coefficient of over 0.55 in Brazil and 0.44 in Argentina (Huber and Stephens 2012). In addition, these reforms aggravated the crisis of social security. In 2004, active contribution to the pension system was 45 percent in Brazil and 24 percent in Argentina (Mesa-Lago 2008, 38).

The discontent generated by market-oriented policies, together with the consolidation of democracy, the rise of left parties, and the commodity export boom of the 2000s paved the road for the expansion of social policies (Huber and Stephens 2012). The Worker's Party (*Partido dos Trabalhadores,* PT) and President Luiz Inácio Lula da Silva in Brazil deepened the trend started by former president Fernando Henrique Cardoso. This party launched Bolsa Família and expanded this conditional cash transfer to cover 23 percent of all Brazilian families in 2011. Primary health care, through Estratégia Saúde da Família, was also strengthened under the PT government.[28] In addition, the pension sector improved its fiscal imbalances and its distribution profile by imposing stronger limits on benefit ceilings and equalizing the benefits for new entrants to the public and private sectors. Finally, the legal minimum wage, which is also used to calculate many transfers targeted to the poor, has consistently increased since Cardoso's administration (Kingstone and Ponce 2010, 113).

In Argentina, the left-of-center faction of the Peronist Party (*Frente Para la Victoria*) also expanded social policies. Similar to Brazil's Bolsa Família, Argentina's Asignación Universal por Hijo is a broadly targeted conditional cash transfer not distributed clientelistically. Primary health care also received emphasis through the distribution of first aid kits and the reimbursement to public clinics and hospitals for services provided to uninsured women, children, and teenagers. The most salient reversal from market-oriented reforms was in the area of pensions. There was an expansion of coverage to those with insufficient contributions in exchange for a payment plan;

---

[28] Estratégia Saúde da Família was launched as a national policy in 1994. The statistical results are not altered when separating the Cardoso and Lula periods (Niedzwiecki 2016, 491).

and the government fully nationalized the pension system in 2008 (Arza 2009; Niedzwiecki 2014a).

In Argentina, the Peronist Party has been the promoter of both retrenchment and expansion policies. This is possible because the Peronist Party has generally enjoyed majorities in both chambers and has a flexible structure that allowed it to change from union-based linkages to personal-based clientelistic linkages (Levitsky 2003). In Brazil, the PT was in open opposition to the implementation of *Partido da Social Democracia Brasileira* (PSDB)-led neoliberal reforms and implemented expansive policies after the commodity boom (Roberts 2014). Both retrenchment and expansion policies were implemented by broad coalitions. This is because there is no majority party in Brazil that can implement policies alone.

The differences in party structure across countries produce variation in the role of political alignments for the implementation of national policies. In particular, political alignments have a stronger effect on policy implementation in Argentina compared with Brazil because the party system is more fragmented, coalitions are more fluid, and there is lower party discipline in the latter compared with the former. These characteristics contribute to blurring attribution of responsibility (Powell and Whitten 1993), thus weakening the effect of political alignments. In addition, governors are more powerful in Argentina and this also contributes to a larger effect of political alignments in this country. In spite of the differences in party systems and the strength of governors across countries, the theory on the effects of political alignments on policy implementation still holds, providing an increased confidence in the results.

The other two independent variables also exhibit differences across countries. Policy legacies are stronger in Brazil than in Argentina, in part because policies have been around for a longer period of time, covered more people, and developed more experience with the provision of conditionalities. These differences allow for testing the effect of the strength of legacies on implementation. Finally, civil society has a prominent role in the implementation of national policies in Brazil, while in Argentina it is mostly absent, with noticeable exceptions. In addition, civil society participated through institutionalized channels in Brazil and in a more ad hoc manner in Argentina. Territorial infrastructure, as a result, also looks different across the two countries.

Case Selection at the Provincial Level

At the intermediate level, I select two states in Brazil and two provinces in Argentina with similar levels of GDP per capita and population density to rule out explanations based on economic development and industrialism. These cases also show variation in the level of subnational democracy, to test for the effect of regime type on social provision. In addition, they exhibit different political alignments with the federal government, which is one of the main independent variables accounting for variation in policy implementation. Finally, there is also variation in policy legacies and the role of civil society in territorial infrastructure across provinces.

In Argentina, I select the provinces of Mendoza and San Luis, two middle-income provinces with similar GDP per capita and population density, as illustrated in Figure 3.5.[29] In terms of electoral trajectories, while Mendoza has generally been an ally to the national government since 2003, San Luis has been in opposition. Table A.3.1 in the Appendix summarizes the coding of Mendoza's and San Luis' political alignments following seven indicators since 2007 across executive and legislative elections. A team of six researchers recruited by myself and three Argentine political science professors coded newspaper articles a month before and a month after each election to decide whether the governor was aligned or opposed to the

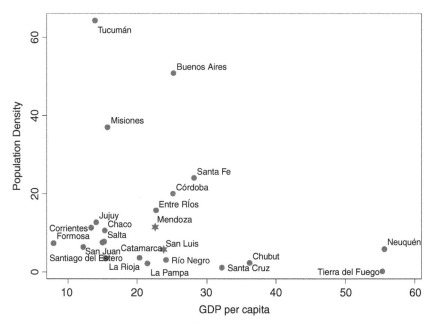

FIGURE 3.5 GDP per capita and population density in Argentina
Note: CABA is not included for presentation purposes, for exhibiting very high levels of both variables. Data of GDP per capita is of 2009, in 1,000 Argentine Pesos, and population density data is of 2012 and per square kilometer.
Sources: Argentina. Ministerio del Interior de la Nación (2011). Equipo Observatorio Económico Territorial Universidad Nacional del Litoral (2014), I thank James McGuire for making this data available.

[29] The most updated available figure for GDP per capita is the year 2009 and I select 2012 for population density because it was the year in which I conducted field research. The choice of year, however, does not alter the fact that Mendoza and San Luis share similar levels of both control variables.

president in that particular election cycle. The profiles in the Online Appendix offer a detailed account of political alignments of all provinces, including Mendoza and San Luis, across seven indicators in each election year covering 2007–15.[30]

Mendoza's governors have been aligned with the national government since 2003. Governors from this province share a party tag with the national government in most elections, have a positive discourse toward the national administration, share meetings and public acts with members of the central government (including the president herself), are assessed by experts (mainly journalists) as being aligned, and their local opposition is also opposed to the national government. Conversely, San Luis' governors score opposite to Mendoza's in these indicators (Table A.3.1). The brothers Adolfo and Alberto Rodríguez Saá handpicked the winning candidates or have been governors themselves in every election cycle since the transition to democracy in 1983. Their governments have been in open competition with the national government. Adolfo Rodríguez Saá ran as a presidential candidate against the Kirchners in 2007 and 2015, and his brother in the 2011 elections.

Table A.3.1 also shows that membership in the Peronist Party does not determine alignment with the federal government in these cases, thus explaining the need for the extensive coding exercise developed for this book. Both Mendoza's and San Luis' governors identified with the Peronist Party, yet their alignments with the national government were different. Moreover, before 2007 Mendoza was part of the *Radicales-K*, the members of the Radical Party (*Unión Cívica Radical*, UCR) who supported the Kirchners. That is why the then governor, Julio Cobos, ran as the vice president of Cristina Kirchner in the 2007 presidential elections. In the wake of a political falling out that resulted in the dissolution of the *Radicales-K* and Cobos' detachment from kirchnerismo in 2008, the elected governors after that used the Frente para la Victoria party tag to show undisputed alignment with the President.

These provinces also show variation in the levels of subnational democracy, a variable that has been important for predicting social provision at the national level (Haggard and Kaufman 2008; McGuire 2010b; Huber and Stephens 2012). Mendoza is considered one of the most democratic provinces, while San Luis is one of the most undemocratic (Chavez 2003; Giraudy 2009, 2014; Gervasoni 2010b). While there has been party alternation in Mendoza, San Luis has been governed by the Rodríguez Saá family or close collaborators since 1983. As a consequence civil society tends to collaborate with the government in the implementation of social assistance policies in Mendoza but not in San Luis. In other words, there is variation in the characteristics of the territorial infrastructure variable across these two provinces.

In Brazil, I select the states of Rio Grande do Sul and Goiás. They are middle-income states, with similar levels of GDP per capita but with somewhat different population densities, as illustrated in Figure 3.6. At the same time,

---

[30] The online appendix is available at saraniedzwiecki.com

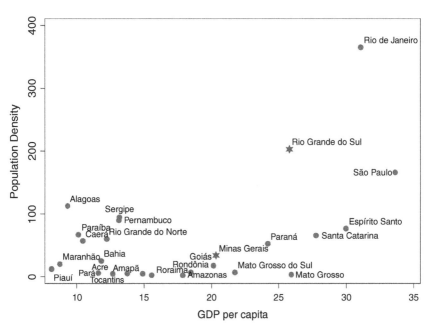

FIGURE 3.6 GDP per capita and population density in Brazil
Note: Federal District of Brasília is not shown for presentation purposes. Data as of 2012. GDP per capita is in 1,000 Brazilian Reais and population density measured per square kilometer.
Sources: Brasil. Ministério da Saúde, DATA (2015); Brasil. Instituto Brasileiro de Geografia e Estatística.

these states show differences in terms of political alignments. While party tags are somewhat meaningless in Argentina, given the large number of provincial parties and the complexities among self-defined Peronist Parties, in Brazil party tags are more meaningful to observe alignments.[31] In Goiás, politics is relatively polarized between the *Partido da Social Democracia Brasileira* (PSDB) and the PMDB (Dias Bezerra, Paiva Ferreira, and Ribeiro 2011, 5). Goiás' governor (PSDB) has presented open opposition to the federal government since 2003, when the PT was elected for the presidency. The state incumbent alliance headed by the PSDB included around eleven parties in the 2010 elections, and its main opposition has been an alliance between the PMDB and the PT. Conversely, in Rio Grande do Sul the PT governor, in power since 2010, is fully aligned with the president. The position of previous governors toward the federal government is more ambivalent since alliances are not long lasting in Rio Grande do Sul, but leaning toward opposition to the federal government. This across-time variation

[31] See Chapter 4 for a discussion of the measurement of political alignments in Brazilian states.

in political alignments, and its effect on the implementation of the CCT, is analyzed in Chapter 5.

These two states also exhibit variation in terms of levels of subnational democracy.[32] Rio Grande do Sul shows high degrees of alternation of power in the governorship, has been defined as pluralist with the left playing a relevant role (Borges 2007), and has been a case of "broadened competition" (Montero 2007). Since 1982, different parties have occupied the seat of the governor, including PMDB, PSDB, PT, and *Partido Democrático Trabalhista* (PDT), and no governor has been reelected. Conversely, Goiás has had less alternation, with PSDB (in coalition with *Partido Progresista,* PP) controlling state politics for the last fifteen years. Goiás has been defined as a "dominant machine" (Borges 2007), as a case of "conservative competition" (Montero 2007), and as a "hyper-presidential region" (Krause 2008). Politics in Goiás has been dominated by Iris Rezende Machado (PMDB) from 1982 to 1997, and Marconi Perillo (PSDB) since 1998. As a result of these different levels of internal democracy, civil society coordinates with the state to a larger extent in Rio Grande do Sul than Goiás, meaning that territorial infrastructure looks different across the two cases.

The main limitation of the intermediate (provincial and state) case selection strategy is that the level of subnational democracy covaries with political alignments: aligned provinces Rio Grande do Sul and Mendoza are also highly competitive and opposition provinces Goiás and San Luis exhibit characteristics of nondemocratic regimes. How can we be sure that it is political alignments, and not regime type, that matters for policy implementation? Theoretically, subnational regime type shapes the way in which policies are implemented but not their ultimate success in terms of coverage. In other words, governors in authoritarian provinces have no political incentives to block national policies if they are politically aligned with the president and if they rest on positive policy legacies. Overall, federal policies can be successfully implemented in democratic and authoritarian places in which executives are aligned with the national government and count on strong territorial infrastructure and positive policy legacies. Subnational regime type matters indirectly for policy implementation.[33] In less democratic provinces such as San Luis, the role of the governor will be more relevant than that of mayors due to the high concentration of power in the executive. In addition, territorial infrastructure in a place like San Luis does not include the

---

[32] Brazilian states do not show the kind of undemocratic characteristics that Argentine provinces do. This difference may be due to the fact that Argentine provinces have the authority to decide on electoral rules, including dates, district designs, and reelection rules, as well as on the organization of municipalities. Brazilian states do not have this option, since all these decisions are constitutionalized. Therefore, there is more room for variation in the level of democracy among Argentine provinces than Brazilian states.

[33] The indirect role of subnational regime on policy implementation is explained in Chapter 2.

collaboration between state and non-state actors; it is achieved through provincial institutions exclusively.

Given that the relationship between subnational regime type and policy implementation is theoretically not a direct one, this variable is not included in the regression analysis. However, subnational case studies show the independent effect of regime type and alignments. In particular, across-time variation in political alignments allows for ruling out the direct role of subnational regime type on policy implementation in the case studies. The state of Rio Grande do Sul in Brazil has been consistently democratic (Borges 2007; Montero 2007), yet its alignment with the national government has changed since the implementation of CCT Bolsa Família. When the national CCT was launched in 2003, the state was headed by an opposition alliance. The governor at the time acted by omission: he decided not to aid the implementation of the federal CCT and even got rid of a subnational CCT that could have been used to complement the national one. When an aligned PT governor was elected in 2009, he created a state cash transfer that directly complemented Bolsa Família by using state funds to increase the amount of the transfer to Bolsa Família recipients with children in high school. Change in political alignments, therefore, changed the state's attitude toward the implementation of the CCT without altering its level of internal democracy. Similarly, municipal cases in Brazil that exhibit variation in political alignments and not subnational regime type show the relevance of the former for policy implementation. The municipality of Canoas in the state of Rio Grande do Sul switched from omission to active participation after the inauguration of a PT mayor in 2009, without altering its level of internal democracy.

Case Selection at the Municipal Level

National policies are also unevenly implemented at the local level. In Brazil, the policies included in this study are designed to be implemented at the local level, making mayors crucial actors. While in Argentina municipalities tend to have a less important role, they nevertheless influence implementation patterns. Therefore, I also include cases at the municipal level. I select two municipalities within each state or province. To analyze municipalities that have potential leverage over social policies, I choose relatively urban and developed units. The two selected municipalities within states are also geographically close to each other.[34] At the same time, I select cases with different political alignments.

---

[34] In terms of population, according to the 2010 census in both countries, the province of Mendoza in Argentina has 1.7 million inhabitants (Las Heras 203,666 and Godoy Cruz 191,903) and San Luis 432,310 (the Department of La Capital that hosts San Luis City has 204,019 and General Pedernera that hosts Villa Mercedes has 125,899 inhabitants). In Brazil, Rio Grande do Sul has 10.7 million inhabitants (Porto Alegre 1.4 million and Canoas 323,827) and Goiás 6 million (Goiânia 1.3 million and Valparaíso de Goiás 132,982). There is no available data at the

TABLE 3.2 *Multilevel political alignments in Argentina and Brazil in 2012*

Province/Municipality	Party of the Mayor	Party of the Governor	Party of the President
Mendoza			
Las Heras	FPV	FPV	FPV
Godoy Cruz	UCR		
San Luis			
San Luis City	FPV	FJUL	
Villa Mercedes	FJUL		
Rio Grande do Sul			
Porto Alegre	PDT	PT	PT
Canoas	PT		
Goiás			
Goiânia	PT	PSDB	
Valparaíso de Goiás	PSDB		

Note: FPV: Frente para la Victoria; UCR: Unión Cívica Radical; FJUL: Frente Justicialista Unión y Libertad. PDT: Partido Democrático Trabalhista; PT: Partido dos Trabalhadores; PSDB: Partido da Social Democracia Brasileira.

Table 3.2 displays political alignments of the selected provinces, states, and municipalities in 2012, the year in which most of the field research was conducted. In these tables I use the indicator of party tag of the governor to represent alignments, with the caveat introduced earlier that this indicator is more valid for Brazil than for Argentina. In 2012, party tags in Argentina in the selected provinces and municipalities actually accurately represent alignments.

For Argentina's Mendoza, I select Las Heras and Godoy Cruz. Las Heras is a Peronist-Frente para la Victoria stronghold and therefore the three levels of government are aligned (Las Heras–Mendoza–national government), as Table 3.2 illustrates. Conversely, the municipality of Godoy Cruz in Mendoza is a Radical bastion, opposing both the provincial and the federal governments in 2012. In the province of San Luis, I select the municipalities of San Luis City and Villa Mercedes. San Luis City is the capital of the province and has been mostly headed by a government in opposition to the province's governors and aligned with the president. Villa Mercedes, in contrast, is a bastion of the Rodríguez Saá family, where no other party has governed the municipality since the return of democracy in Argentina in 1983. Therefore,

municipal level in Argentina for including other social indicators to compare across municipalities.

the municipality was aligned with the governor and in opposition to the federal government in 2012.

In Brazil, in the aligned state of Rio Grande do Sul, I select Porto Alegre and Canoas. Porto Alegre is the capital of the state and the PT governed there for sixteen consecutive years until 2005. In 2012, the local government is in the hands of a PDT mayor. Porto Alegre is a good example of the complexity of alliances throughout territorial levels in Brazil. The municipal government opposes the PT at the state level (in 2012 local elections the PDT competed against the PT) but is part of the PT coalition at the federal level and is thus aligned with the national government. The bordering municipality of Canoas is the second-largest (after Porto Alegre) metropolitan city in the state. It was dominated by PMDB and PSDB groups until a coalition led by the PT won elections in 2008 and 2012. As in the case of Las Heras in the Argentine province of Mendoza, in Canoas the three levels of government are fully aligned.

In the state of Goiás, I choose Goiânia and Valparaíso de Goiás. Goiânia is the capital city and mayors have been mostly aligned with the federal PT and in opposition to the state governor. The municipality has alternated between PMDB and PT leadership since the transition to democracy and until these parties made a coalition in 2008 that continues to control the local government. The mayor in 2012 is from the PT. Goiânia's political alignments are comparable to San Luis City in Argentina. The second municipality in Goiás is Valparaíso de Goiás. It is located in the surroundings of Brasília and was founded as a municipality in 1995, after being separated from its neighboring Luziânia. Since its founding, two of its mayors have been PSDB, aligned to the state's government and in open opposition to the federal government. For these characteristics, Valparaíso de Goiás is comparable to Villa Mercedes, in the Argentine province of San Luis.

CONCLUSIONS

Studying noncontributory policies is relevant in Latin America, given the high percentage of the population who are outside of the formal labor market and therefore would not have access to these benefits if they were contribution-based. As such, these policies can change people's lives. To reach their potential, these policies need first to be successfully implemented. Social policy implementation is the degree to which policies effectively provide social protection, measured as coverage as a percentage of the targeted population. To address the determinants of policy implementation within countries, this book offers a mixed methods research design that combines the breadth given by the statistical analysis with the depth of causal mechanisms provided by case studies. I select cases across countries, provinces, and municipalities. At the national level, I choose the most decentralized countries in the region, Argentina and

Brazil, which also share similar welfare state development trends since their origin in the 1940s to the present. At the subnational levels, I choose middle-income units with different political alignments. Provinces and municipalities also exhibit differences in the forms of territorial infrastructure and the relative presence of policy legacies, a variation that will be analyzed in Chapters 5 and 6. The next chapter presents the quantitative results; it uses cross-sectional time series analysis to study the average effect of political alignments, territorial infrastructure, and policy legacies on social policy implementation in twenty-seven Brazilian states from 1998 to 2015 and twenty-four Argentine provinces from 2008 to 2015.

APPENDIX

TABLE A.3.1 *Coding of political alignment in the Argentine provinces of Mendoza and San Luis*

	Mendoza				San Luis			
	2007	2009	2011	2013	2007	2009	2011	2013
Peronist	Yes	Yes	Yes	Yes	Yes	Yes	Yes	Yes
Party tag	PJ	FPV	FPV	FPV	FPJ	FJP	CF	CF
Discourse	Alignment	Alignment	Alignment	Alignment	Opposition	Opposition	Opposition	Opposition
Public acts/ meetings with national actors	National government	National government	National government	National government	National opposition	National opposition	No	National government and opposition
Assessment of experts	Alignment	Alignment	Alignment	Alignment	Opposition	Opposition	Opposition	Opposition
Previous appointment in national government	No	No	No	No	No	No	No	No
Local opposition aligned with national government	Yes	No	No	No	Yes	Yes	Yes	Yes
Overall	**Aligned**	**Aligned**	**Aligned**	**Aligned**	**Opposition**	**Opposition**	**Opposition**	**Opposition**

Notes: See Online Appendix for a detailed description of the coding scheme and provincial profiles. PJ: Partido Justicialista; FPV: Frente para la Victoria; FPJ: Frente Partido Justicialista; FJP: Frente Justicialista es Posible; CF: Compromiso Federal.

4

Subnational Statistical Analysis

This chapter quantitatively analyzes the factors that shape social policy implementation across states in Brazil and provinces in Argentina over time. These include political alignments, policy legacies, and territorial infrastructure. First, the extent to which social policies are successfully implemented depends on political alignments at the different territorial levels. Opposition subnational governments become interested in hindering the implementation of an upper-level policy when the policy can be easily attributed to the national government. This chapter tests the effects of political alignments on social policy implementation in four different policies: two conditional cash transfers (CCTs) and two health policies in Argentina and Brazil. While recipients of the CCTs can generally attribute them to the federal government, recipients of the health policies tend not to identify who is responsible for the service. Therefore, political alignments are only expected to be significant in the CCTs in each country.

Second, having strong territorial infrastructure allows the state to successfully implement policies. In particular, subnational institutions that are accessible and of good quality enhance implementation by directly implementing policies, monitoring their functioning, or informing the population about their existence. Weaker infrastructure in the territory, in turn, makes the implementation of policies more challenging.

Finally, policy legacies can hinder the implementation of new policies when strong interests from previous policies are contrary to the current one. In these cases, supporters of the previous policy will try to obstruct the implementation of the new policy. Conversely, positive policy legacies are expected to enhance the implementation of social policies. Previous policies that targeted the same population can advance the reach of the current policy by automatically transferring their recipients from the previous to the current policy or by generating institutional mechanisms that facilitate the implementation of the new policy.

The next section presents the measurement of the dependent, independent, and control variables. Then it proceeds with a discussion of the selected statistical models and the robustness tests reported in the Appendix and Online Appendix to this chapter. Finally, it presents the regression results.

VARIABLES AND OPERATIONALIZATION

I have constructed an original dataset that covers the twenty-four provinces in Argentina (including the Autonomous City of Buenos Aires) from 2008 to 2015 and the twenty-seven states in Brazil (including the Federal District of Brasília) from 1998 to 2015.[1] The starting dates in each country mark the first year in which there is available data. The unit of analysis is each province/state year.[2]

Measurement of the Dependent Variable – Social Policy Implementation

The dependent variable, social policy implementation, is defined as the extent to which policies provide social protection to the intended population. This is measured as levels of coverage as a percentage of the targeted population. The targeted population varies by policy. Chapter 3 offered a detailed account of the dependent variable across policies, so a short summary will suffice. Brazil's federal government has determined the number of people who should be included in the Unified Registry (or *Cadastro Único*) due to their level of vulnerability. Successful implementation of *Bolsa Família* is therefore measured as a percentage of this population. The numerator, in turn, is the number of families receiving this policy. Accordingly, Argentine CCT *Asignación Universal por Hijo* is measured as the number of children receiving the policy as a percentage of people living below the poverty line, calculated by the National Statistical Institute's Permanent Household Survey.

The targeted population can also be broader, such as in Brazil's primary health policy *Estratégia Saúde da Família*. This policy targets the entire population and therefore its coverage is calculated as families receiving the policy as a percentage of total estimated population in that area. Finally, the successful implementation of Argentina's health policy *Plan Nacer* is measured by the Argentine Health Ministry as the average of the percentages of coverage

---

[1] Tables A.4.1–A.4.4 in the Appendix of this chapter include summary statistics, description of variables, and sources. Datasets and Stata do-files are available for replication on the author's website: www.saraniedzwiecki.com.

[2] The collection of subnational data in Brazil and Argentina is challenging, particularly due to the high level of missing values. Given that the missingness is non-ignorable and includes continuous series of years, I have decided not to proceed with multiple imputation. When it was safe to assume that the variable is rarely changing, I have proceeded through single imputation. When this assumption was not reasonable, I have done casewise deletion or the automatic dropping of observations due to missingness. Imputation decisions for each variable are described in Tables A.4.3 and A.4.4 in the Appendix.

of medical practices, previously agreed with each province, called tracers. The following percentages are averaged: pregnant women with the first prenatal check-up, newborn health check-ups, newborn babies who are not underweight, vaccine coverage of pregnant women, fully evaluated cases of maternal mortality or death of infant under one year of age, vaccine coverage in babies under eighteen months, children's complete health check-ups, personnel trained in indigenous medicine, sexual and reproductive counseling to puerperal women and teenagers, regular check-ups for teenagers, and uterine and breast cancer prevention.

Measurement of Independent and Control Variables

Political Alignments

To measure political alignments I code the level of opposition of the governor toward the president throughout time. This variable is measured at the moment of elections, thus tapping into electoral alignments or the explicit position of elected candidates at the moment of elections. The main advantage of this measurement decision is that it is straightforward: candidates make their position toward the president explicit at the moment of the election. It therefore keeps the same value for two years in Argentina and four years in Brazil. This is because while gubernatorial and presidential elections are concurrent in Brazil, that is not necessarily true in Argentina, where provinces have the authority to set the date of elections.[3] The coding is effective from the year following the elections because candidates take on their position at that time. Given the different characteristics of the party system in each country, this variable is coded differently across Brazil and Argentina.

The highly fragmented party system in Brazil requires that national and subnational executives form coalitions to win elections. The coding therefore includes electoral coalitions. In addition, party names in Brazil are consistent across local, state, and federal levels, meaning that there are no subnational party labels. This allows for measuring political alignments between the president and the governor by observing party labels. Previous research has shown that it matters for the distribution of resources in Brazil whether subnational executives belong to the president's party, belong to the federal coalition, or are part of the opposition (Bueno 2018). I therefore code the level of opposition as whether the governor and president belong to the same party

[3] The coding assumes that political alignments remain stable from one election to the next. Although alignments can certainly change after an election, measuring changes in-between elections would be problematic both for theoretical and empirical reasons. Theoretically, the measurement would confound political alignments at the moment of elections with actions that show their alignment in nonelection moments (such as hindering the implementation of policies, among other actions). In other words, measuring alignments through actions in-between election years would make it challenging to analyze the consequences of such alignments, which is the main goal of this book. Empirically, measuring political alignments in nonelection moments (such as years, months, or even days) would make coding decisions more arbitrary.

(=0), the governor and the president share an alliance with each other's party or a common third party (=1), or none of these options (=2). In the multivariate regressions, the category aligned (=0) serves as the base category and the other two are included as dummy variables, "middle" and "opposition," respectively.

In Argentina, party labels are less meaningful because of the large number of provincial parties that have unique names. The coding, therefore, cannot be based on party names. In addition, some of these parties self-identify as "Peronist," in spite of being in opposition to the (also Peronist) national government. Therefore, the coding needs to be sensitive to opposition from within the Peronist Party. I use a database that incorporates these complexities.[4] A team of researchers coded newspaper articles a month before and a month after the elections, to decide whether the governor was aligned or opposed to the president in that particular election.[5] The database looks at seven indicators of alignment to assess the overall position of the governor toward the president.

The first step was to identify whether the governor self-identified as Peronist or non-Peronist. In the former case, there was a higher chance that the governor was aligned. However, in the cases in which the governor self-identified as Peronist but decided to break with the federal government, the governor's position was made very explicit in media outlets.[6] In the case of non-Peronist governors, there was a higher chance that they belonged to the opposition. The cases of non-Peronist alignment to the federal government tended to also appear explicit in the newspapers.[7]

The second step was to identify the party tag: if the governor, or the list he or she supported in legislative elections, ran with a *Frente para la Victoria* party tag (the party tag of the president), there was a high chance that the governor was aligned with the president. However, not competing with a Frente para la Victoria party tag did not mean opposition to the president. Third, the coding analyzed expressions of support or opposition from the governor to the president in public speeches and media outlets. Fourth, the researchers looked at whether the governor participated in public acts organized by the president, signaling alignment, or by the national opposition to the president, signaling political opposition. Public acts and meetings took place in the federal capital, the province, or a third location.

Fifth, the coding observed whether the governor had previously held an appointed position at the federal level under the current presidency. If so, there were chances that the president and the governor were aligned. Sixth, the coders

---

[4] Cherny, Freytes, Niedzwiecki, and Scherlis (2015) measure alignments through newspaper coding. See Appendix A.4.5 and the Online Appendix for a full description of the coding of each governor in each election year.

[5] The coding included the two main national newspapers, *La Nación* and *Página12*, as well as one or two provincial newspapers per province when these were available online.

[6] Such is the case of the province of San Luis, a stronghold of the Peronist opposition to the federal government, and thus coded as "opposition" throughout the analyzed period.

[7] This was prominent in 2007 elections, when Cristina Kirchner ran in a coalition platform with a Radical (UCR) governor from the province of Mendoza, Julio Cleto Cobos, as the vice president.

considered the opinions of experts and journalists expressed in newspaper articles on the position of the governor toward the president. Finally, we looked at local politics to analyze the opposition to the governor in the province. If the provincial opposition was aligned with the president, chances were that the governor was in opposition to the president. However, this is not necessarily true and there were cases of governors who had a local opposition aligned with the president while the governor was also aligned with the president.

Overall, the research team analyzed these seven indicators holistically and made a decision for every province and election year. Given that alignment and nonalignment to the federal government is clear at the time of the elections, the variable includes whether the governor is aligned with the president (=0) or the governor is opposed to the president (=1).

Territorial Infrastructure and Policy Legacies

To measure territorial infrastructure, I follow Soifer's (2008) conceptualization of Mann's infrastructural power.[8] I am particularly interested in the aspect of this concept that captures subnational variation in the spatial reach of the state (Soifer 2008, 235).[9] In decentralized countries, the state reaches its territory through subnational institutions. Spatial variation within countries is therefore a key dimension of the concept.

I include a number of direct and indirect measures of territorial infrastructure that are most relevant for the question at hand regarding territorial reach for the implementation of policies across states or provinces. Two separate indicators directly tap into this concept, are space variant, and are available in both countries. First, the proportion of births in private homes, parallel to the indicators proposed by Diaz-Cayeros and Magaloni (2010), is a measure of lack of territorial infrastructure, given that it is expected that births be conducted in health facilities.[10] Second, the percentage of roads that are paved, along the lines of the indicator of road density used by Herbst (2000), represents infrastructure throughout the territory. Data on paved roads and the share of births in private homes are available in both countries (and thus allow for consistency across country regressions) and capture important aspects of state strength that can affect policy implementation. I also include other direct measures of this concept when they are available and relevant for a particular

---

[8] There is a debate in the literature about the best way to measure state capacity. See, for example, the special issue in *Revista de Ciencia Política* 2012 Vol 32, No 3: www.revistacienciapolitica.cl/numero/32-3/ as well as Harbers (2015) and Ziblatt (2008) with a focus on subnational state capacity. Measuring state capacity, especially at the subnational level, is challenging in no small part due to limited data availability.

[9] Given data limitations, I am not able to measure the second dimension of the concept of territorial infrastructure regarding the ties between state and non-state actors. This second dimension is analyzed in the qualitative chapters.

[10] Diaz-Cayeros and Magaloni (2010) propose the share of babies delivered by doctors as a measure of state capacity.

policy: health professionals per capita, public hospital beds (per 1,000 people), and health centers per capita. These indicators are included separately in the regressions and represent direct measures of subnational infrastructure, given that health provision is decentralized in both countries. Access to resources represents an indirect measure of state capacity or territorial infrastructure. This includes access to revenue through transfers from the federal government or through direct subnational taxation.

In terms of policy legacies, this variable varies by policy sector. In the case of the Brazilian primary health care policy, the main impediment to implementation is the preexistence of high-complexity health centers (hospitals), operationalized through the number of hospital beds (public and private) per 1,000 inhabitants and hospital spending (per capita and as a percentage of gross domestic product, GDP).[11] In addition, population density could also serve as a proxy for the development of high-complexity services. This is because more urbanized states and cities tend to have a more developed hospital infrastructure. There are no comparable negative legacies in Argentina's Plan Nacer given that it transfers funds to both primary and high-complexity health centers.

To measure positive feedback effects for the CCTs, I use levels of coverage of previous CCTs. For Bolsa Família in Brazil, I include the level of coverage of *Programa de Erradicação do Trabalho Infantil* (Peti or Child Labor Eradication Program), which included potential recipients to be incorporated into Bolsa Família's registry. Asignación Universal por Hijo in Argentina received automatic beneficiaries from *Plan Familias* (Family Program), which had received recipients from *Plan Jefes y Jefas de Hogar Desocupados* (Unemployed Heads of Households Program). Therefore, the latter workfare program theoretically produced positive feedback for the new policy.

Finally, primary health policies and CCTs in both countries aid each other's implementation by informing the population about the existence of the other policy and through increasing the demand of health services due to health conditionalities in CCTs. This is not a policy legacy in a strict sense and I measure this positive external factor through the inclusion of implementation of CCTs as an independent variable in the primary health policy regressions and implementation of health policies in the CCT regressions in Argentina and Brazil.

Control Variables

The main alternative explanations to successful social policy provision include socioeconomic conditions, geography, and ideology. GDP per capita of provinces,

---

[11] Note that public hospital beds are an indicator of territorial infrastructure in the Bolsa Família regression and hospital beds (including private and public) are a measure of negative policy legacies in the Brazilian primary health policy regression.

percentage of the population without health insurance, and rates of poverty, informality, and underemployment are measures of socioeconomic conditions of the subnational unit.[12] For the policies that were designed to be implemented first in poor areas (such as Bolsa Família and Plan Nacer), the variables that measure affluence are also tapping into program design. In other words, poor areas should show higher levels of coverage as a consequence of the design of the policy. To control for geography, I include population density and distance from the capital of the state or province to the federal capital (Federal District of Brasília or the Autonomous City of Buenos Aires), in kilometers.

Finally, I have included ideology of the party of the governor in Brazil, by following Krause, Dantas, and Miguel (2010) party positioning as left (-1), center (0), or right (1). This coding is the product of the agreement between seventeen experts, who coded parties every four years, from 1990 to 2006. I used 2006 party coding to measure the ideological position of the party of the governor in 2010 and 2014.[13]

STATISTICAL TECHNIQUES AND ROBUSTNESS TESTS

The dependent variables are percentages and linear in nature. Therefore, ordinary least squares and generalized least squares are the appropriate choice of model. Given that we are in a time series context, time trend in the dependent variable needs to be discussed. The coverage of policies as a percentage of the targeted population increases over time for reasons that may not be included in the model, and therefore the models include a time trend (i.e., consecutive numbers for each year) to avoid omitted variable bias. The models are Prais–Winsten regressions: panel-corrected standard errors (PCSE) and first-order autoregressive corrections that deal with contemporaneous correlation of errors across states or provinces (Beck and Katz 1995).[14]

The decision between random versus fixed effects models is also relevant in a time series cross-sectional context. I ran a Hausman test for the models that did not include non-changing variables (such as distance to the capital). This is

---

[12] Previous research has shown the relevance of residential electricity consumption per capita as an alternative measure of affluence (McGuire 2015). I ran the regressions using this measure instead of GDP per capita and the overall results were not altered.

[13] In Argentina, the lack of data on party positioning at the subnational level responds in part to the difficulty of mapping different parties self-identified as Peronists in a left–right continuum. Experts and voters disagree on where to place the Peronist Party along a left–right dimension (Calvo and Murillo 2012, 860). The number of provincial parties self-identified as Peronist aggravates this challenge at the subnational level. I have therefore decided not to control for ideology in Argentina.

[14] I did not include a lagged dependent variable because, as Achen (2000) shows, it can bias the coefficients toward negligible values and artificially inflate the effect of the lagged dependent variable due to high serial correlation and trending in the exogenous variable. Perhaps more importantly, the main focus of the dependent variable is on levels rather than yearly change, for which reason lagging the dependent variable would not be theoretically appropriate.

because fixed effects models only account for variation within units throughout time, and therefore do not allow for the inclusion of invariant or rarely changing variables within units across time.[15] Tables 1 and 3 in the Online Appendix to Chapter 4 show the results of the Hausman test for Brazil and Argentina, respectively.[16] A Prob>chi^2 higher than 0.05 means that the two estimation methods (random and fixed effects) are acceptable and should yield similar coefficients. In these cases I decided to stay with the random effects model reported in the following pages to include control variables that are non-changing or rarely changing across time. In the case in which Prob>chi^2 was lower than 0.05 and I thus could reject the null hypothesis that the coefficients from both models are similar, I report the results from the fixed effects model. The results are not altered, as shown in the Online Appendix, Table 2.

Finally, the models do not suffer from serious multicollinearity. The models with most variables reach variance inflation factors (VIFs) of 5.05 (Estratégia Saúde da Família), 4.22 (Bolsa Família), 4.30 (Asignación Universal por Hijo), and 6.96 (Plan Nacer), which are all below the threshold of 10 (see Tables 4, 5, 7,and 8 in the Online Appendix to Chapter 4).[17] I also performed a modified jackknife by taking one state or province at a time and confirmed that the exclusion of each subnational unit does not alter the overall results.[18]

RESULTS: DETERMINANTS OF SOCIAL POLICY IMPLEMENTATION

Table 4.1 shows bivariate regressions between the dependent variable and political alignments. While CCTs are negatively and significantly (at the 0.01 level) affected by having an opposition governor, the presence of opposition is irrelevant for predicting changes in health policies, for which attribution of responsibility is not clear.

The following models incorporate other independent variables and relevant controls to analyze the determinants of successful social policy implementation. The results of the statistical analysis are consistent overall with the analytic framework that guides this book. The presence of an opposition governor

[15] Random effects models allow for the inclusion of invariant variables by assuming that differences across provinces on social policy implementation are not correlated with any of the mean differences that exist among the independent variables included in the model.

[16] The Online Appendix is located at www.saraniedzwiecki.com

[17] The variables GDP per capita and time trend reach VIFs higher than ten in the Estratégia Saúde da Família regression. High VIFs are also present in the variables GDP per capita and provincial taxes in Asignación Universal por Hijo regression, and these two variables plus population density in Plan Nacer regression. I therefore run the regressions excluding those variables, and the results are not altered, as shown in Tables 6 (Brazil), 9, and 10 (Argentina) in the Online Appendix to Chapter 4.

[18] In particular, the exclusion of the provinces of La Pampa and Santa Cruz, which show very high levels of coverage of Asignación Universal por Hijo in Chapter 3, does not change the results (see Table 11 and 12 in the Online Appendix to Chapter 4).

TABLE 4.1 *Bivariate regression between policy implementation and political opposition*

	Coefficient	Standard error	p>ltl
Conditional cash transfers			
Bolsa Família (Brazil)	−9.31***	1.18	.00
Asignación Universal por Hijo (Argentina)	−64.93***	22.05	.004
Health policies			
Estratégia Saúde da Família (Brazil)	−2.06	1.57	.19
Plan Nacer (Argentina)	−.45	1.52	.77

Note: ***p≤0.01

(Argentina) or an opposition coalition in the governorship (Brazil) has a significantly negative effect on the implementation of social policies when such policies can be attributed to the federal government. Lower levels of territorial infrastructure and negative legacies hinder social policy implementation.

Brazil

Tables 4.2 and 4.3 present the regression results for the implementation of the two national Brazilian policies analyzed in this book: Bolsa Família and Estratégia Saúde da Família, measured through coverage as a percentage of the targeted population. In terms of the CCT Bolsa Família (Table 4.2), it enjoys clear attribution of responsibility. The Brazilian Electoral Panel Study conducted 4,611 interviews with 2,669 voting-age Brazilians throughout 2010, an election year. It found that six months before the presidential election 76 percent of respondents identified the federal government as responsible for the program. By the time of the election, this number had risen to 84 percent (Zucco 2013, 814). In addition, previous analyses have shown that Bolsa Família benefits incumbent presidents by increasing the performance of their party in presidential elections (Hunter and Power 2007; Zucco 2008). The assumption of these studies is that attribution of responsibility is clear. In other words, the electorate can reward the president for Bolsa Família only because they are able to identify Lula as the main actor responsible for this policy.

Accordingly, higher levels of opposition between the state and the national government decrease the level of coverage as a percentage of the targeted population. This effect is consistently significant and negative across all model specifications, from columns 4.2.A through 4.2.E. In particular, a one unit increase in "opposition alliances," from the governor and president belonging

TABLE 4.2 *Determinants of Bolsa Família implementation from 2004 to 2015*

	4.2.A		4.2.B		4.2.C		4.2.D		4.2.E	
Opposition alliances	−5.12*	(2.98)	−5.28*	(2.75)	−7.15***	(2.24)	−4.99**	(1.96)	−5.95***	(1.91)
Middle opposition	−3.45	(2.22)	−3.10	(2.21)	−6.40**	(2.95)	−5.68**	(2.91)	−6.88**	(2.91)
Births private homes	−1.63***	(.36)	−1.95***	(.46)	−2.07***	(.40)	−2.09***	(.42)	−2.14***	(.37)
GDP per capita	−.001***	(.00)	−.0004**	(.00)	−.001***	(.00)	−.001***	(.00)	−.001**	(.00)
Time trend	3.06***	(.19)	2.42***	(.35)	3.57***	(.36)	4.27***	(.46)	3.99***	(.59)
Ideology governor	.98	(.82)	.89	(.74)	2.00***	(.71)	1.68**	(.74)	1.85**	(.75)
Distance to capital	.004***	(.001)	.004***	(.001)	.002**	(.001)	.002**	(.001)	.002**	(.00)
Public hospital beds			5.69*	(3.32)	3.48	(2.71)	3.93	(3.00)	4.92**	(2.20)
ESF implementation			.11	(.09)	.25***	(.07)	.26***	(.08)	.24***	(.08)
Paved roads					−.27***	(.07)	−.24***	(.07)	−.23**	(.07)
Poverty rate					−.12	(.13)	.18	(.15)	.27*	(.15)
Population density					.05***	(.01)	.04**	(.02)	.03**	(.02)
Peti coverage							−.00	(.00)	−.00	(.00)
Informality rate							−.41***	(.14)	−.43***	(.13)
Transfers municipalities									.01	(.01)
Transfers to states									−.002	(.00)
R²	.93		.94		.96		.96		.97	
Rho	.28		.44		.32		.40		.28	
States	27		27		27		27		27	
Observations[a]	321		321		243		243		243	

Note: *** p≤0.01; ** p≤0.05; * p≤0.1 absolute values of standard errors in parentheses.
[a] The difference in the number of observations corresponds to missing data in one or more variables.

to the same party (the baseline category) to not sharing any parties in their coalition, significantly decreases coverage from around 4.99 (4.2.D) to 7.15 (4.2.C) percentage points. In 2015, a 5 percent decrease would be approximately 25,000 families. It is noteworthy that the variable "middle opposition" is also consistently negative, although not always significant and generally with a weaker effect than "opposition alliances." A one unit increase in "middle opposition" means a change from the governor and president sharing the same party to them sharing at least one party in their coalition. Taken together, the first two variables included in the model provide robust evidence to show that opposition coalitions undermine the implementation of Bolsa Família, a CCT with clear attribution of responsibility.

Structural variables also show expected results overall. Territorial infrastructure is measured through three different variables: births in private homes, public hospital beds per 1,000 inhabitants, and percentage of paved roads. First, increases in births at home (as opposed to at a health facility) as a percentage of all births show lower territorial infrastructure. As a result, lower infrastructure significantly decreases the successful implementation of the CCT. These results are consistent across all five models, from 4.2.A to 4.2.E. In particular, a one unit increase in the percentage of births at home reduces the coverage of Bolsa Família by at least 1.63 percentage points (4.2.A). Second, public hospital beds is also an indicator of infrastructure: the more hospital beds per 1,000 people, the stronger the infrastructure in the territory. As such, a one unit increase in this variable consistently increases the coverage of Bolsa Família across models 4.2.B to 4.2.E, although its effect is not always significant. Third, the percentage of federal roads that are paved, as a last direct indicator of territorial infrastructure, has a surprisingly negative effect. Unexpectedly, as the percentage of federal paved roads increases, the implementation of Bolsa Família worsens. This is particularly surprising not only theoretically but also empirically, given that the effect of this variable improves the implementation of the health policy in Table 4.3. Finally, access to resources, measured through federal transfers to states and municipalities per capita, is insignificant for predicting changes in the levels of Bolsa Família coverage.

Policy legacies are measured as coverage of previous CCT Peti. This policy had the aim of eradicating child labor and its nonsignificant effect (columns 4.2. D and 4.2.E) may be related to the fact that it was narrowly targeted to the extreme poor, and therefore its effect may be too small to be significant.

As a positive external factor, the health policy Estratégia Saúde da Família enhances the implementation of Bolsa Família and is significant in most models (models 4.2.C–E). Estratégia Saúde da Família health teams, and particularly health agents in the community, have been important for expanding coverage through distributing information about the CCT, such as where to go to seek information and what to bring to sign up. The Ministry of Health published a document explaining how these teams aid the expansion of Bolsa Família to more than 800,000 families (particularly reaching families with young children)

(Souza 2012). The policies complement one another nicely since check-ups in the patients' house or in the health unit fulfill Bolsa Família's health conditionalities.

Among the main alternative explanations, GDP per capita is consistently negative and significant across all models (4.2.A–E). As GDP per capita increases, the implementation of Bolsa Família worsens. In fact, Bolsa Família is better implemented in the Northeast region of Brazil, a region with the lowest levels of GDP per capita. This is consistent with a program designed for the poorest regions, and is probably a function of program design. The federal government has an active strategy of focusing on these states and thus the highest levels of overall coverage are located in this area. Along similar lines, poverty rate has a positive, and significant in model 4.2.E, effect on Bolsa Família implementation. As poverty rate increases, the level of coverage of Bolsa Família significantly increases. The relationship between the CCT and informality goes in the opposite direction: as informality rates increase, coverage of Bolsa Família decreases.

The ideology of the party of the governor is either insignificant (4.2.A–B) or statistically significant but with the opposite effect as expected by the literature. In models 4.2.C–E, a one unit increase in this variable, from a governor in the center to a governor in the right of the ideological spectrum, predicts increases in the coverage of Bolsa Família as a percentage of the targeted population. This result is surprising given that previous literature on policy implementation predicts that the implementation of more universalistic policies such as Bolsa Família should be supported by left and left-of-center political parties (Turner 2011). Having said that, parties in Brazil are ideologically ill defined and governors join coalitions with very different parties across territorial levels (Krause, Dantas, and Miguel 2010), for which reason this result should be analyzed with caution.

Finally, in terms of geography, the farther away the states are from Brasília, the higher the levels of coverage of the CCT. Population density has a significantly positive effect on the implementation of Bolsa Família, meaning that this policy is better implemented in places with higher concentrations of people.

Table 4.3 shows the factors that shape the implementation of Brazil's primary health policy, Estratégia Saúde da Família. Political alignments do not statistically significantly affect the implementation of this policy, given that users of the service do not identify which territorial level is responsible for its provision – 78 percent of the forty-five users interviewed by the author did not know where the policy was coming from and 15 percent answered that it came from the municipal government. Services such as those provided by this policy have more blurred attribution of responsibility than CCTs because the direct recipients of federal transfers are health facilities and not patients. In addition, Estratégia Saúde da Família has been implemented in Brazil for two decades; the changes in government administration across time and territorial

TABLE 4.3 *Determinants of Estratégia Saúde da Família implementation from 1998 to 2015*

	4.3.A		4.3.B		4.3.C		4.3.D		4.3.E	
Opposition alliances	−.37	(1.30)	−.53	(1.16)	−.33	(1.29)	.24	(1.10)	.43	(1.23)
Middle opposition	−2.51*	(1.53)	−.93	(1.31)	.25	(1.33)	−.21	(1.19)	−.42	(1.40)
Time trend	3.30***	(.34)	1.07***	(.25)	1.00***	(.33)	2.00***	(.38)	1.12**	(.49)
Hospital beds	−6.70***	(2.60)	−6.91***	(1.62)	−7.09***	(1.73)	−4.21***	(1.64)	−2.33	(1.84)
Informality rate			.45***	(.08)	.59***	(.13)	.24**	(.12)	.34***	(.11)
BF implementation			.15***	(.04)	.16***	(.04)	.12***	(.04)	.16***	(.04)
Paved roads			.22***	(.04)	.13***	(.05)	.16***	(.06)	.09*	(.05)
Ideology governor					−.30	(.62)	−.56	(.64)	−.75	(.62)
Births private homes					−.68***	(.20)	−.69***	(.20)	−.91***	(.18)
Poverty rate					.05	(.07)	.15	(.10)	.21**	(.10)
Hospital spending (% GDP)					−.01***	(.002)	−.01***	(.003)	−.004*	(.002)
GDP per capita							−.001**	(.00)	−.0005	(.00)
Population density							−.05***	(.02)	−.06***	(.02)
Distance to capital							.001	(.001)	−.0003**	(.001)
Hospital spending (per capita)			−.0002	(.00)						
Health professionals									1122	(720)
Transfers municipalities									.01*	(.01)
Transfers to states									−.001	(.002)
R^2	.72		.96		.96		.96		.98	
Rho	.78		.77		.99		.82		.72	
States	27		27		27		27		27	
Observations[a]	486	324	297	297	297					

Note: *** p≤0.01; ** p≤0.05; * p≤0.1 absolute values of standard errors in parentheses.

[a] The difference in the number of observations corresponds to missing data in one or more variables.

levels further contribute to blurring attribution of responsibility. Finally, the decentralized implementation of this policy also opens the possibility for attribution of responsibility at different levels of government. The face of the policy is the municipality, although the main source of funding is the federal government. Therefore, governments at all three levels have claimed responsibility for this policy. As a result, opposition parties appear insignificant in the regression, in all five models presented in the table (4.3.A-E), including "opposition alliances" and "middle opposition".

A major result to highlight is the role of negative policy legacies for hindering the implementation of ESF. In agreement with the theoretical framework, the existence of previous high-complexity structures is in direct opposition to the implementation of the primary health policy. Doctors who support high-complexity medicine fight for more resources for their sector, to the detriment of the primary health strategy.[19] Therefore, the higher presence of hospital provision reduces the coverage of Estratégia Saúde da Família. This is measured through three different variables. First, all models (4.3.A–E) show that hospital beds (both public and private) per 1,000 inhabitants consistently and (almost always) significantly worsen the implementation of ESF. An increase in one more hospital bed per 1,000 people decreases coverage at a maximum of 7.09 percentage points (column 4.3.C). In 2015, this decrease would include more than 300,000 people. Second, models 4.3.C–E show that increases in hospital spending as a percentage of GDP also significantly reduce the level of coverage of ESF. Finally, hospital spending per capita has the same effect: it worsens the implementation of the health policy, although its effect is not significant (4.3.B).

The negative effect of policy legacies is also captured in the negative sign of the statistically significant coefficients of population density (4.3.D–E). Given that high-complexity health systems are generally more developed in cities than in rural areas, it is expected that the higher the level of population density the more difficult it will be to implement this primary health policy.

Similar to Bolsa Família's models, stronger territorial infrastructure predicts increases in the coverage of ESF. In particular, as the percentage of births in private homes increases, thus showing lack of institutional strength, the level of coverage of this policy significantly decreases in models 4.3.C–E. A 1 percent increase in the births at home reduces the level of coverage of the health policy by almost 1 percentage point (4.3.E). Additionally, as the percentage of federal paved roads increases, thus improving the infrastructure in the territory, the implementation of this policy is also enhanced, as models 4.3.B–E show. As was the case for Bolsa Família, transfers to states and municipalities are statistically insignificant or barely significant to predict the implementation of ESF, as shown in model 4.3.E.

---

[19] Weyland (1996) made a similar argument about the role of doctors and medical business delaying the implementation of the SUS in 1988.

The variables that tap into wealth also show expected results. Although ESF was conceived of as a universal policy (with the aim of covering all Brazilians), in reality it has been mostly implemented in poorer areas. This is because in less wealthy areas people have less access to health insurance through labor market contributions. As a result, as the rate of informality increases, and thus the amount of people without access to health insurance increases, the implementation of ESF improves (Models 4.3.B–E). The variables GDP per capita and poverty rate show similar results, although the latter is less consistently significant.

The implementation of Bolsa Família provides a positive context for the primary health policy. As the CCT covers more people it increases the levels of coverage of ESF in models 4.3.B–E. In model 4.3.D, a 1 percentage increase in the implementation of Bolsa Família increases the coverage of the health policy by around 0.12 points or roughly 5,400 people in 2015. As more people sign up for Bolsa Família, there is a corresponding increase in participation in the primary health policy both because recipients are more informed about this policy and they must fulfill the health conditionalities of the CCT. This higher demand for services may produce pressure for expansion of primary health coverage.

Finally, the main alternative explanation, ideology of the party of the governor, appears consistently insignificant in these models (4.3.C–E).

Argentina

Tables 4.4 and 4.5 show the determinants of successful social policy implementation in Argentina for conditional cash transfer Asignación Universal por Hijo and health policy Plan Nacer. For the former, the national government successfully claims credit, so as expected the effect of opposition parties is significant and negative. Conversely, having a governor in opposition to the president does not affect the implementation of the health policy, for which attribution of responsibility is blurred. Having stronger infrastructure in the territory enhances both policies, and legacies appear too weak to be significant.

Regarding Asignación Universal por Hijo (Table 4.4), a survey of 2,240 people showed that 96.7 percent knew of this policy and 86.5 percent identified the National Social Security Administration (*Administración Nacional de la Seguridad Social*, Anses) as being in charge of implementing it. This survey was conducted in May 2010 by an independent polling agency, and it was representative of the national population in terms of geographic distribution, age, and gender (Deloitte and Anses 2010).

Since the federal government can successfully claim credit for this policy, it is to be expected that political alignments have a significant effect on its implementation. This is confirmed in the regression analysis, in every model specification. Regressions 4.4.A through 4.4.E show that a one unit increase in the level of opposition, from a governor aligned with the president to a governor

TABLE 4.4 *Determinants of Asignación Universal por Hijo implementation from 2009 to 2015*

	4.4.A		4.4.B		4.4.C		4.4.D		4.4.E	
Opposition	-49.44***	(14.34)	-43.79***	(13.45)	-40.77***	(15.91)	-51.90***	(9.98)	-49.33***	(8.41)
Births in private homes	-16.30**	(6.51)	-22.90***	(8.47)	-25.00***	(8.67)	-24.57***	(6.25)	-20.65***	(5.70)
Time trend	9.19***	(1.08)	11.60***	(1.95)	11.97***	(2.15)	9.88***	(1.75)	24.18***	(.6.74)
GDP per capita			-1.61*	(.83)	-2.21*	(.63)	-7.68***	(.75)	-5.83***	(.98)
Distance to capital					.02*	(.01)	-.003	(.03)	-.04	(.04)
Population density					.01***	(.002)	-.01***	(.002)	-.01**	(.003)
Underemployment rate					-7.19	(6.12)	-22.60***	(7.05)	-18.90**	(7.91)
Plan Nacer implementation							-.49	(.62)	-1.34	(.45)
Transfers to provinces							25.76*	(13.43)	23.35***	(8.90)
Provincial taxes							140.0***	(7.61)	105.3***	(16.87)
Paved roads									-2.22**	(.97)
Employment program[a]									-.00	(.00)
R²	.62		.67		.69		.87		.88	
Rho	.92		.97		.28		-.61		-.49	
Provinces	24		24		24		24		24	
Observations[b]	168		168		146		92		92	

Note: *** p≤0.01; ** p≤0.05; * p≤0.1 absolute values of standard errors in parentheses.

[a] Employment program: *Plan Jefes y Jefas de Hogar Desocupados*.

[b] The difference in the number of observations corresponds to missing data in one or more variables.

opposed to the president, decreases the successful implementation of Asignación Universal por Hijo from 41 (4.4.C) to 52 (4.4.D) percentage points. A 41 percentage point reduction represents almost 60,000 children who do not receive coverage in the year 2015. In the opposition province of San Luis, for instance, this would mean around 13,000 children in that same year.

Territorial infrastructure, measured through percentage of births in private homes, also shows consistent results. Increases in the rate of births in private homes (as an indicator of lack of state infrastructure) reduces the implementation of the CCT in all models from 4.4.A through 4.4.E. A 1 percentage increase in the births at private homes (as opposed to births that take place at health centers) decreases the implementation of Asignación Universal por Hijo by over 16 percentage points at a minimum.

I included a number of additional indicators of territorial infrastructure in Models 4.4.D and 4.4.E. Percentage of roads that are paved shows unexpected results in model 4.4.E. As was the case in Brazil, increases in paved roads actually reduce the implementation of the national CCT. This is surprising given that AUH is not geographically targeted to poorer areas, but instead targeted to poor families, independently of where they live. In addition, a widely used indicator of state capacity or territorial infrastructure is provincial taxes per capita. This indicator shows expected results: as the capacity of the province to raise taxes increases, it significantly enhances the implementation of CCT Asignación Universal por Hijo in models 4.4.D and 4.4.E.[20] Finally, federal transfers to the provinces per capita is positively associated with policy implementation, although the interpretation of this result is not straightforward. This is because federal transfers try to compensate for subnational deficiencies and can therefore be a weak indicator of state capacity. As a result, the positive effect of transfers per capita on the implementation of the CCTs can be understood simply as the importance of resources for the implementation of policies in general.

In terms of policy legacies, the previous workfare national program *Plan Jefes y Jefas de Hogar Desocupados* is insignificant (Model 4.4.E). This is probably because its effect may be too small to have an impact on the implementation of the CCT. Similarly, the implementation of Plan Nacer, a contextual factor that could theoretically enhance the CCT, is either insignificant or shows unexpected results (Models 4.4.D and E). Although during field research it appeared that health agents in the territory informed the population about the CCT and health centers provided conditionalities for Asignación Universal por Hijo, the actual effect of these practices may be smaller than expected.

The measure of wealth (GDP per capita) is consistently negative and significant (Models 4.4.B through 4.4.E), as was the case in Brazil. Although

---

[20] This variable is excluded from the other regressions given that the most recent years are missing and therefore it reduces the sample size.

the policy was designed to target poor families and not poor regions, the policy has been more successfully implemented in provinces with fewer resources. The effect of population density is negative in Models 4.4.D and 4.4.E (but flips sign in Model 4.4.C). Overall, these two variables show that AUH is generally better implemented in more remote places with lower resources.

Table 4.5 shows the regression results for Argentina's main noncontributory health policy, Plan Nacer. As a health service, this policy is not clearly attributed to any government level. A survey conducted by the Ministry of Health in 2007 revealed that among 5,159 eligible pregnant women belonging to indigenous populations, 60 percent of the sample did not know about the existence of Plan Nacer (Argentina. Ministerio de Salud de la Nación, Plan Nacer 2007). In personal interviews with potential recipients, 64 percent of forty-seven respondents did not know where the policy was coming from.[21] In fact, recipients do not even identify that they are beneficiaries of this policy because federal transfers are directed to health centers and not to individuals. Being able to identify the existence of a policy and its responsibility on desirable outcomes (i.e., the visibility of a policy) is necessary for assigning credit. As a result, policy recipients probably do not reward anyone for this policy, and even if they wanted to reward someone, they would probably not know who to reward. Therefore, there is no incentive for opposition provinces to impede the full implementation of this policy. This is reflected in the regression results, which show that the level of opposition of the governor is statistically insignificant for predicting changes in Plan Nacer's coverage in all five models (Models 4.5.A–E).

Territorial infrastructure measured through percentage of births at home shows expected results in the models in which it is significant, 4.5.D and 4.5.E. A 1 percentage increase in the births that take place at private homes (as opposed to at health centers) reduces the implementation of Plan Nacer by around 1 percentage point. An alternative measure of territorial infrastructure, percentage of federal roads that are paved, has a significant and positive effect in Model 4.5.C for the implementation of the health policy, but is mostly insignificant or switches sign in the rest of the models. Two other alternative measures of territorial infrastructure, health centers and health professionals per capita, also show insignificant results or results contrary to expectations in Models 4.5.D and 4.5.E. These results may be related to the poor quality of the data: the total number of health centers corresponds to the year 2001 and is repeated throughout provinces across time, and the data for health professionals is constant within provinces since 2008. For this reason, these variables are excluded for most of the models. Additionally, the variable provincial taxes and federal transfers per capita are insignificant.

All in all, the lack of significance of the variables that tap into territorial infrastructure for explaining Plan Nacer implementation does not necessarily

---

[21] Potential beneficiaries are users of the public system. All interviews were conducted at primary health centers or public hospitals.

TABLE 4.5 Determinants of Plan Nacer implementation from 2008 to 2015

	4.5.A	4.5.B	4.5.C	4.5.D	4.5.E
Opposition	-.09 (2.06)	-.33 (2.17)	.44 (1.84)	.84 (1.14)	-.30 (.67)
Births private homes	.65 (.69)	.24 (.71)	-.35 (.63)	-1.08* (.62)	-.95** (.47)
Time trend	1.22*** (.26)	.48 (.71)	-.39 (.88)	3.07*** (.60)	2.70*** (.41)
AUH coverage	-0.02 (.02)	-.01 (.01)	-.01 (.01)	-.01 (.01)	-.01** (.01)
GDP per capita		-.08* (.04)	-.14 (.09)	-.34*** (.10)	-.28* (.16)
Paved roads		.17 (.13)	.27* (.14)	-.17** (.08)	-.03 (.09)
Distance to capital			.01** (.003)	-.001 (.002)	-.0004 (.002)
Population density			.001 (.0004)	.002*** (.0005)	.002*** (.0004)
Health centers				-1693 (3495)	-9264*** (2837)
Health spending				-.62*** (.21)	-.59*** (.17)
No health insurance				.10 (.10)	.07 (.08)
Health professionals					-2609*** (686)
Transfers provinces					.68 (.51)
Provincial taxes					1.03 (2.23)
R^2	.77	.79	.84	.95	.96
Rho	.64	.28	.61		
Provinces	24	24	24		
Observations[a]	186	186	113		

Note: *** $p \leq 0.01$; ** $p \leq 0.05$; * $p \leq 0.1$ absolute values of standard errors in parentheses.

[a] The difference in the number of observations corresponds to missing data in one or more variables.

mean that these variables do not matter for shaping the implementation of Plan Nacer. Besides the poor quality of the data, this is probably also related to the fact that the federal government negotiates each year with each province the degree of success (measured through coverage) that they should be able to reach. At the end of the year, the level of success (i.e, the coverage of a set of medical practices explained in Chapter 3) is measured relative to the agreed goals. Therefore, it is plausible to think that state capacity is considered when setting the goals at the beginning of the year, thus not appearing significant in the regressions.

Having said that, population density is positive and significant in Models 4.5.D and 4.5.E, meaning that Plan Nacer is better implemented in areas where there is a greater concentration of people. This result could be explained by the fact that the policy needs a minimum infrastructure to be implemented: the capacity to keep a registry of medical procedures and patients through trained personnel with access to a computer. It is reasonable to argue that places with higher population density have access to more trained personnel with access to computers and can therefore keep better registries for the better implementation of the policy.

It should be noted that since Plan Nacer transfers funds to both primary and high-complexity health centers, there are no negative policy legacies coming from hospitals, which is different from the Brazilian health policy analyzed earlier. The main policy legacy for Plan Nacer comes from the 1990s *Programa Materno Infantil y Nutrición* (Maternal and Child Nutrition Program, PROMIN) that helped to develop local capacities for the implementation of the later policy. Unfortunately, there is no data available for the level of implementation of this policy across provinces and time.

The implementation of CCT Asignación Universal por Hijo theoretically provides a positive contextual factor, but it appears insignificant in models 4.5.A through 4.5.D, and with an opposite as expected sign in model 4.5.E. As part of the conditionality for receiving the family allowance, recipients need to attend health check-ups and therefore the actual coverage of Plan Nacer could potentially increase. In fact, since the CCT was implemented in 2009, there was an increase of three million new children signed up for Plan Nacer (Argentina. Ministerio de Salud de la Nación, Plan Nacer 2012c).[22] In addition, the incorporation of pregnant women to the national CCT expanded Plan Nacer's coverage of pregnant women by 14 percent (Argentina. Ministerio de Salud de la Nación, Plan Nacer 2012c, 10).[23] However, it seems that the effect is too small to appear in the regression. In fact, after the expansion of coverage in 2013 to all women, including those

---

[22] Although Plan Nacer's funds are delivered to CAPS and hospitals, the amount of transfers depends on the number of medical practices performed to uninsured adults and children who have signed up to the policy.

[23] Pregnant women receive 80 percent of the monthly transfer and the remaining is given at the end of the pregnancy (when the baby is born or the pregnancy is interrupted) and is conditioned upon health check-ups.

without children, the coverage of Plan Nacer now exceeds that of the CCT, which remains restricted to families with children.

As was the case for the other three policies analyzed earlier, increases in GDP per capita decrease the implementation of Plan Nacer (models 4.5.B, 4.5.D, and 4.5.E). In fact, this noncontributory health policy is intended (by design) to provide good quality health care particularly in the places where people are less wealthy and have no access to health insurance through their formal job. That is one reason why the coefficient for the percentage of workers without health insurance is positive, yet insignificant, in Models 4.5.D and 4.5.E. Along similar lines, a 1 percentage increase in provincial health spending significantly decreases the implementation of Plan Nacer, when all other variables are constant, in Models 4.5.D and 4.5.E. This may be because the higher the priority that the province assigns to health care, the less need there is for a noncontributory policy such as Plan Nacer and therefore the lower the level of implementation of this policy.

CONCLUSIONS

This chapter showed that political alignments matter for social policy implementation when the policy is easily attributable to the national government. Governors opposed to the president are interested in hindering upper-level policies when recipients of the policy can identify where the policy is coming from and thus reward that party or government level in elections. Clear attribution of responsibility is more salient in CCTs compared to social services. Therefore, political alignments statistically significantly predicted lower levels of coverage as a percentage of the targeted population in the cases of Bolsa Família and Asignación Universal por Hijo, policies which can be attributed to the national government. In the cases where the policies could not be attributed to any government level, such as health services Estratégia Saúde da Família and Plan Nacer, opposition from governors was statistically insignificant.

Taken together, the bivariate (Table 4.1) and multivariate regressions (Tables 4.2 and 4.4) seem to show that the effect of political alignments is stronger in the implementation of Argentina's Asignación Universal por Hijo than in Brazil's Bolsa Família.[24] Governors in Argentina are more effective at resisting policy implementation than their counterparts in Brazil in part because political alignments are more blurred in Brazil – the party system is more fragmented and therefore national and subnational governments form

[24] This cross-country comparison comes with two caveats. In Argentina, the implementation of the CCT reaches levels higher than 100 percent because poverty figures are underestimated and they do not include rural populations and nonpoor informal workers. In addition, the variable "political alignments" has two values in Argentina ("alignment" or "opposition") and three in Brazil (including a "middle" category).

coalitions to win elections; and these coalitions vary at the national, state, and local levels. Additionally, parties in Argentina (particularly the Peronist Party) are more centralized and disciplined than in Brazil (with the exception of the PT).[25] This high-level of party fragmentation and lack of discipline also contribute to blurring clear attribution of responsibility (Powell and Whitten 1993), thus further weakening the effect of political alignments.[26]

In addition, the effect of political alignments is stronger when a given social policy is initially launched. Brazil's Bolsa Família began in 2003, six years before Argentina's Asignación Universal por Hijo began in 2009. Moreover, Bolsa Família was based on previous legislation discussed in Congress and on previous subnational programs, while Argentina's Asignación Universal por Hijo was enacted by presidential decree. This means that subnational governments in Brazil were included in the design of the policy, while provinces in Argentina were excluded. As a result of including multilevel shared rule mechanisms in Brazil, Bolsa Família's attribution of responsibility may be lower than Argentina's CCT. Finally, at least since 2012, attribution of responsibility in Bolsa Família is becoming less clear, in part as a result of an active strategy from the federal government to share credit with subnational levels of government. The federal government gives incentives to states to develop programs that complement Bolsa Família. If states agree, then the logo of the state is placed on the ATM card that recipients use every month to withdraw the funds.[27] For all these reasons, we should expect political alignments to have a weaker role in Brazil than Argentina in the successful implementation of these CCTs. With these caveats in mind, this chapter showed that subnational units controlled by opposition parties have hindered the implementation of both Bolsa Família and Asignación Universal por Hijo.

The statistical analysis in this chapter provided evidence to show that territorial infrastructure also matters for shaping the successful implementation of noncontributory social policies. A better reach of the state through its institutions improves the conditions for implementing policies. This was exhibited through the consistently negative effect of the percent of births in private homes. Chapters 5 and 6 incorporate more nuanced measures of territorial infrastructure, including the characteristics of facilities, their personnel, and the relationship of these institutions with local civil society.

---

[25] Nomination and electoral rules boost these differences. In the closed list PR system in Argentina, provincial party leaders control the rank order of the party list, and national party leaders can also intervene. In Brazil, the open list electoral system encourages candidates to employ personal vote strategies through making political alliances with subnational executives (Garman, Haggard, and Willis 2001, 214).

[26] The only institutional characteristic that would favor clearer attribution of responsibility in Brazil is that presidential and gubernatorial elections are concurrent there while in Argentina provinces have the authority to set the date of their elections. Samuels (2004a) argues that in presidential systems, concurrent executive elections promote clarity of responsibility.

[27] See Chapter 5 for a description of this initiative.

Finally, policy legacies are more relevant in Brazil than in Argentina. In particular, negative policy legacies from high-complexity health care hindered the implementation of the primary health policy in Brazil. Policy legacies for all other policies are more challenging to measure quantitatively, and therefore the conclusions were less sound.

The next chapters will show the causal mechanisms that explain these statistical relations through case studies of the national CCTs Asignación Universal por Hijo and Bolsa Família, and health policies Plan Nacer and Estratégia Saúde da Família. While the next chapter analyzes the cash transfers, Chapter 6 focuses on the health policies. These policies' implementation processes are analyzed throughout two states and four municipalities in Brazil and two provinces and four municipalities in Argentina.

APPENDIX

TABLE A.4.1 *Brazil. Summary statistics (1998–2015)*

Variable	Obs	Mean	Std. Dev.	Min	Max
Policy implementation					
Bolsa Família coverage (%)	324	59.35	17.15	1.37	91.56
Estratégia Saúde da Família coverage (%)	483	49.97	25.72	.65	99.52
Political alignments					
Opposition alliances	483	.43	.50	0	1
Middle opposition alliances	483	.38	.49	0	1
Territorial infrastructure					
Births in private homes (%)	483	3.08	4.43	.13	34.35
Paved roads (%)	404	81.66	22.27	10.70	100
Professionals in health (per capita)	483	.01	.002	.005	.02
Public hospital beds (per 1,000 people)	483	1.01	.40	.41	2.75
Policy legacies					
Hospital beds (per 1,000 people)	483	2.33	.47	1.25	3.89
Hospital spending (% GDP)[a]	349	44.51	194.23	0	1,649
Hospital spending (per capita)	349	469.94	1,874	0	17,589
Peti coverage	294	22,251	33,319	0	22,5662
Controls					
Ideology of party of governor	480	−.22	.68	−1	1
GDP per capita	431	13,124	9,851	2,107	64,653
Poverty rate	375	32.76	16.84	4.21	68.82
Informality rate	402	61.28	12.37	33.80	90.50
Federal transfers to states (per capita)	483	633	701	50.53	3,735
Federal transfers to municipalities (per capita)	483	394	227	15.28	1,126
Distance to the capital (km)	483	1,636	872	0	4,123
Population density	483	66.60	94.66	.96	445
Time trend[b]	483	19.54	5.18	11	28

[a] Values reach higher than 100 percent because GDP is measured in 1,000 Brazilian Reais. I did not transform the original data to avoid values close to 0 in the regression coefficients.
[b] Time trend = 1 in 1988, the first year in the original dataset.

TABLE A.4.2 *Argentina. Summary statistics (2008–2015)*

Variable	Obs	Mean	Std. Dev.	Min	Max
Policy implementation					
Asignación Universal por Hijo (%)[a]	168	169	127	16.40	694
Plan Nacer (%)	186	21.97	8.62	.03	38.19
Opposition					
Opposition parties	186	.23	.42	0	1
Territorial infrastructure					
Births in private homes (%)	186	.69	1.01	0	5.17
Paved roads (%)	186	88.71	14.12	44	100
Health professionals (per capita)	186	.002	.002	.001	.01
Health centers (per capita)	186	.0003	.0002	.00001	.001
Policy legacies					
Employment program – Plan Jefes y Jefas de Hogar Desocupados (Total)	115	11,977	32,514	0	262,408
Controls					
GDP per capita (in 1,000)	186	24.28	15.33	6.79	82.99
Transfers to provinces (per capita, in 1,000)	114	1.78	.87	.26	4.78
Provincial taxes (per capita, in 1,000)	113	1.18	.92	.28	5.40
Population density	186	485	2,586	.1	14,775
Distance to Buenos Aires (in km)	186	927	497	0	2,376
Underemployment rate	164	1.57	1.08	0	4.8
Health spending (% of total provincial spending)	137	10.62	2.94	5.3	23.1
Lack of health insurance (%)	114	38.76	10.32	16.90	57.90
Time trend[b]	186	18.60	2.27	15	22

[a] Percent coverage is higher than 100 because population living below the poverty line (i.e., the denominator) is underestimated by official figures and does not include the rural poor and nonpoor workers who are unemployed or in the informal sector. As a result, the denominator can be lower than the numerator (total coverage).

[b] Time trend = 1 in 1994, the first year in the original dataset.

TABLE A.4.3 *Brazil. Variable description and sources*

Variable	Variable description	Source
Policy implementation		
Bolsa Família coverage	Families covered by Bolsa Família as a percentage of poor families (Cadastro Único profile). There is registry of this percentage since 2009. 2004–8: own calculations based on Cadastro Único figures.	Secretaria de Avaliação e Gestão da Informação do Ministerio do Desenvolvimento Social e Combate á Fome – aplicacoes.mds. gov.br/sagi/mi2oo7/tabelas/mi_social.php
Estratégia Saúde da Família coverage	Percentage of population covered by Estratégia Saúde da Família in December of each year.	Departamento de Atenção Básica da Secretaria de Atenção à Saúde dab.saude.gov.br/portaldab/historico_cobertura_sf.php
Opposition alliances		
Opposition and middle opposition alliances	0: governor's party same as president's party, 1: president's party in governor's coalition, or governor's party in president's coalition; or at least one party in the coalition of the president and governor coincide, 2: no party in the coalition of the president and governor coincide. Four year periods, starting the following year of the election.	Own coding based on Tribunal Superior Eleitoral tse.jus.br/ eleicoes/eleicoes-anteriores/eleicoes-anteriores

(continued)

Variable	Variable description	Source
Territorial infrastructure		
Births in private homes	Percentage of babies born at home. Data for 2014–15 taken from 2013.	Instituto Brasileiro de Geografia e Estatística 1998–2002: seriesestatisticas.ibge.gov.br/series.aspx?no=2&op=1&vcodigo=RC68&t=nascidos-vivos-ocorridos-registrados-ano-local 2003–2011: seriesestatisticas.ibge.gov.br/series.aspx?no=2&op=1&vcodigo=RC71&t=nascidos-vivos-ocorridos-ano-local-nascimento 2012–13: sidra.ibge.gov.br/bda/tabela/listabl.asp?z=t&o=27&i=P&c=2680
Paved roads	Percentage of federal roads that are paved. The data for 2015 as of June.	Serviço de Informação ao Cidadão. Departamento Nacional de Infraestrutura de Transportes. Official Data through e-mail exchange – dnit.gov.br/acesso-a-informacao/servico-de-informacao-ao-cidadao-sic
Professionals in health	Total quantity of health professionals (data for August of each year) divided by total population.	Departamento de Informática do Sistema Único da Saude -tabnet. datasus.gov.br/cgi/tabcgi.exe?cnes/cnv/profidbr.def tabnet. datasus.gov.br/cgi/tabcgi.exe?cnes/cnv/prido2br.def
Public hospital beds	Number of public hospital beds related to SUS for every 1,000 people. Given that this variable has low variation across time, 1998 takes on the value of 1999, 2000–1 of 2002, 2003–7 of 2005, and 2008–15 of 2009.	Instituto Brasileiro de Geografia e Estadística seriesestatisticas. ibge.gov.br/series.aspx?vcodigo=MS35&sv=47&t=leitos-mil-habitantes-publico

(continued)

Policy legacies

Hospital beds	Number of hospital beds, private or public, related to SUS for every 1,000 people. Given that this variable has low variation across time, 1998 takes on the value of 1999, 2000–1 of 2002, 2003–7 of 2005, and 2008–15 of 2009.	Instituto Brasileiro de Geografia e Estadística seriesestatisticas. ibge.gov.br/series.aspx?no=2&op=1&vcodigo=MS33&t=leitos-mil-habitantes
Hospital spending	Total spending on hospital and ambulatory care (this variable is calculated as a percentage of GDP and per capita).	Departamento Informático do Sistema Único da Saúde – siops. datasus.gov.br/rel_subfuncaouf.php
Peti coverage	Number of children covered by PETI – Programa da Erradicação do Trabalho Infantil.	Secretaria de Avaliação e Gestão da Informação do Ministerio do Desenvolvimento Social e Combate a Fome – aplicacoes.mds. gov.br/sagi/mi2007/tabelas/mi_social.php

Controls

Ideology	Ideology of the party of the governor. Expert coding for 1998, 2002, and 2006. −1: left, 0: center, 1: right. The coding of party positioning is used for four years. 2006 coding used for 2010 and 2014 elections.	Krause, Silvana; Danta, Humberto; Miguel, Luis Felipe. 2010. Coaligações Partidárias na Nova Democracia Brasileira. Perfis e Tendências. Rio de Janeiro; São Paulo: Ed. UNESP; Konrad-Adenauer-Stiftung.

(continued)

TABLE A.4.3 *(continued)*

Variable	Variable description	Source
GDP per capita	GDP per capita in 2013–15 take on value of 2012.	1998–99: Instituto de Pesquisa Econômica Aplicada – www.ipeadata.gov.br 2000–12: Departamento Informático do Sistema Único da Saúde: tabnet.datasus.gov.br/cgi/tabcgi.exe?ibge/cnv/pibmunuf.def
Poverty rate	Percentage of people with household income per capita below the poverty line. The poverty line considered here is twice the extreme poverty line, an estimate of the value of a basket of food with minimum calories needed to adequately supply a person, based on Food and Agriculture Organization and World Health Organization recommendations. Poverty lines are estimated at different values for the twenty-four regions of the country.	Series calculated from Pesquisa Nacional por Amostra de Domicílios of Instituto Brasileiro de Geografia e Estadística. Instituto de Pesquisa Econômica Aplicada - ipeadata.gov.br
Informality rate	Informality rate = (nonregistered workers + self-employed)/(registered workers + nonregistered workers + self-employed).	Based on Pesquisa Nacional por Amostra de Domicílios of Instituto Brasileiro de Geografia e Estadística. Instituto de Pesquisa Econômica Aplicada ipeadata.gov.br
Transfers to states	Total federal transfers to states divided by population. Data from 2015 as of September 7.	1997–2003 – Tesouro Nacional: tesouro.fazenda.gov.br/estados_municipios/transferencias_constitucionais.asp 2004–15 – Secretaria de Avaliação e Gestão da Informação. Ministério do Desenvolvimento Social e Combate à Fome: aplicacoes.mds.gov.br/sagi/miv/miv.php

(continued)

Transfers to municipalities	Total federal transfers to municipalities divided by population. Data from 2015 as of September 7.	1997–2003 – Tesouro Nacional: tesouro.fazenda.gov.br/estados_municipios/transferencias_constitucionais.asp 2004–15 – Secretaria de Avaliação e Gestão da Informação. Ministério do Desenvolvimento Social e Combate à Fome: aplicacoes.mds.gov.br/sagi/miv/miv.php
Distance to the capital	Distance from capital of the province to Brasília in kilometers.	br.distanciacidades.com
Population density	Population density = population/area in square kilometers.	Instituto Brasileiro de Geografia e Estadística. Population: sidra.ibge.gov.br/ ; Area: ibge.gov.br/home/geociencias/areaterritorial/principal.shtm

Note: Online links were last accessed from June to September 2015.

TABLE A.4.4 *Argentina. Variable description and sources*

Variable	Variable description	Source
Policy implementation		
Asignación Universal por Hijo coverage	Coverage of Asignación Universal por Hijo as a percentage of people living below the poverty line.	Administración Nacional de la Seguridad Social . "Asignación Universal por Hijo para Protección Social. Datos de cobertura por mes y provincia." 2015. Official data. Provided by personal correspondence. Poverty data: Instituto Nacional de Estadísticas y Censos (2014). Compiled by James W. McGuire, Department of Government, Wesleyan University. Contact: jmcguire@wesleyan.edu. Calculated from Argentina. Ministerio de Economía y Finanzas Públicas (2014). "Evolución de la población que habita hogares por debajo de la línea de pobreza – Encuesta Permanente de Hogares (EPH)." The EPH surveys around 80 percent of the population living in metropolitan areas.
Plan Nacer coverage	Average of coverage previously agreed with each province: pregnant women with the first prenatal check-up before the twentieth week of gestation, newborns' health check-ups, newborn babies who are not underweight, vaccine coverage of pregnant women, fully evaluated cases of maternal mortality or death of infant under one year of age, vaccine coverage in babies under	Ministerio de Salud de la Nación, Plan Nacer, Official data. Data as of March of every year. Provided by personal correspondence.

(*continued*)

eighteen months, sexual and reproductive counseling to puerperal women within forty-five days after giving birth, children's complete health check-ups, and personnel trained in indigenous medicine. Added after 2012: sexual and reproductive counseling to teenagers, regular check-ups for teenagers, and uterine and breast cancer prevention.

Opposition

Governor's opposition

Expert coding:
0: governor is aligned with the president;
1: governor is opposed to the president.
This variable is updated every two years from 2007 to 2015, starting the following year of the election. See Table A.4.5 for coding of each province across time and the Online Appendix for detailed provincial profiles. Online appendix available at saraniedzwiecki.com

Cherny, Nicolás, Carlos Freytes, Sara Niedzwiecki, and Gerardo Scherlis. 2015. *Base de Datos de Alineación Política Subnacional, Argentina 2003–2015*. Instituto de Investigaciones Gino Germani, Universidad de Buenos Aires.

Territorial infrastructure

Births in private homes

Births in private homes as a share of all births. 2014–15 take on value of 2013.

Compiled by James W. McGuire, Department of Government, Wesleyan University. Calculated from Argentina. Ministerio de Salud. Dirección de Estadísticas e Información de Salud. Estadísticas vitales. Información básica – 2013. Buenos Aires: Ministerio de Salud. Tabla, Nacidos vivos registrados según local de ocurrencia.

(continued)

TABLE A.4.4 (continued)

Variable	Variable description	Source
Paved roads	Percentage of national roads that are paved. 2015 takes on value of 2014.	Ministerio de Planificación Federal, Inversión Pública y Servicios. Secretaría de Obras Públicas. Dirección Nacional de Vialidad.
Health centers (per capita)	Total public health care facilities divided by population.	Instituto Nacional de Estadísticas y Censos, Dirección Nacional de Estadísticas Sociales y de Población, based on data from Ministerio de Salud y Ambiente de la Nación, Dirección de Estadísticas e Información de Salud.
Health professionals (per capita)	Number of doctors (number of people twenty years or older with completed medical education) divided by population.	Ministerio de Salud – msal.gob.ar/images/stories/pdf/indicadores-basicos-2012.pdf
Policy legacies		
Employment Program – PJJHD	Total coverage of the Programa Jefes y Jefas de Hogar Desocupados (PJJHD).	Dirección de Información Estratégica para el Empleo – Secretaría de Empleo, Ministerio Trabajo, Empleo y Seguridad Social de la Nación.
Controls		
GDP per Capita (in 1,000 pesos)	Gross domestic product divided by population. 2010–15 take on the value of 2009.	Ministerio del Interior de la Nación. 2011. Producto Bruto Geográfico (en miles de pesos) por Provincia mecon.gov.ar/hacienda/dinrep/sidep/indice.php?eje=2&indice=1 Accessed July 1, 2013.

(continued)

Variable	Description	Source
Transfers to provinces (per capita, in 1,000 pesos)	Federal transfer to provinces (Coparticipación Law 23548) in thousands of pesos in constant value of 2004. 2012 takes on value of 2011.	Own calculations based on Ministerio de Economía and Instituto Nacional de Estadísticas y Censos for Price Indexes. mecon.gov.ar/hacienda/dncfp/provincial/recursos/info_consolidada.php
Provincial taxes (per capita, in 1,000 pesos)	Total provincial tax revenues, in a thousand pesos and in current value.	Ministerio de Economía mecon.gov.ar/hacienda/dncfp/provincial/recursos/serie_recursos.php
Population density	Inhabitants per square kilometer.	Compiled by James W. McGuire, Department of Government, Wesleyan University. Contact: jmcguire@wesleyan.edu. Equipo Observatorio Económico Territorial Universidad Nacional del Litoral. "Densidad de Población (habitantes por Km2) por Provincia y Total Nacional 1895–2010." Accessed October 14, 2014, at www.unl.edu.ar/oet/userfiles/image/360Poblacion.xls
Distance to Buenos Aires (in kilometers)	Distance from capital of the province to Ciudad Autónoma de Buenos Aires in kilometers.	ar.lasdistancias.com/calcular?from=Buenos+Aires%2C+Argentina&to=Tucum%C3%A1n%2C+Argentina
Underemployment rate	Percentage of economically active population who are underemployed and not actively looking for a job.	Instituto Nacional de Estadísticas y Censos – Encuesta Permanente de Hogares.
Health spending	Provincial public spending on health care as a percentage of total provincial public spending.	2008–2011:Compiled by James W. McGuire, Department of Government, Wesleyan University. Contact: jmcguire@wesleyan.edu. Calculated from Base de Datos Provinciales del Centro de Investigaciones en Administración Pública, Facultad de Ciencias Económicas, Universidad de Buenos Aires. "Ejecución por finalidad y función 1991–2007."

(continued)

TABLE A.4.4 *(continued)*

Variable	Variable description	Source
		Administración Central, Organismos Descentralizados y Cuentas Especiales." Accessed October 11, 2014, at econ. uba.ar/www/institutos/admin/ciap/baseciap/base.htm 2012–13: Ministerio de Economía y Finanzas Públicas, Dirección Nacional de Coordinación Fiscal con las Provincias, Gasto por Finalidad y Función, Por Jurisdicción. Accessed January 30, 2015, at mecon.gov.ar/ hacienda/dncfp/provincial/info_presupuestaria/ gasto_FIN_FUN/fin_fun_juris_serie_APNF.php
Lack of health insurance	Percentage of population in private homes that do not have health coverage.	2010 National Census. censo2010.indec.gov.ar/ index_cuadros_2.asp pdf Censo 2010 Tomo 1.

Note: Online links were last accessed around January 2015.

TABLE A.4.5 *Political alignments in Argentine provinces (by election year)*

Province	2007	2009	2011	2013
Buenos Aires	Aligned	Aligned	Aligned	Aligned
CABA	Opposition	Opposition	Opposition	Opposition
Catamarca	Aligned	Opposition	Aligned	Aligned
Chaco	Aligned	Aligned	Aligned	Aligned
Chubut	Aligned	Opposition	Aligned	Aligned
Córdoba	Aligned	Opposition	Opposition	Opposition
Corrientes	Aligned	Opposition	Opposition	Opposition
Entre Ríos	Aligned	Aligned	Aligned	Aligned
Formosa	Aligned	Aligned	Aligned	Aligned
Jujuy	Aligned	Aligned	Aligned	Aligned
La Pampa	Aligned	Aligned	Aligned	Aligned
La Rioja	Aligned	Aligned	Aligned	Aligned
Mendoza	Aligned	Aligned	Aligned	Aligned
Misiones	Aligned	Aligned	Aligned	Aligned
Neuquén	Aligned	Aligned	Aligned	Aligned
Río Negro	Aligned	Aligned	Aligned	Aligned
Salta	Aligned	Aligned	Aligned	Aligned
San Juan	Aligned	Aligned	Aligned	Aligned
San Luis	Opposition	Opposition	Opposition	Opposition
Santa Cruz	Aligned	Aligned	Opposition	Opposition
Santa Fe	Opposition	Opposition	Opposition	Opposition
Santiago del Estero	Aligned	Aligned	Aligned	Aligned
Tierra del Fuego	Opposition	Aligned	Aligned	Aligned
Tucumán	Aligned	Aligned	Aligned	Aligned

Source: Cherny, Nicolás, Carlos Freytes, Sara Niedzwiecki, and Gerardo Scherlis. 2015. *Base de Datos de Alineación Política Subnacional, Argentina 2003–2015*. Instituto de Investigaciones Gino Germani, Universidad de Buenos Aires.

Note: The value is kept constant for two years, until the next election, and it starts the following year of the election because elected candidates take on their position the following year. See the Online Appendix for the explanation of the coding for each province-year available at saraniedzwiecki.com.

5

Conditional Cash Transfers in Argentina and Brazil

This chapter analyzes the mechanisms that shape the successful implementation of noncontributory cash transfers in Argentina and Brazil, policies for which government responsibility (what here is referred to as "attribution of responsibility") is clear. For these types of policies, political alignments matter for their implementation. When recipients can identify the national government as the source of a popular policy, and therefore potentially reward it in the elections, opposition governors and mayors will hinder the policy's implementation and aligned subnational politicians will facilitate it. In addition, territorial infrastructure – in the form of subnational state institutions and their collaboration with civil society – also contributes to the implementation of these Conditional Cash Transfers (CCTs). Finally, positive policy legacies can enhance the implementation of CCTs, such as the existence of previous national or subnational policies that automatically transfer recipients to the new policy or that prepare local institutions by providing similar conditionalities.

The focus of this chapter is the implementation of Argentina's *Asignación Universal por Hijo* (Asignación or Universal Child Allowance) and Brazil's *Bolsa Família* (Family Allowance). While Asignación is designed, funded, and implemented by the national government, Bolsa Família is designed and funded by the national government but implemented by municipalities. The provision of conditionalities in the forms of health and education is in the hands of subnational governments in both countries. This chapter analyzes the implementation of these policies in two provinces (Mendoza and San Luis) and four municipalities (Las Heras and Godoy Cruz in Mendoza, and San Luis City and Villa Mercedes in San Luis) in Argentina, and two states (Rio Grande do Sul and Goiás) and four municipalities (Porto Alegre and Canoas in Rio Grande do Sul, and Goiânia and Valparaíso de Goiás in Goiás) in Brazil. These cases have similar levels of GDP per capita but different political alignments to the national and intermediate governments.[1] These cases also exhibit variation in terms of territorial infrastructure and policy legacies.

The role of political alignments is stronger in the implementation of Argentina's Asignación than in Brazil's Bolsa Família. This is in part because political alignments are less clear in Brazil – the party system is more fragmented and therefore national and subnational governments form coalitions to win elections, and these coalitions vary at the national, state, and local levels. Thus, the same party can be aligned with another party at a given territorial level and in opposition to that same party at another level (Krause and Alves Godoi 2010; Peixoto 2010; Ribeiro 2010). Previous research shows that high levels of party fragmentation can blur attribution of responsibility (Powell and Whitten 1993), and this, in turn, weakens the effect of political alignments. In addition, and as is the case in Argentina, the effect of political alignments is stronger when a given social policy is initially launched. As time goes by, and a given policy survives different government administrations, attribution of responsibility starts blurring. It was not until 2012 – nine years after its initiation – that attribution of responsibility in Bolsa Família started to become less clear. Blurring attribution of responsibility was also an active strategy from the federal government to share credit with subnational levels of government. For all these reasons, we should expect political alignments to have a weaker role in Brazil than in Argentina in the successful implementation of these CCTs. With these caveats in mind, subnational units controlled by opposition parties have hindered the implementation of both Bolsa Família and Asignación Universal por Hijo, with strategies including providing direct policy competition and raising bureaucratic obstacles.

The effect of territorial infrastructure and policy legacies also exhibits differences across Argentina and Brazil. While the characteristics of subnational state institutions vary in Argentina depending on each province and municipality, the institutions that provide social assistance in Brazil are more homogenous. This is because the Unified System of Social Assistance (SUAS) in Brazil established clear guidelines for the provision of welfare. This system also regulates the participation of civil society in social assistance, making the relationship between state and non-state actors stronger on average in Brazil than in Argentina. Policy legacies are also stronger in Brazil, yet positive in both cases. Previous social assistance policies enhance the implementation of the national CCTs through automatically transferring recipients to the new policy and through developing experience with the provision of conditionalities. These positive policy legacies are stronger in Brazil than in Argentina because previous policies were implemented for more time, were targeted to a broader segment of the population, and included conditionalities in their design. Differences in length of time, degree of coverage, and actual experience with conditionalities shape the strength of policy legacies across countries. The remainder of this chapter will focus on within-country variation, and the conclusions will further elaborate on differences across countries.

---

[1] For a description of case selection, see Chapter 3.

ASIGNACIÓN UNIVERSAL POR HIJO IN ARGENTINA

Clear Attribution of Responsibility

Asignación was created in 2009 by presidential decree as an addition to the contributory family allowance.[2] It is a broadly targeted cash transfer program of around US$75 per child per month in 2012, up to a maximum of five children per family, and for pregnant women after the third month of pregnancy (Argentina. Presidencia de la Nación 2011).[3] It covers every unemployed or underemployed person (also including single taxpayers since 2016 and domestic service)[4] earning less than the monthly minimum salary (roughly US $480 in 2012) with children under the age of eighteen or handicapped children. It is paid to the parents or legal guardians. While 80 percent of the total sum is paid through an ATM, the other 20 percent is in a bank account, to be transferred at the end of the year and contingent upon health check-ups, vaccination, and school attendance.

This policy centralizes the responsibility to provide social protection in the hands of the federal government. The national institution in charge of signing-up recipients and of administering cash transfers to bank accounts is the *Administración Nacional de Seguridad Social* (National Social Security Administration, Anses). In all provinces and major towns, Anses signs up potential beneficiaries of Asignación and follows their cases through *Unidades de Atención Integral* (Integrated Assistance Unit). The national government funds this policy through the social security reserve fund (called Sustainability Guarantee Fund) and from the social security budget that comes from wage contributions and taxes (Bertranou and Maurizio 2012, 3).

Provinces and municipalities do not have a legal role in the implementation of the policy, although their representatives monitor compliance with health and education conditionalities. Compliance with conditionalities has been loosely enforced.[5] In addition, subnational governments play an unwritten role

---

[2] Contributory family allowances for formal employees were created in 1957, providing a cash benefit for each child (zero to seventeen years old), and a supplement for school supplies, childbirth, and marriage, among other benefits. In 1996, access to family allowances was limited to formal workers in the lowest earning bracket. Asignación Universal por Hijo in 2009 covers those children who are not part of the contributory family allowance system because their parent does not have a formal job (Arza 2016).

[3] Official exchange rate US$1=$6 Argentine pesos, as of November 20, 2013. All conversions are taken at this rate and all values are taken around the time when field research was conducted in 2012. Anses. "Asignación Universal por Hijo" www.anses.gob.ar/destacados/asignacion-univer-sal-por-hijo-1 Accessed November 20, 2013. The value of the transfer has been increased following changes in the highest level of the contributory family allowance system (Anses 2011).

[4] Single taxpayers, self-employed taxpayers, or *monotributistas* refer to people who pay taxes for their small businesses or as individuals.

[5] Compliance is loosely monitored through the *Libreta Nacional de Seguridad Social, Salud y Educación* (Notebook for Social Security, Health, and Education). Although normatively recipients are supposed to lose the entire transfer if they do not comply with conditionalities, from a

in the implementation of this policy. Their territorial infrastructure and previous legacies can aid or hurt the CCT. They can also choose to actively support, hinder, or be indifferent to the policy, and their decision shapes success in its implementation. For instance, subnational governments can hinder implementation by not sharing databases of eligible recipients or can enhance implementation by designing policies that complement the national one.

Figure 5.1 shows levels of coverage of Asignación across provinces in 2009, 2012, and 2015 as a percentage of people living in poverty. Percent coverage can reach levels higher than one hundred because official poverty figures are known to be underestimated in Argentina since 2007. In addition, coverage also includes the rural poor and nonpoor workers in the informal sector or unemployed who are not included in the poverty figure. As a result, total coverage can be larger than the targeted population (people living below the poverty line). This figure shows that the two provincial case studies, Mendoza and San Luis, exhibit different values of the dependent variable. When the policy was first launched in 2009, coverage in the province of Mendoza reached almost 70 percent of the poor, while in the province of San Luis it reached less than 16 percent. By 2015, Mendoza exhibited one of the highest rates of coverage with 525 percent of the poor and San Luis' coverage reached over 150 percent. Table 5.1 summarizes the variables that account for differences in the degree of implementation of Asignación in the selected provinces and municipalities. The province of Mendoza combines a strong territorial infrastructure and positive (yet weak) policy legacies with the will to enhance the national CCT that comes from its alignment with the national government. Conversely, San Luis uses its strong territorial infrastructure to hinder Asignación due to its opposition to the national government.[6]

Political alignments matter for the implementation of Asignación because attribution of responsibility is clear for recipients. The National Social Security Administration agency, Anses, conducted a survey among 2,240 people and found that 96.7 percent of respondents know of this policy and 86.5 percent identify Anses as in charge of implementing it.[7] This survey was conducted in May 2010 by an independent polling agency, and it is representative of the national population in terms of geographic distribution, age, and gender

---

practical standpoint it is only possible to withhold the 20 percent that was not included in the monthly ATM payment (Bertranou and Maurizio 2012; Fenwick 2016).

[6] Political alignments in these two provinces have been roughly constant since the left segment of the Peronist Party (*Frente para la Victoria*) won the presidency in 2003 and until 2015. For a description of the political trajectories in the selected provinces and municipalities, see Chapter 3. The Online Appendix includes a detailed account of political alignments in each of the Argentine provinces across time. It is available at www.saraniedzwiecki.com.

[7] Anses is known by a large majority of the sample (99.3 percent). Of these people, 75.3 percent agree with the idea that this institution represents every Argentine, almost half agree with the idea that it is "controlled" by the Kirchners, and more than half think that it is not independent from politics.

TABLE 5.1 *Implementation of Asignación Universal por Hijo in selected provinces and municipalities*

Subnational unit	Alignment with national government	Territorial infrastructure	Level of implementation[a]
San Luis	**Opposition**	**Strong**	**Low**
San Luis City	Alignment	Weak	n/a[b]
Villa Mercedes	Opposition	Weak	n/a[b]
Mendoza	**Alignment**	**Strong**	**High**
Las Heras	Alignment	Strong	High
Godoy Cruz	Opposition	Weak	Low

Note: Policy legacies are excluded from this table because they are weak (yet positive) in all cases.

[a] Level of implementation measured in relation to the national average (provinces) and compared to the other municipality in the province (due to the lack of data for all municipalities).

[b] There is no available data on the level of implementation of the CCT at the municipal level in San Luis. However, local variation is expected to be minimal across municipalities given the province's strong resistance to this policy and the high concentration of authority in the hands of the province.

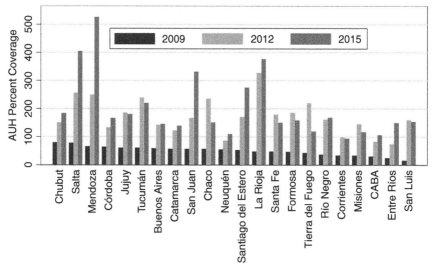

FIGURE 5.1 Asignación Universal por Hijo percent coverage in 2009, 2012, and 2015
Note: The order of provinces is from highest to lowest coverage in the first year of implementation. The share of the population in poverty covers only the thirty-one largest metropolitan areas, about 80 percent of the population. For clarity purposes, due to their high value, the provinces of La Pampa and Santa Cruz have been excluded.
Sources: Argentina. Administración Nacional de Seguridad Social (2015); Argentina. Instituto Nacional de Estadísticas y Censos (2014).

(Deloitte and Anses 2010). In addition, in individual interviews with the author, 90 percent of the sixty-three eligible recipients who were asked the questions "Where do you think this policy comes from?" or "Who do you think funds it?" identified the provider of this policy as the federal government. The answers varied, including things such as "Cristina," "Kirchner," "The President," "the national government," or "Buenos Aires." Along the same lines, a report published by the Argentine Ministry of Education reproduced a conversation between a mother and her daughter in the province of Buenos Aires as they were withdrawing Asignación money from an ATM (Argentina. Ministerio de Educación de la Nación 2011, 35):

- Mom, Who is paying for this?
- Cristina [Kirchner], my child, she is helping us – the mother answers
- But, Why? If you work ...
- She helps us so that you can go to school. Besides, the money I earn from ironing clothes is not enough.

As a consequence of this clear attribution of responsibility, opposition subnational governors, such as those in the province of San Luis, have an incentive to hinder the implementation of this policy.

Political Alignments and Territorial Infrastructure

Province of San Luis

The opposition province of San Luis hinders the implementation of Asignación with both bureaucratic obstacles and direct policy competition. To begin, the province refused to share lists of beneficiaries of provincial social policies. This imposed a challenge to the implementation of Asignación, since the national government determined that the national CCT was incompatible with the principal provincial workfare program, *Plan de Inclusión Social* (Social Inclusion Program, PIS). In other words, if a person receives either Asignación or PIS, they are legally ineligible for the other program. Given the incompatibility between the two policies, people living in the province of San Luis and recipients of Asignación had to deal with an extra formality: every six months they had to present a certificate of negativity, a proof signed by both Anses and the Provincial Department of Social Development,[8] located in the capital of the province, that shows they are not beneficiaries of the provincial workfare program. Every six months, Asignación is canceled and it can only be reactivated after each recipient provides this piece of paper. The coordinator of the provincial program explained this situation in a personal interview:

[8] For clarity purposes, I refer to the institution in charge of providing social assistance at the provincial or municipal levels as the Department of Social Development. However, this institution has a different name in each particular subnational unit.

It is ridiculous what the national government makes us do, I have two people working exclusively signing these certificates of negativity ... The national government wanted us to share with them the databases of all the beneficiaries of provincial programs; and we will not give them that information ... You never know what they [the national government] can do with that information (Interview Di Cristófano).

The decision to not share the databases, which creates the need to present extra paperwork every six months, imposes an obstacle for every recipient of Asignación in the province of San Luis. It produces a "compliance cost" that obstructs the take-up of the national policy (Moynihan, Herd, and Harvey 2014). This challenge is worse for those recipients who do not live in the capital city, where the provincial Department of Social Development is located and the certificates of negativity are signed. Recipients throughout the province have to travel to the capital city every six months to avoid the cancelation of their national cash transfer. The representative of Anses in the City of Villa Mercedes remembered the difficulty that recipients faced traveling the sixty-two miles that separate Villa Mercedes from the City of San Luis: "For us it was even more difficult because the certificate of negativity was only handled in the City of San Luis. Therefore, these people who were unemployed had to go all the way to the city" (Interview Medaglia). More than one year after Asignación was implemented, a representative of the provincial program provides certificates also in Villa Mercedes, but not in other municipalities.

Besides not sharing the databases of recipients, the principal way San Luis hinders the implementation of Asignación is by providing direct policy competition through the provincial workfare program, Plan de Inclusión Social, which has existed since 2003. Recipients of this program work six hours per day, five days a week, in exchange for a monthly stipend of US$142 in 2012. The majority of beneficiaries work planting trees by the road, in public safety activities, in health centers, schools, or municipalities. This policy was fully designed and funded by the provincial government, and according to a former governor and creator of this policy, it represented 20 percent of the provincial budget in 2003, when unemployment was unusually high, and around 3 percent in 2012 (Interview Rodríguez Saá).

None of the twenty-two recipients of the workfare program responded positively when I asked whether they would change to the national Asignación.[9] One of the justifications for this answer was that after comparing the two programs they realized they would lose money. In the words of a woman who had been a recipient of the provincial workfare program since 2003, "It is not in my best interest to change. Here [with the provincial program] I earn 855 pesos and there [with the national program] I

[9] In addition, when I asked them who was responsible for this policy, twenty (out of twenty-two) referred to the provincial government, most of them directly referring to the former governor, Alberto Rodríguez Saá.

would earn 200 pesos" (Interview Argentina #44).[10] Some recipients I interviewed answered that they did not have enough information about the national program to make an informed decision, and other recipients responded that they did not qualify for the national policy because their children were older than eighteen. It is also possible that some recipients may think it is beneath their dignity to receive a noncontributory transfer, and prefer to be paid for work. In fact, many explained that they actually enjoyed participating in the workfare program, in part because there was the promise of a potential permanent position. The reasons for choosing the subnational program over the national one show that this policy competition can actually be positive when it fills a gap in the national policy and provides alternative options for recipients. The national policy does not incorporate poor families without children, for instance, while Plan de Inclusión Social does. As a result, childless poor people in San Luis are not covered by the national policy, but by the provincial policy.[11]

This policy succeeded at providing effective policy competition against the national CCT. This is partly because the Province of San Luis has strong provincial *territorial infrastructure*. Social assistance institutions are strong: facilities are in good condition; they are evenly distributed throughout the province or include mobile units to reach remote areas; and they are staffed by relatively well-trained and well-paid personnel. Compared with other provinces in Argentina, San Luis has an efficient bureaucracy in terms of size and meritocratic hiring. The governors have historically aimed to hire the most qualified professionals. In Giraudy's (2014, 116) words: "Highly competitive salaries and generous benefits not only attracted the province's most skilled technocrats, but also exerted a pull on prestigious professionals living in neighboring provinces." One of these skilled bureaucrats, a former governor's principal advisor on the provincial program, described the subnational reach of this capable provincial state: "We reached the entire province; the whole territory of the province ... the province goes directly and individually to each person" (Interview Baylac).

San Luis exhibits a nondemocratic political regime – the Peronist Party has won executive elections by a landslide since the return of democracy in 1983 (Gervasoni 2010b; Gibson 2012, 75; Giraudy 2014). This undemocratic subnational political regime has two consequences for the implementation of the CCT. On the one hand, civil society organizations do not collaborate with the state in reaching high levels of territorial infrastructure. There are very few

---

[10] Although the comparison on amount of transfers across policies may not be entirely accurate, families with just one child tend to receive a higher transfer in the provincial program.

[11] However, in general, national–subnational policy competition is a waste of resources when both policies provide similar benefits to a similar population. If these governments worked together instead of competing, the provincial resources used to create the subnational policy could be used for other things, such as improving the quality of social services.

instances of autonomous civil society and those voices are very weak. As a result, strong territorial infrastructure is achieved by high provincial institutional capacity alone, without the aid of non-state actors.

On the other hand, the province concentrates authority in its own hands and therefore the political opposition of the province overrides the efforts to support the policy made by aligned municipalities. In spite of this diminished role of municipalities, they are part of the story in the implementation of Asignación, since the national government uses local representatives in Anses to sign up the population. When comparing municipalities, local representatives in the aligned city of San Luis are more active than in the opposition city of Villa Mercedes.[12] While Anses in San Luis City has had an active strategy to contribute to the implementation of the national CCT, the Villa Mercedes Anses office has had a more passive role (Interviews Témoli, Medaglia).[13]

San Luis City, as the rest of the municipalities, receives few provincial transfers (Giraudy 2014, 115). This means that the municipality has few resources to train or pay the salaries of local bureaucrats. In addition, representatives of the municipal government in the local branch of Anses attempt to coordinate with churches, NGOs, and members of the community to reach the poorest neighborhoods for the implementation of the national CCT. The local government promotes its outreach activities (including sign-up campaigns) on Facebook, Twitter, and local radio stations not affiliated with the provincial government. Nevertheless, the weakness of the local state and of civil society makes these collaborations unsuccessful; few people show up to their sign-up campaigns. Additionally, the overwhelming control of the provincial government throughout the territory, including newspapers and radio stations, makes it challenging to reach out the population (Interviews Di Chiacchio, Témoli). When local representatives try to reach the population outside of the municipalities aligned with the national government, the job is even more challenging. In the words of the Director of Anses in the City of San Luis: "We are not present in those municipalities, because most mayors are aligned with the province" (Interview Témoli).

Unlike the case of San Luis City, where the mayor is aligned with the national government and in opposition to the provincial government, in the municipality of Villa Mercedes there is no real possibility for a party in opposition to the governor's to win. Villa Mercedes is a long-standing bastion of the party of the governor, exhibiting an allied media and bureaucratic apparatus. Therefore, the role of Anses in Villa Mercedes is very limited. It promoted the initial signing up

---

[12] Unfortunately, there is no available data on levels of coverage of Asignación at the municipal level in the province of San Luis. Nevertheless, the provincial obstacles are too strong to overcome them through local efforts, so variation in coverage is expected to be minimal.

[13] There are two local branches of Anses in the province of San Luis – one in Villa Mercedes (in charge of four departments) and one in the City of San Luis (in charge of five departments), and they divide the area of the province between these two offices.

to Asignación in 2009 through diffusion campaigns, but it stopped engaging in an active promotion strategy soon after that. The local branch of Anses in this municipality is staffed by people aligned with the national government, and therefore ostracized by the local government. In the words of the Director of Anses in Villa Mercedes: "We [Anses] have no relationship with the municipality; they ignore us to the point that we are not even included in the protocol lists ... [The municipal government] has no role in Asignación because it provides no political payoff; they are constantly trying to keep the national government from interfering in the province" (Interview Medaglia). In a personal interview, the current mayor of the city confirmed that the municipality had no role in the implementation of Asignación, and explained that the national government does not have access to this opposition municipality. "The federal government has not reached this territory ... It is a political issue ... They want to jump over the province ... But the federal government needs to respect the province" (Interview Merlo). This opposition municipality acts by omission to limit the implementation of the CCT: it relies on the weakness of the local branch of Anses and on the active obstruction of the provincial government.

Overall, the combination of an opposition province with strong territorial infrastructure has the effect of successfully limiting the implementation of the national CCT. At the same time, aligned municipalities (such as the City of San Luis) do not count on a strong territorial infrastructure to overcome the limits imposed by the province.

Province of Mendoza

The province of Mendoza has been aligned with the national government since 2006, when Governor Julio Cobos was part of the *Radicales-K* ("K" from Kirchner), the members of the Radical Party who supported the national government. In 2007, Cobos ran for vice president with Cristina Kirchner, and a Peronist aligned with the federal government was elected as governor. In the words of a current Under Secretary of Social Development in the province of Mendoza: "We not only support the national model, we *are* the model" (Interview Alfonso). In addition to being closely aligned with the national government, Mendoza exhibits high levels of territorial infrastructure through the combination of strong provincial institutions and active collaboration with non-state actors. Being aligned with the national administration and its ties to non-state actors for achieving strong institutional capacity differentiates Mendoza from San Luis. Figure 5.1 shows that this province has been one of the most successful in the implementation of Asignación Universal por Hijo, partly due to its alignment with the national government and its strong infrastructure in the territory (Table 5.1).

Unlike San Luis, Mendoza signed the original agreement in which the province shares the list of recipients of provincial programs with the national government. In this way, the national government can determine incompatibilities between Asignación and other provincial programs without imposing extra bureaucratic steps on recipients. Besides signing basic agreements, the province goes a step further: it adapts its provincial program to complement Asignación Universal por Hijo.

Before Asignación was enacted, the government of Mendoza had been developing a program of scholarships of US$17 per month for low-income children who attended school. It is called *De la Esquina a la Escuela* (From the Corner to School). When Asignación was implemented, the provincial government decided to provide this scholarship (which is defined by the national government as incompatible with Asignación) only to those not eligible for the national CCT. The subnational government further complements the national policy by providing tutors for children who are going back to school thanks to the national policy (Goldar 2012). In addition, Mendoza contributes to the national CCT by making sure that the population has access to the national IDs needed to receive the cash transfer.[14]

Besides the predisposition to enhance the national CCT that stems from its political alignment, the province of Mendoza rests on a strong *territorial infrastructure* that includes strong state institutions in collaboration with non-state actors. Mendoza is a relatively wealthy province that can afford to pay good salaries to its public employees. Resources are administered efficiently, since it has one of the most capable state structures in the country: there is a clear distinction between the private and public domains, rulers tend not to appropriate state resources, and societal groups are autonomous (Giraudy 2014, 48). High levels of coverage of the national CCT were rapidly achieved in part due to strong provincial institutions: local representatives of Anses have access to trained human resources and to computers necessary for signing up the population (Potenza Dal Masetto 2011, 37). Additionally, local institutions staffed with trained personnel (including social workers, psychologists, and lawyers) coordinate with autonomous non-state actors for the implementation of the policy (Goldar 2012, 110).

Most NGOs that work with issues related to children in the province are organized around an umbrella organization called *Federación de Entidades No Gubernamentales de Niñez y Adolescencia* (Federation of NGOs for Children and Teenagers, Fedem). This group of organizations worked to ensure that the transfers were not discretionally interrupted. For example, in 2012 Fedem, in coordination with the provincial government, realized that the cash transfer was sometimes interrupted when the adult recipient was a parent who did not live with the family, and it could only be reactivated after providing legal proof of residence with the child recipient. The success of this collaboration led to a

---

[14] This is not unique to Mendoza. The aligned province of Buenos Aires, for instance, has also adapted or canceled provincial programs, and promoted the distribution of national IDs to enhance the implementation of Asignación (Mazzola 2012, 121–23).

change in the national legislation: when in doubt of the residence of the parent there was no need to go through judicial channels. Proof of who lived in the house with the child recipient could be achieved through faster means (Interviews Manoni, Spoliansky; Goldar 2012, 109).

In the opposition province of San Luis, we saw a difference in the attitude of municipalities toward the implementation of Asignación, although the local government's role was more limited, given their overall weakness. Conversely, in the aligned and more democratic province of Mendoza, municipal governments can make a difference in the implementation of the national CCT. In this province, the municipal governments have a real impact in expanding coverage of the national policy (Interviews Alfonso, R. Miranda, R. Moyano, U. Moyano, Serú). Accordingly, the next paragraphs focus on municipal variation between the two selected municipalities, Godoy Cruz and Las Heras.

Goldar (2012) analyzes the level of coverage of Asignación among young people (zero to seventeen years old) across municipalities in Mendoza.[15] Las Heras scores higher than Godoy Cruz in terms of coverage of Asignación as a percentage of the young population – while 29 percent are covered in Las Heras, only 14 percent are covered in Godoy Cruz.[16] This difference in implementation is in part due to differences in political alignments. While Las Heras is aligned with the provincial and national governments, Godoy Cruz is in opposition to both.

Las Heras is the only case in my analysis of Argentina in which the three levels of government – municipal, provincial, and national – are aligned. This triple alignment enhances the implementation of national social policies. When Asignación first appeared in December 2009, the municipality engaged in a full-scale diffusion campaign that included promoting the policy in community centers, and through *delegados territoriales* (territorial delegates; Interviews Quintana, Serú). The role of the municipal government is central for informing the population about this new policy, its eligibility requirements, and the documentation needed to sign up. The municipality acts as the entry point of social demands, and therefore provides accurate information to those who might have been excluded from the policy and are potential recipients. In the words of the Secretary of Social Development in Las Heras:

When the program [Asignación Universal por Hijo] started, we needed to sign up the community, make sure that they met the eligibility criteria to access that universal

---

[15] Municipal data in Argentina are scarce. The level of coverage as a percentage of targeted age group is the best proxy of successful implementation of the national CCT at the municipal level in Mendoza that I could find. The level of coverage as a percentage of young population is a valid measure in Las Heras and Godoy Cruz, since socioeconomic characteristics are comparable. The percentage of illiteracy among the population older than ten years is around 1 percent in both cases. In addition, 5 percent of the households do not have access to public sanitation in Godoy Cruz, compared to a bit more than 10 percent in Las Heras. Finally, the proportion of the population younger than seventeen years is roughly similar across the two municipalities (Argentina. Instituto Nacional de Estadísticas y Censos 2010).

[16] The average coverage of Asignación across municipalities in Mendoza is 26 percent.

allowance right. We coordinated with Anses, we provided the territorial structure here in Las Heras ... everybody participated, municipal employees, territorial delegates ... and we started explaining what the policy was all about ... At the beginning we needed to inform the majority of the people ... So we organized two weeks of sign-up campaigns in different parts of the municipality, with neighborhood organizations, pensioners' organizations, centers of social and cultural development, sports clubs ... in two weeks we went neighborhood by neighborhood informing everybody (Interview Serú).

The municipality combined the political will to inform citizens about Asignación and a strong *territorial infrastructure* to do so. The latter includes both municipal institutions (territorial delegates and community centers) evenly distributed throughout the territory in coordination with a number of nongovernmental organizations. There are ten territorial delegates representing the mayor in each of the ten districts within the municipality. The delegates are generally appointed by the mayor. Their main focus is public sanitation, but they also develop social activities in the community and distribute information. A current territorial delegate explained his role in Asignación: "We went home by home to let people know the date and place when Anses would come to sign up for Asignación, and we had a list of paperwork they had to bring that day" (Interview Quintana). The same delegate remembered that many people said they did not have national IDs, and so they worked with provincial and national institutions to distribute national IDs, a prerequisite for receiving Asignación. These territorial delegates exist in other Peronist municipalities in Mendoza. In the words of the Under Secretary of Social Development in the province and former Secretary of Social Development in the Peronist municipality of Guaymallén: "The national government reaches the territory through the provinces. Provinces through the municipalities and municipalities through delegates. They are the ones who know Pedro and Juan ... and they need to be known by the community ... that person is a common fellow" (Interview R. Moyano).

Centros de Intergración Comunitaria (Community Centers, CICs) are also part of the state infrastructure in the municipality of Las Heras that contributed to the implementation of Asignación. Community centers are built with funds from the national government and staffed with personnel paid by the municipality. They include professionals such as doctors, nurses, teachers, and social workers. The CIC is also the place where the local state and civil society meet and coordinate joint strategies. Its aim is to promote community participation in a place that combines a health center, day care, and all-purpose rooms. The mayor of Las Heras described the CIC in the following terms: "Before the CIC, people thought that the health center had nothing to do with the day care, with a place for recreation and culture, or with a place for community debate and participation ... Those who want to, can participate in the CIC ... and we promote that" (Interview Miranda).

There were three CICs in Las Heras alone (in the neighborhoods of Plumerillo, Algarrobal, and Borbollón) and there were plans to build three more in the following years (Interviews Serú, E. Martínez). From the four municipal cases studied in Argentina (two in Mendoza and two in San Luis), only Las Heras had functioning CICs. The CICs include *mesas de gestión y desarrollo local* (similar to an open community forum), where the community discusses needs and projects. Both individuals and groups participate in these roundtable discussions, including neighborhood organizations, pensioners' organizations, churches, social leaders, and municipal officials, among others. These community meetings facilitated the role of the municipality both for designing local projects and for disseminating information, including information on the national CCT (Interview Serú).

In contrast to the municipality of Las Heras, the process of implementation of Asignación in the opposition municipality of Godoy Cruz can be described as one of indifference. High-ranking officials in the municipality confirmed that Godoy Cruz did not have an active role in the implementation of Asignación, since the implementation was purely the responsibility of the national government through Anses (Interviews Cornejo, Fernandez, Salomón). In the words of the mayor of Godoy Cruz: "the municipal government has no role in Asignación. It does not have a specific role; the national government has not given us a specific role. It is a direct relationship between the beneficiaries and Anses" (Interview Cornejo). In practice, then, the municipal government in Godoy Cruz did not engage in any diffusion campaign to promote the policy when it was first launched, and it is not involved in finding new recipients for the national CCT. It should nevertheless be noted that Godoy Cruz, and most municipalities throughout the country, cannot provide policy competition the way that the opposition province of San Luis does. This is because municipalities, as might be expected, are weaker than provinces throughout Argentina, both in terms of formal authority and actual access to resources (Gibson 2012; Hooghe et al. 2016).

The lack of a desire to enhance Asignación in Godoy Cruz that stemmed from political opposition is combined with a weaker *territorial infrastructure* in the municipality, compared to that of Las Heras. First, the position of a territorial delegate does not exist in this municipality. In the words of a former mayor of Godoy Cruz when asked about territorial delegates: "We [Mendoza] have 18 departments, and 18 Mayors, and that's it" (Interview Biffi). As a result, the territorial reach of the municipality is limited. Second, there are no functioning CICs in the municipality, mainly due to local resistance to this federal initiative, and therefore there is no stable place for the community to meet with local representatives (Interviews Berrios, Cornejo, Lecaro, Salomon).[17] Finally, and as a result of weak state infrastructure, the articulation with non-state actors is not effective.

---

[17] The only CIC in the municipality was located inside a hospital and was not functioning at the time of field research in 2012.

The municipal government engages in some minor social assistance activities such as distributing food and clothes through what is called *efectores* (providers), NGOs located in the poorest areas of the municipality, where the municipal government is not present. The Secretary of Social Development in Godoy Cruz expressed her dissatisfaction with these providers in a personal interview: "the model with providers does not give me hope ... I would like to conduct direct intervention in these places ... because we [the municipal government] are not reaching those who need it the most" (Interview Fernandez). Interviews with leaders of these NGO providers and high-ranking municipal authorities confirmed the municipality's lack of significant support to these NGOs (Interviews Cornejo, Fernandez, Reales). The co-director of the main NGO in the municipality of Godoy Cruz, Coloba, explained that the institution is located where there is a complete absence of the state: the municipal government is not present in the territory and Coloba does not articulate regularly with the local government (Interview Reales). These institutions do not receive significant funds from the municipality and they do not report to the mayor in any respect (Interviews Bautista, Cornejo, Reales). As a result, even if the mayor had the desire to enhance the implementation of the national CCT, she would not have the territorial infrastructure to carry it out.

Weak Policy Legacies

Political alignments and territorial infrastructure at the provincial and municipal levels shape the successful implementation of Asignación Universal por Hijo. The role of policy legacies is more marginal in this case because previous national social assistance policies were narrowly targeted and did not develop the institutional capacity to ensure compliance with health and education conditionalities. In Mendoza, provincial programs were very narrowly targeted, thus providing a positive yet weak legacy, and in San Luis the subnational workfare program was in direct opposition to Asignación, thus providing a negative legacy.

A number of previous national social assistance programs were the precursors of Asignación, and transferred most of their recipients to the new policy. Most notably, 40 percent of Asignación coverage in 2009 came from direct transfers from *Jefes y Jefas de Hogar Desocupados* (Unemployed Heads of Households, PJJHD) and *Famílias por la Inclusión Social* (Families for Social Inclusion or Familias). These two programs provided an initial basic coverage (Basualdo 2010, 8–9; Bertranou 2010, 19; Bertranou and Maurizio 2012, 3; Mazzola 2012, 114).[18] PJJHD was a workfare program implemented in 2002

---

[18] Plan Jefes y Jefas de Hogar Desocupados was preceded by *Programa Trabajar, Servicios Comunitarios,* and *Programa de Emergencia Laboral* in the 1990s (Chiara and Di Virgilio 2005, 133–35; Andrenacci et al. 2005, 186). Compared to all previous policies, Asignación increases the level of coverage and the amount of cash transfer (Basualdo 2010).

and targeted to unemployed heads of households, prioritizing households with children, handicapped people, and pregnant women, as well as unemployed young people with no children, and seniors over sixty. Since 2004, recipients of PJJHD who qualified as "unemployable" (poor women with children and pregnant women) could choose to transfer to Familias.[19] These two previous programs were legally incompatible with Asignación, and therefore its recipients stopped receiving the transfer from PJJHD or Familias and started receiving the transfer from Asignación.

Nevertheless, these previous policies were narrowly and ineffectively targeted, making their effect on Asignación limited. In 2009, in the province of Mendoza, less than 5 percent of people living with unsatisfied basic needs were recipients of the national PJJHD; around 16 percent in San Luis were recipients (Neffa and Brown 2011).[20] In addition to these two previous cash transfers, the program *Vale Más* incorporated the use of ATM cards for cash transfers to buy food, but its effect was limited. In Mendoza, for example, it only covered around 11 percent of those living with unsatisfied basic needs and the transfer was not enough to cover a basic food basket (Ruggeri 2012, 68).

Legacies in terms of complying with conditionalities were also weak. Although Familias did have health and education conditionalities, they were not effectively monitored. Therefore, there were limited previous capacities developed at schools, health centers, or social assistance institutions to regulate the compliance with conditionalities. This is one reason why the conditions required by Asignación have been poorly monitored. In particular, municipal institutions in charge of social development mostly conduct social assistance activities (as opposed to the development of social capital), including handing out goods such as mattresses, blankets, food, clothes, and plastic to cover holes in houses, particularly after heavy rainfall.[21]

Finally, previous provincial programs left legacies for the implementation of Asignación. In Mendoza, provincial programs covered 24 percent of the population living with unsatisfied basic needs, although these programs varied widely in type and sustainability (Dirección de Estadísticas e Investigaciones Económicas de Mendoza 2011). As explained earlier, the scholarship program (De las Esquina a la Escuela) complemented Asignación, but it covered only 528 children throughout the province in 2011 and the transfer was of only US$17 per month (Ministerio de Desarrollo Humano, Familia y Comunidad de

---

[19] Those recipients of Jefes considered "employable" could choose to transfer to a training program called *Seguro de Capacitación y Empleo* (Employment and Training Insurance). Campos, Faur, and Pautassi (2007) evaluate Plan Familias under the light of (the lack of) social rights' standards.

[20] The data for unsatisfied basic needs are taken from the 2010 Census (Argentina. Instituto Nacional de Estadísticas y Censos 2010).

[21] Municipal social assistance institutions are also in charge of enrolling people for the national program of noncontributory pensions. The final decision on who receives these pensions lies with the national government.

Mendoza 2011b). Although more than half of the population in San Luis living with unsatisfied basic needs was covered by the provincial workfare program in 2009, this policy was in direct competition with Asignación, as was explained in the previous section, and therefore left a negative legacy for the implementation of the CCT (Ministerio de Inclusión Social, San Luis 2012).

While for Argentina's CCT policy legacies are more limited, they are central in the expansion of Brazil's Bolsa Família, particularly through the automatic incorporation of recipients of previous policies and through building local capabilities for the provision of conditionalities. In addition, strong territorial infrastructure through social assistance institutions and councils also enhanced the implementation of the Brazilian national policy. Finally, political alignments were central in the implementation of Bolsa Família given that recipients can identify the national government as the entity responsible for the policy. The next section analyzes the implementation of Brazil's main CCT across the selected states and municipalities.

BOLSA FAMÍLIA IN BRAZIL

Changes in Attribution of Responsibility

Bolsa Família is a CCT enacted in 2003 by a Provisional Measure and codified into Law in 2004 (Brasil. Presidência da República, Casa Civil 2004). It is targeted at all Brazilian families with a monthly per capita income of less than half a minimum salary (US$70) and included in a master database called *Cadastro Único* (Unified Registry).[22] The transfer is conditioned upon school enrollment and minimum school attendance of 75–85 percent (depending on the age of the child), completion of required vaccinations, regular health check-ups (for children and pregnant women), and keeping updated information in the Unified Registry every two years. By 2014, families in extreme poverty received a fixed monthly transfer of US$35; those in extreme poverty with young children and pregnant women received, in addition to the fixed monthly transfer, a variable transfer of US$16 per child for up to five children; and families with teenagers (sixteen to seventeen years old) received US$19 per teenager up to a maximum of two teenagers.[23] This means that the transfer varies between US$35 and US$150.

As a noncontributory social policy, Bolsa Família has been part of the legislation of the *Sistema Único de Assistência Social* (Unified Social Assistance System, SUAS) since 2005, by which all levels of government (national, state, and

---

[22] Exchange rate US$1=R$2, as of January 24, 2013. All conversions are taken at this rate and all values are taken around 2012, when field research was conducted. Monthly income per capita is self-declared and is calculated by the sum of each family member's income divided by the total number of family members (Brasil. Presidência da República, Casa Civil 2004, 2; Brasil. Ministério do Desenvolvimento Social e Combate à Fome 2012a).

[23] Brasil. Ministério do Desenvolvimento Social e Combate à Fome: mds.gov.br/bolsafamilia/beneficios, Accessed January 4, 2014.

municipal) are responsible for social provision.[24] The general administration of the policy is in the hands of the *Secretaria Nacional de Renda de Cidadania* (National Secretariat of Citizen Income, SENARC) within the Ministério do Desenvolvimento Social e Combate à Fome (Ministry of Social Development and the Fight against Hunger, MDS). The federal government is in charge of administering and funding the CCT. In particular, it determines eligibility, sets targets, pays recipients through an ATM card, and monitors states and municipalities through the transfer of federal funds with strings attached to them.

The federal government transfers municipalities US$1.25 per month per Bolsa Família family to support administrative efforts, and the municipality receives a double transfer for the first 200 families that the local government signs up. This value is multiplied by the *Índice de Gestão Descentralizada* (Index of Decentralized Management, IGD), which varies from 0 to 1 and measures the quality of management (Brasil. Congreso Nacional, 12; Soares and Sátyro 2010, 40).[25] The resources transferred through Bolsa Família are increasingly important for municipalities, especially for the poorer ones. In 2006, for example, Bolsa Família transfers to municipalities equaled 15 percent of all federal transfers and up to 23.5 percent in some municipalities (Da Silva e Silva and Santos de Almada Lima 2010, 86). Municipal institutions (in particular, the Reference Center of Social Assistance, *Centro de Referência da Assistência Social*, CRAS) use these transfers to identify potential recipients, supervise the fulfillment of conditionalities, and keep an updated registry of poor families in the Unified Registry (Rizzotti, Almeida, and Albuquerque 2010, 142; Baddini Curralero et al. 2010, 147). All families with monthly income per capita below half a minimum salary should be included in this registry. In this way, the registry keeps track of potential recipients of national social policies, one of which is Bolsa Família. Municipalities are also in charge of providing health and education services by which Bolsa Família recipients can meet the

---

[24] Previous legislation set the context for launching Bolsa Família. The 1988 constitution raised social assistance to the same status as health, education, and pensions. The Organic Law of Social Assistance (1993) and the National Policy of Social Assistance (2003) also contributed toward the construction of a legal framework for the creation of Bolsa Família. Since 1985 Brazil's social assistance has been funded by the *Fundo Nacional de Assistência Social* (National Fund of Social Assistance), as well as mandatory contributions from states and municipalities (Brasil. Congreso Nacional, 27–28). In addition, three previous experiences of conditional cash transfers developed in Campinas, Distrito Federal, and Riberão Preto in 1995 were then replicated throughout the country (Sugiyama 2007, 94–103; Soares and Sátyro 2010, 28–30; Bandeira Coêlho 2012, 62–66).

[25] The IGD takes into consideration the following indicators: quality of the Unified Registry data, registry update, and information on education and health conditionalities. Only the municipalities with IGD higher than 0.5 receive federal resources in a given month (Brasil. Ministério do Desenvolvimento Social e Combate à Fome 2012b).

conditions for the transfers. They also monitor federal transfers through a local council.[26]

While municipalities are central actors in the implementation of Bolsa Família, the role of states is less clear. The legislation declares that states are in charge of coordinating and training municipalities, thus giving them a secondary role, but they also have the authority to design and implement their own social policies (Brasil. Congreso Nacional, 27–28). As a result, cooperation from states is important for complementing Bolsa Família, in spite of their diminished legal role.

Figure 5.2 shows levels of coverage of Bolsa Família as a percentage of the targeted population, as measured by people who show socioeconomic deprivation and are therefore included in the Unified Registry.[27] Coverage has been lower than the Brazilian mean in the state of Goiás. When the policy was first launched, for instance, only around a quarter of the targeted population was covered in Goiás. In 2015, coverage was lower than 60 percent of the targeted population. The state of Rio Grande do Sul has scored better than the state of Goiás since the policy was first launched, reaching almost 40 percent of the targeted population in 2004. Political alignments, territorial infrastructure, and policy legacies explain these

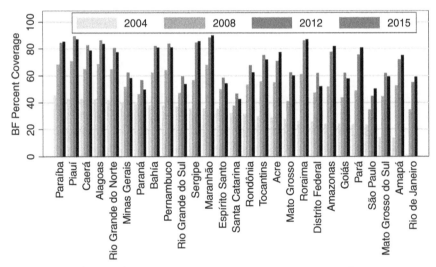

FIGURE 5.2 Bolsa Família percent coverage in 2004, 2008, 2012, and 2015
Note: Order of states from highest to lowest coverage the first year of available data.
Source: Brasil. Secretaria de Avaliação e Gestão da Informação do Ministerio do Desenvolvimento Social e Combate á Fome (2015).

---

[26] Since 2005, municipalities have been required to develop local councils, composed of government and civil society members, for monitoring the use of federal funds (Baddini Curralero 2012, 117).
[27] For a description of the measurement of the dependent variable, see Chapter 3.

differences. Table 5.2 presents a summary of the dependent and independent variables across the selected states and municipalities, and across time.

As a CCT, attribution of responsibility is clear in Bolsa Família. The Brazilian Electoral Panel Study project conducted 4,611 interviews with 2,669 voting-age Brazilians throughout 2010, a presidential election year. It found that six months before the presidential election 76 percent of respondents identified the federal government as responsible for the program. By the time of the election this number had risen to 84 percent (Ames et al. 2010, 37; Zucco 2013, 814). Additionally, Bolsa Família has improved the performance of the incumbent's party in presidential elections (Hunter and Power 2007; Zucco 2008, 2013). The assumption of these studies is that attribution of responsibility is clear. In other words, the electorate can reward presidents

TABLE 5.2 *Implementation of Bolsa Família in selected states and municipalities*

Subnational unit	Alignment with national government[a]	Territorial infrastructure	Subnational policy legacies[b]	Level of implementation[c]
Goiás	Opposition	Weak	Negative	Low (2004–11) Medium (2012–)
Goiânia	Alignment	Weak	Negative	Medium (2004–5) Low (2006–)
Valparaíso de Goiás	Opposition (2003) Alignment (2004–8) Opposition (2009–)	Weak	Weak	Low (2004–11) High (2012–)
Rio Grande do Sul	Opposition (2003–9) Alignment (2010-)	Strong	Positive	Medium
Canoas	Opposition (2003–8) Alignment (2009–)	Weak	Negative	Medium (2004–9) Low (2010–12) Medium (2013–)
Porto Alegre	Alignment (2003–4) Opposition (2005–9) Alignment (2010–)	Strong	Negative	Medium (2004–6) Low (2007–8) High (2009–)

[a] Alignments from 2003, when the PT was elected for the presidency, to 2012. By 2012, Bolsa Família started to lose its clear attribution of responsibility, so alignments are expected to become irrelevant; see explanation below.
[b] Policy legacies at the national level are overall positive; see Table 5.3
[c] Level of implementation measured in relation to the national average (for states) and to the state average (for municipalities).

from the Workers' Party (PT) for Bolsa Família only because they are able to identify this party as primarily responsible for this policy. An editorial in Goiás' local newspaper announced Bolsa Família in the following terms:

Government programs have names and logotypes that have been carefully studied by marketing teams advising the government. This happens during elections at the local, state and, most importantly, federal levels. With the arrival of Lula, this sequence is repeated ... The government is trying to put its own stamp on social assistance by announcing yet another program, Bolsa Família (Weinberg, October 22, 2003).

Others have also explained the change in program name – from Cardoso's flagship program Bolsa Escola to Lula's Bolsa Família – as a strategy to increase policy ownership (Melo 2008).

Although it is true that attribution of responsibility is clear in this CCT, a number of factors have contributed to blurring such clarity and therefore improving levels of coverage since 2012, as exhibited by increases in coverage across states in Figure 5.2. To begin with, as time goes by, there are changes in government administration but the policy sticks around, so people start forgetting where the policy came from in the first place. In addition, conditionalities have the effect of blurring the policy provider and therefore the potential electoral gains. Since recipients have to keep up with health check-ups, school attendance, and updating of the registry, the municipal as well as the state and federal levels have some participation in Bolsa Família and can claim some credit.

Last, but certainly not least, the federal government has had an active strategy to share responsibility with the aim of improving the implementation of the CCT. The federal government actively asked states to complement Bolsa Família with their own subnational programs. In exchange for this, the logo of the state would be placed on the ATM card used by recipients to withdraw the funds (see Niedzwiecki 2014b for an example). In addition to adding the state logo, the federal government also proposed to provide a document to each beneficiary family, where the separate contributions from the federal and state governments would be shown. Although these pacts have not been completely successful in terms of durability and scope, more states are slowly signing up (Interview Mariz de Medeiros). In 2010, only two states – both with PT governors – were part of these agreements, Acre and Distrito Federal. By mid-2012, a total of eleven states decided to sign such agreements, and some of these states were opposition states.[28] By expanding attribution of responsibility, the federal government

---

[28] By August 2012, the following states had joined the federal government's proposal of complementing Bolsa Família with the state programs (in parenthesis): Acre (*Programa Adjunto da Solidariedade*), Amapá (*Programa Família Cidadã*), Distrito Federal *(DF Sem Miséria)*, Espírito Santo (*Programa Bolsa Capixaba),* Goiás (*Renda Cidadã*), Mato Grosso *(Programa Panela Cheia)*, Rio de Janeiro (*Programa Renda Melhor),* Rio Grande do Sul (*Programa RS Mais Igual*), Rondônia *(Programa Bolsa Futuro),* Santa Catarina (*Santa Renda*), and São Paulo (*Programa Renda Cidadã*) (Brasil. Ministério do Desenvolvimento Social e Combate à Fome

enhances the implementation of Bolsa Família. In the words of the National Secretary for Citizen Income:

States have the prerogative to develop their own programs ... the federal government is now offering state governments ... more visibility ... The problem was the identity of Bolsa Família was very strong, so now we try to divide the identity by including the state, so that their participation becomes stronger; and integration is actually increasing ... We knew we had to give visibility to state governments for a joint effort, so dividing the ATM card is good because it gives more space to the partner state, making it clear that the benefit is being divided ... *That contributed to the fact that states led by the opposition would agree to participate* [emphasis added] (Interview Silva de Paiva).

In my own qualitative interviews with Bolsa Família recipients throughout the second half of 2012, this change in attribution of responsibility has slowly started to appear in numbers. When asked about where Bolsa Família came from and who funded it, 63 percent (24 out of 38) of the respondents answered that they did not know, or had the wrong answer. These answers included: "I don't know," "from the government ... I don't know which one," "from the municipality," "from the governor," "from the state government of Rio Grande do Sul," or "from the government of Iris Rezende and then Marconi Perillo [former governors in the state of Goiás]." As attribution of responsibility progressively fades away and opens up the possibility of sharing credit, the effect of political alignments on the implementation of Bolsa Família is also starting to disappear.[29] As the coordinator of Bolsa Família in the municipality of Porto Alegre commented,

[t]he political issue does not weigh in Bolsa Família any longer, because all other parties know how to make political use of this cash transfer ... Today, there is much less identification with a particular government ... At the beginning, the political issue was important because it was directly associated with Lula's government ... But in 2012, that is not the case (Interview L. Souza)

The following section analyzes this transition from a strong to weaker effect of political alignments on the implementation of Bolsa Família, in the opposition state of Goiás.

Political Alignments and Changes in Attribution of Responsibility

State of Goiás

The state of Goiás has been in opposition to the federal government since the PT candidate won the presidency in 2003. Elected governors have belonged to the

---

2011; Brasil. Secretaria Nacional de Assistência Social, Departamento de Benefícios 2012; Brasil. Secretaria Nacional de Renda de Cidadanía 2012).

[29] This very recent policy to blur attribution of responsibility (and its effect on the diminished role of political alignments) is only now appearing in the case studies for which I conducted field research in 2012. Therefore, it does not show up in the statistical analysis in Chapter 4.

opposition parties PSDB (*Partido da Social Democracia Brasileira*) and PP (*Partido Progressista*), at least since the PT won the presidency in 2003.[30] As a consequence, Goiás originally hindered the implementation of Bolsa Família by presenting direct policy competition through its own cash transfer program called *Renda Cidadã* (Citizen Income) and through refusing to share the list of recipients of this state policy with the federal government. Nevertheless, as attribution of responsibility for Bolsa Família became less clear, competition gave way to cooperation. In 2012 the state signed an agreement with the federal government to collaborate with the implementation of Bolsa Família by which Renda Cidadã started complementing the national cash transfer.

When Bolsa Família was launched in 2003, the state of Goiás already had its own noncontributory cash transfer: Renda Cidadã was established in 2000, and was designed, implemented, and fully funded by the state. This subnational CCT was used in direct competition to the federal policy. From the beginning Renda Cidadã had been the centerpiece strategy of the state for the provision of social assistance and it had high approval rates from the electorate.[31] It is targeted at poor families and entails a cash transfer of US$40 (raised from US$23 to US$30) paid through an ATM card that includes the logo of the state government.

The funds from Renda Cidadã can only be used for buying designated items, including bread, milk, flour, beans, soap, medicine, and propane tanks (Faria 2005, 53; Vieira 2005, 83). Municipalities have a supervisor in charge of ensuring that the transfer is only used for buying items on the list.[32] The supervisor is appointed by the governor, generally with the approval of the mayor and the federal and state deputies from that municipality (Interviews Arantes, Lobo). This person represents the governor in the neighborhoods and is the main channel through which the policy is implemented, thus avoiding the need to coordinate implementation with opposition groups (Interviews Abreú,

---

[30] The PSDB headed a coalition that included eleven parties in the 2010 elections, when it competed against an alliance headed by the PMDB (*Partido do Movimento Democrático Brasileiro*) and the PT. The confrontation between these two coalitions at the state level has remained stable at least since 2003 (Interview Rezende Machado).

[31] The policy was announced a few months after the new PSDB governor, Marconi Perillo, began his term in 1998. It was a way to differentiate himself from the previous opposition PMDB governorship, which had implemented a program providing baskets of food (*O Popular*, December 24, 1999; *O Popular*, October 12, 1999). Renda Cidadã had an approval rate of 73 percent in 2001. Therefore, in 2002 gubernatorial elections, the PMDB contender assured in the campaign he would keep the transfer (Chuahy, May 17, 2002).

[32] A couple of days after giving the funds to families, they need to present receipts, showing that they bought food and not alcohol or cigarettes (Botão, December 25, 2002). The policy also includes health and education conditionalities, which were given priority in 2009, but overall only the type of goods bought are monitored and can cause exclusion from the program (Faria 2005, 58; Vieira 2005, 83).

Ribeiro Guimarães).[33] In the past, the supervisor was also in charge of mobilizing recipients for political rallies in support of the governor.

As in the Argentine opposition province of San Luis, Goiás refused to provide the federal government with the list of people included in Renda Cidadã and banned these recipients from receiving any federal policy. To receive the state cash transfer, people could not be included in the Unified Registry, a fact that excluded them from any policy that came from the federal government such as Bolsa Família. The state determined that potential beneficiaries of Renda Cidadã had to receive written proof from their municipal government stating that they were not recipients of Bolsa Família. This added a burden to municipal governments, which were dealing with the initial registration for Bolsa Família. Not sharing databases also excluded the national government from accessing a list of potential recipients for Bolsa Família. The coordinators of Bolsa Família in the municipality of Goiânia (first) and the state of Goiás (second) remembered this time of competition:

It was very difficult because there was rivalry between programs. For the federal government, if the person was in a vulnerable situation, he or she could receive Bolsa Família. But for the state government, it asked families to not be included in Bolsa Família to receive Renda Cidadã. So, to receive Renda Cidadã, we had to give families a declaration from the municipality saying that they were not included in Bolsa Família's registry ... Bolsa Família tried to have a registry of vulnerable families, but we had a large number of families that were excluded from the registry because they chose Renda Cidadã (Interview Artiaga).

If you had Bolsa Família you could not receive Renda Cidadã ... Those who had Renda Cidadã were excluded from the Unified Registry ... and if a person is excluded from the Unified Registry it means they will be excluded from every other federal program ... this was a complete des-information ... it completely disoriented people (Interview Barra de Azevedo).

In order to convince people to stay in the state program, Goiás offered a higher cash transfer than Bolsa Família. In 2007, for example, Bolsa Família recipients received from US$7 to US$47, while Renda Cidadã offered around US$40 (*O Popular*, February 19, 2007; Oliveira, March 19, 2008). The state program reached a maximum of 160,000 families in 2004–5 or roughly half of all families living with less than one minimum salary in 2002 (Faria 2005, 85; Rodríguez da Cunha, June 29, 2005; Estado de Goiás 2010). By 2012, Bolsa Família was the preferred policy; it not only offered a higher transfer for families with children, but it also appeared to be more stable in the minds of recipients. Of the thirty-six Bolsa Família recipients interviewed, 60 percent said they thought the cash transfer would not end in the future. For Renda Cidadã,

---

[33] The state does not coordinate with opposition municipalities for the implementation of this and other state cash transfers (Interviews Accorsi, Arantes, Bezerra, De Nacimento, Edson, Lobo, Ribeiro Guimarães).

eight of eleven recipients who were asked the same question said they thought this policy would be canceled in the future.

Since July 2012, competition has given way to the first steps toward cooperation between Renda Cidadã and Bolsa Família, although the state government is still in the hands of politicians opposed to the national government. This is reflected in the higher levels of coverage, exhibited in Figure 5.2 since 2012. Renda Cidadã now complements the transfer of Bolsa Família recipients to reach at least US$35. In addition, the state cash transfer covers those excluded from Bolsa Família: people above extreme poverty with no children and populations excluded from the labor market, such as the elderly. High-level bureaucrats explained that the goal in the long run is for Renda Cidadã to cease to exist (Interviews Arante, Ribeiro Guimarães; Silva, March 29, 2012).

This transition from competition to collaboration with the implementation of Bolsa Família reflects a move toward less clear attribution of responsibility, or a lesser degree to which the PT and the president at the federal level can claim credit for this policy. As explained earlier, this weaker attribution of responsibility is in part a result of an active strategy by the federal government (sharing logos in the ATM card), but also the effect of conditionalities and the passing of time. The Planning Director at the Secretary of Social Development in Goiás expressed this shift in the following terms:

We are now in a process of unifying both programs . . . which did not exist before because it was not technically or politically propitious . . . In Goiás, Bolsa Família has lost its exclusive personality as a federal program. Nobody says that it is from Dilma [Rousseff, the current President], or from Lula [Da Silva, the former President] . . . it has lost that attribute . . . Cash transfers before were used for political gain because they were new; now it brings less political dividends than what they used to ten years ago (Interview Lobo).

This change in attribution of responsibility has also weakened the effect of political alignments on the successful implementation of Bolsa Família across municipalities. The municipality of Goiânia has been aligned with the federal government since 2003, and the municipality of Valparaíso de Goiás has been in opposition to the federal government and aligned with the state government for most of the period. Figure 5.3 shows how the municipality of Valparaíso de Goiás has consistently scored lower in the percentage of eligible people covered by Bolsa Família than the average for the state of Goiás until 2012, and lower than the municipality of Goiânia until 2009. By 2012, when attribution of responsibility was becoming blurred, Valparaíso de Goiás was performing better than the state average and Goiânia. This figure also shows that both municipalities score lower than the average for the state, at least until 2012, which responds to the relatively weak territorial infrastructure and negative policy legacies in both cases, depicted in Table 5.2, and explained in the next sections.

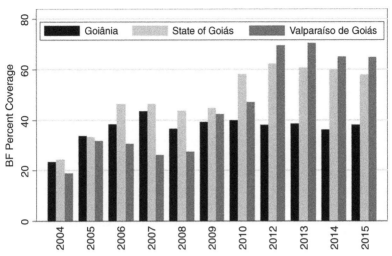

FIGURE 5.3 Bolsa Família percent coverage in the state of Goiás and the municipalities of Goiânia and Valparaíso de Goiás
Note: Year 2011 not available at the municipal level.
Source: Brasil. Secretaria de Avaliação e Gestão da Informação do Ministerio do Desenvolvimento Social e Combate á Fome (2015).

The municipality of Goiânia has been mostly aligned with the federal government since 2003. It was led by a PT governor from 2000 to 2004 and also since 2010, and by a PMDB governor during 2005–9 (in coalition with PT since 2008). This close political connection with the federal government has made Bolsa Família a priority for the local government. Goiânia was one of the few subnational governments to sign an agreement with the federal government in 2004 to help co-fund the policy through local initiatives (Licio 2012, 189). In 2006, the municipality received an award from the federal government for the implementation of Bolsa Família, called *Prêmio Práticas Inovadoras na Gestão do Programa Bolsa Família* (Innovative Practices in the Administration of Bolsa Família). The award recognizes the successful implementation of a local program that developed cooperatives among actual and potential Bolsa Família recipients, as a possible way of incorporating these recipients into the labor market (Brasil. Ministério do Desenvolvimento Social e Combate à Fome 2006, 92–97). In spite of being aligned with the national government, the local government has been unable to fully implement Bolsa Família due to the combination of weak territorial infrastructure and strong and negative policy legacies, which will be analyzed in subsequent sections.

Valparaíso de Goiás has changed its political alignments since its creation as an independent municipality in 1995, but has mostly been in opposition to the national government and aligned with the state government.[34] As such, Bolsa Família has not been a priority for the local government until very recently. As was the case in Argentina, while states may have the resources to temporarily compete with the federal government through their own subnational policies, municipalities generally do not have this option. Opposition municipalities can hinder the implementation of national policies more by omission than by action. Figure 5.3 shows a stark increase in Bolsa Família coverage, particularly from 2012 onward. Around the time when Bolsa Família started losing its clear attribution of responsibility and the state government signed an agreement with the national government, this municipality started having a more active commitment to this policy. Every fifteen days, the Secretary of Social Development moved her activities from her central office to a highly populated neighborhood (called Santa Rita) to cover those who were unable to go to the central office. In addition, the secretary developed a campaign using the local television network to promote Bolsa Família (Interview Machado Freitas). The Secretary of Social Development in the municipality referred to this higher commitment:

We increased the number of people directly working with recipients, we bought a car specifically for Bolsa Família with money from the federal government ... We started making weekly visits to families ... So we basically increased the service ... and because the service was better people started coming more ... We also started disseminating more information to mothers about courses offered through Bolsa Família, so they had more incentives to sign up (Interview Tabosa).

State of Rio Grande do Sul

While the state of Goiás represents uninterrupted political opposition to the federal government, Rio Grande do Sul's alignment with the federal government changed after Lula won the presidency in 2003. This change in political alignments allows for analyzing the effect of this variable across time in a given subnational unit. The governors of Rio Grande do Sul had been mostly in opposition to the federal government until 2010 when a PT governor was elected. Therefore, we should expect that the state government would change its commitment toward Bolsa Família after 2010. The state of Rio Grande do Sul showed medium levels of coverage in Bolsa Família, particularly in the initial years after Lula was elected president (Figure 5.2). This was due in part to a strong territorial infrastructure, built upon robust civil society organizations throughout the state, and also to the fact that opposition to the federal government was weak in Rio Grande do Sul, compared with Goiás, reacting with omission rather than action against Bolsa Família. While previous governments had been mostly indifferent to

---

[34] Between 2004 and 2008 Valparaíso de Goiás had a weakly aligned mayor belonging to the PTB (*Partido Trabalhista Brasileiro*).

Bolsa Família in Rio Grande do Sul, the commitment toward this policy became stronger after a PT governor was elected. This stronger commitment had a minor effect on levels of coverage at the state level, as depicted in Figure 5.2, partly because of local opposition to the state program that will be analyzed below.

When Bolsa Família was launched, the state was led by an opposition PMDB–PSDB coalition (2002–6). This opposition government eliminated its cash transfer program targeted at poor families (called *Família Cidadã*, Citizen Family) that had been implemented by the previous PT governor in 1998 (Interview M. I. Nunes; Dualibi, November 22, 2009).[35] Therefore, when the federal policy was launched, the state government remained indifferent: it neither complemented the federal policy nor provided policy competition. When an aligned PT governor was elected in 2009, one of the first measures was to create a new policy that would directly complement Bolsa Família, called *RS Mais Renda Mais Igual* (Rio Grande do Sul More and Fairer Income). The program targets Bolsa Família families with children in high school, and complements their transfer. Recipients of Bolsa Família who qualify for this extra transfer receive a card with the state's logo. The high level of commitment from the state in designing and fully funding this program is explained by the director of the program:

Policies such as Mais Renda were promoted by the federal government so that states could start to complement Bolsa Família. That is what we are doing here ... While some states followed the federal government's suggestion, others did not ... We were one of the first ones with Tarso's government [Rio Grande do Sul's PT governor] ... We feel very close to the federal government, and that is why we work for the improvement of Bolsa Família ... The main characteristic of the state government is our complete alignment with the federal government (Interview Bauer).

This complementarity produced only small increases in coverage partly due to local resistance to the program. Echoing the role of political alignments in the implementation of federal policies, the implementation of this state program also encountered resistance in opposition municipalities and support in aligned municipalities. While the PT municipality of Canoas fully implemented the state program by informing eligible families and adding them to the Unified Registry, the opposition government of Porto Alegre, the capital of Rio Grande do Sul, resisted it (Interviews Boniatti, Mardemattos, Seadi, L. Souza). This is somewhat complicated by the fact that the government of Porto Alegre is in opposition to the PT at the state level but part of the PT coalition at the federal level. As a result, this local government refuses to sign agreements with the state for the implementation of RS Mais Renda Mais Igual, but fully implements

---

[35] Família Cidadã entailed a transfer of around US$100 and reached 100,000 families in January 2002 (Cidades do Brasil, January 2002).

Bolsa Família, thus providing strong evidence for the multilevel political alignment argument.

According to high-level bureaucrats at the local and state levels, the resistance to the state cash transfer reflected political opposition, particularly throughout the electoral year of 2012. The municipality opposed the idea of adding the state logo to the Bolsa Família ATM card, arguing that it would confuse recipients (Interviews Bauer, L. Souza). A concrete effect of not signing the agreement with the state government is that those who theoretically would be in charge of signing up potential recipients for the state policy in Porto Alegre were unaware of the state program (Interviews J. Mallmann, J. Ribeiro, Velloso).

Municipalities in the state of Rio Grande do Sul are crucial actors in the implementation of the national cash transfer. Figure 5.4 shows the levels of coverage of Bolsa Família in the municipalities of Porto Alegre and Canoas across time and compared with the state average. Political alignments vary throughout the analyzed period in these municipalities and we should therefore expect variation in their position toward Bolsa Família's implementation. Canoas was in opposition to the national government until a PT governor was inaugurated in 2009. This is reflected in the levels of coverage, with a significant recovery after 2010. The still low levels of coverage in 2010 respond to the previous opposition government's lack of compliance with Bolsa

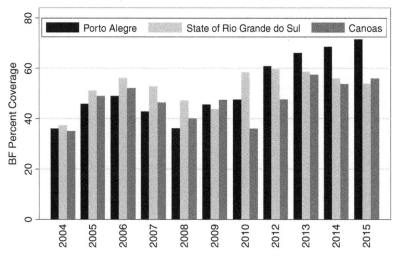

FIGURE 5.4 Bolsa Família percent coverage in the state of Rio Grande do Sul and the municipalities of Porto Alegre and Canoas
Note: Year 2011 not available at the municipal level.
Source: Brasil. Secretaria de Avaliação e Gestão da Informação do Ministerio do Desenvolvimento Social e Combate á Fome (2015).

Família's requirements to update the Unified Registry. It took the new government a couple of years to recover from this omission. Conversely, Porto Alegre had PT governors until 2004, when the levels of coverage were initially increasing. After that, an opposition alliance between PPS (*Partido Popular Socialista*) and PMDB was elected at the local level. These changes in alignments led to a significant decrease in the levels of coverage from 2007 onward, which jumped again in 2009–10 with an aligned PDT (*Partido Democrático Trabalhista*) mayor.

The municipality of Canoas switched from a lack of commitment to Bolsa Família to active participation when a PT mayor was inaugurated in 2009. The previous opposition government did not comply with the obligation to update the Unified Registry and therefore the new government did not receive federal transfers in their first year in office. In the words of the Coordinator of Social Protection in Canoas: "We did not receive transfers from the federal government in 2009 because the registry was not updated, only since 2010 we have started to reverse that situation" (Interview Mardemattos). As a result, the year 2010 exhibits low levels of coverage because it took some time to recover from the lack of federal transfers in 2009. In addition, the previous opposition government underspent the budget by around US$1,000, which had been transferred by the federal government for human capital development and institutional building to expand Bolsa Família (Interview Mardemattos). The previous opposition government had agreed to build one CRAS in 2007, as a response to pressures from civil society groups. Nevertheless, it did not provide any public space for building this CRAS and the CRAS was built inside a church-associated NGO, *Grupo da Ação Social Nossa Senhora Aparecida* (Interviews Mardemattos, Pisonique). The Secretary of Social Development in Canoas at the time recalled that "Bolsa Família was never a priority" for the PSDB mayor (Interview Pisonique).

Since the election of a PT mayor, the municipality of Canoas has shown an active involvement with Bolsa Família along the lines proposed by the federal government (Da Silva 2011, 36). One of the ways in which this commitment can be seen is the expansion of the number of CRAS from one to five, and closing down the one located inside the NGO because it did not comply with the minimum requirements defined by the federal government. The new local government also hired more professionals and started to actively look for new recipients to sign up. These actions increased the territorial infrastructure in the municipality, a topic that will be further developed in the next section, thus increasing the level of coverage in the last couple of years, as shown in Figure 5.4.

The process of implementation of Bolsa Família has been different in Porto Alegre. When Bolsa Família was launched the PT municipal government modified its local cash transfer to complement the national policy, to reach a maximum total of US$100 per household. For doing so, in 2004 Porto Alegre signed an agreement with the federal government to co-fund the policy through local initiatives (Licio 2012, 189). The local program was called *Núcleo de Apoio Socio Familiar* (Support for the Family). It had been created in the late 1990s and was targeted to families at risk of domestic violence or drug addiction. Since the transfer was never updated, the program slowly disappeared. The years between 2005 and 2009, under an opposition government, were characterized by poor performance, as shown in Figure 5.4. The PMDB opposition mayor had an approach of nonconfrontation and of keeping only the "good" ideas from the PT and changing the "bad" ones. He did not engage in any open opposition to the federal policy but he also did not actively promote it (Interviews Olegário, Verle). He acted by omission. Since 2010, the aligned PDT governor has been fully committed to the expansion of Bolsa Família by further signing up potential recipients and by following up on the fulfillment of conditionalities. This is reflected in increasing levels of coverage of the national CCT in Figure 5.4.

Territorial Infrastructure
Political alignments couple with territorial infrastructure to explain the variation in the implementation of Bolsa Família across states and municipalities. Strong territorial infrastructure can be achieved through strong state institutions and through their collaboration with civil society. Municipalities are in charge of implementing Bolsa Família and, therefore, the strength of social assistance institutions and their relationships with civil society at the *local* level are particularly important. While infrastructure in the state of Rio Grande do Sul is comparatively stronger than in Goiás, there is significant variation across municipalities. Within Rio Grande do Sul, the municipality of Porto Alegre is an example of strong local institutional capacity in collaboration with civil society organizations. There is fruitful collaboration between governmental and nongovernmental institutions for the implementation of Bolsa Família. The neighboring municipality of Canoas lags behind due to the combination of structurally precarious and understaffed municipal social assistance institutions, and weak collaboration with civil society. Local variation is also present in the state of Goiás. The municipality of Goiânia has lagged behind in the development of social assistance institutions, in part due to a previous local infrastructure that only partly implemented Bolsa Família, and in part as a result of weak linkages with civil society. Finally, Valparaíso de Goiás is a relatively new municipality that lacks significant development of social assistance institutions.

Territorial infrastructure is relatively strong in the wealthy state of Rio Grande do Sul. Most civil servants have accessed their job through meritocratic means (passing an exam) and receive comparatively high salaries. For the implementation of Bolsa Família, the state offers training to municipal civil servants and engages in campaigns to increase the amount of national IDs, a prerequisite for receiving the transfer (Interviews Bauer, Brito, Capitanio, Nunes, Ninov). Strong social assistance institutions are strengthened through close collaboration with non-state actors. Throughout Rio Grande do Sul, civil society is vital for monitoring the use of Bolsa Família funds. Such monitoring is conducted through state and municipal councils, as well as agreements (*convenios*) between civil society, the state, and municipalities. Territorial infrastructure at the municipal level is crucial for explaining implementation patterns.

The provision of social assistance in Porto Alegre through the government *Fundação de Assistência Social e Cidadanía* (Social Assistance and Citizen Foundation, FASC) rests on strong material and human resources.[36] In 2012, Porto Alegre decentralized the implementation of Bolsa Família in twenty-two CRAS divided into nine regions and staffed by professionals who have passed public service exams. CRAS facilities are in adequate condition and are distributed relatively evenly throughout the territory. This increases their accessibility. The work of CRAS is monitored and enhanced by an active participation of civil society. The relationship between CRAS professionals and civil society allows for monitoring the use of federal funds and the quality of the service, for reaching recipients who are not complying with conditionalities, and for finding new recipients. In particular, grassroots organizations have a role in monitoring the fulfillment of conditionalities for Bolsa Família. CRAS directors assign NGOs a number of families living in the area that are not complying with conditionalities. The NGO, who knows the territory, is best equipped to assess the reasons for the lack of compliance (Interview M. Medeiros). Civil society monitors the overall implementation of the CCT in the municipality. The Secretary of Social Development in Porto Alegre summarized the monitoring role of civil society:

Every single thing is discussed mainly with civil society ... clause by clause ... you open up the discussion and therefore you take longer, but it is more democratic ... They work towards accountability ... We are held accountable every week throughout the year ... Every week I have to go to the CMAS [Municipal Council of Social Assistance] before implementing any change in the street ... They are partners, they make a good debate (Interview Seadi).

Since its creation in 1994, the Municipal Council of Social Assistance has been comprised of forty-four members, half of which represent civil society and half of which represent the municipal government. The Council meets every other week, while its special commissions (including a Bolsa Família Commission) meet weekly. Porto Alegre is the only one of the four Brazilian municipal cases included in this book that subdivides the Municipal Council of Social Assistance into sixteen regions that follow the participatory budgeting regions. The *Conselho Regional de Assistência Social* (Regional Councils of Social Assistance, CORAS) take the discussions to a smaller scale. These regional councils are then present in the municipal council. The Municipal

---

[36] Despite the name, FASC is a fully funded government institution.

and Regional Councils have a central role in Bolsa Família. They are active in the definition of the location of new CRAS in the territory and they receive complaints from users of social assistance if they feel their rights have been violated. In these cases, councilors visit the involved institution (generally the CRAS) and take the complaint to the regional or municipal councils (Interviews Dariva, L. Souza).

Compared to Porto Alegre, the neighboring municipality of Canoas has more fragile municipal institutions and poor synergy with civil society. CRAS facilities are inadequate in that they do not provide comfort for populations with special needs, such as a bathroom for children or handicapped people. In addition, three quarters of these facilities are rented, which is a problem because the municipality does not invest in improvements and there is always the risk of moving to another location, a fact that challenges the sustained work in a given neighborhood. Moreover, the specific neighborhoods for which each CRAS is responsible is not clear, which is a major challenge for monitoring the fulfillment of conditionalities. The families that are not complying with Bolsa Família conditionalities do not receive a visit to their house, as is the case in Porto Alegre. Instead, they just receive a letter from the CRAS informing them that they must go to an appointment with the CRAS to explain the situation. Many families never show up, however, thus risking the interruption of the benefit. Finally, human resources in the CRAS are not enough and some CRAS workers are not familiar with the people they assist. Overall, the CRAS is not a recognized institution in the territory, and thus it has not become the entry point for social assistance (Interviews Boniatti, Mardemattos; Vieira Ferrarini, Deitos Giongo, and Silva Silveira 2010).

The administration inaugurated in 2009 implemented a number of changes to start strengthening territorial infrastructure in Canoas. The CRAS expanded their activities by actively looking for new recipients (*busca ativa*), following up on those who were not fulfilling conditionalities, increasing business hours, installing internet access, and hiring additional personnel. The new government hired professionals through a public competition, and incorporated a coordinator, two social assistants, one psychologist, and four administrators. In addition, it made efforts to keep the Unified Registry updated, and the transfer of funds was routinized. Finally, the new local government also implemented a "mobile unit," a van that could register people who live far from the CRAS, thus lowering barriers for access (Interview Mardemattos; Canoas Secretaria Municipal de Desenvolvimento Social 2009; Vieira Ferrarini, Deitos Giongo, and Silva Silveira 2010). For these improvements, after 2010 Canoas expanded coverage, as shown in Figure 5.4, and received a national award.[37] However, investments in state

---

[37] *Colegiado Nacional de Gestores Municipais de Assistência Social* (National Association of Municipal Social Assistance Administrations) (Da Silva 2011, 48).

territorial infrastructure take time to be consolidated, and they do not produce changes overnight.

Besides having a comparatively weaker state infrastructure than Porto Alegre, another major difference is that local institutions have weak relationships with grassroots organizations for the implementation of the national CCT (Interviews Dutra, Fagundes, Mardemattos, Rosa). Although a Municipal Council – that combines both state and non-state actors – has existed in Canoas since 1997, the level of participation is low (and lower than in Porto Alegre). There are eighteen councilors, nine representing civil society and nine representing the municipal government. There are no regional councils to raise concerns from the neighborhoods. The institutional weakness of the CRAS undermines the legitimacy of the Council, since CRAS members rarely participate in Council meetings. As the director of a CRAS in Canoas acknowledged: "The truth of the matter is that the CRAS is not very much involved in the Council, we participate only if they call us ... we know it would be important to participate but we do not have the time to do so" (Interview Boniatti). Until 2009, there was very little dialog between the Council and the Department of Social Development, a situation both have been trying to reverse since the new PT governor was elected (Interview Rosa). As a result, civil society is not a partner of the municipality in the implementation of Bolsa Família. They do not help the CRAS in the supervision of conditionalities or in finding potential recipients (Interview Mardemattos).

Compared with the state of Rio Grande do Sul, the state of Goiás faces the challenge of a relatively weak subnational territorial infrastructure, coupled with fragile linkages to civil society. The state is not particularly wealthy and a significant amount of resources for social assistance have been invested in the subnational cash transfer described in the previous section. Those in charge of the subnational program Renda Cidadã hold political rather than meritocratic positions. In more general terms, most middle- and upper-level bureaucrats in the main state social assistance office (*Secretaria de Cidadania e Trabalho)* accessed their position through personal or political connections, rather than through meritocratic channels (Interviews Abreú, Arantes). In addition, the state fails at coordinating joint strategies with civil society for the implementation of Bolsa Família (Interviews P. García, Arantes).

Goiás' weak pluralistic regime (Borges 2007; Montero 2007) does not promote the development of an independent civil society that can effectively monitor the use of Bolsa Família funds. There is a state council composed of members representing the state government (50 percent) and civil society (50 percent). Nevertheless, the council does not meet regularly (Interview Arantes);[38] and since it was created in 1995, most of the council's presidents have been representatives of the government as opposed to civil society

---

[38] In fact, during my two months living in this state, I was not able to participate in any of the meetings because their schedule was uncertain.

(Interview de Jesus). The President of the Municipal Council of Social Assistance in Goiânia explained the limited relationship of civil society with the state government: "The state council was implemented very politically, and institutions never had real presence ... they never had much participation ... Participation is really minimal, councilors were always very few ... the Presidency of the council has always been appointed by the governor" (Interview Regina de Moraes).

The two municipal case studies within the state of Goiás also exhibit weak territorial infrastructure. In the municipality of Goiânia, weak territorial infrastructure is the main factor to account for an overall poor performance of Bolsa Família, as Figure 5.3 shows. Goiânia implemented Bolsa Família through fifteen CRAS and to a lesser extent through fifteen *Unidades Municipais de Assistência Social* (Municipal Units for Social Assistance, UMAS) that have existed since the late 1990s. UMAS only existed in Goiânia: they were a legacy of a previous policy in the municipality called *Cidadão 2000* (Citizen 2000), and therefore this institution did not receive any transfers from the federal government. Given the strong legacy of UMAS, the CRAS structure has only been in place since 2009 and remains very weak. There is a lack of professional personnel working at the Department of Social Development, and the CRAS do not have the human and material resources (such as a car in larger territories) necessary to conduct an active sign up of potential Bolsa Família recipients (Interviews de Nacimento, de Oliveira, Edson, Regina de Moraes).

The weakness of state institutions in Goiânia affects the lack of coordination between the local state and civil society for the implementation of the national CCT (Interviews Accorsi, Barra de Azevedo, de Nacimento, P. García). The Municipal Council of Social Assistance faces a number of challenges, such as being viewed as irrelevant by the municipal government, unable to monitor the use of federal transfers for social assistance, and lacking infrastructure and human resources (Pio de Santana, Dilma 2007, 210). As a consequence, the council does not have the capacity to monitor the Department of Social Development and its CRAS in the implementation of Bolsa Família (Interview De Nacimento). The President of the Goiânia Council of Social Assistance explained it in the following terms:

There does not exist monitoring or evaluation of Bolsa Família, there are processes that should be working but are not working ... there exists a systematic way of monitoring but this Council is not carrying it out ... we just don't have a functioning evaluation system ... the evaluation process of the program is not working ... only a few councilors are involved in the daily activities, because most of them prioritize their own institutions, so it is difficult for the council to make demands, to complain (Interview Regina de Moraes).

The municipality of Valparaíso de Goiás exhibits an even weaker territorial infrastructure. Although there are two CRAS in the municipality, they have remained inactive for the implementation of Bolsa Família, which is centralized in the Secretary of Social Development (Interview Tabosa). This clearly has limited further expansion of Bolsa Família.[39] The few CRAS in the territory and the centralization of the implementation of Bolsa Família in the Department of Social Development mean that potential and actual recipients of Bolsa Família in this municipality have to travel to the neighborhood where the Department of Social Development is located, imposing an extra barrier to access. At the same time, and similar to Goiânia, the role of organized civil society is also limited in Valparaíso de Goiás. The council does not regularly meet and is not very active in Bolsa Família (Interviews Baddini Curralero, Machado Freitas).

Policy Legacies

Besides the role of political alignments and territorial infrastructure for the successful implementation of Bolsa Família, policy legacies are also central for understanding the overall success of this policy. Some policy legacies have been general and have affected all subnational units (such as the unification of previous national cash transfers), while others have been specific for each subnational case study.

Brazil's previous noncontributory social policies have shaped the implementation of Bolsa Família. The main legacies from previous policies are the incorporation of recipients from other programs to the Unified Registry, institutional learning (including the practices of schools, health centers, and municipal institutions in working with conditionalities), and recipients' use of ATM cards in previous cash transfers.[40] Table 5.3 presents a description of previous policies and their legacies for the implementation of Bolsa Família.

The novelty of Bolsa Família was to unify programs that were not coordinated and registries that were incomplete. It unified the CCTs that had been created since 2001 (*Bolsa Escola, Cartão Alimentação, Auxílio-Gás,* and *Bolsa Alimentação*) and incorporated programs from the 1990s (*Programa de Erradicação do Trabalho Infantil,* Peti). This means that the implementation of Bolsa Família did not start from scratch. There already were 4.2 million families receiving benefits from other programs, such as Bolsa Escola (3,601,217), Bolsa Alimentação (327,321), Cartão Alimentação (346,300), and Programa de Erradicação do Trabalho Infantil (1,000) (Soares and Sátyro 2010, 43). Many of these families were incorporated into Bolsa Família.

---

[39] The lack of decentralization of Bolsa Família implementation to CRAS is not necessarily negative. This municipality has almost 150,000 inhabitants, compared to Goiânia, which has more than 1.3 million. Still, the ratio of population to social assistance institutions is significantly lower in Valparaíso de Goiás.

[40] Bither-Terry (2013) argues that it is precisely this building on legacies from previous policies that made Bolsa Família such a successful social policy.

TABLE 5.3 *Previous social policies and their legacies for Bolsa Família implementation*

Policy	Description	Legacy for Bolsa Família implementation
Programa de Erradicação do Trabalho Infantil – Peti (1996)	• *Target:* families with children under sixteen currently working or in risk of child labor • *Transfer:* roughly US$30 (rural) and US$45 (urban) • *Conditionality:* 85 percent school attendance • *Responsible:* Ministry of Social Development	• Registered recipients: 1,000 • Schools working with conditionalities
Bolsa Escola Federal (2001)	• *Target:* families with income per capita below US$45 with children between seven and fifteen years old • *Transfer:* roughly US$7.5 per child and a maximum of US$23 (three children) • *Conditionality:* 85 percent school attendance • *Responsible:* Ministry of Education	• Registered recipients: 3.6 million • Schools working with conditionalities • Municipalities in charge of implementation
Bolsa Alimentação (2001)	• *Target:* families with income per capita below US$45 and with children between zero and six years old or pregnant women • *Transfer:* roughly US$7.5 per child and a maximum of US$23 (three children) • *Conditionality:* health controls for pregnant women and children • *Responsible:* Ministry of Health	• Registered recipients: 327,000 • Health centers and hospitals working with conditionalities

Auxílio-Gás/Vale-Gás (2001)	• *Target:* families with per capita income lower than half a minimum salary and beneficiaries of Bolsa Escola or Bolsa Alimentação • *Transfer:* US$4 per month, every two months • *Conditionality:* fulfill conditionalities from Bolsa Escola and Bolsa Alimentação • *Responsible:* Mines and Energy Ministry	• Registered recipients: 9.7 million
Cartão Alimentação (2003)	• *Target:* families with per capita income below half a minimum salary • *Transfer:* roughly US$25 per family • *Conditionality:* funds can only be used for food • *Responsible:* Extraordinary Ministry of Food Safety	• Registered recipients: 346,000 • Recipients start using ATM cards

Sources: Brasil. Ministério do Desenvolvimento Social e Combate à Fome (2008); Da Silva e Silva and Santos de Almada Lima (2010); Soares and Sátyro (2010); Sposati (2010); Baddini Curralero (2012).

The transfer of recipients from previous programs to Bolsa Família was particularly important when the national CCT was launched. In personal interviews with CRAS directors across the states of Goiás and Rio Grande do Sul, they explained that the first recipients included in the unified registry were those who already received another program, such as subsidies for gas, milk, and food (*Auxílio-Gás, Vale Leite,* and *Cesta Básica*), and cash transfers targeted to families with children who were working, malnourished, or in school (Peti, Bolsa Alimentação, and Bolsa Escola, respectively). Some of these programs had a registry that dated from the 1990s and were incorporated (after arduous work updating and adapting information) into the Unified Registry (Interviews Baddini Curralero, Bartholo, Boniatti, Camara Pinto, L. Souza, Mallmann, Silva de Paiva, Teixeira; Cotta and Paiva 2010, 61; Modesto and Abrahão de Castro 2010, 15). The Unified Registry was launched in July 2001 in the context of Bolsa Escola, and the unification of registries started in October 2003 and ended in 2011 (Interviews Baddini Curralero, Teixeira). As the National Secretary for Citizen Income put it:

> The existence of previous programs assisted Bolsa Família to get started on a database ... but it was a very arduous process ... the large majority of people who were receiving these previous benefits, also qualified for Bolsa Família, so it was simply a matter of unifying it, of paying a single benefit for all families ... that allowed Bolsa Família to reach 11 million people in 2006 ... It would have been very difficult to start from scratch (Interview Silva de Paiva).

Previous policies do not only leave a paved road for the transfer of recipients, they also encourage institutional learning, particularly for the implementation of conditionalities. These previous policies are present in the great majority of the municipalities (Da Silva e Silva and Santos de Almada Lima 2010, 113). Therefore, many of these municipalities had already prepared institutions for the provision of national social policies (through Departments of Social Development, for example) that enhanced Bolsa Família when it was launched. In addition, Peti and Bolsa Escola had school attendance conditionalities, and Bolsa Alimentação had health check-up conditionalities. Therefore, Bolsa Família's conditionalities were not a complete novelty for schools, health centers, and municipal officials. In 2004, critics of the lack of control over the fulfillment of conditionalities in Bolsa Família compared it with the success of Bolsa Escola at registering school attendance. As a response to this criticism, the government started exercising stricter control over the compliance with conditionalities (Cotta and Paiva 2010, 61).

Legacies from previous policies are also specific to each state and municipality. The state of Rio Grande do Sul designed and implemented CCT programs before Bolsa Família. These are Pia 2000 (1996–2000) and Citizen Family (*Família Cidadã*, 1998–2003). These programs were cash transfers to poor families under the condition of school attendance and health check-ups. When Bolsa Família was implemented, Rio Grande do Sul's health centers and schools had developed practices that made the implementation of conditionalities a smoother process. In the words of a former Secretary of Social Development in the state of Rio Grande do Sul:

We had already developed linkages with Família Cidadã and Pia 2000 ... In the case of Pia 2000, for example, other state agencies had to work towards the provision of national i.d's ... The banks had to learn to include this new population ... All this already existed at the level of the state since 1997 ... The work with health and education ministries, who had to check school attendance and vaccination, already existed here ... When Bolsa Família was launched we already had a process underway (Interview M.I. Nunes).

However, not all policy legacies were positive. Porto Alegre's initial below-average success in implementing Bolsa Família, depicted in Figure 5.4, is partly related to the legacy of a previous system for social provision. This previous structure took some time to be converted to the standards defined by the national government through the Unified System, namely that signing up for Bolsa Família has to be conducted at CRAS or at social development departments. The city had developed a network of nine social assistance centers, some of which were slowly transformed to CRAS. Nevertheless, this transformation is still being completed (Interviews Brito, L. Souza, Timmen).

Social assistance legacies in Canoas, also in the State of Rio Grande do Sul, are even more challenging than those in Porto Alegre. Until 2001, social assistance did not have the status of department; it had been a subdepartment within the Department of Health since 1970 and therefore developed the activities that the Health Department mandated, such as distributing prosthesis and coordinating ambulances. Between 1995 and 2000, this subdepartment started training personnel for the distribution of "benefits that were only received by those who took a personal initiative" (Interview Pisonique). It is only in 2001 that social assistance is upgraded to department status and separated from health. Due to the historic secondary position that social development has in Canoas, the Department lacked human resources when Bolsa Família was launched; the first CRAS was opened in 2005 in a space that had to be borrowed from an NGO (in the neighborhood of Guajuviras). The rest of the CRAS were built after the PT mayor assumed power in 2009 (Da Silva 2011, 33–50).

In the state of Goiás, the initial meager performance of Bolsa Familia's implementation reflects in part the direct competition through the state cash transfer and the refusal to share databases of state programs with the federal government, explained earlier in this chapter. Within the state of Goiás, Goiânia and Valparaíso de Goiás represent negative and weak legacies, respectively.

In Goiânia, social assistance was run by an NGO, the *Fundação Municipal de Desenvolvimento Comunitário* (Municipal Foundation for Community Development, FUNDEC) and directed by the wife of the mayor. This foundation provided social assistance between the 1970s and 2009. Therefore, until very recently, social assistance in Goiânia was linked to the first lady (*primero damismo*) and had a charitable and philanthropic characteristic. As the Executive Secretary of the Municipal Council of Social Assistance put it: "changing that philanthropic and first lady characteristic is not a simple thing ... you don't change that easily ... but at least we have a Department now ... whereas before we did not have almost any psychologists or social assistants" (Interview Edson). In addition, and as was explained in the previous section, UMAS provide an alternative infrastructure for social assistance. They hinder the expansion of Bolsa Família because they are not supported by the federal government and limit the development of the CRAS. In the municipality of Valparaíso de Goiás, institutional legacies are weak. As a new municipality (it was founded in 1995), the Department of Social Development dates back to 1997. Although the question of spouses as heads of social assistance was never an issue, there has not been strong institutional learning for providing conditionalities before Bolsa Família (Interview Tabosa). As a result, the implementation of Bolsa Família is done in a somewhat empty context.

CONCLUSIONS

In Argentina and Brazil political alignments affect the successful implementation of CCTs because attribution of responsibility is clear. The aligned province of Mendoza and state of Rio Grande do Sul complement Asignación Universal por Hijo and Bolsa Família with their own programs. Conversely, the opposition province of San Luis and state of Goiás hinder the implementation of the national CCTs by providing direct policy competition and by refusing to share the list of recipients of state policies. Nevertheless, while San Luis in Argentina is still obstructing the implementation of Asignación by 2012, Goiás signed an agreement with the federal government to collaborate with Bolsa Família for the first time that same year. This reflects the fact that attribution of responsibility is more blurred in Bolsa Família both due to the passing of time and because of an active effort by the federal government to share credit. The federal government proposed to incorporate the state logo into the ATM card in exchange for cooperation. Overall, when comparing Brazil and Argentina, the effect of political alignments is stronger in the latter because alignments are clearer and the CCT has a stronger attribution of responsibility.

In terms of territorial infrastructure, the two countries also show differences in their forms, though not necessarily in their results. In Argentina the institutions that provide social protection vary throughout the territory, including municipal territorial delegates and community centers in some municipalities, and centralizing social protection in the province in others. Conversely, Brazil has engaged in a process of homogenization of the territory – the Unified System of Social Assistance provides clear guidelines for how the territory should be organized, and on the specific roles of the national, state, and local governments. Such territorial organization is relatively new and builds from the *Sistema Único de Saúde* (Unified Health System, SUS), which will be analyzed in the next chapter.

Strong territorial infrastructure can be achieved through capable government institutions and through their connections with civil society. In general, Brazil exhibits higher levels of collaboration between state and non-state actors for the implementation of CCTs, partly due to the existence of legally mandated councils. However, there is also variation across subnational units. While the municipality of Porto Alegre is an example of strong municipal institutions and active civil society participating in the monitoring of Bolsa Família, all the other cases lag behind. This is in part because state institutions are weaker in these other cases than in Porto Alegre and because municipal agencies are less receptive to joint participation with non-state actors.

Besides political alignments and territorial infrastructure, policy legacies are also central for explaining the successful implementation of Bolsa Família and more marginal in Argentina. The effect of previous national social assistance policies is stronger in Brazil compared with Argentina because previous policies were implemented for a longer period of time, they were more broadly targeted, and they required health and education conditionalities. The latter produced institutional learning for the implementation of Bolsa Família. Policy legacies are both common throughout the territory and at the same time specific to each locale. States, provinces, and municipalities had previous policies that competed with or complemented Asignación and Bolsa Família when they were launched. At the same time, the national cash transfers benefitted from previous national social assistance policies, and the implementation of these previous policies was uneven throughout the territory. As a result, their legacies also exhibit subnational variation.

6

Health Care Policies in Argentina and Brazil

Chapter 5 analyzed policies with clear attribution of responsibility. In those cases, political alignments shaped implementation. This chapter presents the opposite case – when *attribution of responsibility* is not clear, *political alignments* are irrelevant for shaping the successful implementation of national social policies. This is the case of the selected health policies in Brazil (*Estratégia Saúde da Família*, Family Health Strategy, ESF) and Argentina (*Plan Nacer*, Birth Plan, PN). For each country, I first analyze the sources of blurred attribution of responsibility and, as a consequence, the irrelevance of political alignments.

Second, I focus on the role of *policy legacies* within each national health policy. Entrenched interests from a previous primary health care strategy and from hospital health provision are crucial for understanding the challenges in the implementation of Estratégia Saúde da Família in Brazil. The states and municipalities that had a more developed health structure before the implementation of ESF present the greatest resistance to this policy. In Argentina, Plan Nacer is implemented in health facilities that provide both preventive and curative health care (including high-complexity hospitals), and therefore the policy does not generate a conflict between the different strategies for the provision of health care. In other words, there are no negative legacies for the implementation of Plan Nacer.

Finally, *territorial infrastructure* is central for understanding the successful implementation of national health policies. There are differences in the types of territorial infrastructure for health provision across countries and within countries across provinces and municipalities. In Brazil, municipalities – in coordination with civil society – are in charge of implementing primary health care, and states are more or less present in coordinating such provision. In Argentina, provinces provide health care, but some municipalities in some provinces have also taken on health responsibilities. In addition, non-state actors are absent in the implementation of health policies in Argentina.

ESTRATÉGIA SAÚDE DA FAMÍLIA IN BRAZIL

Brazil's health system is called *Sistema Único de Saúde* (Unified Health System, SUS) and is two-tiered – it includes a public tier financed by general taxes and a private tier financed by individuals. Decentralization of the public tier since the 1980s has given states and municipalities room for innovation while leaving the definition of broad parameters to the federal government (Chapman Osterkatz 2013). These broad parameters are enforced through federal transfers to subnational governments with strings attached to them. Subnational governments also partly co-fund health care, as well as participate in designing the system through health councils. In terms of health provision, the federal government is in charge of high-complexity health care, states deal with medium-complexity procedures, and municipalities administer primary health care. In practice, big cities and some states have also taken on high-complexity health administration.[1]

Within the Unified Health System, Estratégia Saúde da Família or ESF is the main policy for primary health provision. The national government launched the policy in 1994 to decrease health spending while overcoming the lack of de facto access to health care despite the constitutional mandate of universal coverage.[2] The aim of this policy is to substitute curative (and more expensive) health care for universal, easily accessible, and good quality preventive health care. This is done by increasing immunization rates, nutritional controls, and basic medical and dental assistance for children; prenatal care, cancer prevention, and dental controls for women; and health check-ups for populations at risk, such as people with high blood pressure, diabetes, or tuberculosis. It is expected that good quality preventive health care decreases illnesses that require complex and expensive services. In this way, the policy aims at reorganizing the provision of health around preventive care, and thus decreasing health spending.

The federal government is in charge of setting minimum standards by legislating and monitoring ESF implementation, which is guaranteed through the transfer of funds called *Piso de Atenção Básica* (Primary Care Baseline). These transfers include a fixed portion based on population and a variable portion to promote the implementation of ESF, among other national health policies. States monitor the implementation of ESF and provide training to

---

[1] In 2008, 44 percent of health spending came from the federal government, 28 percent from the states, and 29 percent from municipalities. In theory, 30 percent of the national, state, and municipal social security income should be invested on health care, as well as a percentage of the income from taxes at the state (15 percent) and municipal (12 percent) levels. The federal government has to increase health spending at the same rate as GDP increases. These percentages are rarely respected (Levi and Scatena 2011, 82).

[2] In 1987, the *Programa Agentes Comunitarios* (Community Agents Program) was implemented in the state of Ceará and then folded into the national program in 1991. This national program was then transformed into *Programa Saúde da Família* (Family Health Program) in 1994 and then renamed *Estratégia Saúde da Família* in 2006 (Tendler 1997).

municipalities. Municipalities are in charge of implementation. A team of professionals at the municipal level is responsible for the health of no more than 4,000 people in a defined territory located at a *Unidade Saúde da Família* (Family Health Facility, USF).[3] According to an official document, "[t]his organization favors the establishment of bonds of responsibility and trust between professionals and families and enables a better comprehension of the health/disease process and the necessary interventions" (Brasil. Ministério da Saúde, Departamento de Atenção Básica 2005, 15). At a minimum, the multi-professional team includes a primary care physician, a nurse, a nursing assistant, and four health agents (*Agente Comunitário de Saúde*).[4] This team is in charge of offering health assistance, registering the population, formulating a local health plan, monitoring diseases, developing educational activities, engaging with community organizations, boosting health councils, and getting to know each family (Brasil. Ministério da Saúde, Departamento de Atenção Básica 2005, 21). ESF is characterized by so-called active search (*busca ativa*) to find and register patients as well as visit them in their home, an activity for which the health agent is mainly responsible.

Health agents are crucial actors in the implementation of ESF. They are the link between the families and the health facility, and they decrease barriers of access to the health system. I asked forty-four users of ESF whether they had received house visits from health agents. Sixty-five percent (twenty-nine people) answered positively and 35 percent (fifteen people) answered negatively.[5] Of the ones who answered positively, almost 70 percent said that health agents visited their house at least once a month. They summarized the role of health agents in the following way: "Health agents come very often to my house, sometimes even twice a week. They let us know if it is time for the vaccines or weight controls for Bolsa Família" (Interview Brazil #10); "Sometimes I call them [health agents] and sometimes they come directly. They know me already" (Interview Brazil #23); "[health agents come] once a month now; they came more often when my children were newborns" (Interview Brazil #54); "They [health agents] came more often before, because my mother had HIV, but now I go directly to the health facility for pregnancy controls" (Interview Brazil #19).

Users of this primary health care system participate through health councils, which are mandatory for the implementation of ESF. There are health councils at many ESF facilities, and at the municipal and state levels. In fact, almost 40 percent of ESF units throughout the country participated in local or

---

[3] Each USF can host one or more teams, depending on the concentration of the population in that territory.

[4] Since 2000, some teams also include a dental team (*Equipe de Saúde Bucal*). According to local needs and possibilities, a psychologist, nutritionist, social assistant, and physical therapist can be incorporated to the team.

[5] All interviews were conducted from August to December 2012, mostly in Family Health Facilities while patients were waiting for assistance, and also in their house together with health agents who were carrying out their regular visits.

municipal health councils in 2002 (Brasil. Ministério da Saúde, Departamento de Atenção Básica 2004, 21). The composition of the health councils at the state and municipal levels follows specific guidelines – 50 percent of its members should be users of the system (organized in neighborhood associations or other NGOs), 25 percent should be government representatives, and 25 percent should represent health workers.

ESF is a right with no political manipulation. If health services do not reach adequate standards (for example, if the doctor of the health facility is often absent, the health facility is in poor condition, or politicians try to manipulate the policy) users of the system can complain at the health councils or through a free hotline. In addition, of all the policies included in this study, ESF is the only universal policy. All Brazilian citizens are eligible for this policy, regardless of their income levels. In spite of its universal ideals, ESF's actual coverage is still much lower than universalism and the users of ESF are mostly poor people. As a result, the policy is commonly referred to as "poor medicine for poor people" (*medicina pobre para pobre*). The Coordinator of Health in the research institute *Instituto de Pêsquisa Econômica Aplicada* (IPEA) in Brasília explained this idea: "The organization of the public health system in which preventive health care is an entry port is only used by poor people. The middle class and rich people are not users of the SUS for primary health care; they have private coverage for primary health care ... And they use the SUS for high-complexity procedures" (Interview Servo).

Figure 6.1 shows the levels of ESF coverage as a percentage of the total population in Brazil, including the selected states of Rio Grande do Sul and Goiás. The levels of coverage consistently increased in Brazil until 2015, although at different paces across states. While Rio Grande do Sul is among the poorest performers, with 56 percent coverage in 2015, Goiás had a very successful start and reached almost 70 percent of the population in 2015. This is noteworthy since Goiás has been in opposition to the national government throughout this period. This lack of correlation between political alignments and ESF coverage is also true at the local level. Figures 6.2 and 6.3 show levels of coverage within Rio Grande do Sul's and Goiás' selected municipalities. Figure 6.2 shows that both Canoas and Porto Alegre are below Rio Grande do Sul's average. At the same time, Canoas only started implementing ESF after 2003 and scores lower than Porto Alegre, at least until 2014. Figure 6.3 shows that Valparaíso de Goiás scores generally higher than Goiânia and even higher than the state average since 2009. Conversely, Goiânia scores below both. At the same time, Goiânia has been generally aligned with the national government and Valparaíso de Goiás has been in opposition. The levels and changes in ESF coverage are not correlated with political alignments in these municipalities.[6]

---

[6] For a description of political alignments across the selected states and municipalities, see Chapter 3.

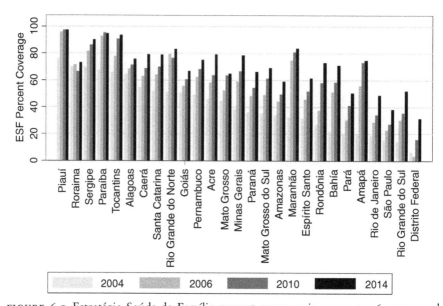

FIGURE 6.1 Estratégia Saúde da Família percent coverage in 2004, 2006, 2010, and 2014

Source: Brasil. Departamento de Atenção Básica da Secretaria de Atenção à Saúde (2015).
Note: Population covered by ESF in December of each year. States ordered from highest to lowest coverage in 2004.

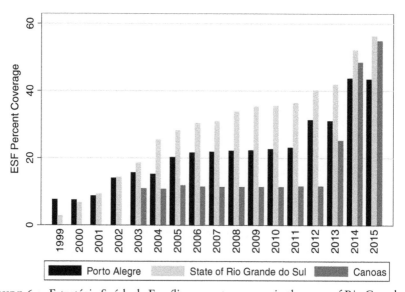

FIGURE 6.2 Estratégia Saúde da Família percent coverage in the state of Rio Grande do Sul and the municipalities of Porto Alegre and Canoas

Source: Brasil. Departamento de Atenção Básica da Secretaria de Atenção à Saúde (2015).
Note: Population covered in December of each year.

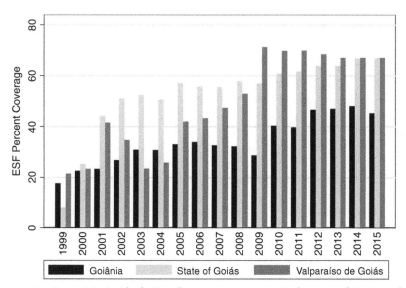

FIGURE 6.3 Estratégia Saúde da Família percent coverage in the state of Goiás and the municipalities of Goiânia and Valparaíso de Goiás
Source: Brasil. Departamento de Atenção Básica da Secretaria de Atenção à Saúde (2015).
Note: Population covered in December of each year, except 2015 for state of Goiás, which corresponds to July.

Blurred Attribution of Responsibility and Irrelevance of Political Alignments

As a health policy, attribution of responsibility in ESF is expected to be less clear than in the cash transfers analyzed in Chapter 5. Although the policy is mostly funded and designed by the federal government, a great majority of the users of the system do not attribute this policy to this government level. Of the forty-five people whom I asked where ESF came from, only one answered that it came from the national government – 78 percent answered they did not know where the policy came from, 15 percent thought the municipal government was primarily responsible, 5 percent identified the state government as the main responsible actor, and only 2 percent identified the national government as the main provider. Along similar lines, in interviews with medium- and high-level bureaucrats at the local, state, and national levels, many expressed the idea that ESF does not belong to any particular government (Interview J. Pinto) or that any government could self-attribute it (Interview Rousselet de Alencar). These ideas show the same underlying fact – attribution of responsibility is fuzzy in this health policy and it can therefore belong to no government or to any government. A permanent member of the health council in the city of Porto Alegre put it in the following terms: "People think that the mayor or council person gives Estratégia Saúde da Família, and not the national government ... And that is what the SUS wants, that people identify the municipality as the entry port ... no matter where most of the resources come from" (Interview Rousselet de Alencar).

This lack of clear attribution of responsibility is a quality of the policy – as a service the direct recipients of federal transfers are health facilities and not patients. As a result, patients tend not to identify receiving any particular policy. In fact, 86 percent (out of a total of forty-four) users of ESF answered they did not know which services the policy provided.[7] Identifying the benefits of a policy with the policy itself is necessary for attributing responsibility. Relatedly, the "good" provided by the policy (accessible primary health care) is less tangible than in the case of CCTs (cash). When a new health center is inaugurated, it is initially visible for the community; however, recognizing that the center is a product of ESF is not obvious and eventually the building is taken for granted and the policy becomes an effort toward – less visible – good quality primary health care provision. Moreover, the fact that the policy has been implemented for around twenty years means that it has survived changes in national, state, and municipal administrations. ESF was implemented in the midst of economic adjustment policies in 1994, for which reason some initially mischaracterized it as a neoliberal policy (Interview Fagundes). The policy was strengthened by the left-leaning PT government from 2003 to 2016 (Chapman Osterkatz 2013, 248). These changes in government administration across time and territorial levels further contribute to blurring attribution of responsibility. Finally, the decentralized implementation of ESF also opens the possibility for self-attribution at different levels of government. The face of the policy is the municipality, although the federal government defines minimum standards, and state governments provide training. As a result, governments at the three levels have self-attributed, or self-claimed responsibility for this policy.[8]

The main outcome of this blurred attribution of responsibility is that users of ESF cannot shape their voting decision based on satisfaction with this policy. As a result, opposition subnational governments have no political incentive to hinder this policy, and therefore political alignments are irrelevant for predicting the successful implementation of ESF. This idea was confirmed by politicians at the local, intermediate, and national levels (Interviews Alvarenga, Bosio, Britzke, Castilhos Gomes, De Camargo, Dhein, Frantz, Rassi, I. Rodriguez, Rousselet Alencar, Sant'ana de Lima, Toazza Tura).

While political alignments are irrelevant predictors of the degree of implementation of ESF, the two other variables analyzed in this book are crucial for explaining subnational variation – policy legacies and territorial infrastructure, which are summarized in Table 6.1. While policy legacies affect the *level* of ESF coverage, territorial infrastructure shapes the *quality* of provision.

---

[7] The 14 percent who answered they knew the services provided by ESF identified the policy only with house visits from health agents.

[8] The main street in the City of Porto Alegre, for instance, was filled with life-size pictures of the mayor holding ESF signs.

TABLE 6.1 *Implementation of Estratégia Saúde da Família in selected states and municipalities*

Subnational unit	Policy legacies (negative)	Territorial infrastructure	Level of implementation[a]
Rio Grande do Sul	Strong	Strong	Low coverage High quality
Porto Alegre	Strong	Strong	Low coverage Medium quality
Canoas	Strong	Weak	Low coverage Low quality
Goiás	Medium	Weak	Medium coverage Medium quality
Goiânia	Strong	Weak	Low coverage Low quality
Valparaíso de Goiás	Weak	Weak	High coverage (1999–2000) Low coverage (2001–8) High coverage (2009-) n/a quality[b]

[a] Level of implementation based on national average (for states) and state average (for municipalities). Quality based on PMAQ (Programa Nacional de Melhoria do Acesso e da Qualidade da Atenção Básica) and in relation to the included subnational units (Brasil. Ministério da Saúde, Departamento de Atenção Básica (2011), Accessed on June 29, 2016).
[b] Data not available either because Valparaíso de Goiás did not request external evaluation or because there was no professional at the time of the PMAQ survey.

Policy Legacies

The implementation of ESF faces strong resistance from supporters of the previous primary health strategy and of high-complexity or hospital health care. The SUS did not always organize the provision of primary health through ESF; it was previously organized through *Unidades Básicas Tradicionais* (Traditional Basic Health Units, UBS).[9] This previous model was comparatively more expensive than ESF and had more limited coverage. In addition, UBS did not include health agents, a central characteristic of ESF that increases access for those patients who cannot go to the health facility for different reasons. These patients would not receive health care through the previous system. In addition, the UBS system is centered

---

[9] The term UBS throughout this chapter refers to health facilities aimed at providing primary health care through the traditional system.

on access to health assistance (as opposed to prevention) and incorporates more specialized doctors, including pediatricians, gynecologists, and clinical doctors. This means that generations of doctors were trained for this previous system and did not change their training to become less specialized to adapt to ESF. Instead, some of these doctors became even more specialized to work in the hospital system. Partly for this reason, it has been a challenge for ESF to find doctors trained in family medicine (Brasil. Ministério da Saúde and Fundação Oswaldo Cruz 2005, 18). It has also been challenging to convince patients of the old system to adapt to the new one. A previous user of UBS who moved to a neighborhood that had ESF expressed this idea: "I was used to the other health unit where there were more doctors ... I would still choose that other one because I felt more accompanied" (Interview Brazil #12).

In 2009, almost half of the municipalities that implemented ESF did so in combination with the UBS system (Brasil. Ministério da Saúde 2009, 27). The most successful cases of ESF implementation were those that could replace the old UBS system with the new ESF system, taking advantage of the previous infrastructure and resources (Giovanella et al. 2009). At the same time, the places that had the highest density of UBS found it harder to transition to the new system than the places that did not have any system before. A government report (first) and the National Director of the Basic Health System (second) evaluate the challenges of implementing ESF in the presence of strong UBS legacies:

In municipalities with more structured health systems and preventive health provision the resistance to the implementation of ESF was higher, compared to cases where there was no previous health provision. In other words, changing the existent model, by substituting already existent traditional basic units, generates more resistance than creating new family health facilities in areas without coverage (Brasil. Ministério da Saúde and Fundação Oswaldo Cruz 2005, 54).

There are places where Estratégia Saúde da Família coexists with the basic unit of the traditional system ... Today we have a third of basic health provision under the traditional system ... In the 90s, we had the idea of complete replacement of the previous system, but decades go by and that is still missing ... Of course, we still keep pushing for Estratégia Saúde da Família (Interview H. Pinto).

Doctors and patients interested in keeping the old system can use health councils to organize and voice their demands. As a result, health councils that are crucial for monitoring the implementation of ESF (as it will be analyzed in the section on territorial infrastructure) can also hinder the expansion of ESF. Nevertheless, some municipalities also use the health councils to raise awareness of the benefits of the new policy compared to the traditional system (Brasil. Ministério da Saúde and Fundação Oswaldo Cruz 2005, 53–54). The role of health councils for hindering or enhancing ESF varies across and within municipalities and is shaped by the strength of the previous UBS and high-complexity systems.

High-complexity health provision is another structure that challenges ESF implementation, particularly with regard to the struggle for material and human resources. When a health system is structured around curative and hospital health provision, municipal governments have little incentive to invest in basic health of any kind. Municipalities have autonomy in deciding how to spend their own resources, and investment in hospitals is generally a smart electoral strategy since it is very visible (Interview Servo). More people see and benefit from a hospital than from a small health facility. In addition, federal transfers for health reinforce medium- and high-complexity health structures. In 2008, almost half of the national health transfers were for medium- and high-complexity health care, and less than 20 percent were for primary health care (Brasil. Ministério da Saúde, Datasus 2009). Finally, hospital health provision holds back the expansion of ESF through offering higher salaries to general practitioners, and therefore making it difficult for the primary health system to compete for personnel. Health professionals can receive a higher salary by working part-time in hospitals, and particularly in private ones, than by working exclusively in ESF. Given these salary differences, many medical students choose not to follow preventive health training and instead specialize in curative health care.

In general, UBS and high-complexity health systems are more developed in larger cities compared to smaller towns. As a result, smaller municipalities have implemented ESF faster and with better results than larger ones. In 2002, small municipalities had more than double the coverage of large municipalities (Brasil. Ministério da Saúde and Fundação Oswaldo Cruz 2005, 20; Brasil. Ministério da Saúde, Departamento de Atenção Básica 2006, 18).[10] To overcome this gap, since 2002 the federal government developed a program called *Programa de Expansão e Consolidação da Saúde da Família* (Program for the Expansion and Consolidation of Family Health). This program seeks to expand ESF coverage in cities with more than 100,000 inhabitants with the aim to transform the UBS system to ESF, train students in family medicine, and promote monitoring mechanisms. In addition, the fixed portion of the federal transfers for the provision of primary health care is calculated based on population, a fact that benefits municipalities with large populations (Ferla et al. 2002, 16; Brasil. Ministério da Saúde, Departamento de Atenção Básica 2005, 21; Viana et al. 2009, 17; Do Nascimento and Da Costa 2009, 75).

Besides the negative legacies that stem from alternative health systems, ESF also faces a challenging neoliberal legacy – The Fiscal Responsibility Law (*Lei*

---

[10] It should also be mentioned that reaching higher percentage coverage requires less effort in a small municipality, compared to a larger one. The smaller the municipality, less family health teams are needed to reach higher coverage percentages.

de Responsabilidade Fiscal). Since 2000, this law has determined that no more than 60 percent of net fiscal revenues of states and municipalities could be spent on personnel (Brasil. Câmara dos Deputados May 4, 2000, 19).[11] This affects every sector of the public bureaucracy but particularly those that are human resource intensive, such as health and education. To not exceed the 60 percent limit, municipalities are forced to find alternatives to hiring ESF teams. In 2006, 60 percent of municipalities outsourced hiring for ESF to nonprofit private organizations. In addition, 80 percent of municipalities hired doctors through temporary contracts, and 70 percent of doctors and more than half of nurses had a temporary contract (Brasil. Ministério da Saúde 2009, 5). Such precarious contracts contributed to the high turnover rate of doctors in ESF – almost 80 percent of all doctors and dentists stay for less than one year (Brasil. Ministério da Saúde, Departamento de Atenção Básica 2004, 18). This legacy challenges the essence of ESF based on the importance of personal knowledge between health professionals and patients in the community.

State of Rio Grande do Sul

The state of Rio Grande do Sul had a legacy of strong development of UBS and hospitals before ESF was implemented. By 2012, roughly 70 percent of primary health care was provided through UBS and only 30 percent through ESF (Interview Castilhos Gomes). In addition, the state had already developed a strong hospital infrastructure by the time ESF was launched, most of which was nonpublic.[12] Given that a majority of the population in this state receives health care through systems other than ESF, the implementation of ESF has not been a priority. As a result, Figure 6.1 shows that Rio Grande do Sul scores lower than most other states in Brazil. A former director of a conglomerate of health institutions in Rio Grande do Sul explained the reasons why the hospital system expanded at the expense of preventive health care:

> There is a constant political pressure from hospital administrators to receive the resources they want ... No health secretary has ever had the courage to ... allocate more resources to ESF and reduce the resources to hospitals ... Medical entities in Rio Grande do Sul are also very strong, and they constantly criticize primary care ... They generate an impossible pressure ... While the hospitals organize banquets in *Plaza San Rafael* [expensive hotel in Porto Alegre], primary care organizes a picnic in the *Parque da Rendenção* [public park in Porto Alegre] (Interview Sanzi Souza).

---

[11] The law also sets specific minimums for each branch of government. At the municipal level, no more than 54 percent of revenues can be spent on personnel in the executive branch and no more than 6 percent on personnel in the legislative branch. Violation of these rules is subject to criminal penalties, fines, and even jail (Liu and Webb 2011, 39).

[12] In 2001, only 7 percent of hospital beds in Rio Grande do Sul were public. The rest were philanthropic (55 percent), university-owned (21 percent), and private (17 percent) (Ferla et al. 2002, 19).

Supporters of hospital- and UBS-based health strategies use councils to exercise political pressure. In particular, every time there is a proposal to transform an UBS to an ESF unit, that proposal needs to be first approved by the local UBS council, then by the district council, and finally by the municipal council. While popular participation enhances the quality of health provision, as it is analyzed in the section on territorial infrastructure, it can also hold back ESF's coverage. These three instances of debate (local, district, and municipal) are also veto points that can push the proposal back. The municipality of Porto Alegre, with its high levels of popular participation (Baiocchi 2005), is the best representative of the benefits of health councils for improving the service of ESF and the potential costs of health councils for providing a platform for those willing to maintain the old UBS system – especially organized doctors.[13]

Porto Alegre developed a strong UBS and hospital infrastructure before the implementation of ESF. Figure 6.2 shows that Porto Alegre has had an overall poor performance compared to the state levels, with a more noticeable increase in coverage since 2012, when the city improved the working conditions of ESF teams. Overall, changes in coverage have been slow because these previous health systems are challenging to modify.

The city was a pioneer in primary health care training (through *Centro de Saúde Escola de Murialdo* and *Grupo Hospitalar Conceição*) since the mid-1970s and by 1990 there were already twelve UBS in the city (Goulart 2002). As a result, when ESF was implemented in Porto Alegre it had to coexist parallel to the UBS system, and always occupying a secondary role. The first twenty-four ESF teams in 1996 were located in a space that had to be borrowed from neighborhood associations (Woltmann 2012, 45). In 2013, there were fifty-four UBS, each covering between 5,300 and 116,000 people (Prefeitura Municipal de Porto Alegre, Secretaría Municipal de Saúde 2013, 145). Therefore, in Porto Alegre the mainstream primary health strategy is still UBS. The Secretary of Health in Porto Alegre expressed the challenges of implementing ESF in the presence of these strong negative legacies:

After that health structure was in place, we tried to implement Estratégia Saúde da Família. In other municipalities, you did not have that structure before the implementation of ESF … And that initial moment defined the outcome, because it was too late; you already had too many resources in another health structure and it was hard to change those resources … The big structures will remain … When we started implementing Estratégia Saúde da Família, we wanted to make a complete replacement; that is, make

---

[13] On September 4, 2012, I participated in a meeting of the district council in the East Region in Porto Alegre (Bom Fim). In that case, the proposal to change a particular UBS to an ESF unit was approved by majority vote. Most of the debate was around the strategy for mobilizing the local population to exercise pressure at the municipal health council, where other groups would present open opposition to the transition to ESF.

all UBS disappear. But as time went by we realized that could not be the way ...
The system will remain mixed (Interview Bosio).

Besides the struggle with the UBS system, ESF competes for resources against
the hospital system. In 2014, the municipality of Porto Alegre had twenty-seven
private and public hospitals of medium- and high-complexity (Prefeitura
Municipal de Porto Alegre 2014). Given that hospitals are more expensive to
maintain and that they organize a stronger lobby, they receive a larger amount
of resources than primary health care strategies. These budget priorities have
proven challenging to modify. A former Secretary of Health in Porto Alegre
expressed this struggle over resources between the different health strategies:

Porto Alegre always had a health structure that highly valued emergency care, and that
received most of the financial resources ... When health care was municipalized in
1991–1992, Porto Alegre responded with emergency units ... and that is a very expensive system ... Only later Porto Alegre focused on primary health care ... but only
through unidades básicas tradicionais in the late 1990s ... Since 2000s the municipality
started working toward the implementation of ESF, but the municipality was already
financially strangled (Interview Fagundes).

Primary health care in Porto Alegre also competes with the hospital system
for employees. Salaries for family doctors are lower than salaries for specialized
doctors, making it difficult to convince students of medicine to choose that
career path. This couples with the fact that the Fiscal Responsibility Law
promotes precarious contracting of ESF professionals. Most doctors who
participate in ESF have an unstable contract (renewable every year) and their
contracting is outsourced. As a result, of the 189 ESF teams in 2013, forty-five
of them were incomplete, mostly lacking general practitioners (Prefeitura
Municipal de Porto Alegre, Secretaría Municipal de Saúde 2013, 149). Gibson
(2016) also finds that Porto Alegre's weak contracting partly explains the
meager results in the implementation of ESF until 2010.

To improve these conditions, since 2011 ESF professionals in Porto Alegre
have a contract that follows the *Consolidação das Leis do Trabalho*
(Consolidation Labor Law) that is the same legal framework that regulates all
hires in the private sector, a fact that improved labor conditions of ESF workers.
However, contracting is still outsourced, meaning that they are not municipal
workers. The institution in charge of hiring ESF doctors is a publicly owned
foundation governed by private law (*Fundaçõe Pública de Direito Privado*) that
reports to the municipality of Porto Alegre.[14] The initial result of this more stable

---

[14] ESF personnel were hired by neighborhood associations from 1996 to 2000, by the public State
University from 2000 to 2007 (*Fundação de Apoio da Universidade Federal do Rio Grande do
Sul*), and by a public interest nongovernmental organization (*Organização da Sociedade Civil de
Interesse Público*) from 2007 to 2010. Serious corruption accusations form the media and local
councils against this organization (called *Sollus*) forced the municipality to change the out-
sourcing entity in 2010 to the private Cardiology University Foundation (*Fundação
Universitaria de Cardiologia*) until it changed again in 2011 to a publicly owned foundation

labor contract has been an increase in professionals interested in ESF, and a subsequent increase in ESF coverage since 2012, shown in Figure 6.2.

The bordering municipality of Canoas in the state of Rio Grande do Sul also exhibits obstacles in the implementation of ESF. This policy was not implemented until 2003 and its coverage levels are lower than the state and Porto Alegre (Figure 6.2). Previous UBS and hospital infrastructure, as well as precarious contracts for ESF professionals, explain this poor performance. Canoas had developed a strong infrastructure of twenty UBS when ESF was implemented. The last UBS was built in 2000 and thirteen were still used in 2012 for the provision of primary health care. The remaining seven of the original twenty UBS were transformed into ESF units. However, all new ESF units have been exclusively built in poor neighborhoods where the previous system was never implemented. As a result, ESF in Canoas is accepted as "medicine for poor people" (Interviews Camargo, F. Santos, L. Santos).

The main resistance against ESF comes from doctors. Doctors who work in UBS earn a higher salary than ESF professionals and have a more stable contract. In addition, they do not have to work forty hours a week (as in ESF), and therefore they can choose to work twenty hours a week at the UBS and the rest of the time at another place, such as an emergency room. While ESF doctors earned US$25 per hour in 2012, a doctor in the emergency room earned more than US$35 (Interview Camargo).[15] Therefore, the working conditions in ESF are more precarious than in UBS. Finally, to respect the Fiscal Responsibility Law, Canoas outsources the hiring of health professionals to a cooperative since 2003; their contracts are renewable yearly and vacations are not included. As a result, "recently graduated doctors may start working at Estratégia Saúde da Família, but only until they find something better" (Interview F. Santos).

The developed hospital system also gives doctors a more attractive alternative to ESF. The hospital infrastructure includes the private sector, which is also highly developed in Canoas – around 30 percent of the population in Canoas has private insurance. Following the idea that ESF should be targeted at poor neighborhoods, in places where many people have private insurance, the municipal government has decided not to expand ESF (Interview L. Santos).

State of Goiás

The state of Goiás also presents health systems that compete against ESF, including UBS and hospitals. However, both competing systems are less

governed by private law. Throughout this period, all ESF employees continued to be outsourced, with the exception of health agents, who had to be hired by open bid since the 2006 Constitutional Amendment 51 (Woltmann 2012; Gibson 2016).

[15] Exchange rate US$1=R$2, as of January 24, 2013. All conversions are taken at this rate.

developed than in Rio Grande do Sul, and therefore Goiás exhibits higher levels of ESF coverage, as shown in Figure 6.1. On the one hand, the coverage of UBS is lower than in Rio Grande do Sul because primary health care was never a priority in this state. On the other hand, the development of public and private hospitals is also more limited. In fact, with the exception of the largest cities (Goiânia and Anápolis), most municipal health secretaries perceive the development of the hospital network as being low throughout the state (Governo de Goiás, Secretaria de Estado da Saúde 2011).[16]

Within Goiás, the municipality of Valparaíso de Goiás is among the most successful in implementing ESF, reaching around 70 percent of coverage since 2009, and surpassing both the state's and Goiânia's coverage, as exhibited in Figure 6.3. The municipality was founded in 1995 and therefore it lacks the development of a strong previous UBS and hospital infrastructure.[17] There are only six UBS (none of which could be transformed into ESF units) and only one medium-complexity hospital that was recently inaugurated. These weak negative legacies allow for restructuring health provision around primary health care – it is mandatory to see a general practitioner before being transferred to a specialized doctor. Such administration strengthens the primary health care system, and ESF in particular, since it increases the actual take-up rate. The Coordinator of Basic Health care in Valparaíso de Goiás explained the successful performance of ESF in the following terms: "Saúde da Família is the base of the system; it is the entry port to the health system ... We have had a hospital for one year, but it is embryonic, it has very few specializations. Serious health cases are transferred to Brasília" (Interview Chaveiro).

In spite of the absence of negative legacies in terms of hospitals and UBS development, Valparaíso de Goiás cannot escape the requirements of the Fiscal Responsibility Law. As a consequence, professionals are not municipal employees and they have unstable contracts that need to be renewed every year. As in Rio Grande do Sul's municipalities, the precariousness of contracts and the low salaries produces a high turnover rate of ESF doctors. This volatility damages the implementation of this policy in the sense that "the community is most affected because they lose the linkage with the ESF unit" (Interview Chaveiro).

In contrast to Valparaíso de Goiás, Goiânia shows low relative levels of ESF coverage in Figure 6.3. The development of a previous UBS system together with the presence of a strong (mostly private) hospital infrastructure explains this poor performance. The municipality has always

---

[16] I am using this measure for the lack of comparable data on the development of high-complexity and UBS systems in the state of Goiás.
[17] This lack of strong development of previous health infrastructure makes Valparaíso de Goiás comparable to low-income municipalities and states that also lacked this infrastructure when ESF was implemented.

implemented ESF parallel to the UBS system and never had the plan to completely substitute it. It originally implemented a modified version of ESF – from 1998 to 2001 Goiânia had mobile teams (without family health facilities) that went house by house to reach the population that the other systems could not reach. These efforts proved ineffective, and since 2001 all future ESF teams were based at health centers, some of which were shared with the UBS system (Brasil. Ministério da Saúde and Fundação Oswaldo Cruz 2005, 76). Since 2011, the municipal Secretary of Health has tried to modify ESF to look a bit more similar to the UBS strategy that was widely accepted in the city. In particular, some ESF units agreed to extend the opening hours from 5 to 7 p.m. and to open on Saturdays. The aim in the long run is to convince those excluded from the ESF facility schedule (Monday to Friday 9 a.m. to 5 p.m.), particularly full-time workers, that ESF is a better alternative to the UBS system. The results of this new strategy have slowly started to affect the numbers since 2012, as shown in Figure 6.3.

Besides the UBS system, the existence of a strong previous hospital infrastructure further accounts for the low ESF coverage. The private sector is particularly strong in this municipality – more than 80 percent of hospital beds belong to the private system (Brasil. Ministério da Saúde and Fundação Oswaldo Cruz 2005, 45). The strong presence of private providers hinders the expansion of ESF because "rich people who have private insurance will never choose ESF" (Interview Batista). The Secretary of Health in Goiânia expressed this idea in different terms:

> In Goiânia there is a primacy of the private sector, and the primary health strategy cannot be implemented outside of that context ... It is possible to expand ESF coverage but not much more than we have now ... the private system imposes a limit because public provision is of worse quality ... And in a city with such a strong private system, people buy services in the private sector (Interview Rassi).

This hospital, UBS, and private provision also produce a competition for professionals. In general, doctors choose to specialize in disciplines other than family medicine in part because most ESF workers have an unstable contract – of the 181 doctors who were part of ESF teams in 2012, only 22 had a stable contract; the other 159 had a contract that was renewable every year (Interviews Batista, Belem).

Overall, the strength of negative legacies across Goiás, Rio Grande do Sul, and their selected municipalities puts limits on the expansion of ESF's coverage.

Territorial Infrastructure

Territorial infrastructure refers to the spatial reach of the state through subnational state institutions, as well as the connections of these institutions to non-state actors. Estratégia Saúde da Família is implemented through professional teams located at family health facilities or USF. The key to successful implementation of the policy is partly the quality of the USF and the team that participates in that health facility. This has to do with the training that these professionals receive, which is partly under the authority of states, as well as with the quality of their contract and salary, which are the responsibilities of municipalities. In 2009, the average monthly salary for ESF doctors was US$3,150, US$1,150 for nurses, and US$270 for health agents (Brasil. Ministério da Saúde 2009, 95). These salaries are relatively low and contracts tend to be temporary.

To monitor the quality of the service, civil society supervises ESF implementation through health councils at the USF, and at the municipal and state levels. The combination of strong state institutions collaborating with active civil society contributes to the successful implementation of the policy, particularly in terms of good quality provision. For measuring quality of service provision, the Ministry of Health developed a National Program for the Improvement of Access to and Quality of Primary Health Care (Programa Nacional de Melhoria do Acesso e da Qualidade da Atenção Básica, PMAQ). In 2011, the program included interviews in 15,095 primary health facilities (both UBS and USF) across 65,000 municipalities (Brasil. Ministério de Saúde, Departamento de Atenção Básica 2011).[18] The last column of Table 6.1 summarizes the results of the survey for the selected states and municipalities. In Rio Grande do Sul, most (64 percent) primary health facilities provide above-average quality of health, while in Goiás a majority of facilities (52 percent) fall in the below-average category. When comparing municipalities, only Porto Alegre exhibits primary health facilities with some above-average quality provision (25 percent of facilities). In Canoas and Goiânia, nearly all primary health facilities have average or below-average provision. In Valparaíso de Goiás, there is no available data.

State of Rio Grande do Sul

Following national legislation (Law 7058) passed in 2011, the state of Rio Grande do Sul has divided health administration into thirty regions, with the aim of enhancing the coordination of the system. To promote ESF in particular, since 2003 the state has provided a monetary incentive of US$1,000 for each ESF team conditioned upon health targets. This state program is called *Saúde para Todos* (Health for All), and it resulted in increases in ESF coverage (Sanzi Souza et al. 2003 and Figure 6.2). The state also complements ESF through a policy called *Primeira Infância Melhor* (Better Early Childhood), which trains municipal health agents in providing care to young children during house visits.[19] In addition, the state

---

[18] Given that this is a new measurement instrument, indicators and results change in every wave.

[19] Porto Alegre implements this state program since 2004, adapting its name to *Primeira Infância Alegre* (Happy Early Childhood). Since 2010, this program was officially approved through

participates in meetings of the health council since its creation in 1994 to enhance the coordination of municipalities and with civil society.[20] This investment in human capital and synergy between the state and the council partly explains the good quality of ESF provision summarized in Table 6.1. In spite of these efforts, the state is comparatively secondary in this policy; the central actors are the municipality for its implementation and the federal government for funding it and defining general guidelines.

Porto Alegre divides its territory into seventeen health districts, with eight regional administrations that report to the municipal health secretariat. As it was explained earlier, the city enjoys a developed health infrastructure of previous UBS and hospitals, but this hinders ESF coverage. In addition, this infrastructure and ESF facilities are concentrated in the center and northern parts of the city, leaving vacuums of health coverage in the south of the city (Prefeitura Municipal de Porto Alegre 2014). The unevenness of health provision in Porto Alegre couples with the fact that the professional teams in charge of ESF are poorly paid and their contracts are unstable, a fact that affects most cities in Brazil. These obstacles partly explain the comparatively lower levels of coverage depicted in Figure 6.2.

At the same time, Porto Alegre offers comparatively higher quality of provision than the other municipalities included in this study. Although most health facilities have average or below-average quality, Porto Alegre is the only municipal case that shows a quarter of its facilities with above-average quality (Brasil. Ministério de Saúde, Departamento de Atenção Básica 2011). The active participation of civil society through health councils is crucial for understanding differences in quality in the provision of ESF. Porto Alegre has been singled out for its vibrant civil society, and the health sector is no exception (Baiocchi 2005). Most ESF facilities have a health council, which aggregates demands into nineteen district councils, which are then represented at the Municipal Council. The Municipal Council was created in 1992 from pressures from civil society, and particularly from the sanitarista movement since the 1970s. Civil society organized around the health councils monitors the implementation of ESF. These groups make sure that funds are spent correctly and that the functioning of ESF facilities is adequate. In particular, they notify the government if health professionals are late or absent, if they do not conduct house visits, if there is not enough medicine in a particular health facility, or if the health facility is not in adequate condition, among other failings. Civil society also helps the government identify places for

---

municipal law. Nevertheless, the program is very small – in July 2013 it covered only 468 people (Prefeitura Municipal de Porto Alegre, Secretaría Municipal de Saúde 2013, 161).

[20] The health council in Rio Grande do Sul is among the most democratic forums throughout the country. The president of the health council has always been elected among its members and most of its members belong to civil society organizations (Pereira, Côrtes, and Barcelos 2009, 111–12).

setting up new ESF facilities. Roughly half of all ESF units were proposed by civil society in participatory budgeting processes (Interviews Bosio, Frantz, H. Pinto, Rousselet de Alencar, Toazza Tura, Vilar da Cunha).

Compared to Porto Alegre, the collaboration between state and non-state actors is not as developed in Canoas. The opening of new ESF units has always been suggested by the municipal government, and not by the health council (Interview Dhein). The council is less vibrant than the one in Porto Alegre.[21] Nevertheless, the inauguration of each new ESF unit has to be approved by the council. In addition, council members meet regularly to voice demands for improvements on ESF implementation, and the SUS more generally (Interviews F. Santos, Camargo, Dhein).[22] This lower collaboration between the local state and civil society partly responds to weaker municipal institutions. The municipality's main problem is hiring and maintaining ESF professionals – in particular, health agents. There were forty-two health agents in the municipality in 2012, but many of them were not yet registered in the system because they did not have the necessary qualifications. This is because very few people sign up to take the qualifying exam in Canoas. The problem is that without credited health agents the ESF team is incomplete and cannot receive the transfers from the federal government (Interviews F. Santos, L. Santos). This is partly the reason why ESF performance in Canoas is below average both in terms of coverage (Figure 6.2) and quality (100 percent of health facilities are average or below average; Brasil. Ministério de Saúde, Departamento de Atenção Básica 2011).

State of Goiás

As is the case in Rio Grande do Sul, the state of Goiás has a limited role in the administration of primary health care. While Rio Grande do Sul divides the territory for better administration, Goiás has not done so yet. In addition, there are no state policies similar to those in Rio Grande do Sul to develop human resources and thus strengthen the infrastructure in the territory. For the implementation of ESF, the states' role is to provide training support and to help co-fund it. The opinion on the extent to which the state complies with these

---

[21] The origins of the Municipal Council date back to 1996 and respond to pressures from the national government by conditioning health transfers to the creation of such council. All twenty-eight council members are appointed as opposed to elected (Interview Martins). In addition to the Municipal Council there are also local councils at some ESF facilities, but there is no district council.

[22] In one of the meetings of the municipal health council of Canoas in which I participated on October 8, 2012, members of the council discussed two main issues. On the one hand, the hospital *Nossa Senhora das Graças* was being held accountable on a particular spending. On the other hand, members of the council discussed that the hospital at the state university had a bad smell, and the council had contacted the hospital but nobody had provided an answer. Representatives of that hospital were present in the meeting to answer the members of the council's concerns.

activities is controversial. Such disagreement partly responds to the fact that the state funds poorer municipalities more than larger cities, assuming that larger cities have enough resources to face ESF implementation (Interview Batista). The former Director of ESF in Goiânia (first) and the current Director of Basic Health Care in Valparaíso de Goiás (second) represent this disagreement:

There is very little coming from the state in terms of training. For example, the introductory course on family health is a 40-hour course for people without background on family health but who are interested in joining ESF ... the state performs poorly in providing this course. That is why universities need to step in (Interview Batista).

The state is reference for us ... The state conducts most training activities ... Most funding comes from the federal government and the states co-funds 25 percent (Interview Chaveiro).

The state of Goiás also participates in meetings of the state health council for monitoring ESF implementation. However, the role of the council is more limited in Goiás compared to Rio Grande do Sul. In particular, Goiás' health council is less organized and has had periods in which it was closed or had limited influence (Interviews Alvarenga, De Jesús).[23] Partly as a result of this weaker territorial infrastructure the quality of the provision of ESF is lower in Goiás compared with Rio Grande do Sul, with more than half of health facilities falling in the average or below-average category (Brasil. Ministério de Saúde, Departamento de Atenção Básica 2011).

While the collaboration between local state and non-state actors mostly improves the quality of service provision, it can also expand its coverage. Health councils can improve the coverage of ESF, particularly in places where there are no strong negative legacies from UBS or hospitals. This is the case of the municipality of Valparaíso de Goiás. In this municipality, since 2009 the Secretary of Health sought input from the council and from civil society to determine the places where the first ESF facilities would be located. This strategy proved to be successful, as shown by the increased level of coverage since 2009 (Figure 6.3), in no small part because the municipality was able to reach remote areas with little previous access to health care. The Coordinator of Basic Health Care in Valparaíso de Goiás remembered the reaction from neighbors and organizations:

The mayor organized one meeting in each community ... The neighbors, the government, and the council participated in these meetings ... this was particularly important in far-away areas where, for example, neighborhood associations participated ... The community was interested because they had to walk long distances to the first health

[23] In a session of the state health council I attended on November 6, 2012, the council discussed the requirements for organizations that wanted to be a part of the council. Twenty people attended this session and it was challenging to find volunteers to work on this topic. By the end of the session, there were no volunteers from the health workers.

center ... The ESF facility is very important in these places ... The municipal government went to the neighborhoods rather than the neighbors to the government (Interview Chaveiro).

This initial high level of participation and increased accessibility in remote areas faded away after the system was expanded in 2009. In 2012, there were still neighborhoods that lacked ESF facilities, but the system did not continue expanding. In addition, none of the ESF facilities have a local council, the municipal council does not meet regularly, and most of their debates are exclusively centered on the salary of doctors. This topic of debate is relevant given that a serious issue in this municipality, as in all others, is the difficulty in finding doctors for ESF. Most ESF doctors in Valparaíso de Goiás are recent graduates who leave the job after a year, when they take their residency exam. A particular characteristic of this municipality is its closeness to Brasília (eighteen miles away), which provides a bigger market for recent graduates. This makes it even more difficult to find ESF doctors and for doctors to stay in this municipality (Interview Rassi).[24] The lack of trained professionals hinders the development of municipal infrastructure necessary for the expansion of ESF and the improvement of the quality of health provision. To deal with this issue, Valparaíso de Goiás hires part-time ESF doctors who can complement their salary with their work at emergency rooms, a practice that is discouraged by the national government but seems the only option for this municipality (Interview Chaveiro).

Compared to Valparaíso de Goiás, the municipality of Goiânia has a more structured health administration. The municipality divides health administration into seven health regions, each of which has a representative from the municipal government. These regions are in charge of monitoring the quality of the service, which is a priority for the local government.[25] Higher quality is prioritized over expanding coverage (Interviews Belem, Rassi). Nevertheless, their efforts have been less than successful, as 97 percent of facilities have average or below-average quality (Brasil. Ministério de Saúde, Departamento de Atenção Básica 2011). The Department of Health in the municipality decides where to open ESF facilities, and so far it has decided to open facilities where there is a higher concentration of poverty, thus reinforcing the stereotype of ESF as "poor medicine for poor people." This is partly the reason why quality of ESF provision is overall low.

The lower quality of provision also partly responds to the fact that the relationship between the local government and civil society is not fully developed in Goiânia. People can raise concerns about the quality of the service at the local and municipal councils, and there is a complaint commission that serves

[24] The proximity to Brasília could potentially provide a steady supply of recent medical school graduates; however, it has not been a common destination for recent graduates.
[25] The division of health administration into regions in Goiânia, compared with Valparaíso de Goiás, is understandable given that the former has over one million inhabitants, while the latter only 132,982.

as the platform for such concerns (Interviews Belem, De Jesús, Lima, Rassi). Nevertheless, the level of participation is low (Brasil. Ministério da Saúde and Fundação Oswaldo Cruz 2005, 69–70).[26] There were between 60 and 130 local councils in Goiânia in 2012,[27] which were then represented at the municipal council. There are no regional councils between the local and municipal councils. The quality of local councils varies widely – while some are actively involved in every detail of health provision, others are more passive.

The participation of civil society in the provision of health care through councils is a particular characteristic of the Unified Health System in Brazil. Having strong state–society collaborations partly depends on the existence of participatory institutions such as councils and on the strength of subnational state institutions. In Argentina, having strong territorial infrastructure also shapes the implementation of health policies. However, civil society does not actively participate in health care. There are no participatory health institutions comparable to Brazil's health councils. Another difference between Brazil and Argentina is that while in the former municipalities are in charge of primary health care, in the latter health administration is mostly under the authority of provinces. In addition, there are no negative legacies for Argentina's Plan Nacer compared to Brazil's ESF.

PLAN NACER IN ARGENTINA

Argentina's health system includes three components – social insurance funds financed by formal workers (*obras sociales*, administered by unions and provinces), a private sector, and a publicly financed sector.[28] The main institution in charge of providing public preventive health care is the *Centro de Atención Primaria de la Salud* (Primary Health Center, CAPS). Fully staffed CAPS include a doctor, nurse, pharmacist, obstetrician, therapist, dentist, social worker, and health agents (*agentes sanitarios*). Health agents are the nexus between the community and the health center, but they receive more limited training and resources compared to health agents in Brazil. In addition, primary health care administration is not unified as in Brazil: the characteristics and quality of CAPS vary widely, and primary health care is generally administered by provinces but sometimes also by municipalities.

---

[26] The municipal council has existed since 1993, but there are no elected council members; they are all appointed by the municipal government or by organizations.

[27] The number varies depending on the source. The president of the municipal council said that there are 130 local councils, and the director of ESF in the municipality counted 60 (Interviews Belem, De Jesús).

[28] Around 40 percent of the population were exclusive users of the public system in 2009 (Cortez et al. 2012, 1). For a description of the health system in Argentina, see Niedzwiecki (2014a).

Plan Nacer has directly intervened in the provision of primary health since 2004 by increasing access to basic services. It represented around 10 percent of the health public budget in 2009 and covered five million people in 2012. The policy was first introduced in nine provinces and then expanded to the rest of the country (World Bank 2006a; McGuire 2010b, 142–43; Argentina. Ministerio de Salud de la Nación, Plan Nacer 2012b; Cortez et al. 2012). It is targeted at men and women up to sixty-four years old without health insurance.[29] The policy finances medical procedures at no cost for the patient. Most of these procedures fall in the realm of preventive health care, such as health check-ups, immunizations, and sexual and reproductive health. For the provision of these health procedures, Plan Nacer transfers funds from the federal government to all provinces and the municipalities in charge of administering health, and these funds are then transferred to providers – CAPS and hospitals. While 60 percent of the funds are transferred monthly after a subnational unit enters the program (and starts signing up patients), the other 40 percent is conditioned on agreed-upon targets between the national government and each province. These health targets are called *trazadoras*.[30] The province or municipality then transfers the resources to health providers based on the quantity and type of medical services actually offered the previous month. The amount of transfer for each particular medical procedure is set by the province or municipality, based on an equation that cannot surpass the total amount of transfers from the federal government.

To implement Plan Nacer, the federal government signs an agreement (called *Convenio Marco* or Umbrella Agreement) with each province and the municipalities in charge of administering health care, and then that province or municipality signs an agreement with each public health provider (CAPS or hospital) called *Compromiso de Gestión* (management agreement). First, the umbrella agreement defines the responsibilities and health targets of each territorial level and is implemented through a contract that is renegotiated each year. Second, the management agreement between the subnational government and each health provider defines the providers' responsibilities, including signing up recipients, providing medical services, billing the province or municipality for these services, and maintaining clinical and financial records. Finally, the World Bank and the Argentine Supreme Audit Institution (*Auditoría General de la Nación*) develop regular monitoring activities to hold the national government, subnational governments, and health providers accountable; they

---

[29] Plan Nacer expanded its target population in late 2012 (and changed its name to *Sumar* or Addition). Until 2012, it covered pregnant women and children up to six years old. Senior citizens in Argentina (sixty-five and older) are covered through the *Programa de Atención Médica Integral* (Comprehensive Medical Attention Program).

[30] The degree of compliance with each health target determines the percentage of funds transferred. If the province or municipality does not comply with the previously agreed minimum results for three consecutive months, a new agreement needs to be signed.

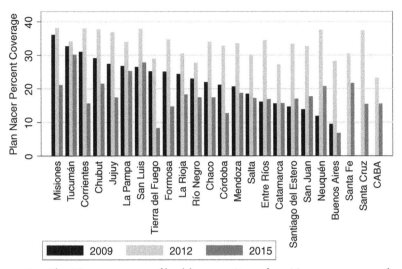

FIGURE 6.4 Plan Nacer coverage of health targets (*trazadoras*) in 2009, 2012, and 2015
Source: Argentina. Ministerio de Salud de la Nación, Plan Nacer (2015).
Note: Order of provinces from highest to lowest coverage in 2009. Data as of March of
every year.

ensure that funds are used according to the policy's guidelines, and contribute to
building capacity for adequate health provision (World Bank 2006b, 11;
Auditoría General de la Nación 2008; Cortez et al. 2012, 8).

The policy aims at strengthening the public provision of health care in the
long term. This is promoted through a monetary incentive for improving CAPS
and hospitals' facilities, filling out forms, and developing good quality medical
histories of uninsured people, something that used to be a reality for insured
patients only. There is an incentive to keep accurate records because if the
doctor does not fill in the medical history of a given patient, then that medical
procedure does not receive the transfer from Plan Nacer. As a former Secretary
of Health of the province of Mendoza put it: "[Plan Nacer] pays us to do our
job ... We improve the registry and the quality of medical procedures"
(Interview Saracco). As a result of these changes, the experience of going to
the health center is improved, and thus even some patients who have low-
quality health insurance benefit from this policy by going to the CAPS for
treatment (Interviews Arce, Heguiabehere, Mattar, Mercado, Musri, Nuñez,
Varcalcel).[31]

Figure 6.4 shows the implementation of Plan Nacer in 2009, 2012, and 2015,
using the government's indicator. The Ministry of Health measures the degree of
implementation as the average of the percentages of coverage of different medical

---

[31] If a person has health insurance, treatment in the CAPS will not be reimbursed by Plan Nacer.

procedures.[32] Until 2012, the following ten percentages were averaged: pregnant women with the first prenatal check-up before the twentieth week of gestation, sexual and reproductive counseling, newborns' health check-ups (Apgar score of six or higher five minutes after delivery), newborn babies who are not underweight, vaccine coverage of pregnant women (including tetanus and test for sexually transmitted diseases), vaccine coverage in babies under eighteen months (measles–mumps–rubella), health check-ups for children under age one, health check-ups for children under six years old, fully evaluated cases of maternal and child mortality, and personnel trained in indigenous medicine.[33] Since 2013, the following health targets were added: the capacity to detect congenital heart disease in children under one year old, health check-ups for children between one and nine years old, health check-ups for teenagers between ten and nineteen years old, vaccine coverage for seven-year-old children, and prevention of cervical cancer and treatment of breast cancer for women up to sixty-four years old (Argentina. Ministerio de Salud de la Nación 2013).

Some of the most successful provinces in Figure 6.4 (Misiones, Tucumán, Corrientes, Jujuy, and Formosa) are some of the places where the policy was implemented first (in 2004), for being the poorest provinces in the country, with the highest levels of maternal and child mortality. Therefore, their coverage starts higher in 2009. Most of the provinces were incorporated in 2007, after some of the original nine provinces had reached at least 25 percent of the target population, 20 percent of the World Bank loan had been disbursed, monitoring had been successful, and at least five new provinces were ready to join (Cortez et al. 2012, 3). However, there is more to the story than just starting early. Some early implementers such as Santiago del Estero and Catamarca lag behind, while new implementers such as Chubut and San Luis have reached high coverage levels.[34]

A salient characteristic of this policy is that it is implemented in aligned and opposition provinces alike. As Figure 6.4 shows, the opposition province of San Luis and the aligned province of Mendoza implement this policy at similar levels,

---

[32] The target levels vary by province and are negotiated (partly considering wealth and capacity) between the national and subnational governments. In these negotiations, the national government tries to set as high levels as it is reasonably possible to encourage high coverage (Cortez et al. 2012). This indicator was updated in 2013 after Plan Nacer expanded its target population, thus explaining the overall decrease in implementation in 2015.

[33] While the first eight objectives are services delivered to women or children, the ninth refers to the investigation of why a mother or child died with the aim of reducing preventable deaths in the future. The last indicator applies to indigenous populations, which comprise 3 percent of the total population in Argentina, and are traditionally poor and excluded; it aims at promoting culturally and linguistically equipped health professionals for pregnancy, births, and childcare procedures (Cortez et al. 2012, 15).

[34] The province of Santa Cruz implemented Plan Nacer last because salaries for the administration of this policy were lower than salaries paid by the province. Therefore, it took a longer time to reach an agreement. In the case of the province of Santa Fe, it decided that it was too costly to start signing up children, and therefore focused almost entirely on providing good quality health coverage for pregnant women, and thus its low coverage (Interview Mercado).

with San Luis being slightly more successful across time. By 2015, San Luis reached almost 30 percent of coverage, while Mendoza was closer to 20 percent. San Luis has consistently been among the best performers. In addition, there is no record of a province that has decided not to sign the agreement with the federal government. The opposition province of San Luis, for example, signed the agreement with the national government on January 1, 2007, and was among the first provinces to join the expansion of Plan Nacer in 2012 (Interview Mercado; Argentina. Ministerio de Salud de la Nación, Plan Nacer 2012b). Finally, Chapter 4 showed that political alignments are not a statistically significant predictor of successful implementation of Plan Nacer across provinces and time. I argue that political alignments do not explain Plan Nacer's degree of implementation due to a lack of clear attribution of responsibility, the focus of the next section.

Blurred Attribution of Responsibility and Irrelevance of Political Alignments

Attribution of responsibility is not clear in Plan Nacer. Eligible patients do not generally recognize the services that this policy provides or that they are actual or potential beneficiaries of it, and therefore it is not clear to them whom they should reward for it in the elections (Interviews Calderón, Carrizo, Mattar, Sabignoso, Varcalcel). Being able to recognize the existence of a policy is a necessary first step for attributing credit to a particular government. In an official document, the National Ministry of Health referred to this lack of visibility in the following terms: "Given that Plan Nacer's design aims at improving human resources in health facilities, the population hardly attributes the benefits that Plan Nacer generates to this policy" (Ministerio de Salud de la Nación 2013, 6). As a result of this challenge, the National Ministry of Health can only measure users' satisfaction through changes in satisfaction with the public health system in general (including satisfaction with the health facility and professionals) in the places where the policy has been implemented.[35] In fact, a survey conducted by that same ministry in 2007 among 5,159 eligible pregnant women belonging to indigenous populations revealed that 60 percent of the sample did not know Plan Nacer at all (Argentina. Ministerio de Salud de la Nación, Plan Nacer 2007). In personal interviews with potential recipients, of the forty-seven potential beneficiaries who I asked about the responsibility for Plan Nacer or where the policy came

---

[35] During 2012–2013, the Ministry of Health conducted a representative survey of 9,633 pregnant women and women with young children who received Plan Nacer. The aim was to measure the level of satisfaction of users with the public health system during pregnancy and after the baby was born. Although the survey could not ask users directly about Plan Nacer (because they generally do not recognize which services it provides), the results showed that in the health facilities where Plan Nacer was more present, users tended to have a more positive image of the health system in general. Around 90 percent of the respondents were satisfied (or very satisfied) with heath care provided by the public system during pregnancy or after their babies were born (Argentina. Ministerio de Salud de la Nación 2013).

from, 64 percent (30) answered they did not know and only 34 percent referred to the national government.[36] In contrast to the Argentine conditional cash transfer, analyzed in Chapter 5, where beneficiaries directly identify the policy with the federal government, in Plan Nacer there is no clear attribution of responsibility, and therefore political credit is not assigned to any particular government or politician. In the words of a Regional Director of Primary Health Care in the Province of San Luis: "People are not aware that they have Plan Nacer, they do not know what benefit it gives them ... They do not see that the benefit is for them. Some people even say 'I do not have anything, I have that thing called Plan Nacer, but I do not have anything' ... [it works so well] because people do not identify where it is coming from" (Interview Mattar).

As a service, compared to a cash transfer, it is expected that attribution of responsibility is less clear. To begin with, there is no direct relationship between Plan Nacer and the patient. The monetary incentive is given to health centers and hospitals, and not to patients. The indirect benefit for patients is that they receive more medical monitoring (because the health facility receives money for each medical procedure), complete medical records, and that the conditions of the building improve (because the transfers from the federal government can be invested in enhancing the health facility). Nevertheless, more health check-ups, complete health records, and better facilities are a less tangible "good" than cash, and patients do not necessarily connect these improvements with Plan Nacer.

Another characteristic in the design of this policy that blurs attribution of responsibility is that at every level, ranging from the federal government to a small health center, actors expressed the idea that each of them is autonomous and independent in the implementation of the policy (Interviews Cardello, Farjado, C. García, Mattar, Mercado, Miatello, Mussoto, Musri, Nuñez, Rodriguez Assaf, Sabignoso, Saracco; Cortez et al. 2012, 36). This is true within reasonable boundaries: the national government and the World Bank set the general guidelines through establishing a list of health prescriptions and conducting monitoring activities; provincial governments give a monetary value to those prescriptions and monitor the use of transfers;[37] and health providers receive money for each medical service offered and can spend that money toward the enhancement of the health center or hospital.[38] With these many levels of implementation, it is expected that attribution of responsibility is blurred. The Director of Primary Health Care in the opposition province of San Luis (first) and the

---

[36] I identified potential beneficiaries as women who were users of the public system. All interviews were conducted at CAPS or public hospitals.

[37] In assigning a monetary value to medical procedures, the province is also shaping the primary health strategy. For instance, while San Luis assigned one of the highest monetary values to early pregnancy check-ups (Interview Nuñez), Mendoza emphasized postpartum check-ups to babies and mothers (Interview Saracco).

[38] The transfers from Plan Nacer can be used to improve the building, to buy medical and general supplies, and to pay bonuses or incentives for the staff (Cortez et al., 19).

Director of Plan Nacer at the national level (second) expressed this idea in the following terms:

We work very well with the national government in health care … Because one thing is to try to reach an agreement with the province and a different thing is to try to implement a pre-packaged (*enlatado*) program which will not work because we need to adapt them to our local reality … We consider Plan Nacer as our own child, our own child that we have to defend (Interview Fajardo).

The program is very cooperative, particularly in the way we incorporate the province … And that has been favorable for the way it works … But the provinces will never take on 100 percent of the funding, because otherwise the national government would lose its leadership in the program … If we want to keep on maintaining the principles of the program, the national government needs to maintain that leadership (Interview Sabignoso).

Given that the primary beneficiaries are not the patients, that the "good" provided is less tangible, and that participation of multiple levels of government contributes to blurring attribution of responsibility, national and subnational governments can in some cases share responsibility and in others dispute responsibility. Provincial governments share responsibility in television advertisements, where they include the logos of both the national and subnational governments.[39] The same is true for sign-up, health targets, billing, and medical history forms, which generally include the logos of Plan Nacer, the national government, and the provincial government. At the same time, blurred attribution of responsibility also means that credit can be disputed. For this reason, the national government develops print and television advertisements with the national logo only, trying to claim responsibility for Plan Nacer.[40] Nevertheless, given the characteristics of the design of the policy described earlier, the efforts to claim credit are not effective. No matter how much money is spent on television and print ads, patients still do not clearly identify any government level as responsible for this policy.

As a result of such blurred attribution of responsibility, opposition provinces and municipalities do not hold back the implementation of Plan Nacer. In an official document, the World Bank explains that "Plan Nacer enjoys an unprecedented level of ownership and political support from national and provincial governments" (World Bank 2006b, 22). For opposition subnational governments the implementation of Plan Nacer is a win-win

[39] See, for example, advertisements of Plan Nacer in the provinces of Catamarca (youtube.com/watch?v=oriLLjBgwww&feature=related), Formosa (youtube.com/watch?v=bmVPEs8SJXA&feature=related), and La Rioja (youtube.com/watch?v=_sF81FsYuX8&feature=related). Last accessed on April 23, 2016.
[40] See, for example, advertisements from the national government (youtube.com/watch?v=52Ad_fNfsXU; youtube.com/watch?v=c6bgBVozHtw; vimeo.com/11175775). Last accessed April 23, 2016.

situation – they receive the transfers from the policy at no electoral cost. Therefore, the opposition province of San Luis does not attempt to undermine the implementation of this policy (Interviews Mercado, Mussoto, Nuñez). In fact, the software developed in San Luis for billing medical procedures and signing up recipients for Plan Nacer was so advanced that the federal government invited the responsible developer to present it in Buenos Aires in 2010 with the aim to reproduce this methodology in other provinces. Around 15 provinces agreed to adopt a similar software by 2012 (Interview Nuñez; Argentina. Ministerio de Salud de la Nación, Plan Nacer 2012a). In addition, the province of San Luis considers the federal government a partner in the implementation of this policy (Interviews Mercado, Nuñez).

The irrelevance of political alignments for the successful implementation of Plan Nacer finds a correlate at the municipal level. In the words of a former Health Secretary in the Province of Mendoza: "Every province and municipality accepts Plan Nacer; Why wouldn't you accept it if it gives you money ... In fact, we sometimes implemented Plan Nacer better in opposition than in aligned municipalities" (Interview Saracco). High-level health bureaucrats in opposition municipalities confirmed the inexistence of political considerations for the implementation of Plan Nacer (Interview Maccio, Martinez, Varcalcel). While political alignments do not shape the implementation of Plan Nacer, territorial infrastructure and – to a lesser extent – policy legacies impact the way in which this policy is implemented. The next two sections analyze these variables in each of the provinces and municipalities included in this study. Table 6.2 summarizes the characteristics of territorial infrastructure and policy legacies found in the selected provinces and municipalities. Compared with Brazil, territorial infrastructure is as important for shaping the outcome, while policy legacies are weaker, yet positive, for influencing the implementation of the health policy.

Territorial Infrastructure

The infrastructure in the territory shapes the successful implementation of Plan Nacer, in particular the presence and characteristics of health centers and hospitals. The quantity of health facilities is not the only component of state infrastructure; the proximity to poor areas (with high percentages of uninsured populations) and the quality of these facilities also matter. In addition, it is important that the personnel (doctors, nurses, health agents, and assistants) are trained, earn good salaries, and have access to the necessary medical devices. While civil society is a central actor in the implementation of Brazil's primary health care strategy, it is irrelevant in the implementation of Plan Nacer and in health care in Argentina more generally. As a result, the success of health policies depends only on strong state institutions.

Both provincial cases, San Luis and Mendoza, developed a robust primary health infrastructure through Primary Health Services (*Atención Primaria de la*

TABLE 6.2 *Implementation of Plan Nacer in selected provinces and municipalities*

Subnational unit	Territorial infrastructure	Policy legacies (positive)	Level of implemen- tation[a]
San Luis	Strong primary health and hospitals Centralized health care	National Policies: PROMIN, *Remediar*	High
San Luis City	Strong provincial primary health facilities and hospitals Moderate presence of health agents	Provincial CCT *Plan de Inclusión Social*	
Villa Mercedes	Strong provincial primary health facilities and hospitals Moderate presence of health agents		
Mendoza	Strong primary health facilities and hospitals Decentralized health care	National Policies PROMIN, *Remediar*	Medium
Las Heras	Strong primary health and hospitals Low presence of health agents CAPS within community centers	Provincial Food program *Comer Juntos en Familia*	
Godoy Cruz	Strong primary health and hospitals Low presence of health agents Uneven distribution of CAPS		

[a] There is no comparable data on the level of coverage across municipalities. This is not problematic since provinces, and not municipalities, are mostly in charge of health care in Argentina. See Tables 6.3 and 6.4 for alternative municipal indicators.

Salud) since the Federal Health Plan (*Plan Federal de Salud*) was implemented in 2004. Plan Nacer works directly through these health institutions, and particularly through CAPS, most of which are funded by provinces and big municipalities. Within CAPS, health agents are crucial for signing up uninsured people to Plan Nacer, as well as for identifying populations in risk, such as pregnant women, elderly people, and newborns. Besides CAPS, hospitals also participate in Plan Nacer, both through the provision of primary health care and through more complex procedures such as assisting births. Overall, the provinces of San Luis and Mendoza implement Plan Nacer successfully, as exhibited in Figure 6.4, because they can rely on a developed infrastructure of CAPS and hospitals. However, the strategies for administering the provision of health care (and therefore of Plan Nacer) are different in Mendoza and San Luis. San Luis centralizes health provision in the province and Mendoza partly decentralizes primary health care to large municipalities. Decentralizing health care to the municipalities is not necessarily positive, since it can make coordination more difficult.

Province of San Luis

The province of San Luis administers the provision of health care almost entirely. The province is responsible for all hospitals and CAPS; there are no municipal health providers.[41] The coordination of Plan Nacer is conducted from its offices in the Provincial Ministry of Health. The province transfers Plan Nacer funds to each health provider and is in charge of monitoring the use of such funds.[42] Therefore, successful implementation of Plan Nacer in San Luis is reached by the efforts of the provincial Health Ministry, CAPS, and hospitals, all of which fall under provincial control.

San Luis had 131 CAPS, 28 medium-complexity hospitals (_centros de referencia_), and two high-complexity hospitals (_hospitales de cabecera_) in 2012.[43] Most of the CAPS (97) and all 30 hospitals had signed agreements with the provincial government to implement Plan Nacer (Ministerio de Salud de la Provincia de San Luis 2012). There is only one community health agent per 10,000 inhabitants, which is much lower than the average in Brazil. Health agents are required to have completed high school and are paid US$530 per month for thirty hours of work per week (Interview Leyes).[44] Doctors must be working at the CAPS exclusively; they may not complement their salaries with work in an ER or private practice.[45] Although health professionals are well trained for their jobs, their salaries are low, less than US$1,000 per month with almost any level of experience (_El Diario de la República, San Luis_, January 14, 2009). The exclusivity requirement and relatively low salaries discourage some professionals from working at the CAPS.

The provision of health care in the province of San Luis is divided into six geographical areas for better administration; each geographical area includes a number of municipalities. The municipality of San Luis belongs to region V (Capital region) and Villa Mercedes belongs to region VI (Pedernera region).

[41] The only exception is one CAPS within a community center in the municipality of Merlo.

[42] The Systems' Analyst of Plan Nacer in the province of San Luis provided an illuminating example of why centralizing the administration of health care in the province is a good strategy – if the province has planned to buy stretchers with its own funds and sees in the system that a health unit has budgeted to buy stretchers with money from Plan Nacer, the province suggests the health center wait until the stretchers from the province arrive, and to use Plan Nacer money for something else (Interview Nuñez).

[43] The areas that are not covered by these health units receive either a health post with a nurse or a community health worker, or a temporary team of doctors and nurses carrying vaccines and conducting preventive health activities (Interview Fajardo).

[44] Official exchange rate US$1=$6, as of November 20, 2013. All conversions in Argentina are taken at this rate and all values are taken around the time when field research was conducted in 2012.

[45] Aside from the work at the CAPS, health professionals can teach at universities for a limited amount of hours.

TABLE 6.3 *Implementation of Plan Nacer in San Luis City and Villa Mercedes (Province of San Luis) in 2012*

	Percent coverage	Agreements signed with health units as a percentage of eligible health units	Level of spending (as a percentage of funds transferred)
San Luis City	119%	100%	58%
Villa Mercedes	110%	100%	53%

Source: Ministerio de Salud de la Provincia de San Luis (2012).
Note: The data include the departments of capital (which includes San Luis City among other municipalities) and General Pedernera (which includes Villa Mercedes among other municipalities). San Luis City and Villa Mercedes are the largest cities within those departments.

The province is responsible for the administration of each of these six areas. The province funds and designs health strategies, and trains medical and nonmedical personnel for the implementation of Plan Nacer. This includes, for instance, training in filling in medical histories and billing of medical procedures. Table 6.3 presents data on the implementation of Plan Nacer in San Luis City and Villa Mercedes in 2012. The level of implementation of this health policy across these two municipalities is almost identical, with the City of San Luis marginally surpassing Villa Mercedes in the level of coverage as a percentage of the targeted population and the percentage of the federal budget that has been already spent. The similarity in the implementation of this policy has to do in part with similar provincial territorial infrastructure and the same provincial health administration.

Both municipalities have comparable health infrastructures. In the City of San Luis, there are thirteen CAPS and four hospitals, one of which (Hospital San Luis) is a high-complexity hospital. Comparatively, there are twelve CAPS and three hospitals in Villa Mercedes. Overall, health units are evenly distributed across the territory of both municipalities, thus exhibiting no clear gaps in access. In addition, given that the province administers the whole territory, there is coordination among all public health providers. Finally, there are twenty-two health agents in the City of San Luis and eighteen in Villa Mercedes, all of whom are trained by the provincial Ministry of Health (Interview Leyes).

Province of Mendoza
As depicted in Figure 6.4, the province of Mendoza is relatively successful in the implementation of Plan Nacer, although slightly less successful than San Luis. This is in part because both San Luis and Mendoza have similarly adequate state territorial infrastructure for the provision of health care. Nevertheless, their strategies for health provision are different; San Luis

concentrates the implementation of health care in the province, while in Mendoza the province and municipalities share its administration. Within each of the eighteen municipalities, there is a Director of Health who represents the province, and some of the larger municipalities have a parallel health care structure dependent on the municipal level. Ideally, the entry port is the CAPS (administered by the province or large municipalities) distributed throughout the neighborhoods, the patient is then referred to medium-complexity centers (one per municipality, administered by the province), and subsequently to one of the four high-complexity hospitals across the province. Three of these four hospitals are under the realm of the province and one of them is the responsibility of the federal government. There are 21 of the 22 hospitals implementing Plan Nacer, as well as around 219 CAPS (Potenza Dal Masetto 2011, 40).

Since both municipal and provincial levels of government are responsible for the administration of CAPS, both territorial levels have a role in the implementation of Plan Nacer in Mendoza. There are more than 300 CAPS located throughout the province, 80 percent of which are administered by the province, while the rest are administered by the municipalities.[46] To implement Plan Nacer, these health centers need to have minimum infrastructure, such as the capacity to keep a registry of medical procedures and patients. The current Director of Maternal Health in the province of Mendoza (and former Director of Plan Nacer in the same province) expressed this idea in the following terms:

Some health centers do not have an agreement with Plan Nacer because they do not have the capacity to administer this policy. This may seem like Plan Nacer excludes the most vulnerable centers, but the truth is that these places do not even have the capacity to bill their medical procedures, because they do not even have computers (Interview Cardello).

Given that most health providers are provincial, we should not expect significant differences across municipalities with similar levels of GDP per capita and population density, as is the case of the selected municipalities of Las Heras and Godoy Cruz. Table 6.4 presents the indicators for the implementation of Plan Nacer across the two selected municipalities. The first two columns compare the total spending of health units dependent on the province (first column) and on the municipality (second column) funded by Plan Nacer transfers. The third column shows the total quantity of recipients of Plan Nacer within the territory of the municipality. While Godoy Cruz has higher rates of spending, Las Heras is a better performer in terms of quantity of recipients. Overall, both municipalities end up being similarly successful at the implementation of Plan Nacer, but in different aspects.

---

[46] Provincial CAPS are fully funded and administered by the provincial government and municipal CAPS are theoretically fully funded and administered by the municipal government. However, there are a number of municipal CAPS that receive joint funding from the municipal and provincial governments.

TABLE 6.4 *Implementation of Plan Nacer in Godoy Cruz and Las Heras (Province of Mendoza) in 2007–2011*

	Total spending in provincial health facilities (2007–11)	Total spending in municipal health facilities (2007–11)	Total recipients of Plan Nacer (2010)	Total population (2010)
Las Heras	US$88,986	US$19,128	10,350	203,666
Godoy Cruz	US$175,196	US$25,060	7,055	191,903

Sources: Plan Nacer Mendoza (2012); Goldar (2012), Argentina. INDEC, National Census (2010).

In the municipality of Las Heras, there were three hospitals and twenty-two CAPS in 2012, fourteen of which were provincial and eight of which were municipal. CAPS in Las Heras are concentrated in the south of the municipality, leaving gaps of access in the northernmost neighbors.[47] Of the twenty-two CAPS, twenty-one are part of Plan Nacer.[48] However, some of these CAPS do not have the capacity to fill in forms and provide good quality health care, and that hinders the implementation of Plan Nacer. In particular, almost half of the provincial CAPS did not have the personnel to fill in patients' registries and bill medical procedures necessary to receive the transfers from Plan Nacer. As a result, these CAPS constantly received only a portion of the transfers from the policy, a situation that the province has solved through centralizing the filling of forms of those CAPS in the provincial government (Interview Musri).

Compared to Brazilian health units, CAPS in Argentina do not have an active strategy of looking for the patients outside of the health facility. There are seven health agents that work in the twenty-four CAPS, but most of their activities are limited to work inside the health centers (Interview Musri). The situation is different for the three municipal CAPS located within *centros de intergración comunitaria* (community centers, CICs), where the community meets in a single place for the provision of health, early childhood education, and social development (Interviews Berrios, Miranda, Musri). The CAPS within the community centers have been successful at reaching out to the community outside of the CAPS and signing up most eligible recipients of Plan Nacer. In addition, the quality of the service is better, since community centers are relatively new buildings and are informally monitored by the population who participates in their activities (Interviews Musri, Quintana). Overall, the

[47] See: Niedzwiecki (2014b).
[48] The one CAPS excluded from Plan Nacer does not reach the minimum requirements (including a landline telephone) to access the policy (Interview Musri).

municipality of Las Heras lacks the infrastructure to fill in forms but is more successful than Godoy Cruz at reaching out to the population.

The implementation of Plan Nacer in the municipality of Godoy Cruz surpasses that of Las Heras in the administration of spending, as Table 6.4 shows. Provincial and municipal CAPS in Godoy Cruz have more personnel for completing forms and keeping updated registries. The municipal government, for instance, invested in a team exclusively in charge of administering the funds from Plan Nacer. This strategy enhanced spending indicators. However, Godoy Cruz had more limited reach to the population compared to Las Heras, as I analyzed in Chapter 5. For the provision of health care, there are eighteen CAPS and two hospitals within this municipality, and only two of these CAPS were municipal.[49] Thirteen provincial and both municipal CAPS implement Plan Nacer. Nevertheless, none of the CAPS are within community centers as in Las Heras, a model that is proving to be successful for the implementation of Plan Nacer. In addition, there are four health agents, and they have a limited role in the community.[50] Finally, the municipal CAPS in Godoy Cruz show the challenge of coordination across levels when decentralizing primary health care provision to the municipality. In particular, one of these municipal CAPS is located in a middle-class neighborhood (where most people are not users of the public system) and the other one is surrounded by provincial health services. For the latter, "there is superposition of supply between the province and the municipality because there is no coordination between the two levels" (Intreview Martinez).

Positive – yet Weak – Policy Legacies

Plan Nacer does not affect any entrenched interests from previous policies, as Estratégia Saúde da Família in Brazil does, and actually benefits from the legacies of previous policies. As is the case in Brazil, most health resources in Argentina correspond to hospitals' spending. Nevertheless, this does not affect Plan Nacer given that it transfers resources to both hospitals and CAPS. In this way, Plan Nacer avoids a conflict between the high-complexity and primary care strategies for the provision of health care, and in fact benefits from the expansion of hospital infrastructure. In other words, one of the main challenges for the expansion of ESF in Brazil (i.e., hospital infrastructure) actually aids the implementation of Argentina's Plan Nacer. Given the absence of strong negative legacies for this policy, it exhibits less temporal and spatial variation than its Brazilian counterpart – while the standard deviation for

[49] There were also a number of municipal health posts that do not reach the minimum qualifications for accessing Plan Nacer.

[50] Health agents have to live in the neighborhood where they work and have to pass exams. However, municipal health agents only leave the CAPS once a week (Interviews Saralago, Zamora).

Estratégia Saúde da Família's coverage is over 25 percent, Plan Nacer exhibits less than 10 percent. In spite of the lack of opposition from hospitals, the transfers of Plan Nacer represent a significantly higher percentage of the budget of CAPS than hospitals. Hospitals have such a high budget already that the money from Plan Nacer is marginal. Conversely, for CAPS, Plan Nacer is "a blessing; if it wasn't for Plan Nacer, we would not have money even for the basic things" (Interview Musri).

The most direct positive policy legacy to Plan Nacer is the *Programa Materno Infantil y Nutrición* (Maternal and Child Nutrition Program, PROMIN), which was implemented in the mid-1990s. It was targeted to women and children younger than six years old who lived in areas where the poverty level was higher than 25 percent. In these places, CAPS and hospitals were in charge of implementing this policy that aimed at funding projects on infrastructure, training, communication, and buying medical supplies for health providers. This policy was also funded mostly by the World Bank and partly by the federal, provincial, and municipal governments (Chiara and Di Virgilio 2005, 130–33; Auditoría General de la Nación 2008). Although the program covered few people, it did develop initial capacities in health centers, hospitals, provinces, and municipalities that Plan Nacer would benefit from.

Another national health policy that enhances the implementation of Plan Nacer is the Medicine Program *(Programa Remediar)*. Since 2002, this policy has supported the delivery of a first aid kit from the central government to CAPS, to be then directly delivered to the population. Both Plan Nacer and Remediar aim at strengthening the primary health network by increasing the take-up rate of public primary health services – Remediar through providing medicine resources and Plan Nacer through transferring funds for the improvement of the service in the CAPS (Tobar 2004, 13). In addition, most CAPS where Plan Nacer is implemented also have Remediar, which allows for delivering free medicine to Plan Nacer recipients. In this way, the transfers from Plan Nacer do not generally need to be used for buying medicine.

It is not only national health policies that provide positive legacies for the implementation of Plan Nacer, provincial policies in San Luis and Mendoza also enhance Plan Nacer's implementation. The main positive legacy for the implementation of Plan Nacer in the province of San Luis is the provincial workfare program *(Plan de Inclusión Social* or PIS) analyzed in Chapter 5. The administration of Plan Nacer initially hired twenty-seven PIS workers for signing up patients and for data entry activities (*El Diario de la República, San Luis*, February 15, 2007). In addition, most of the administrative and cleaning staff working at the CAPS is also funded by the provincial workfare program. These workers are very necessary for the normal functioning of the CAPS. For example, in a CAPS located in the City of San Luis, the two cleaning staff and four of the five administrative staff members are paid by the provincial program (Interview Arce).[51]

Plan Nacer in the province of Mendoza is marginally enhanced by a provincial program called *Comer Juntos en Familia* (Meals with Family). This provincial program has been implemented since 2009 and entails a basket of food handed out every other week with the aim of transitioning to an ATM card in the future. It is implemented through civil society organizations and some municipalities (Interviews Martin, Massolo, Spoliansky). The provincial food program targets families under the poverty line (and who previously participated in soup kitchens) and covered more than 1,000 families (5,500 people) in 2011 (Ministerio de Desarrollo Humano, Familia y Comunidad de Mendoza 2011a). The basket of goods is conditioned upon participation in training activities that include cooking courses as well as basic courses on preventive health and hygiene. In these courses, recipients are trained on the importance of health checkups conducted by CAPS and covered by Plan Nacer. In this way, the beneficiaries of the food program are encouraged to attend the local CAPS on a regular basis, thus marginally aiding Plan Nacer's implementation.

CONCLUSIONS

This chapter analyzed the determinants of the successful implementation of national health policies in Brazil and Argentina. One of the main findings is that political alignments do not matter for the implementation of these policies because thy do not carry clear attribution of responsibility. This is different from the conditional cash transfers analyzed in Chapter 5, where recipients could identify who was responsible for these policies and could therefore potentially reward that party or government level in the elections. In those cases, the alignment between national and subnational governments shaped their implementation. Conversely, the health policies analyzed in this chapter do not carry clear attribution of responsibility because recipients do not generally identify the existence of these policies. And being able to identify the existence of a policy (i.e., its visibility) is necessary for attributing credit. The fact that they are social services, that transfers go to health centers and not to patients, and the decentralized implementation of health policies, all contribute to blurring attribution of responsibility.

This chapter has also highlighted the relevance of policy legacies and territorial infrastructure for implementing national health policies. As was the

[51] The working conditions of these people are precarious since they do not enjoy access to the same salaries and the same benefits as workers included in the formal labor market who conduct similar activities (Interviews Bragagnolo, Carrizo, J. Gomez, Mattar). As it was analyzed in Chapter 5, beneficiaries of the provincial program work for very low wages (US$140 per month), with no pension contributions, and with no health insurance for their families. They work side by side and develop the same activities as workers hired by the formal labor market who earn around US$580 per month and enjoy full benefits (Interview Arce).

case in the CCTs analyzed in the previous chapter, policy legacies are stronger in Brazil than Argentina. In Brazil, the presence of previous health systems that compete against the new system of primary health care hinders the implementation of the policy. This is generally the case in subnational units where large sectors of the population are users of alternative health systems, be it the previous primary health structure, private insurance, or hospitals. Conversely, Plan Nacer does not face opposition from competing health strategies since it transfers funds to both primary health centers and hospitals, thus avoiding conflicts over resources. In addition, while the Brazilian health policy aims at reorganizing the provision of the entire health system, the Argentine health policy is just an incentive for enhancing the quality in the provision of existing public health structures.

Besides the role of policy legacies, territorial infrastructure played a central role in the implementation of both of these health policies. Estratégia Saúde da Família and Plan Nacer are enhanced by health facilities in adequate condition, distributed evenly throughout the territory, and staffed by trained personnel with adequate salaries. In Brazil, ESF also benefits from close collaboration between state and non-state actors through participatory councils. In Argentina, civil society does not participate in the provision of health care, and in Plan Nacer specifically. The different participation of civil society in Argentina and Brazil is due to both legal and historical factors. On the one hand, primary health care in Brazil requires by law the development of health councils that incorporate the state, health providers, and civil society. As a result, almost half of all Family Health Facilities participate in local or municipal health councils (Brasil. Ministério da Saúde, Departamento de Atenção Básica 2004, 21). In Argentina, the implementation of Plan Nacer does not include a law mandating the participation of civil society. On the other hand, the participation of civil society for pushing toward universalistic health reforms has a long tradition in Brazil compared to Argentina. The incorporation of the Unified Health System in the 1988 constitution was partly the product of pressures from the sanitarista movement, a civil society movement that spread through the state since the 1970s. As a result of these societal pressures, the health sector became more participatory, with councils and forums that monitor the implementation of the SUS across all levels of government (Côrtes 2009; Côrtes et al. 2009; Falleti 2010b; Niedzwiecki 2014a; Niedzwiecki and Anria Forthcoming; Mayka 2019).

A major implication of these primary health policies is that they contribute to narrowing the gap between the quality of health services in the public and private systems. In this way, they advance social rights. The challenge is to modify the idea that the public system is "poor medicine for the poor" and raise the quality of the service to a level in which the middle class chooses to use the public system for primary health care.

7

Conclusions

Uneven Social Policies analyzed policies that represent a breakthrough in the expansion of social protection. For the first time, health policies and cash transfers are broadly targeted, are nondiscretionarily distributed, and aim at enhancing the quality of provision. These policies are also not dependent on work contributions, and therefore include those who have no job or who work in the informal sector. These characteristics give the policies the potential to improve the well-being of the population. In particular, good quality primary health care can reduce infant mortality, strengthen human capital, and have a redistributive impact; and CCTs have proven successful at decreasing poverty and extreme poverty (Handa and Davis 2006; McGuire 2010b).

The missing link between policy design and transformative outcomes in the welfare state literature is the implementation of policies. National policies can improve the lives of their populations only if they are able to actually reach these populations. This book shows that implementation is uneven within decentralized countries – in some provinces and municipalities policies are implemented better than in others. In other words, national policies are more transformative in some places than in others. This uneven implementation requires an explanation that includes factors at multiple territorial levels.

One of the main contributions of this book is to highlight how the interaction between national and subnational politics shapes implementation patterns. In a world in which subnational officials are increasingly elected and no longer appointed, national policy makers and executives should expect that they will face opposition from mayors and governors. In democratic and decentralized countries, it is rare that presidents and their parties control all subnational governments, so multilevel cooperation cannot be taken for granted. One way to promote cooperation across subnational levels is through blurring the attribution of responsibility of national policies.

Another central contribution of this book is the distinction between policies with clear national attribution of responsibility and policies in which attribution of responsibility is not clear. Clarity of responsibility differentiates

CCTs from social services such as health care. CCTs have clear attribution of responsibility because the good provided (cash) is tangible and provision is centralized at the national level. For health care, recipients may not associate the benefits provided by the policy with the policy itself. This lower visibility of the policy makes credit claiming harder. Given that opposition subnational executives only hinder policies with clear attribution of responsibility, central governments should be ready to share credit to successfully implement policies. While clarity of responsibility may increase the popularity of a leader and her party, it decreases the chances of that policy succeeding in opposition subnational units.

The policy recommendation to decrease credit claiming begs the related question of whether politicians will enact policies that do not provide them with a clear electoral payoff. In other words, are social services destined to disappear? No – politicians will keep on enacting social services for self-interested or altruistic reasons. Policies with blurred attribution of responsibility can still provide indirect electoral payoffs: a healthier population is more productive and less poor and this can indirectly benefit the incumbent, even if the voter does not associate her improvement in living conditions with the national policy itself. In addition, there are particular aspects in the provision of social services that carry clear attribution of responsibility, such as building a new school or hospital. Those provide direct electoral payoffs. Finally, presidents and policy makers can sincerely care about the well-being of the population and therefore decide to implement policies that enhance human capital development, independently of their political gain.

Besides making an original connection between multilevel politics and attribution of responsibility, this book also broadens our understanding of where state capacity comes from. It underscores the relevance of state–society relations for state capacity, and hence for the implementation of national policies. Subnational states that have strong institutional capacity and are able to develop synergic relations with non-state actors can succeed at policy implementation. The state can contribute to these relationships by building participatory institutions that allow capable subnational states to identify specific needs and better serve the population. In particular, councils in some Brazilian municipalities facilitate implementation by deliberation. Among other things, municipalities can make sure that national funds are not discretionarily used, that the quality of the service provision is adequate, and that anybody who should access a policy can do so.

This last chapter seeks to summarize the main arguments of *Uneven Social Policies* and analyze their theoretical and practical implications. Next, it expands one of its core arguments – the role of political alignments – to other decentralized countries. I will draw on examples from Mexico, Bolivia, Ecuador, Peru, Spain, and the United States, and focus on the implementation of the Affordable Care Act in the latter. Finally, the last section will discuss avenues for further research.

SUMMARY OF FINDINGS AND POLICY IMPLICATIONS

Attribution of responsibility, political alignments, territorial infrastructure, and policy legacies shape the implementation of national policies. This framework was tested through a mixed methods research design. The regression analysis in Chapter 4 showed that having weak institutional capacity hinders the implementation of all national policies, while opposition governors only obstruct the implementation of CCTs but not of health policies. Having strong state institutions, positive policy legacies, and aligned subnational executives enhances the implementation of national policies. The case studies of four provinces and eight municipalities across four national policies illustrated the causal mechanisms that link politics, capacities, and legacies with implementation and the qualitative chapters also showed the ways in which the independent variables can be related to each other. Chapters 5 and 6 showed three ways in which the independent variables interact.

First, opposition governors and mayors benefit from having strong territorial infrastructure to block national initiatives. The opposition governor of San Luis in Argentina, for instance, uses the territory's strong infrastructure to implement a subnational policy that competes against the national CCT. While having strong capacity provides subnational executives with specific tools (such as implementing competing policies) not available to those in weaker units, subnational executives in contexts of weaker territorial infrastructure have other options at hand. In weaker municipalities and provinces, governors and mayors can act by omission: they can simply decide not to put their institutions and personnel at the service of the national policy, thus hindering its implementation. The option to act by omission does not require significant capacity or resources.

Second, the legacy of previous subnational policies can be positive or negative depending on the political affiliation of the executive. Previous subnational policies can be used to hinder or enhance national policies, as the Brazilian cases of the opposition states of Goiás and the aligned state of Rio Grande do Sul, respectively, showed. Finally, territorial infrastructure and policy legacies are also related. Deliberative forums that strengthen territorial infrastructure can also serve as a venue for resistance to change. In particular, when previous policies empower actors who oppose the new policy (i.e., negative policy legacies), councils can provide a microphone to these groups to resist implementation. At the same time, those same public forums can help those who want to promote the new policy. Whether councils are used to hinder or enhance a policy varies by city, policy area, and particular topic of discussion, thus showing the relevance of studying policy legacies through subnational lenses. The next four sections analyze each of the independent variables separately, to understand their individual effect on implementation and their broader implications.

Attribution of Responsibility

National politicians can only benefit electorally from policies that "belong" to the national government, meaning that attribution of responsibility is clear. Voters cannot reward a particular government if they do not identify where the policy is coming from. Clarity of attribution of responsibility differentiates CCTs from social services. CCTs are generally distributed directly by the national government and the provider's logo appears on the ATM card that recipients use to withdraw funds every month. That is how recipients identify where the policy is coming from and they can choose to reward the provider in elections. Conversely, social services carry more blurred attribution of responsibility. In the case of health care, it is challenging for voters to associate the benefits of a particular policy with the policy itself. This low visibility makes it hard to reward any particular government in elections. In addition, health services tend to be implemented by provinces and municipalities, thus further blurring national credit claiming. Finally, attribution is blurred because it is generally health centers (and not users) that receive national transfers and the good distributed by health policies (such as better quality of service) is less tangible than money.

The analysis in this book focuses on CCTs *Bolsa Família* (Family Grant, Brazil) and *Asignación Universal por Hijo* (Universal Child Allowance, Argentina) and health policies *Estratégia Saúde da Família* (ESF, Family Health Strategy, Brazil) and *Plan Nacer* (Birth Plan, Argentina). Given that they provide access to basic income and services, these are policies for which national governments want to claim credit as opposed to avoid blame. In Argentina, recipients can clearly identify where the CCT is coming from. In contrast, they do not recognize the existence of Plan Nacer, and thus are unable to assign credit. The difference in attribution of responsibility across policies is also present in Brazil, when comparing CCT Bolsa Família with health policy ESF.

While having strong versus weak attribution of responsibility is a characteristic of the type of policy – transfers versus services – the case of Brazil's Bolsa Família shows the relevance of the passing of time and the government's strategies for sharing credit. This CCT has been implemented for fifteen years and it has therefore survived changes in national and subnational administrations. As time goes by and the policy sticks around, people start forgetting where it came from in the first place. In addition, and perhaps most importantly, the federal government has had an active strategy of sharing credit with subnational governments and this has decreased clarity of responsibility. The federal government enables subnational governments to include the logo of their states on the ATM card recipients use to withdraw funds in exchange for developing programs or using existing programs to complement Bolsa Família. By 2012, this strategy was relatively successful, since many states had decided to sign such agreements, and some of these states had opposition governors. The experience with Bolsa Família shows that policy makers have the option to decrease credit claiming, even for policies that carry clear attribution of responsibility by design.

On the other hand, decreasing attribution of responsibility has the additional implication of creating a tension with programmatic politics – accountability demands some degree of attribution. Rewarding governments in elections for good policy decisions is a crucial form of accountability that becomes harder in the absence of clarity of responsibility (Harding 2015). The need for accountability partly explains why the public administration and practitioner literature on decentralization tends to advocate for clear attribution of responsibility in the division of tasks between levels of government (e.g., Agrawal and Ribot 1999; Burki, Perry, and Dillinger 1999; Manor 1999). Clear attribution of responsibility across levels, according to this literature, avoids ambiguity and overlapping responsibilities. Therefore, the choice is between even territorial implementation, on the one hand, and accountability and clear responsibilities, on the other.

Political Alignments

The difference in attribution of responsibility across CCTs and health policies augurs different effects for political alignments. For opposition governors and mayors, policies with blurred attribution of responsibility are a win-win situation – they receive federal money at no electoral cost. The regression analysis in Chapter 4 showed that across Brazilian states and Argentine provinces, having a governor who is opposed to the president has a statistically insignificant effect on the implementation of health policies ESF and Plan Nacer. The qualitative case studies presented in Chapter 6 showed similar results. Because of the lack of clarity of responsibility, government officials in opposition subnational units confirmed that the policy was not implemented differently due to political considerations. The opposition province of San Luis is a clear example of the absence of politics in the implementation of Plan Nacer. This province is one of the most successful in implementing the health policy.

The effect of political alignments is crucial for the implementation of policies with clear attribution of responsibility. Both the national government and its subnational allies have gained electorally from the implementation of CCTs (Borges 2007, 129–30; Hunter and Power 2007; Queirolo 2010; Baez et al. 2012; De La O 2013; Zucco 2013; Souza 2015). As a result, opposition governors and mayors have incentives to obstruct policy implementation, while aligned governors and mayors are motivated to facilitate it. The opposition state of Goiás in Brazil, for instance, refused to share the lists of beneficiaries of its subnational cash transfer with the national government and this slowed down the initial signing up. This opposition government also used its subnational program to compete with the national one. Politically aligned provinces not only shared the list of recipients of subnational programs with the national government but also complemented the national CCTs by developing new policies or adapting their existing ones. The aligned province of Mendoza in Argentina adapted its existing scholarship program to provide tutors to recipients of the national CCT who were going back to school, thanks to the national policy. Similarly, the aligned state of Rio Grande do Sul in Brazil created a new CCT called *RS Mais Renda Mais Igual* (RS More and Fairer Income) to increase the level of transfers of Bolsa Família recipients who had children in high school.

Contrary to welfare state theories where the focus is on the design of policies (e.g., Esping-Andersen 1990; Huber and Stephens 2001), I argue that opposition to the implementation of national policies does not follow ideological lines. It is not the ideology of subnational governments that shapes the implementation of national policies, but rather multilevel political alignments. In decentralized Latin American countries, coalitions between ideologically ill-defined parties may vary at the national and subnational levels. In Brazil, for example, 60 percent of coalitions for gubernatorial elections are between right and left parties. In addition, the same party can join ideologically different coalitions at the three territorial levels (Krause and Alves Godoi 2010; Borges 2016). This means that if governors oppose national policies it is not due to ideological conviction but rather because of a rational calculation of whether policies can provide them with electoral dividends. The fact that coalitions in Brazil are not consistent across national and subnational levels of government makes political alignments more blurred than in Argentina, and therefore their effect on policy implementation is weaker. In other words, Argentina's more disciplined party system produces a stronger effect of political alignments on the implementation of the national CCT than Brazil's more fragmented system.

While incongruence of partisanship also matters for the distribution of clientelistic policies – the president can choose to benefit subnational co-partisans, and parties can strategically select recipients to improve their election chances – *Uneven Social Policies* shows that politics also matters for the distribution of nondiscretionary policies. The CCTs and health policies analyzed here are not targeted by the provider for electoral reasons, in part because these policies have a more stringent design. However, they are still unevenly implemented as a result of opposition from subnational governors and mayors. In addition, brokers in the territory have a different role than in clientelistic policies. While networks of brokers and activists mediate access to particularistic goods (Calvo and Murillo 2012), they can actually enhance the implementation of nondiscretionary policies by providing information. The local broker is in an invaluable position to reach the most vulnerable population – the broker knows the neighbors by name, where they live, and which are their most pressing problems. Without having the authority to distribute patronage-free policies, brokers' knowledge can be put at the service of these policies. For instance, the broker can tell people about the launching of a new cash transfer or can use her car to take an ill child to the nearest clinic. This does not mean that nondiscretionary policies will end clientelism, as Montero (2010, 149) convincingly argues for the case of Brazil. Clientelistic machines continue serving the interests of incumbents, and therefore vote-buying will probably continue being a prominent practice, at least in the short term. In the long run, however, the implementation of nondiscretionary social policies may have the effect of weakening clientelistic networks and thus strengthening citizenship rights.

Territorial Infrastructure

This book analyzes a specific aspect of state capacity: territorial infrastructure, which is related to Michael Mann's definition of infrastructural power as the capacity to actually implement political decisions throughout the territory (Mann 1988, 5). The concept of territorial infrastructure incorporates two dimensions: the spatial reach of state institutions, which is particularly relevant in large and decentralized countries, and the relationship between state and non-state actors (Soifer and Vom Hau 2008). Subnational health, education, and social assistance facilities that are accessible, in adequate condition, and staffed by trained personnel are the basis of strong territorial infrastructure. This means that cash transfers and social services need to be accompanied by investment in infrastructure that generates good quality service provision. Only good quality services can improve human capital development. For instance, higher levels of school attendance produced by CCTs do not guarantee better education outcomes, including higher cognitive abilities and academic achievement, and consequently better work opportunities (Jones 2016). To achieve these aims, governments should concentrate on improving the quality of schooling.

Strong state infrastructure can be complemented by collaboration between state and civil society. Having a capable state and an autonomous civil society are necessary for positive collaboration. This synergy between state and non-state actors produces deliberative processes that mutually reinforce each other for the successful implementation of policies (Evans 1995; Evans and Heller 2015). Deliberative institutions set up by the state can advocate for these types of deliberation to be sustained in the long run. The state of Rio Grande do Sul and its municipality of Porto Alegre are examples of active civil society participation, in combination with strong institutions, for the implementation of national policies. Most ESF facilities in Porto Alegre include a health council in which representatives voice their concerns. These local councils aggregate demands and take them to the district councils, which report to the municipal Health Secretariat, and are then represented at the municipal council. The municipal health council has been an active participant in health policies since its creation in 1992, aggregating demands and monitoring the implementation of primary health care.

When comparing Brazil and Argentina, state–society participation in the implementation of social policies is institutionalized in the former through mandated councils at all levels of government, while in Argentina state–society collaboration is more limited, takes place though more informal channels, and is conducted on an ad hoc basis. However, this does not mean that territorial infrastructure is weak in Argentine provinces and municipalities, because strong capacity can also be achieved through good quality and accessible state institutions in the territory. The Argentine province of San Luis is an example of strong territorial infrastructure without coordination with civil society. The province centralizes the delivery of health care and therefore controls the implementation of Plan Nacer. All institutions and personnel are provided, funded, and monitored by the province. This monopolistic control of health activities in the Provincial Ministry of Health has a successful outcome: there is no superposition of activities and Plan Nacer is implemented evenly throughout the province.

Policy Legacies

This book confirms the relevance of policy legacies on social policies (Pierson 1993, 2004; Huber and Stephens 2001; Pribble 2013) and underscores the importance of this variable's within-country variation. Previous policy choices generate institutional dynamics and empower actors that influence the implementation of current ones. Policy legacies can be positive or negative, and vary across policy sectors, countries, and subnational units. While the primary health policy in Brazil faces negative legacies from the previous system, national CCTs in both countries benefit from the experience of previous social assistance policies. Brazil's policy legacies are stronger than in Argentina because previous policies have been around for a longer period of time and they targeted a larger percentage of the population.

In Brazil, the implementation of primary health care policy ESF generates opposition from those interested in defending hospital provision and in advocating for an alternative primary health system – UBS (*Unidades Básicas Tradicionais*, Traditional Basic Health Units). The more a state or municipality is structured around hospital provision, the more challenging it is to increase investment in basic health care of any kind, given that most health federal transfers are allocated to medium- and high-complexity health provision. In the case of UBS, whole generations of doctors were trained following the guidelines of this system and strongly oppose ESF. In at least half of the municipalities, ESF has to be implemented side by side with the old UBS system (Brasil. Ministério da Saúde 2009, 27). The places that have the highest density of UBS found it hardest to transition to the new system, while in those municipalities where no UBS was implanted, the implementation of ESF is smoother. Hospitals and UBS offer higher salaries to general practitioners than ESF, and therefore the latter loses in the competition for professionals.

The difficulty of recruiting human resources for ESF also responds to the legacy of the Fiscal Responsibility Law of 2000, which determined that no more than 60 percent of revenue could be spent on personnel, a fact that particularly affected labor-intensive sectors such as health care. To respect the law, many subnational governments in Brazil rely on the precarious contracting of ESF workers. Contrary to ESF, Plan Nacer in Argentina does not generate any opposition from entrenched interests in alternative systems because Plan Nacer transfers resources to both primary health facilities and hospitals. As a result, previous hospital infrastructure actually enhances Plan Nacer.

CCTs rest on the (positive) legacies of previous national and subnational policies. One of the main explanations for the rapid success of Bolsa Família is that the policy builds on previous efforts (Bither-Terry 2013). When Bolsa Família was implemented, 4.2 million families were receiving other programs (Soares and Sátyro 2010, 43). This CCT incorporated some of these recipients, schools and health centers learned how to successfully fulfill conditionalities from previous policies, and the banking system had already incorporated a number of recipients of previous cash transfers. Argentina's Asignación Universal por Hijo, compared to Brazil's CCT, has weaker policy legacies because previous policies had lower coverage and did not develop the institutional learning to ensure compliance with health and education conditionalities.

BEYOND ARGENTINA AND BRAZIL

The challenges and opportunities analyzed in the process of implementation of CCTs and health policies in Argentina and Brazil may be applied to the study of any decentralized country in any policy area for which attribution of responsibility is either clear or blurred. Any democratic country in which subnational levels of government enjoy high levels of authority will potentially face challenges in the implementation of policies when their attribution of responsibility is clear and subnational governments belong to the opposition. Following Hooghe et al. (2016), democracies with high levels of regional authority include Argentina, Australia, Austria, Belgium, Brazil, Canada, Germany, Malaysia, Mexico, the Netherlands, Singapore, Switzerland, and the United States.[1] This section and the next assess the attribution of responsibility and political alignment argument to cases beyond Argentina and Brazil.

In Mexico, the PRI (*Partido Revolucionario Institucional,* Institutional Revolutionary Party) implemented a CCT program in 1997 called *Progresa* (Progress), which was rebranded first as *Oportunidades* (Opportunities) in

[1] This list includes countries in which non-asymmetric intermediate regions (such as states in the United States) score higher than fifteen points in the Regional Authority Index in 2010 (Hooghe et al. 2016).

2002 after the PAN (*Partido Acción Nacional*, National Action Party) won the presidential elections, and then as *Prospera* (Prosper) after the PRI regained the presidency in 2012. This CCT is not implemented in a discretionary manner; it follows stringent targeting rules. Because of its clear attribution of responsibility, it has benefitted the presidential incumbent in elections (De La O 2015). Partly as a result of this, the opposition government of Mexico City, led by the PRD (*Partido de la Revolución Democrática*, Party of the Democratic Revolution) since 1997, has been distancing itself from the national CCT by establishing its own social policy approach. Luccisano and Macdonald (2014, 341) explain:

Mexico City PRD governments have turned to social policy as a site to legitimize their administration, appeal to voters, contest federal neoliberal approaches to poverty alleviation, and achieve progressive social reform. Successive mayors have also attempted to use the popularity they have won through these policies to launch federal presidential campaigns.

Mexico City promoted an alternative policy that competes against the national one, producing a lower level of coverage by the national CCT. The 2000 Law of Social Development for Mexico City is the umbrella for the alternative social policy approach. The policies that emerged from this law include support for housing, scholarships, food, and noncontributory pensions for residents through the *Programa Integrado Territorial de Desarrollo Social* (Integrated Territorial Social Development Program). In 2010, the municipal government unified fifteen social policies. Three of these policies accounted for 19 percent of the municipal budget (Luccisano and Macdonald 2014). Contrary to the Argentine *Frente para la Victoria* and the Brazilian *Partido dos Trabalhadores*, the PAN government that introduced the national CCT in Mexico is considered a right-wing government, and opposition to this policy was headed by a left-wing party in Mexico City (Luccisano and Macdonald 2014). As a result, this case shows that the theory developed in this book concerning the relevance of political alignments for national policy implementation can be applied to non-left national presidencies.

Regions in Bolivia, Ecuador, and Peru have also been defying national policies. Eaton (2017) shows that local authorities who defend a market-oriented policy regime have been challenging national state-centered models of economic development in Bolivia and Ecuador. Santa Cruz in Bolivia and Guayaquil in Ecuador are the most economically developed regions and, in alliance with business elites, have incentives to maintain the existing successful neoliberal subnational model. The opposite happens in Peru, where challenges to the national neoliberal model include measures such as support for regional research and development and the suspension of mining projects in Arequipa. Overall, subnational officials who challenge national economic models do not belong to the president's party. Eaton (2017) shows that while Peru's subnational governments have failed to produce their own policy regimes, the story in Santa Cruz and Guayaquil seems to be one of success. Subnational policy experimentation can be more adequate for local contexts and more stable than national models of development; however, different policy regimes across levels (what Eaton calls "policy regimes juxtaposition") can also generate contradictions and important political conflict over resources that could be devoted to other priorities.

Beyond Latin America, Spanish *comunidades autónomas* (autonomous communities) have a margin of action in welfare and economic policies that allows them to make their own policy choices. In the aftermath of the 2008 financial crisis, the conservative party (*Partido Popular*, Popular Party) won the general elections of 2011, and immediately implemented austerity policies. Autonomous regions in Spain reacted in three different ways to these measures. Harguindéguy (2015) explains that some accepted the measures enacted by the government of Mariano Rajoy. Most of these regional governments, including Castile-La Mancha and Valencia, belonged to the *Partido Popular* or parties aligned with the national government. Others actively opposed the central government, in part through appeals made to the Constitutional Council with the argument that the reforms proposed by the central government were either unconstitutional or exceeded the central government's jurisdiction. This group of autonomous communities included mostly opposition governments, such as Andalusia, the Basque Country, the Canary Islands, and Navarre. Catalonia has followed a different path of resistance, by seeking independence through a referendum. Overall, the autonomous communities that belonged to the Popular Party mostly supported the policies of the central government, while most of the Socialists and/or Nationalists regions hindered the implementation of national austerity policies (Harguindéguy 2015, 17–18).

To exhibit the generalizability of the theory on social policy implementation, political alignments, and attribution of responsibility, I focus next on the Affordable Care Act in the United States.

The Affordable Care Act (United States)

After a year of congressional debate, the Patient Protection and Affordable Care Act (commonly called Affordable Care Act, ACA) became law on March 23, 2010. That year, there were approximately thirty-two million Americans without health insurance due to its high costs (Jacobs and Skocpol 2010, 4). The aim of this policy is to increase health coverage, affordability, and quality. To achieve these aims, the policy mandates that every US resident should have health coverage (and provides subsidies for low-income individuals), that businesses with more than fifty employees provide health insurance to full-time workers, and that insurance companies meet minimum standards and not discriminate against patients based on preexisting conditions or sex.[2] Failure to comply with the law can carry a penalty. The policy has two components. On the one hand, health insurance marketplaces (or exchanges) operate in every state to provide services to individuals and companies. On the other hand, states can expand Medicaid, a health care program for low-income individuals.

The Affordable Care Act is commonly called "Obamacare" by both supporters and opponents. This shows the strong association between the policy and the US president, who staked an enormous amount of his political capital in this reform in the critical, opening years of his presidency. In addition, the bill was passed in the context of a high level of polarization across party lines where the majority party (Democrats) claimed credit for it and the opposition party (Republicans) rejected it. Not a single Republican representative voted in favor of the law. Partly as a result of this, the policy enjoys strong attribution of responsibility directed to the majority party at the federal level and, more specifically, to the president. This clear attribution of responsibility means that those who evaluate the policy in positive terms may vote for the president or his party.[3] As a result, the implementation of the policy has been uneven throughout the territory due to challenges from opposition states. While 16.4 million uninsured had gained health insurance by early 2015, those who still lack health insurance tend to live in poor, Southern, and Republican states (Bui and Sanger-Katz, October 30, 2015; Obamacare Facts March 16, 2015). Rigby (2012) shows that Republican Party control of the state legislature or state executive is the dominant factor in explaining resistance to the policy.[4]

While the original version of the law required that states expand Medicaid, a Supreme Court ruling in 2012 (National Federation of Independent Business

---

[2] Insurance companies have to offer the same premium price to all potential patients of the same age and geographic location.

[3] Surveys show that a majority of those enrolled in the ACA are satisfied with the policy. A 2015 nationally representative survey of 4,881 adults from the Commonwealth Fund found that over 90 percent of the newly insured were somewhat satisfied or very satisfied with their new insurance (The Commonwealth Fund 2015). A 2016 Kaiser Foundation survey of 786 adults found that over 60 percent of those insured rated their coverage as "good" or "excellent" (Kaiser Family Foundation 2016c). On the other hand, the ACA was "extremely important" for shaping the vote of only 23 percent of the population in 2016 presidential elections, ranking eighth after terrorism and the economy, among others (Kaiser Family Foundation 2016b). However, it does not matter for the theoretical framework in this book whether people actually vote for the Democrats or not based on the ACA, as long as Republicans *think* that supporting the ACA will hurt their party in elections. Republicans could also be punished in elections if they chose to support Obamacare due to the costs associated with the policy, as will be explained later.

[4] While in Latin America the role of subnational executives is key for explaining implementation patterns, the role of subnational legislatures is also relevant in the US context. In general, previous scholarship measures Republican-dominated states where the Republican Party dominates at least two of the three following institutions: governorship, lower chamber, and upper chamber (e.g., Hertel-Fernandez, Skocpol, and Lynch 2016, 242).

v. Sebelius) opened the door for states to reject Medicaid expansion. The effects of this ruling have been damaging for the implementation of the ACA – around three million people would have gained health insurance in the states that decided not to expand Medicaid, if expansion was not optional. These people remain uninsured because they do not qualify for either the existing Medicaid or for subsidized coverage. They fall into a "coverage gap" (Garfield 2016). In 2014, all Democratic governors supported Medicaid expansion, while governors that opposed the expansion belonged to the Republican Party (Barrilleaux and Rainey 2014, 440).[5]

In addition to the refusal of some Republican states to expand Medicaid, opposition states have hindered the implementation of the ACA through a number of additional measures. Between 2010 and 2015, around half of state legislatures issued hundreds of bills and resolutions that challenged the health reform.[6] The mechanisms and legal language to oppose the ACA vary across states – nine states opted for passing restrictions to ACA compliance, eighteen states incorporated constitutional language for not enforcing the individual or business mandate to purchase health insurance, nine states passed laws to create Interstate Health Compacts that would enable a group of states to create broad health care programs outside of the ACA, twenty-three states tried unsuccessfully to nullify the legal validity of the ACA, and over a dozen states restricted the function of state government personnel assisting consumers in choosing health insurance (Cauchi 2016).[7]

Republicans also opposed the creation of their own health exchanges. In the words of Jones, Bradley, and Oberlander (2014, 127): "Exchanges became controversial largely because they suffered from guilt by association – with Democrats, President Obama, and Obamacare." Opposition to health exchanges was not obvious since Republican-led states could have decided to develop their own health exchanges to protect their current policy autonomy (Haeder and Weimer 2013; Rigby and Haselswerdt 2013). Developing state

---

[5] Eleven Republican states did expand Medicaid (while nineteen did not) by 2017, in part because its expansion involved large financial stakes and thus activated lobbies on behalf of hospitals and other business associations. In addition, there is strong public support in some states for Medicaid expansion (Haeder and Weimer 2015; Hertel-Fernandez, Skocpol, and Lynch 2016; Castele, January 23, 2017). Finally, Medicaid's expansion in Republican states may be related to the fact that people may fail to recognize this as part of the ACA given that Medicaid has existed for a long time and has been expanded in the past without major opposition (US Centers for Medicare and Medicaid Services 2017). This low clarity of responsibility and strong legacies may partly explain expansion in Republican states.

[6] At the national level, House Republicans attempted to delay ACA implementation in October 2013 through a "government shutdown" (refusing to approve funds for 2014 fiscal year) and through more than sixty attempts at repealing parts or all of the ACA. There have also been a large number of Supreme Court and Federal Court Actions that pose challenges to the law (Cauchi 2016; Obama 2016, 6).

[7] The effect and legality of these provisions will be made clear with time.

health exchanges can be used as a way of decreasing national attribution of responsibility and appropriating a potentially popular policy. Kentucky's Healthcare Connection, Kynect, is one such example of a state re-branding of the national policy. The state integrated eligibility systems between Kynect and Medicaid, engaged in an expansive local enrollment effort, and developed a broad marketing campaign through TV, radio, and social media. These efforts have produced a highly successful ACA implementation experience. In December 2015, however, a newly elected Republican governor announced a transition from a fully state-based marketplace to a federally supported state-based marketplace (Kaiser Family Foundation 2016a). This type of resistance to the ACA has a direct effect on limiting competition in the exchanges and therefore increasing the cost of premiums (Goodnough and Abelson, 2017). Places with only one insurer in the exchanges are overwhelmingly Republican: 40 million of those living with only 1 insurer reside in states with Republican governors, compared with 10.7 million in states with Democratic governors (Dew and Baker 2017).

As a noticeable example of politically motivated obstacles to the national policy, the state of Missouri enacted a statute that forbids state and local officials to cooperate with ACA implementation unless specifically required to by federal law; a fact that results in poor information among this state's residents (Pear, August 02, 2013). The lack of cooperation with ACA was made evident when decisions by independent courts in 2014, 2015, and 2016 struck down a Missouri law for illegally obstructing "navigators," federally designated personnel in charge of assisting consumers on how to select health care in marketplaces. This state required navigators to obtain state licenses and limited what they could say to consumers. Similar measures were passed in Tennessee (which settled the state court case, now allowing navigators to carry out their job) and Texas (Jost 2014; Cauchi 2016). The state of Missouri also decided not to expand Medicaid, a decision that meant that many low-income residents of the state did not have access to affordable health insurance. Over 60 percent of adults with no health coverage in the state are in the income range for Medicaid expansion (Kaiser Family Foundation 2015).

Conversely, Democratic states aided the implementation of the ACA by expanding Medicaid (Barrilleaux and Rainey 2014). In addition, most of the states that decided to implement their own health exchanges, as opposed to going through the federally facilitated marketplace,[8] have Democrat governors (Haeder and Weimer 2013). Another way of aiding the implementation of ACA is by distributing information through canvassing and media campaigns. In Colorado, for instance, employees of the state health exchange traveled around the state informing and enrolling residents. The governor of the state, John W. Hickenlooper, is a Democrat and a strong supporter of the ACA. He

[8] A third alternative is to enter a state–federal partnership.

expressed: "We'll do whatever it takes, I'll ride around the state on a bicycle if I have to" (Goodnough, August 02, 2013).

The implementation of Obamacare has been shaped by national and subnational political alignments (Rigby 2012; Haeder and Weimer 2013, 2015; Rigby and Haselswerdt 2013; Barrilleaux and Rainey 2014). There is enthusiastic implementation by Democratic states and opposition by many Republicans. This is in part because the policy has clear attribution of responsibility, it "belongs" to Obama and the Democratic Party, and therefore the Republican Party cannot – and probably does not choose to – claim credit for any benefit that the policy may provide. In this context, Republican states have incentives to criticize the ACA and hinder its implementation. However, Obamacare is different from the policies analyzed in *Uneven Social Policies* because besides the potential for credit claiming, the ACA also faces costs associated with the design of the policy (i.e., it is mandatory to buy health care). As a result, those who evaluate the policy negatively may vote for the Republican opposition, who is therefore interested in assigning blame for the individual cost generated by this policy. In fact, Republican voters who evaluate the ACA negatively may penalize their local representatives in elections if they support the policy.[9]

In addition, the electoral motivation to hinder the ACA should incorporate ideological considerations. Opposition to the expansion of the welfare state can partly explain Republican states' resistance, a factor that was not present in Argentina and Brazil. However, the relationship between ideology, party polarization, and opposition to the ACA is not straightforward; the concept of insurance exchanges – but not the expansion of Medicaid – has been advocated by the conservative Heritage Foundation, proposed by Republican legislators before the ACA, and was operational in Massachusetts and Utah under Republican governors (Jacobs and Skocpol 2010, 6; Haeder and Weimer 2013, 35). Overall, it is reasonable to argue that the propositions in *Uneven Social Policies* travel to other decentralized democracies, although they may require the incorporation of ideology as a relevant variable. In other words, we would expect subnational governments to hinder or enhance national policies also based on their ideological affinity to the proposed reforms.[10] This may be a relevant addition to the analytic framework when it travels to countries such as Australia, Austria, Belgium, Canada, Germany, the Netherlands, Spain, Switzerland, and the United States. Ideology may also be an important addition when studying entire economic policy regimes, as opposed to individual social policies (Eaton 2017).

---

[9] Additionally, those who benefit the most from Obamacare tend not to vote (Lichtenstein 2017, 122).

[10] Recent works analyzed the extent to which partisanship ideology at subnational levels influence national policy implementation, subnational policy initiatives, and their outcomes (Turner 2011; Chapman Osterkatz 2013; Kleider 2014).

ISSUES FOR FUTURE RESEARCH

By scaling down the study of the welfare state to the subnational level and by differentiating policies with regard to their attribution of responsibility, the findings in this study provide a number of avenues for future research. Perhaps the most politically relevant area involves the association between social policies and welfare outcomes within countries. The main explanation for differences in welfare outcomes at the national level is economic development – advanced industrial democracies fare better than developing countries. However, between-country differences show the significant effect of policies and politics. At the national level, type of social provision, democracy, and left partisanship partly account for lower levels of infant mortality, poverty, and inequality (McGuire 2010b; Huber and Stephens 2012). While across-country differences have received some attention in comparative politics, the political causes of human development disparities *within* countries has been only studied by a handful of researchers (Pushkar 2012; McGuire 2015; Singh 2015; Touchton, Borges Sugiyama, and Wampler 2017). This is surprising given the drastic inequalities found within countries, especially in large and decentralized ones. Therefore, further research should focus on the political and policy factors that shape welfare outcomes within countries.

One of the factors that shapes the success of national policies and their effect on socioeconomic outcomes within countries is subnational policy making. This study has called attention to subnational policies, a topic that has been neglected in the literature, with noticeable exceptions. The causes of subnational variation in policy-making include diffusion effects (Sugiyama 2013), subnationally based identification or subnationalism (Singh 2015), active state government (Tendler 1997), elite cohesion (Montero 2002), interest group arrangements (Snyder 2006), fiscal resources (Post 2014), and access to subnational resources, state capacity, and electoral competition (Bonvecchi 2008). The effect of subnational regime type on subnational social policies can be particularly promising. By bringing together the literatures on subnational regimes (Gervasoni 2010a; Gibson 2012; Giraudy 2013, 2014) and on the effect of democracy on welfare development at the national level (Haggard and Kaufman 2008; McGuire 2010b; Huber and Stephens 2012), we may find an alternative explanation for the divergence of subnational social policies and outcomes in decentralized countries. Some states in Argentina and Brazil have designed and funded noncontributory cash transfers that have widely different characteristics, ranging from discretionary to citizenship-based. The more authoritarian states tend to choose the former and the more democratic the latter. Initial interviews with politicians and policy recipients in the most authoritarian and democratic states in these countries show a possible causal relationship between subnational regime type and policy-making that is worth investigating.

Welfare states become more fragmented because subnational governments design policies of their own, while national policies are unevenly implemented.

Eaton (2017) uses the term "regime juxtaposition" to refer to the existence of different economic policy regimes in Bolivia, Ecuador, and Peru. Does the focus on multiple "social policy regimes" merit a revision of typologies of welfare states? Recent studies argue that types of welfare states can also be found at the subnational level (Armingeon, Bertozzi, and Bonoli 2004; Rodrigues-Silveira 2012). However, subnational social policy divergence is not significant enough to warrant the concept of types of welfare regimes. National levels of governance still standardize social insurance schemes as well as more universalistic social policies. This is true not only for Brazil and Argentina but also for federal OECD countries (Mathias 2005). Central governments intervene in the affairs of subnational units, so subnational levels of government remain embedded within the national welfare state. What we see is different degrees to which national and subnational social policies are implemented throughout the territory, but not different types of subnational welfare states. It is worth continuing the theoretical discussion of the effect of multilevel social policies for the study of welfare regimes.

Uneven Social Policies shows why research on the implementation of popular social policies should take attribution of responsibility seriously. A policy's clarity of responsibility matters for implementation but also for the possibility of retrenchment. The potential electoral gains for the previous government that came from claiming credit for popular policies may make them the first target of retrenchment when an opposition national administration is inaugurated. On the other hand, policies that have clear attribution of responsibility also have high visibility – only if recipients recognize the existence of a policy will they give credit to a particular government, which often makes them resistant to retrenchment. Taking away popular benefits is an unpopular decision, especially for policies that are easy to recognize. The Affordable Care Act in the United States has both high visibility (previously uninsured people recognize that accessing health insurance is associated with the policy) and clear attribution (it is called "Obamacare" in reference to the Democratic President Barack Obama). These characteristics help explain why the Republican national government tried to repeal it in 2017 but failed due to popular backlash. Recently elected right-leaning governments in Latin America have also sought to reform previously expanded policies, and their strategies have also been shaped by the visibility of extant policies. In Chile and Argentina, new administrations have engaged in policy drift for less visible policies, yet have expanded highly visible cash transfers (Niedzwiecki and Pribble 2017). These examples show why research on social policy reform should take a policy's visibility and attribution seriously, especially in moments of potential retrenchment. In this new political context, the stakes are particularly high since these policies have improved the lives of those excluded.

References

Abrahão de Castro, Jorge and Modesto Lúcia, eds. 2010. *Bolsa Família 2003–2010: Avanços e desafios* Volume 1. Brasília: Instituto de Pesquisa Econômica Aplicada (IPEA). Volume 1. www.ipea.gov.br/portal/images/stories/PDFs/livros/livros/livro_bolsafamilia_vol1.pdf.

Abramowitz, Alan I., David J. Lanoue, and Subha Ramesh. 1988. "Economic Conditions, Causal Attributions, and Political Evaluations in the 1984 Presidential Election." *The Journal of Politics* 50 (4): 848–63.

Achen, Cristopher. 2000. "Why Lagged Dependent Variables Can Supress Explanatory Power of Other Independent Variables." *Annual APSA Meeting*, July 20–22. https://www.princeton.edu/csdp/events/Achen121201/achen.pdf.

Agrawal, Arun, and Jesse Ribot. 1999. "Accountability in Decentralization: A Framework with South Asian and West African Cases." *The Journal of Developing Areas* 33 (4): 473–502.

Albertus, Michael. 2015. "The Role of Subnational Politicians in Distributive Politics: Political Bias in Venezuela's Land Reform under Chavez." *Comparative Political Studies* 48 (13): 1667–710.

Aldrich, John H. 2011. *Why Parties? A Second Look*. Chicago: The University of Chicago Press.

Alves, Jorge Antonio. 2015. "(Un?) Healthy Politics: The Political Determinants of Subnational Health Systems in Brazil." *Latin American Politics and Society* 57 (4): 119–42.

Alzúa, María Laura, Guillermo Cruces, and Laura Ripani. 2013. "Welfare Programs and Labor Supply in Developing Countries: Experimental Evidence from Latin America." *Journal of Population Economics* 26 (4): 1255–84.

Amengual, Matthew. 2016. *Politicized Enforcement in Argentina: Labor and Environmental Regulation*. New York, NY: Cambridge University Press.

Amenta, Edwin. 1998. *Bold Relief: Institutional Politics and the Origins of Modern American Social Policy*. Princeton, NJ: Princeton University Press.

Ames, Barry. 2001. *The Deadlock of Democracy in Brazil: Interests, Identities, and Institutions in Comparative Perspective*. Ann Arbor, MI: University of Michigan Press.

Ames, Barry, Fabiana Machado, Lucio Rennó, David Samuels, Amy Erica Smith, and Cesar Zucco. 2010. "The Brazilian Electoral Panel Studies (BEPS): Brazilian Public Opinion in the 2010 Presidential Elections." *IDB Technical Note 508*.

Anderson, Cameron D. 2006. "Economic Voting and Multilevel Governance: A Comparative Individual-Level Analysis." *American Journal of Political Science* 50 (2): 449–63.

Andrenacci, Luciano, Lidia Ikei, Elina Mecle, and Alejandro Corvalán. 2005. "La Argentina de pie y en paz: Acerca del Plan Jefes y Jefas de Hogar Desocupados y del modelo de política social de la Argentina contemporánea." In Andrenacci 2005 *Problemas de política social en la Argentina contemporánea*. Buenos Aires: Prometeo, 181–211.

Anria, Santiago and Sara Niedzwiecki. 2016. "Social Movements and Social Policy. The Bolivian Renta Dignidad." *Studies in Comparative International Development* 51 (3): 308–327.

Argentina. Anses (Administración Nacional de la Seguridad Social). 2011. "Asignación Universal por Hijo para Protección Social: Una política de inclusión para los más vulnerables." *Observatorio de Seguridad Social*. http://observatorio.anses.gob.ar/ documento-trabajo.

  2015. Asignación Universal por Hijo para Protección Social. Datos de cobertura por mes y provincia. Estadísticas Oficiales.

Argentina. Equipo Observatorio Económico Territorial Universidad Nacional del Litoral: Inhabitants per square kilometer. Compiled by James W. McGuire, Department of Government, Wesleyan University from Equipo Observatorio Económico Territorial Universidad Nacional del Litoral- OET. "Cuadro 2: Densidad de Población (habitantes por Km2) por Provincia y Total Nacional 1895–2010." Accessed October 14, 2014, at "http://www.unl.edu.ar/oet/userfiles/image/3601Poblacion.xls" www.unl.edu.ar/oet/userfiles/image/3601Poblacion.xls.

Argentina. Instituto Nacional de Estadísticas y Censos. 2010. "Censo 2010." www.censo2010.indec.gov.ar/.

Argentina. Ministerio de Economía y Finanzas Públicas. 2014. "Evolución de la población que habita hogares por debajo de la línea de pobreza – EPH." Table 22, LP-Pers. Accessed January 27, 2015, at www.mecon.gov.ar/download/infoeco/apendice3a .xls. Compiled by James W. McGuire, Department of Government, Wesleyan University. Contact: jmcguire@ wesleyan.edu

Argentina. Ministerio de Educación de la Nación. 2011. *Análisis y evaluación de los aspectos educativos de la AUH*. Buenos Aires: Casano Gráfica. http://portal .educacion.gov.ar/asignacion-universal-por-hijo-para-proteccion-social/.

Argentina. Ministerio de Salud de la Nación. 2012. "Programa Sumar."Accessed April 23, 2016. www.msal.gob.ar/sumar/index.php/institucional/programa-sumar-mas-salud-publica.

Argentina. Ministerio de Salud de la Nación. 2013. "Metas Sanitarias (o Trazadoras): Programa Sumar." Accessed April 23, 2016. www.msal.gob.ar/sumar/index.php/ institucional/metas-sanitarias.

Argentina. Ministerio de Salud de la Nación, Plan Nacer. 2007. "Diseño y realización de la encuesta de condiciones de salud materno infantil de los pueblos originarios: Informe Final. Documento conteniendo el análisis de la información relevada durante la encuesta." Julio Aurelio Aresco Consultoría.

Argentina. Ministerio de Salud de la Nación, Plan Nacer . 2012a. "Evaluación de medio término del Plan Nacer APL II. Resultados identificados, acciones en curso y acciones previstas."

Argentina. Ministerio de Salud de la Nación, Plan Nacer. 2012b. "Memoria Anual: Programa Sumar 2012." www.msal.gov.ar/sumar/index.php/institucional/ programa-sumar-mas-salud-publica.

Argentina. Ministerio de Salud de la Nación, Plan Nacer. 2012c. "Reporte de Gestión del Plan Nacer." www.msal.gov.ar/sumar/.

Argentina. Ministerio de Salud de la Nación, Plan Nacer. 2015. *Plan Nacer. Datos de Cobertura por Mes y Provincia*. Estadísticas Oficiales.

Ministerio de Salud de la Nación. 2013. "El Plan Nacer y su efecto en la satisfacción de los usuarios de los sistemas de salud provinciales." www.msal.gob.ar/sumar/ images/stories/pdf/el-plan-nacer-y-su-efecto-en-la-satisfaccion-de-los-usuarios-de-lossistemas-de-salud-provinciales.pdf.

Argentina. Ministerio del Interior de la Nación. 2011. *Producto Bruto Geográfico (en miles de pesos) por Provincia*. Estadísticas Oficiales.

Argentina. Presidencia de la Nación. 2011. "Decreto 446/2011. Asignación por Embarazo para Protección Social."

Armingeon, Klaus, Fabio Bertozzi, and Giuliano Bonoli. 2004. "Swiss Worlds of Welfare." *West European Politics* 27 (1): 20–44.

Arza, Camila. 2009. "Back to the State: Pension Fund Nationalization in Argentina." UNRISD Social and Political Dimensions of the Global Crisis: Implications for Developing Countries. Geneva 12–13 November.

2016. "All children equal? Between expansion and segmentation in social policies for early childhood in Argentina." Paper prepared for the RC19 Symposium, August 25–27, San Jose, Costa Rica.

Atkeson, Lonna Rae and Cherie Maestas. 2012. *Catastrophic Politics: How Extraordinary Events Redefine Perceptions of Government*. New York, NY: Cambridge University Press.

Auditoría General de la Nación. 2008. "Informe de auditoría de gestión sobre el Plan Nacer: Convenio de préstamo BIRF No 7409-AR y 7225-AR."

Baddini Curralero, Cláudia. 2012. "O enfrentamento da pobreza como desafio para as políticas sociais no Brasil: Uma análise a partir do Programa Bolsa Família." Ph.D Dissertation, Instituto de Economia, Universidade Estadual de Campinas.

Baddini Curralero, Cláudia, Ana da Silva, Daniel Ximenes, Ana Vasconcellos, Kelva Carvalho Aquino, Kathleen Souza Oliveira, Ana Carolina Feldenheimer da Silva, Fernandes Nilson, and Eduardo Augusto. 2010. "As Condicionalidades do Programa Bolsa Família." In Abrahão de Castro and Modesto Lúcia 2010, 151–78.

Baez, Javier E., Adriana Camacho, Emily Conover, and Román A. Zárate. 2012. "Conditional Cash Transfers, Political Participation, and Voting Behavior." *The World Bank Policy Research Working Paper* 6215.

Baiocchi, Gianpaolo. 2005. *Militants and Citizens: The Politics of Participatory Democracy in Porto Alegre*. Stanford, CA: Stanford University Press.

Bandeira Coêlho, Denilson. 2012. "Brazil Basic Income: A New Model of Innovation Diffusion." In *Basic Income Worldwide: Horizons of Reform*, edited by Matthew N. Murray and Carole Pateman. International political economy series. New York, NY: Palgrave Macmillan.

Barrilleaux, Charles and Carlisle Rainey. 2014. "The Politics of Need: Examining Governors' Decisions to Oppose the 'Obamacare' Medicaid Expansion." *State Politics & Policy Quarterly* 14 (4): 437–60.

Basualdo, Eduardo. 2010. "La Asignación Universal por Hijo a un año de su implementación." Centro de Investigación y Formación de la República Argentina (CIFRA) *Documento de Trabajo 7*.

Battaglini, Monica and Olivier Giraud. 2003. "Policy Styles and the Swiss Executive Federalism: Comparing Diverging Styles of Cantonal Implementation of the Federal Law on Unemployment." *Swiss Political Science Review* 9 (1): 285–308.

Bechtel, Michael M. and Jens Hainmueller. 2011. "How Lasting Is Voter Gratitude? An Analysis of the Short- and Long-Term Electoral Returns to Beneficial Policy." *American Journal of Political Science* 55 (4): 852–68.

Beck, Nathaniel and Jonathan N. Katz. 1995. "What to Do (and Not to Do) with Time-Series Cross-Section Data." *American Political Science Review* 89 (3): 634–47.

Behrend, Jacqueline. 2011. "The Unevenness of Democracy at the Subnational Level: Provincial Closed Games in Argentina." *Latin American Research Review* 46 (1): 150–76.

Behrman, Jere R. and Susan Wendy Parker. 2010. "The Impacts of Conditional Cash Transfers Programs on Education." In *Conditional Cash Transfers in Latin America*, edited by Michelle Adato and John Hoddinott, 191–211. Baltimore: The John Hopkins University Press.

Bertranou, Fabio. 2010. *Aportes para la construcción de un piso de protección social en Argentina: El caso de las asignaciones familiares*. Buenos Aires: OIT.

Bertranou, Fabio and Roxana Maurizio. 2012. "Monetary Transfers for Children and Adolescents in Argentina: Characteristics and Coverage of a 'System' with Three Components." Research Brief. International Policy Centre for Inclusive Growth 30.

Bither-Terry, Russell. 2013. "Zero Hunger: The Politics of Anti-Hunger Policy in Brazil." Ph.D Dissertation, Political Science Department, University of North Carolina, Chapel Hill.

Bonvecchi, Alejandro. 2008. "Políticas sociales subnacionales en países federales: Argentina en perspectiva comparada." *Desarrollo Económico* 48 (190/191): 307–39.

Borges, André. 2007. "Rethinking State Politics: The Withering of State Dominant Machines in Brazil." *Brazilian Political Science Review* 1 (2): 108–36.
   2016. "Subnational Hybrid Regimes and Democratization in Brazil: Why Party Nationalization Matters." In *Illiberal Practices: Territorial Variance within Large Federal Democracies*, edited by Jacqueline Behrend and Laurence Whitehead, 162–96. Baltimore: Johns Hopkins University Press.

Botão, Alexandre. 2002. "Combate à fome: Com ajuda dos tucanos." *Correio Braziliense*, December 25, 2002.

Brasil. Departamento de Atenção Básica da Secretaria de Atenção à Saúde. "Historico Cobertura." Accessed 2015. http://dab.saude.gov.br/portaldab/historico_cobertura_sf.php.

Brasul. Congreso Nacional. "Lei 8742 and 12435, Lei Orgânia da Assistência Social (LOAS)." 1993, 2011. www.planalto.gov.br/ccivil_03/_Ato2011-2014/2011/Lei/L12435.

Brasil. Instituto Brasileiro de Geografia e Estatística. "Populacao e Territorio." www.sidra.ibge.gov.br; www.ibge.gov.br/home/geociencias/areaterritorial/principal.shtm.

Brasil. Ministério da Saúde. 2009. "Monitoramento da qualidade do emprego na Estratégia Saúde da Família." *Secretaria de Gestão do Trabalho e da Educação na Saúde – Relatório Preliminar*.

Brasil. Ministério da Saúde, and Fundação Oswaldo Cruz. 2005. "Saúde da Família: avaliação da implementação em dez grandes centros urbanos: Síntese dos principais resultados." *Projetos, Programas e Relatórios* Série C.

Brasil. Ministério do Desenvolvimento Social e Combate à Fome, Secretaria Nacional de Assistência Social. 2005. "Norma Operacional Básica NOB/SUAS."

Brasil. Ministério da Saúde, Datasus. 2009. "Indicadores de recursos: Gasto do Ministério da Saúde com atenção à saúde como proporção do gasto total do Ministério da Saúde." Accessed February 20, 2014. http://tabnet.datasus.gov.br/cgi/idb2009/e20.htm.

Brasil. Ministério da Saúde, Departamento de Atenção Básica. 2004. "Avaliação normativa do programa saúde da família no Brasil: Monitoramento da implantação e funcionamento das equipes de saúde da família 2001–2002." *Série C. Projetos, Programas e Relatórios*.

2005. "Evaluation for Quality Improvement of the Family Health Strategy." *Textos Básicos de Saúde* Série B.

2006. "Saúde da Família no Brasil: Uma análise de indicadores selecionados 1998–2004." *Série C. Projetos, Programas e Relatórios*.

2011. "Sistema de Nota Técnica do DAB." Accessed June 29, 2016. http://dab2.saude.gov.br/sistemas/notatecnica/frmListaMunic.php.

2011. "Programa de Melhoria do Acesso e da Qualidade na Atenção Básica (PMAQ)." Accessed June 29, 2016. http://dab.saude.gov.br/portaldab/cidadao_pmaq2.php.

Ministério da Saúde, DATASUS. 2015. "Produto Interno Bruto per capita." http://tabnet.datasus.gov.br/cgi/tabcgi.exe?ibge/cnv/pibmunuf.def.

Brasil. Ministério do Desenvolvimento Social e Combate à Fome. 2006. *Material elaborado a partir do Prêmio de Práticas Inovadoras na Gestão do Programa Bolsa Família*. Brasília.

2008. "Financiamento da Assistência Social no Brasil." *Caderno SUAS* 3 (2).

2011. "Informações sobre Pactuações." Dados Oficiais.

2012a. "Bolsa Família." Accessed January 23, 2012. www.mds.gov.br/bolsafamilia.

2012b. "Bolsa Família Program." Accessed September 16, 2012. www.ipc-undp.org/doc_africa _brazil/6.SENARC_Overview_PBF.pdf.

2012c. "Matriz de Informação Social." http://aplicacoes.mds.gov.br/sagi/mi2007/tabelas/mi_social.php.

Brasil. Presidência da República, Casa Civil. "Decreto 5209." 2004. www.planalto.gov.br/ccivil_03/_ato2004-2006/2004/decreto/d5209.htm.

1993. "Lei 8742." Lei Orgânica Da Assistência Social.

2004. "Lei 10836: Crie o Programa Bolsa Família e dê Outras Providências." www.planalto.gov.br/ccivil_03/_ato2004-2006/2004/lei/l10.836.htm.

Brasil. Secretaria de Avaliação e Gestão da Informação do Ministerio do Desenvolvimento Social e Combate á Fome. "Matriz de Informação Social." Accessed 2015. http://aplicacoes.mds.gov.br/sagi/mi2007/tabelas/mi_social.php.

Brasil. Secretaria Nacional de Assistência Social, Departamento de Benefícios. 2012. "Pactuações Para Complementação Financeira do PBF."

Brasil. Secretaria Nacional de Renda de Cidadanía. 2012. "Apresentação. Integração de Programas de Transferência de Renda – Pactuação."

Brookes, Marissa. 2015. Evaluating Causal Mechanisms in Mixed-Methods Research. Paper prepared for the First Southwest Workshop on Mixed-Methods Research, 12–13 November 2015, Albuquerque.

Brown, David S. and Wendy Hunter. 1999. "Democracy and Social Spending in Latin America, 1980–92." *The American Political Science Review* 93 (4): 779–90.

Bueno, Natália. 2018. "Bypassing the Enemy. Distributive Politics, Credit Claiming, and Non-State Organizations in Brazil" Comparative Political Studies 51 (3): 304–340.

Bui, Quoctrung and Margot Sanger-Katz. 2015. "We Mapped the Uninsured. You'll Notice a Pattern: They Tend to Live in the South, and They Tend to Be Poor." *The New York Times*, October 30.

Burki, Shahid Javed, Guillermo Perry, and William Dillinger. 1999. *Beyond the Center: Decentralizing the State.* Washington, DC: World Bank.

Calvo, Ernesto and Marcelo Escolar. 2005. *La nueva política de partidos en la Argentina: Crisis política, realineamientos partidarios y reforma electoral.* Buenos Aires: Prometeo.

Calvo, Ernesto and Maria Victoria Murillo. 2012. "When Parties Meet Voters: Assessing Political Linkages Through Partisan Networks and Distributive Expectations in Argentina and Chile." *Comparative Political Studies* 46 (7): 851–82.

2014. "Partisan Linkages and Social Policy Delivery in Argentina and Chile." In *Clientelism, Social Policy, and the Quality of Democracy,* edited by Diego Abente Brun and Larry J. Diamond, 17–38. Baltimore, MD: The Johns Hopkins University Press.

Cammett, Melani Claire and Lauren M. MacLean. 2014. "The Political Consequences of Non-State Social Welfare: An Analytic Framework." In *The Politics of Non-State Social Welfare,* edited by Melani C. Cammett and Lauren M. MacLean, 31–53. Ithaca: Cornell University Press.

Campbell, Andrea and Kimberly J. Morgan. 2005. "Federalism and the Politics of Old-Age Care in Germany and the United States." *Comparative Political Studies* 38 (8): 887–914.

Campbell, James. 1986. "Presidential Coattails and Midterm Losses in State Legislative Elections." *The American Political Science Review* 80 (1): 45–63.

Campos, Luis, Eleonor Faur, and Laura Pautassi. 2007. *Plan Jefes y Jefas: ¿Derecho social o beneficio sin derechos?* Buenos Aires: Centro de Estudios Legales y Sociales (CELS).

Canoas Secretaria Municipal de Desenvolvimento Social. 2009. *Gestão 2009–2012. Plano de Ações.*

Carmines, Edward G. and James A. Stimson. 1980. "The Two Faces of Issue Voting." *American Political Science Review* 74 (1): 78–91.

Carsey, Thomas M. and Gerald C. Wright. 1998. "State and National Factors in Gubernatorial and Senatorial Elections." *American Journal of Political Science* 42 (3): 994–1002.

Castele, Nick. 2017. "Meet the Republican Governors Who Don't Want to Repeal All of Obamacare." *National Public Radio (NPR)*, January 23. www.npr.org/2017/01/23/510823789/meet-the-republican-governors-who-dont-want-to-repeal-all-of-obamacare.

Cauchi, Richard. 2016. "State Laws and Actions Challenging Certain Health Reforms." Accessed June 24, 2016. www.ncsl.org/research/health/state-laws-and-actions-challenging-ppaca.aspx.

CEPAL. 2013. "Programas de transferencias condicionadas: Asignación Universal por Hijo para Protección Social (2009-)." Base de datos de programas de protección social no contributiva en América Latina y el Caribe. Accessed July 10, 2013. http://dds.cepal.org/bdptc/programa/?id=33.

Chapman Osterkatz, Sandra. 2013. "Commitment, Capacity, and Community: The Politics of Multilevel Health Reform in Spain and Brazil." Dissertation, Political Science, University of North Carolina, Chapel Hill.

Charbit, Claire. 2011. "Governance of Public Policies in Decentralised Contexts: The Multi-level Approach." *OECD Regional Development Working Papers* 4.

Chavez, Rebecca Bill. 2003. "The Construction of the Rule of Law in Argentina: A Tale of Two Provinces." *Comparative Politics* 35 (4): 417–37.

Cherny, Nicolás, Carlos Freytes, Sara Niedzwiecki, and Gerardo Scherlis. 2015. "Base de Datos de Alineación Política Subnacional, Argentina 2003–2015." Instituto de Investigaciones Gino Germani, Universidad de Buenos Aires. Available at: www.saraniedzwiecki.com

Chhibber, Pradeep K. and Ken Kollman. 2004. *The Formation of National Party Systems: Federalism and Party Competition in Canada, Great Britain, India, and the United States.* Princeton, NJ: Princeton University Press.

Chiara, Magdalena and Mercedes Di Virgilio. 2005. "La política social en la crisis de la convertibilidad (1997–2001): Mirando la gestión desde las coordenadas municipales en el Gran Buenos Aires." In Andrenacci 2005, *Problemas de política social en la Argentina contemporánea.* Buenos Aires: Prometeo, 125–56.

Chuahy, Carolina. 2002. "Maguito admite que manteria programa." *O Popular,* May 17.

Cidades do Brasil. 2002. "Família Cidadã: Programa do governo do Rio Grande do Sul soma o assistencialismo à qualificação profissional." Cidades do Brasil, 28 January 2002.

Collier, Ruth B. and David Collier. 1991. *Shaping the Political Arena: Critical Junctures, the Labor Movement, and Regime Dynamics in Latin America.* Notre Dame, IN: University of Notre Dame Press.

Coppedge, Michael. 1997. *A Classification of Latin American Political Parties.* Notre Dame, IN: The Helen Kellogg Institute for International Studies.

  1998. "The Dynamic Diversity of Latin American Party Systems." *Party Politics* 4 (4): 547–68.

Cornelius, Wayne A. 1999. "Subnational Politics and Democratization: Tensions Between Center and Periphery in the Mexican Political System." In Cornelius, Eisenstadt, and Hindley 1999, *Subnational Politics and Democratization in Mexico.* La Jolla: Center for U.S.-Mexican Studies, University of California, San Diego 3–16.

Corrêa, Diego Sanches and José Antonio Cheibub. 2016. "The Anti-Incumbent Effects of Conditional Cash Transfer Programs." *Latin American Politics and Society* 58 (1): 49–71.

Côrtes, Soraya Vargas, ed. 2009. *Participação e saúde no Brasil.* Rio de Janeiro: Fiocruz.

Côrtes, Soraya Vargas, Marcelo Kunrath Silva, Janete Cardoso Réos, and Márcio Barcelos. 2009. "Conselho Nacional de Saúde: Histórico, papel institucional e atores estatais e societais." In Côrtes 2009, 41–71.

Cortez, Rafael, Daniela Romero, Vanina Camporeale, and Luis Perez. 2012. "Results-Based Financing for Health in Argentina: The Plan Nacer Program." *Health, Nutrition, and Population Family of the World Bank's Human Development Network*. Washington, DC: The World Bank.

Cotta, Tereza Cristina and Luis Henrique Paiva. 2010. "O Programa Bolsa Família e a proteção social no Brasil." In Abrahão de Castro and Modesto Lúcia 2010, 57–99.

Cruces, Guillermo, Nicolás Epele, and Laura Guardia. 2008. "Los programas sociales y los objetivos de desarrollo del Milenio en Argentina." *CEPAL, Serie Políticas Sociales* 142.

Cruz Saco, María Amparo, and Carmelo Mesa-Lago, eds. 1998. *Do Options Exist? : the Reform of Pension and Health Care Systems in Latin America*. Pittsburgh, PA: University of Pittsburgh Press.

Cyr, Jennifer M. 2017. *The Fates of Political Parties. Crisis, Continuity, and Change in Latin America*. Cambridge: Cambridge University Press.

Da Silva, Eberta. 2011. "Da planta a obra final: O serviço social contribuindo no processo de participação de famílias nos cursos de profissionalização." B.A Thesis, Faculdade de Serviço Social, Pontifícia Universidade Católica do Rio Grande do Sul.

Da Silva e Silva, Maria Ozanira, and Valéria Ferreira Santos de Almada Lima. 2010. *Avaliando o Bolsa Família: Unficação, focalização e impactos*. São Paulo: Cortez Editora.

De La O, Ana Lorena. 2013. "Do Conditional Cash Transfers Affect Electoral Behavior? Evidence from a Randomized Experiment in Mexico." *American Journal of Political Science* 57 (1): 1–14.

  2015. *Crafting Policies to End Poverty in Latin America: The Quiet Transformation*. New York, NY: Cambridge University Press.

Deloitte and Anses. 2010. Investigación Cuantitativa Externa. Asignación Universal por Hijo.

Derthick, Martha. 1972. *New Towns in-Town: Why a Federal Program Failed*. Washington, DC: Urban Institute.

  2001. *Keeping the Compound Republic: Essays on American Federalism*. Washington, DC: Brookings Institution Press.

Dew, Brian and Dean Baker. 2017. "The Collapse of Obamacare: Big Problem in Republican States." http://cepr.net/blogs/cepr-blog/the-collapse-of-obamacare-big-problem-in-republican-states.

Dias Bezerra, Heloísa, Denise Paiva Ferreira, and Pedro Floriano Ribeiro. 2011. "Crônica de uma vitória anunciada: A reeleição de Íris Rezende em Goiânia." In *Como o eleitor escolhe seu prefeito: Campanha e voto nas eleições municipais*, edited by Lavareda, Antonioç and Telles, Helcimara. Rio de Janeiro: Fundação Getúlio Vargas.

Diaz-Cayeros, Alberto. 2004. "Do Federal Institutions Matter? Rules and Political Practices in Regional Resource Allocation in Mexico." In *Federalism and Democracy in Latin America*, edited by Edward L. Gibson. Baltimore, London: The John Hopkins University Press.

Diaz-Cayeros, Alberto and Beatriz Magaloni. 2010. "Saving Lives: The Design of Social Programs and Infant Mortality Rates in Mexico." Paper presented at "Better Governance for Better Health" Stanford University, April 26-27. Available online at: iis-db.stanford.edu/docs/458/IMRPublicHealthStanford.pdf

Dirección de Estadísticas e Investigaciones Económicas de Mendoza. 2011. "Miembros de hogares beneficiarios de programas sociales del Ministerio de Desarrollo Humano, Familia y Comunidad."

Do Nascimento, Vânia and Ieda Da Costa. 2009. "PSF, descentralização e organização de serviços de saúde no Brasil." In Cohn 2009, *Saúde da família e SUS. Convergências e dissonâncias*. Rio de Janeiro: Beco do Azougue, 67–92.

Dualibi, Julia. 2009. "PSDB resiste a modelo do Bolsa-Família. Tucanos apostam em projetos sociais, mas fogem do repasse de dinheiro à população de baixa renda." *Estadão*, November 22. www.estadao.com.br/noticias/impresso,psdb-resiste-a-modelo-do-bolsa-familia,470187,0.htm.

Eaton, Kent. 2004. *Politics Beyond the Capital: The Design of Subnational Institutions in South America*. Stanford, CA: Stanford University Press.

2012. "The State of the State in Latin America: Challenges, Challengers, Responses and Deficits." *Revista de Ciencia Política* 32 (3): 643–57.

2017. *Territory and Ideology in Latin America: Policy Conflicts between National and Subnational Governments*. Oxford: Oxford University Press.

Elazar, Daniel. 1987. *Exploring Federalism*. Tuscaloosa, AL: University of Alabama Press.

Esping-Andersen, Gøsta. 1990. *The Three Worlds of Welfare Capitalism*. Princeton NJ: Princeton University Press.

Estado de Goiás. 2010. *Programa Renda Cidadã. Histórico*. Dados Oficiais.

Evans, Peter. 1995. *Embedded Autonomy: States and Industrial Transformation*. Princeton, NJ: Princeton University Press.

1996. "Government Action, Social Capital and Development: Reviewing the Evidence on Synergy." *World Development* 24 (6): 1119–32.

Evans, Peter and Patrick Heller. 2015. "Human Development, State Transformation, and the Politics of the Developmental State." In Leibfried, Nullmeier, Huber, Lange, Levy, and Stephens 2015, *The Oxford Handbook of Transformations of the State*. Oxford: Oxford University Press, 691–713.

Evans, Peter; Huber, Evelyne; Stephens, John D. 2017. "The Political Foundations of State Effectiveness." In Centeno, Kohli, Yashar (Eds.): *States in the Developing World*. Cambridge: Cambridge University Press, 380–408.

Falleti, Tulia G. 2004. "Federalism and Decentralization in Argentina: Historical Background and New Intergovernmental Relations." In Tulchin and Selee 2004 *Decentralization and Democratic Governance in Latin America*. Washington: Woodrow Wilson International Center for Scholars Latin American Program.

2010a. *Decentralization and Subnational Politics in Latin America*. New York, NY: Cambridge University Press.

2010b. "Infiltrating the State: The Evolution of Health Care Reforms in Brazil, 1964–1988." In *Explaining Institutional Change: Ambiguity, Agency, and Power*, edited by James Mahoney and Kathleen A. Thelen, 38–62. New York, NY: Cambridge University Press.

Faria, Mary Nise. 2005. "Políticas sociais em Goiás. Os programas Cesta Básica de Alimentos e Renda Mínima." Masters Thesis, Faculdade de Ciências Humanas e Filosofía, Universidade Federal de Goiás.

Fenwick, Tracy. 2009. "Avoiding Governors: The Success of Bolsa Familia." *Latin American Research Review* 44 (1): 102–31.

2016. *Avoiding Governors: Federalism, Democracy, and Poverty Alleviation in Brazil and Argentina*. Notre Dame, IN: University of Notre Dame Press.

Ferla, Alcindo Antônio, Doris Yadota de Souza, Maria Elisa Mello de Freitas, Maria Letícia Machry de Pelegrini, and Valeska Holst Antunes. 2002. "Regionalização da atenção à saúde na esperiência de gestão estadual do SUS no Rio Grande do Sul." In *O Fazer em Saúde Coletiva: Inovações da atenção à saúde no Rio Grande do Sul*, edited by Alcindo A. Ferla and Sales Fagundes, Sandra Maria, 13–29. Porto Alegre: Dacasa.

Fernandez, Manny. 2012. "Perry Declares Texas' Rejection of Health Care Law 'Intrusions'." *The New York Times*, July 9. Accessed March 02, 2014. www .nytimes.com/2012/07/10/us/politics/perry-says-texas-rejects-health-law-intrusions .html.

Filgueira, Fernando. 2007. "Latin American Social States: Critical Junctures and Critical Choices." In *Democracy and Social Policy*, edited by Yusuf Bangura. Basingstoke: Palgrave Macmillan.

Filgueira, Fernando, Carlos Molina, Jorge Papadopulos, and Federico Tobar. 2005. *Universalismo Básico. Una alternativa posible y necesaria para mejorar las condiciones de vida en América Latina*. Washington, DC: BID.

Filippov, Mikhail, Peter C. Ordeshook, and Olga Shvetsova. 2004. *Designing Federalism: A Theory of Self-sustainable Federal Institutions*. New York, NY: Cambridge University Press.

Filmer, Deon and Norbert Schady. 2011. "Does More Cash in Conditional Cash Transfer Programs Always Lead to Larger Impacts on School Attendance?" *Journal of Development Economics* 96 (1): 150–57.

Fiszbein, Ariel and Norbert Schady. 2009. "Conditional Cash Transfers: Reducing Present and Future Poverty." *A World Bank policy research report*. Washington DC. World Bank.

Freytes, Carlos and Sara Niedzwiecki. 2016. "A Turning Point in Argentine Politics: Demands for Change and Territorial Cleavages in the 2015 Presidential Election." *Regional & Federal Studies* 26 (3): 381–94.

Garay, Candelaria. 2017. *Social Policy Expansion in Latin America*. New York, NY: Cambridge University Press.

Garfield, Rachel. 2016. "The Coverage Gap: Uninsured Poor Adults in States that Do Not Expand Medicaid – An Update." Accessed June 24, 2016. http://kff.org/health-reform/issue-brief/the-coverage-gap-uninsured-poor-adults-in-states-that-do-not-expand-medicaid-an-update/.

Garganta, Santiago. 2011. "Asignación Universal por Hijo: Impacto sobre la formalidad laboral." Masters, Economía, Universidad Nacional de La Plata.

Garman, Christopher, Stephan Haggard, and Eliza Willis. 2001. "Fiscal Decentralization: A Political Theory with Latin American Cases." *World Politics* 53 (2): 205–36.

Gélineau, Francois and Karen L. Remmer. 2006. "Political Decentralization and Electoral Accountability: The Argentine Experience, 1983–2001." *British Journal of Political Science* 36 (01): 133–57.

George, Alexander L., and Andrew Bennett. 2005. *Case Studies and Theory Development in the Social Sciences.* Cambridge, MA: MIT Press.

Gerring, John. 2007. *Case Study Research: Principles and Practices.* New York: Cambridge University Press.

Gervasoni, Carlos. 2010a. "A Rentier Theory of Subnational Regimes: Fiscal Federalism, Democracy, and Authoritarianism in the Argentine Provinces." *World Politics* 62 (02): 302.

2010b. "Measuring Variance in Subnational Regimes: Results from an Expert-Based Operationalization of Democracy in the Argentine Provinces." *Journal of Politics in Latin America* 2 (2): 13–52.

Gibson, Christopher L. 2016. "Sanitaristas, Petistas, and the Post-Neoliberal Public Health State in Porto Alegre." *Latin American Perspectives* 43 (2): 153–71.

Gibson, Edward L. 2012. *Boundary Control: Subnational Authoritarianism in Federal Democracies.* New York, NY: Cambridge University Press.

Giovanella, Ligia, Maria Helena Magalhães de Mendonça, Patty Fidelis de Almeida, Sarah Escorel, Mônica Maia Senna, Márcia Cristina Rodrigues Fausto, Mônica Mendonça Delgado. 2009. "Saúde da família: Limites e possibilidades para uma abordagem integral de atenção primária à saúde no Brasil." *Ciência & Saúde Coletiva* 14 (3): 183–794.

Giraudy, Agustina. 2007. "The Distributive Politics of Emergency Employment Programs in Argentina (1993–2002)." *Latin American Research Review* 42 (2): 33–55.

2009. "Subnational Undemocratic Regime Continuity After Democratization: Argentina and Mexico in Comparative Perspective." PhD Dissertation, University of North Carolina at Chapel Hill.

2013. "Varieties of Subnational Undemocratic Regimes: Evidence from Argentina and Mexico." *Studies in Comparative International Development* 48 (1): 51–80.

2014. *Democrats and Autocrats: Pathways of Subnational Undemocratic Regime Continuity Within Democratic Countries.* Oxford. Oxford University Press.

Giraudy, Agustina, Eduardo Moncada, and Richard Snyder. Forthcoming. "Subnational Research in Comparative Politics: Achievements and Future Directions." In *Inside Countries: Subnational Research in Comparative Politics*, edited by Agustina Giraudy, Eduardo Moncada, and Richard Snyder. New York, NYÑ Cambridge University Press.

Giraudy, Agustina and Jennifer Pribble. 2018. "Rethinking Measures of Democracy and Welfare State Universalism. Lessons from Subnational Research" *Regional & Federal Studies*.

Goertz, Gary. 2017. *Multimethod Research, Causal Mechanisms, and Case Studies. An Integrated Approach.* New Jersey: Princeton University Press.

Goertz, Gary, and James Mahoney. 2012. *A Tale of Two Cultures: Qualitative and Quantitative Research in the Social Sciences.* Princeton: Princeton University Press.

Goldar, María Rosa. 2012. "Impacto e implicancias de la Asignación Universal por Hijo en políticas públicas provincial y municipales en Mendoza: Propuestas a futuro." Informe Final. *Asociación Ecuménica de Cuyo, Mendoza.*

González, Lucas I. 2016. *Presidents, Governors, and the Struggles over the Distribution of Power: Primus contra Pares in Argentina and Brazil*. Routledge studies in federalism and decentralization. New York, NY: Routledge.

Goodnough, Abby. 2013. "Colorado Presses for Uninsured to Enroll." *The New York Times*, August 2. www.nytimes.com/2013/08/03/us/colorado-presses-for-uninsured-to-enroll.html.

Goodnough, Abby and Reed Abelson. 2017. "Affordable Care Act: A Tale of Two States." *The New York Times*, 2017. https://mobile.nytimes.com/2017/04/21/health/how-gop-in-2-states-coaxed-the-health-law-to-success-or-crisis.html.

Gormley, William T. 2006. "Money and Mandates: The Politics of Intergovernmental Conflict." *Publius: The Journal of Federalism* 36 (4): 523–40.

Goulart, Flavio Andrade. 2002. "Experiências em saúde da família: Cada caso é um caso?" Doctoral Dissertation, Escola Nacional de Saúde Pública, Fundação Oswaldo Cruz.

Governo de Goiás, Secretaria de Estado da Saúde. 2011. "Mapa da saúde municipal segundo percepção dos secretários municipais da saúde." www.saude.go.gov.br/templates/superintendencia/splangeo/mapa_saude/mapa-saude.

Grogan, Colleen M. 1999. "The Influence of Federal Mandates on State Medicaid and AFDC Decision-Making." *Publius: The Journal of Federalism* 29 (3): 1–30.

Haeder, Simon F. and David L. Weimer. 2013. "You Can't Make Me Do It: State Implementation of Insurance Exchanges Under the Affordable Care Act." *Public Administration Review* 73 (s1): S34–S47.

    2015. "You Can't Make Me Do It, but I Could Be Persuaded: A Federalism Perspective on the Affordable Care Act." *Journal of Health Politics, Policy and Law* 40 (2): 281–323.

Haggard, Stephan and Robert R. Kaufman. 2008. *Development, Democracy, and Welfare States: Latin America, East Asia, and Eastern Europe*. Princeton: Princeton University Press.

Hagopian, Frances, Carlos Gervasoni, and Juan Andres Moraes. 2008. "From Patronage to Program: The Emergence of Party-Oriented Legislators in Brazil." *Comparative Political Studies* 42 (3): 360–91.

Ham, Andrés. 2014. "The Impact of Conditional Cash Transfers on Educational Inequality of Opportunity." *Latin American Research Review* 49 (3): 153–75.

Handa, Sudhanshu and Benjamin Davis. 2006. "The Experience of Conditional Cash Transfers in Latin Ameria and the Caribbean." *Development Policy Review* 24 (5): 513–36.

Handlin, Samuel and Ruth Collier. 2011. "The Diversity of Left Party Linkages and Competitive Advantages." Levitsky, Steven and Kenneth Roberts. (Eds.) 2011. *The Resurgence of the Latin American Left*. Baltimore: Johns Hopkins University Press.

Harbers, Imke. 2015. "Taxation and the Unequal Reach of the State: Mapping State Capacity in Ecuador." *Governance* 28 (3): 373–91.

Harding, Robin. 2015. "Attribution and Accountability: Voting for Roads in Ghana." *World Politics* 67 (04): 656–89.

Harguindéguy, Jean-Baptiste. 2015. "Les régions espagnoles face aux mesures d'austérité de l'Etat central. Convergence ou divergence?" Prepared for delivery at 2015 European Consortium for Political Research Conference, Section on Comparative Territorial Politics, August 26–29, Montreal, Canada.

Herbst, Jeffrey Ira. 2000. *States and Power in Africa: Comparative Lessons in Authority and Control*. Princeton studies in international history and politics. Princeton, NJ: Princeton University Press.

Hertel-Fernandez, Alexander, Theda Skocpol, and Daniel Lynch. 2016. "Business Associations, Conservative Networks, and the Ongoing Republican War over Medicaid Expansion." *Journal of Health Politics, Policy and Law* 41 (2): 239–86.

Holbrook-Provow, Thomas M. 1987. "National Factors in Gubernatorial Elections." *American Politics Quarterly* 15 (4): 471–83.

Hooghe, Liesbet and Gary Marks. 2003. "Unraveling the Central State, but How? Types of Multi-level Governance." *American Political Science Review* 97 (2): 233–43.

Hooghe, Liesbet, Gary Marks, and Arjan Schakel. 2010. *The Rise of Regional Authority: A Comparative Study of 42 Democracies*. New York: Routledge.

Hooghe, Liesbet, Gary Marks, Arjan Schakel, Sara Niedzwiecki, Sandra Chapman Osterkatz, and Sarah Shair-Rosenfield. 2016. *Measuring Regional Authority: A Postfunctionalist Theory of Governance, Volume I*. Oxford: Oxford University Press.

Huber, Evelyne. 1995. "Assessments of State Strength." In *Latin America in Comparative Perspective: New Approaches to Methods and Analysis*, edited by Peter Smith and Peter H. Smith, 163–93. Boulder: Westview Press.

  1996. "Options for Social Policy in Latin America: Neoliberal Versus Social Democratic Models." In *Welfare States in Transition: National Adaptations in Global Economies*, edited by Gøsta Esping-Andersen, 141–91. London, Thousand Oaks, CA: SAGE.

Huber, Evelyne, Thomas Mustillo, and John D. Stephens. 2008. "Politics and Social Spending in Latin America." *The Journal of Politics* 70 (2): 420–36.

Huber, Evelyne and Sara Niedzwiecki. 2015. "Emerging Welfare States in Latin America and East Asia." In Leibfried, Nullmeier, Huber, Lange, Levy, and Stephens 2015, 796–812.

Huber, Evelyne and John D. Stephens. 2001. *Development and Crisis of the Welfare State: Parties and Policies in Global Markets*. Chicago: University of Chicago Press.

  2010. "Successful Social Policy Regimes? Political Economy, Politics, and Social Policy in Argentina, Chile, Uruguay and Costa Rica." In *Democratic Governance in Latin America*, edited by Scott Mainwaring and Timothy R. Scully, 155–210. Stanford, CA: Stanford University Press.

  2012. *Democracy and the Left: Social Policy and Inequality in Latin America*. Chicago: The University of Chicago Press.

Hume, David. 1975 [1777]. *Enquiries concerning Human Understanding, and Concerning the Principles of Morals*. Oxford: Oxford University Press.

Hunter, Wendy. 2010. *The Transformation of the Workers' Party in Brazil, 1989–2009*: New York, NY: Cambridge University Press.

Hunter, Wendy and Robert Brill. 2016. "'Documents, Please': Advances in Social Protection and Birth Certification in the Developing World." *World Politics* 68 (02): 191–228.

Hunter, Wendy and Timothy Power. 2007. "Rewarding Lula: Executive Power, Social Policy, and the Brazilian Elections of 2006." *Latin American Politics & Society* 49 (1): 1–30.

International Labour Organization. 2016. "Share of informal employment by sex, rural/urban, agriculture/non-agriculture (%)." Accessed March 17, 2016.

Iyengar, Shanto. 1989. "How Citizens Think About National Issues: A Matter of Responsibility." *American Journal of Political Science* 33 (4): 878–900.

Jacobs, Lawrence R. and Theda Skocpol. 2010. *Health Care Reform and American Politics: What Everyone Needs to Know.* New York: Oxford University Press.

Jones, David, Katharine W. V. Bradley, and Jonathan Oberlander. 2014. "Pascal's Wager: Health Insurance Exchanges, Obamacare, and the Republican Dilemma." *Journal of Health Politics, Policy and Law* 39 (1): 97–137.

Jones, Hayley. 2016. "More Education, Better Jobs? A Critical Review of CCTs and Brazil's Bolsa Família Programme for Long-Term Poverty Reduction." *Social Policy & Society* 15 (03): 465–78.

Jones, Mark P. and Scott Mainwaring. 2003. "The Nationalization of Parties and Party Systems: An Empirical Measure and an Application to the Americas." *Party Politics* 9 (2): 139–66.

Jones, Mark P., Sebastián Saiegh, Pablo Spiller, and Mariano Tommasi. 2002. "Amateur Legislators – Professional Politicians: The Consequences of Party-Centered Electoral Rules in a Federal System." *American Journal of Political Science* 46 (3): 656–69.

Jones, Mark P., Pablo Sanguinetti, and Mariano Tommasi. 1999. "Politics, Institutions, and Public-Sector Spending in the Argentine Provinces." In *Fiscal Institutions and Fiscal Performance*, edited by James M. Poterba and Jürgen v. Hagen, 135–50. Chicago: University of Chicago Press.

Jost, Timothy. 2014. "Implementing Health Reform: Court Blocks Missouri Restrictions on ACA Navigators." Accessed March 25, 2014. http://healthaffairs .org/blog/2014/01/23/implementing-health-reform-court-blocks-missouri-restrictions-on-aca-navigators/.

Kaiser Family Foundation. 2015. "Being Low-Income and Uninsured in Missouri: Coverage Challenges During Year One of ACA Implementation." http://kff.org/ report-section/being-low-income-and-uninsured-in-missouri-introduction-8727/.

    2016a. "Implementation of the ACA in Kentucky: Lessons Learned to Date and the Potential Effects of Future Changes." Accessed June 23, 2016. http://kff.org/report-section/implementation-of-the-aca-in-kentucky-issue-brief/.

    2016b. "Kaiser Health Tracking Poll: January 2016." Accessed June 22, 2016. http:// kff.org/health-reform/poll-finding/kaiser-health-tracking-poll-january-2016/.

    2016c. "Survey of Non-Group Health Insurance Enrollees, Wave 3." Accessed June 23, 2016. http://kff.org/health-reform/poll-finding/survey-of-non-group-health-insurance-enrollees-wave-3/.

Kapiszewski, Diana, Lauren M. MacLean, and Benjamin Lelan Read. 2015. *Field Research in Political Sience: Practices and Principles.* Strategies for social inquiry. New York: Cambridge University Press.

Kay, Stephen J. 1999. "Unexpected Privatizations: Politics and Social Security Reform in the Southern Cone." *Comparative Politics* 31 (4): 403–22.

Keefer, Philip and Stuti Khemani. 2005. "Democracy, Public Expenditures, and the Poor: Understanding Political Incentives for Providing Public Services." *The World Bank Research Observer.* http://documents.worldbank.org/curated/en/ 182371468326383728/pdf/767480JRN0WBR0o0Box374387B00PUBLIC0..pdf.

King, Gary, Robert O. Keohane, and Sidney Verba. 1994. *Designing Social Inquiry: Scientific Inference in Qualitative Research.* Princeton, NJ: Princeton University Press.

Kingstone, Peter and Aldo Ponce. 2010. "From Cadoso to Lula: The Triumph of Pragmatism in Brazil." In *Leftist Governments in Latin America: Successes and Shortcomings*, edited by Wendy Hunter, Raúl L. Madrid, and Kurt G. Weyland. New York: Cambridge University Press.

Kitschelt, Herbert, Kirk A. Hawkins, Juan Pablo Luna, Guillermo Rosas, and Zechmeister Elizabeth J. 2010. *Latin American Party Systems*. New York, NY: Cambridge University Press.

Kitschelt, Herbert and Steven Wilkinson, eds. 2007. *Patrons, Clients, and Policies: Patterns of Democratic Accountability and Political Competition*. New York, NY: Cambridge University Press.

Kleider, Hanna. 2014. "Decentralization and the Welfare State: Territorial Disparities, Regional Governments and Political Parties." Ph.D Dissertation, Department of Political Science, University of North Carolina, Chapel Hill.

Kohli, Atul. 1987. *The State and Poverty in India: The Politics of Reform*. South Asian studies. New York, NY: Cambridge University Press.

Koivu, Kendra. 2016. "The Necessity of Sufficient Condition Counterfactuals: Combined counterfactuals analysis and the New History of World War I." *Manuscript*.

Korpi, Walter. 1989. "Power, Politics, and State Autonomy in the Development of Social Citizenship: Social Rights During Sickness in Eighteen OECD Countries Since 1930." *American Sociological Review* 54 (3): 309–28.

Krane, Dale. 2007. "The Middle Tier in American Federalism: State Government Policy Activism During the Bush Presidency." *Publius: The Journal of Federalism* 37 (3): 453–77.

Krause, Silvana. 2008. "Governadores na 'era PMDB' em Goiás (1982–1998): Hiperpresidencialismo regional." In *Panorama da política em Goiás*, edited by Denise Paiva Ferreira and Heloísa Dias Bezerra, 44–80. Goiânia: Editora da UCG.

Krause, Silvana and Pedro Paulo Alves Godoi. 2010. "Coaligações Eleitorais para os Executivos Estaduais (1986–2006). Padrões e Tendências." In Krause, Dantas, and Miguel 2010, 41–97.

Krause, Silvana, Humberto Dantas, and Luis Felipe Miguel, eds. 2010. *Coaligações Partidárias Na Nova Democracia Brasileira. Perfis E Tendências*. Rio de Janeiro, São Paulo: Ed. UNESP; Konrad-Adenauer-Stiftung.

El Diario de la República, San Luis. 2007. "Lanzan un proyecto que reforzará la atención primaria de la salud." February 15.

2009. "Aseguran que los médicos cobran como mínimo un sueldo de $4850: Lo confirmaron desde el Ministerio de Hacienda Pública." January 14.

Larcinese, Valentino, Leonizio Rizzo, and Cecilia Testa. 2006. "Allocating the US Federal Budget to the States: The Impact of the President." *The Journal of Politics* 68 (2): 447–56.

Lau, Richard R. and David O. Sears. 1981. "Cognitive Links Between Economic Grievances and Political Responses." *Political Behavior* 3 (4): 279–302.

Layton, Matthew L. and Amy E. Smith. 2015. "Incorporating Marginal Citizens and Voters: The Conditional Electoral Effects of Targeted Social Assistance in Latin America." *Comparative Political Studies* 48 (7): 854–81.

Leibfried, Stephan, Francis G. Castles, and Herbert Obinger. 2005. "'Old' and 'New' Politics' in Federal Welfare State." In *Federalism and the Welfare State: New World and European Experiences*, edited by Herbert Obinger, Stephan Leibfried, and Francis G. Castles, 307–55. New York, NY: Cambridge University Press.

Leiras, Marcelo. 2007. *Todos los caballos del rey. La integración de los partidos políticos y el gobierno democrático de la Argentina, 1995–2003.* Buenos Aires: Prometeo Libros, Pent.

Levi, Maria Luiza and João Henrique Scatena. 2011. "Evolução recente do financiamento do SUS e considerações sobre o processo de regionalização." *In* Regionalização e relações federativas na política de saúde do Brasil, edited by Viana, Ana Luiza D'Avila, Luciana Dias de Lima, and Cristiani V. Machado, 81–113. Rio de Janeiro: Contra Capa.

Levitsky, Steven. 2003. *Transforming Labor-Based Parties in Latin America: Argentine Peronism in Comparative Perspective.* New York, NY: Cambridge University Press.

Levitsky, Steven and Kenneth M. Roberts. 2011. "Latin America's "Left Turn": A Framework for Analysis." In Levitsky and Roberts. *The Resurgence of the Latin American Left.* Baltimore: Johns Hopkins University Press, 2011b, 1–28.

Leyden, Kevin M. and Stephen A. Borrelli. 1995. "The Effect of State Economic Conditions on Gubernatorial Elections: Does Unified Government Make a Difference?" *Political Research Quarterly* 48 (2): 275–90.

Lichtenstein, Nelson. 2017. "Who Killed Obamacare?" *Dissent* 64 (2): 121–29.

Licio, Elaine Cristina. 2012. "Para além da recentralização: Os caminhos da coordenação federativa do Programa Bolsa Família (2003–2010)." Doctoral Dissertation, Instituto de Ciências Humanas, Universidade de Brasília.

Lieberman, Evan S. 2005. "Nested Analysis as a Mixed-Method Strategy for Cross-National Research." *The American Political Science Review* 99 (3): 435–52.

2015. "Nested Analysis: Toward the Integration of Comparative-Historical Analysis with Other Social Science Methods." In *Advances in Comparative-Historical Analysis*, edited by James Mahoney and Kathleen A. Thelen, 240–63. *Strategies for social inquiry.* New York, NY: Cambridge University Press.

Liu, Lili and Steven B. Webb. 2011. "Laws for Fiscal Responsibility for Subnational Discipline: International Experience." *The World Bank Policy Research Working Paper* 5587.

Lloyd-Sherlock, Peter. 2000. *Healthcare Reform and Poverty in Latin America.* London: Institute of Latin American Studies.

Lowry, Robert C., James E. Alt, and Karen E. Ferree. 1998. "Fiscal Policy Outcomes and Electoral Accountability in American States." *American Political Science Review* 92 (4): 759–74.

Lucas, Kevin and David Samuels. 2010. "The Ideological Coherence of the Brazilian Party System, 1990–2009." *Journal of Politics in Latin America* 2 (3): 39–69.

Luccisano, Lucy and Laura Macdonald. 2014. "Mexico and Social Provision by the Federal Government and the Federal District: Obstacles and Openings to a Social Protection Floor." *Global Social Policy* 14 (3): 333–51.

Lustig, Nora. 2009. "Poverty, Inequality and the New Left in Latin America." *Woodrow Wilson Center Update on the Americas* October (5): 1–28.

Lustig, Nora, Luis F. Lopez-Calva, and Eduardo Ortiz-Juarez. 2013. "Declining Inequality in Latin America in the 2000s: The Cases of Argentina, Brazil, and Mexico." *World Development* 44: 129–41.

Lyne, Mona M. 2005. "Parties as Programmatic Agents: A Test of Institutional Theory in Brazil." *Party Politics* 11 (2): 193–216.

Maestas, Cherie, Lonna Rae Atkeson, Thomas Croom, and Lisa A. Bryant. 2008. "Shifting the Blame: Federalism, Media, and Public Assignment of Blame Following Hurricane Katrina." *Publius: The Journal of Federalism* 38 (4): 609–32.

Magaloni, Beatriz, Alberto Diaz-Cayeros, and Federico Estévez. 2007. "Clientelism and Portfolio Diversification: A Model of Electoral Investment with Applications to Mexico." In *Patrons, Clients, and Policies: Patterns of Democratic Accountability and Political Competition*, edited by Herbert Kitschelt and Steven Wilkinson, 182–205. New York, NY: Cambridge University Press.

Mainwaring, Scott. 1995. "Brazil: Weak Parties, Feckless Democracy." In *Building Democratic Institutions: Party Systems in Latin America*, edited by Scott Mainwaring and Timothy R. Scully, 354–98. California: Stanford University Press.

Mainwaring, Scott and Timothy R. Scully, eds. 1995. *Building Democratic Institutions: Party Systems in Latin America*. California: Stanford University Press.

Mainwaring, Scott and Mariano Torcal. 2005. "Party System Institutionalization and Party System Theory after the Third Wave of Democratization." *Kellogg Institute Working Paper* 319.

Malloy, James. 1979. *The Politics of Social Security in Brazil*. Pittsburgh, PA: University of Pittsburgh Press.

Manacorda, Marco, Edward Miguel, and Andrea Vigorito. 2011. "Government Transfers and Political Support." *American Economic Journal: Applied Economics* 3 (3): 1–28.

Mani, Anandi and Sharun Mukand. 2007. "Democracy, Visibility and Public Good Provision." *Journal of Development Economics* 83 (2): 506–529.

Mann, Michael. 1988. *States, War, and Capitalism: Studies in Political Sociology*. Oxford, New York: Basil Blackwell Ltd.

Manor, James. 1999. *The Political Economy of Democratic Decentralization*. Washington DC: The World Bank.

Marsh, Michael and James Tilley. 2010. "The Attribution of Credit and Blame to Governments and Its Impact on Vote Choice." *British Journal of Political Science* 40 (01): 115.

Marshall, Thomas Humphrey. 1950. *Citizenship and Social Class, and Other Essays*. New York, NY: Cambridge University Press.

Martínez-Franzoni, Juliana and Diego Sánchez-Ancochea. 2016. *The Quest for Universal Social Policy in the South: Actors, Ideas and Architectures*. New York, NY: Cambridge University Press.

Mathias, Jörg. 2005. "Welfare Management in the German Federal System." In *The Territorial Politics of Welfare*, edited by Nicola McEwen and Luis Moreno, 62–84. London, New York: Routledge.

Mayhew, David R. 1974. *Congress: The Electoral Connection*. New Haven: Yale University Press.

Mayka, Lindsay. 2019. Building Participatory Institutions in Latin America: Reform Coalitions and Institutional Change. New York: Cambridge University Press.

Mazzola, Roxana. 2012. *Nuevo paradigma: La Asignación Universal por Hijo en la Argentina*. Buenos Aires: Prometeo Libros.

McGuire, James W. 2010a. "Political Factors and Health Outcomes. Insight from Argentina's Provinces." United Nations Development Programme, Human Development Reports Research Paper 2010/25: 1–73.

2010b. *Wealth, Health, and Democracy in East Asia and Latin America.* New York, NY: Cambridge University Press.

2015. "Politics, Gender, and Health: Insight from Argentina's Provinces." Paper prepared for delivery at American Political Science Association Meeting, San Francisco, September 3–6.

Medeiros, Marcelo, Tatiana Britto, and Fábio V. Soares. 2008. "Targeted Cash Transfer Programmes in Brazil: BPC and the Bolsa Família." International Poverty Center, Working Paper (46).

Melo, Marcus André. 2008. "Unexpected Successes, Unanticipated Failures: Social Policy from Cardoso to Lula." In Kingstone, Peter R. and Timothy Power. *Democratic Brazil Revisited.* Pittsburgh: University of Pittsburgh Press, 161–84.

Mesa-Lago, Carmelo. 1978. *Social Security in Latin America: Pressure Groups, Stratification, and Inequality.* Pittsburgh, PA: University of Pittsburgh Press.

1989. *Ascent to Bankruptcy: Financing Social Security in Latin America.* Pittsburgh, PA: University of Pittsburgh Press.

2008. *Reassembling Social Security: A Survey of Pensions and Health Care Reforms in Latin America.* Oxford, New York: Oxford University Press.

Miguel, Luis and Carlos Machado. 2010. "De partido de esquerda a partido de governo: O PT e suas coaligações para prefeito (2000 a 2008)." In Krause, Silvana, Humberto Dantas, and Luis Felipe Miguel (Eds.): *Coaligações partidárias na nova democracia Brasileira. Perfis e tendências.* Rio de Janeiro, São Paulo: Ed. UNESP; Konrad-Adenauer-Stiftung, 345–71.

Miller, Edward A. and David Blanding. 2012. "Pressure Cooker Politics: Partisanship and Symbolism in State Certification of Federal Stimulus Funds." *State Politics & Policy Quarterly* 12 (1): 58–74.

Ministerio de Desarrollo Humano, Familia y Comunidad de Mendoza. 2011a. "Detalle de beneficiarios del programa Comer Juntos en Familia." Datos Oficiales.

2011b. "Plan de Inclusión en Derecho para Jóvenes 2011." Datos Oficiales.

Ministerio de Inclusión Social, San Luis. 2012. Cantidad de Beneficiarios del Plan de Inclusión Social. Datos Oficiales.

Ministerio de Salud de la Provincia de San Luis. 2012. "Lista de efectores del Plan Nacer. Información de contacto: Sistema de Gestión del Programa Sumar." http://64.215.200.28/nacer/login.php.

Modesto, Luis and Jorge Abrahão de Castro. 2010. "Introdução." In Abrahão de Castro, Jorge and Lúcia Modesto (Eds.) 2010. *Bolsa Família 2003–2010. Avanços e desafios.* Brasília: Instituto de Pesquisa Econômica Aplicada (IPEA).

Molina, Carlos. 2006. *Universalismo Básico: Una Nueva Política Social Para America Latina.* Washington, DC: Inter-American Development Bank.

Molyneux, Maxine. 2006. "Mothers at the Service of the New Poverty Agenda: Progresa/Oportunidades, Mexico's Conditional Transfer Programme." *Social Policy & Administration* 40 (4): 425–49.

Montero, Alfred P. 2002. *Shifting States in Global Markets: Subnational Industrial Policy in Contemporary Brazil and Spain.* University Park, PA: Pennsylvania State University Press.

2007. "Uneven Democracy? Subnational Authoritarianism in Democratic Brazil." Paper presented at the 2007 Latin American Studies Association meeting, Montréal, Canada.

2010. "No Country for Leftists? Clientelist Continuity and the 2006 Vote in the Brazilian Northeast." *Journal of Politics in Latin America.* 2: 113–53.

Montero, Alfred P. and David Samuels, eds. 2004. *Decentralization and Democracy in Latin America.* Notre Dame, IN: University of Notre Dame Press.

Moynihan, Donald, Pamela Herd, and Hope Harvey. 2014. "Administrative Burden: Learning, Psychological, and Compliance Costs in Citizen-State Interactions." *Journal of Public Administration Research and Theory* 25 (1): 43–69.

Murillo, Maria Victoria. 2009. *Political Competition, Partisanship, and Policy Making in Latin American Public Utilities.* Cambridge: Cambridge University Press.

Neffa, Julio César and Brenda Brown. 2011. *Empleo, Desempleo y Políticas de Empleo No 7: Poliíticas Públicas de Empleo III (2002–2010).* Buenos Aires: CEIL-PIETTE. Accessed November 1, 2011. www.ceil-piette.gov.ar/docpub/revistas/empleo/7politicasempo210.pdf.

Nicholson-Crotty, Sean. 2012. "Leaving Money on the Table: Learning from Recent Refusals of Federal Grants in the American States." *Publius: The Journal of Federalism* 42 (3): 449–66.

Niedzwiecki, Sara. 2014a. "The Effect of Unions and Organized Civil Society on Social Policy. Pension and Health Reforms in Argentina and Brazil (1988–2008)." *Latin American Politics & Society* 56 (4): 22–48.

2014b. "Multilevel Social Policies and Partisan Alignments. Cash Transfers and Healthcare in Argentina and Brazil." Dissertation, Political Science, University of North Carolina, Chapel Hill.

2015. "Social Policy Commitment in South America: The Effect of Organized Labor on Social Spending from 1980 to 2010." *Journal of Politics in Latin America* 7 (2): 3–42.

2016. "Social Policies, Attribution of Responsibility, and Political Alignments: A Subnational Analysis of Argentina and Brazil." *Comparative Political Studies* 49 (4): 457–98.

Niedzwiecki, Sara and Anria, Santiago. Forthcoming. "The Participatory Politics of Social Policies in Bolivia and Brazil" *Latin American Politics & Society*

Niedzwiecki, Sara, Sandra Chapman Osterkatz, Gary Marks, and Liesbet Hooghe. 2018 "The RAI Travels to Latin America: Measuring Regional Authority Under Regime Change." *Regional & Federal Studies*

Niedzwiecki, Sara and Evelyne Huber. 2013. "Soziale Sicherungssysteme in Lateinamerika und Ostasien: Hin zu einer universellen Grundsicherung?" *Zeitschrift fr Sozialreform* 59 (Heft 2): 255.

Niedzwiecki, Sara and David Nunnally. 2017. "Mixed-Methods Research in the Study of Welfare States." *PS: Political Science & Politics* 50 (4).

Niedzwiecki, Sara, and Jennifer Pribble. 2017. "Social Policies and Center-Right Governments in Argentina and Chile." *Latin American Politics & Society* 59 (3): 72–97.

Norris, Pippa. 2012. *Making Democratic Governance Work: How Regimes Shape Prosperity, Welfare, and Peace.* New York, NY: Cambridge University Press.

O Popular. 1999. "Senador critica mudança na cesta básica." December 24.

Obama, Barack. 2016. "United States Health Care Reform: Progress to Date and Next Steps." *The Journal of the American Medical Association.*

Obamacare Facts. March 16, 2015. "ObamaCare Enrollment Numbers As of March 2015." http://obamacarefacts.com/2015/03/16/obamacare-enrollment-numbers-as-of-march-2015/.

O'Donnell, Guillermo. 1993. "On the State, Democratization and Some Conceptual Problems: A Latin American View with Glances at Some Postcommunist Countries." *World Development* 21 (8): 1355–69.

Oliveira, Carla de. 2008. "Renda só para 10% dos beneficiários." *O Popular*, March 19.

Ostrom, Elinor. 1996. "Crossing the Great Divide: Coproduction, Synergy, and Development." *World Development* 24 (6): 1073–87.

Palazzolo, Daniel, Vincent G. Moscardelli, Meredith Patrick, and Doug Rubin. 2007. "Election Reform after HAVA: Voter Verification in Congress and the States." *Publius: The Journal of Federalism* 38 (3): 515–37.

Pear, Robert. 2013. "Missouri Citizens Face Obstacles to Coverage." *The New York Times*, August 2. www.nytimes.com/2013/08/03/us/missouri-citizens-face-obstacles-to-coverage.html?_r=0.

Peixoto, Vitor de Moraes. 2010. "Coalizações eleitorais nos municípios Brasileiros: Competição e estratégia." In Krause, Silvana, Humberto Dantas, Luis Felipe Miguel (Eds.) *Coalizações partidárias na nova democracia Brasileira. Perfis e tendências.* Rio de Janeiro, São Paulo: Ed. UNESP; Konrad-Adenauer-Stiftung, 277–300.

Pereira, Elisabete Oliveira, Soraya Vargas Côrtes, and Márcio Barcelos. 2009. "Conselho estadual de saúde do Rio Grande do Sul: Histórico, funcionamento, atores e dinâmica das relações sociais." In Côrtes, Soraya Vargas (Ed.) *Participação e saúde no Brasil.* Rio de Janeiro: Fiocruz, 111–44.

Petrocik, John R. 1996. "Issue Ownership in Presidential Elections, with a 1980 Case Study." *American Journal of Political Science* 40 (3): 825–50.

Piereson, James E. 1975. "Presidential Popularity and Midterm Voting at Different Electoral Levels." *American Journal of Political Science* 19 (4): 683–94.

Pierson, Paul. 1993. "When Effect Becomes Cause: Policy Feedback and Political Change." *World Politics* 45 (4): 595–628.

1994. *Dismantling the Welfare State? Reagan, Thatcher, and the Politics of Retrenchment.* New York, NY: Cambridge University Press.

1995. "Fragmented Welfare States: Federal Institutions and the Development of Social Policy." *Governance* 8 (4): 449–78.

2001. "Coping with Permanent Austerity: Welfare State Restructuring in Affluent Democracies." In *The New Politics of the Welfare State*, edited by Paul Pierson, 410–56. Oxford: Oxford University Press.

2004. *Politics in Time: History, Institutions, and Social Analysis.* Princeton: Princeton University Press.

Pio de Santana, Dilma. 2007. "O papel do controle social na política de assistência social em Goiânia." Masters Thesis, Facultade de Ciências Humanas e Filosofía, Universidade Federal de Goiás.

Plan Nacer Mendoza. 2012. Facturación Liquidadas a Efectores. Informe Acumulado al 13/03/2012. Datos Oficiales.

Posner, Paul. 2007. "The Politics of Coercive Federalism in the Bush Era." *Publius: The Journal of Federalism* 37 (3): 390–412.

Post, Alison E. 2014. *Foreign and Domestic Investment in Argentina: The Politics of Privatized Infrastructure.* Cambridge: Cambridge University Press.

Potenza Dal Masetto, María Fernanda. 2011. "Los Principales Programas de Protección Social en la Provincia de Mendoza." Programa de Protección Social, Área de Desarrollo Social, CIPPEC. *Documento de Trabajo.* 71.

Powell, Bingham and Guy D. Whitten. 1993. "A Cross-National Analysis of Economic Voting: Taking Account of the Political Context." *American Journal of Political Science* 37 (2): 391–414.

Power, Timothy. 2008. "Centering Democracy? Ideological Cleavages and Convergence in the Brazilian Political Class." In Kingstone, Peter and Timothy Power (Eds.) *Democratic Brazil Revisited*. Pittsburgh: University of Pittsburgh Press, 81–106.

Prefeitura Municipal de Porto Alegre. 2014. "Observatorio da Cidade de Porto Alegre: Territorialidades da Cidade. Mapas Saúde." Accessed April 23, 2016. http://www.observapoa.palegre.com.br/default.php?p_secao=46.

Prefeitura Municipal de Porto Alegre, Secretaría Municipal de Saúde. 2013. "Plano Municipal de Saúde 2014–2017." http://www2.portoalegre.rs.gov.br/sms/default.php?p_secao=927.

Pribble, Jennifer. 2013. *Welfare and Party Politics in Latin America*. New York, NY: Cambridge University Press.

2015. "The Politics of Building Municipal Institutional Effectiveness in Chile." *Latin American Politics and Society* 57 (3): 100–121.

Pushkar. 2012. "Democracy and Infant Mortality in India's 'Mini-Democracies': A Preliminary Theoretical Inquiry and Analysis." *Journal of South Asian Development* 7 (2): 109–37.

Putnam, Robert. 1003. Making Democracy Work. Civic Traditions in Modern Italy. Princeton: Princeton University Press.

Queirolo, Rosario. 2010. "El rol de las transferencias monetarias en la reelección del Frente Amplio en 2009." In *Del cambio a la continuidad: Ciclo electoral 2009–2010 en Uruguay*, edited by Daniel Buquet and Niki Johnson, 195–212. Montevideo: Editorial Fin de Siglo.

Ragin, Charles C. 1989. *The Comparative Method: Moving Beyond Qualitative and Quantitative Strategies*. Berkeley: University of California Press.

Regan, Priscilla M. and Cristopher J. Deering. 2009. "State Opposition to REAL ID." *Publius: The Journal of Federalism* 39 (3): 476–505.

Ribeiro, Pedro Floriano. 2010. "Velhos e novos companheiros: Coaligações eleitorais nos municípios do G79 (1996–2008)." In Krause, Silvana, Humberto Dantas, and Luis Felipe Miguel (Eds.) *Coaligações partidárias na nova democracia Brasileira. Perfis e tendências*. Rio de Janeiro, São Paulo: Ed. UNESP; Konrad-Adenauer-Stiftung, 309–23.

Rigby, Elizabeth. 2012. "State Resistance to 'ObamaCare'." *The Forum* 10 (2).

Rigby, Elizabeth and Jake Haselswerdt. 2013. "Hybrid Federalism, Partisan Politics, and Early Implementation of State Health Insurance Exchanges." *Publius: The Journal of Federalism* 43 (3): 368–91.

Riker, William H. and Ronald Schaps. 1957. "Disharmony in Federal Government." *Behavioral Science* 2 (4): 276–90.

Rizzotti, Maria Luiza Amaral, Aidê Cançado Almeida, and Simone Aparecida Albuquerque. 2010. "Sistema Único de Assistência Social: Sua Contribuição na Proteção Social Brasileira." In *Bolsa Família 2003–2010: Avanços e desafios*, edited by Jorge Abrahão de Castro and Lúcia Modesto. Brasília: Instituto de Pesquisa Econômica Aplicada (IPEA), 137–50.

Roberts, Kenneth M. 2002. "Social Inequalities Without Class Cleavages in Latin America's Neoliberal Era." *Studies in Comparative International Development* 36 (4): 3–33.

2013. "Market Reform, Programmatic (De)alignment, and Party System Stability in Latin America." *Comparative Political Studies* 46 (11): 1422–52.

2014. *Changing Course in Latin America: Party Systems in the Neoliberal Era.* Cambridge studies in comparative politics. New York, NY: Cambridge University Press.

Rock, David. 1985. *Argentina, 1516–1982: From Spanish Colonization to the Falklands War.* Berkeley: University of California Press.

Rodden, Jonathan. 2006. *Hamilton's Paradox: The Promise and Peril of Fiscal Federalism.* New York, NY: Cambridge University Press.

Rodrigues-Silveira, Rodrigo. 2012. *Gobierno local y estado de bienestar: Regímenes y resultados de la política social en Brasil.* Salamanca: Fundación Manuel Giménez Abad de Estudios Parlamentarios y del Estado Autonómico.

2013. "The Subnational Method and Social Policy Provision: Socioeconomic Context, Political Insttutions and Spatial Inequality." www.desigualdades.net/ Working_Papers/index.html.

Rodriguez da Cunha, Rosane. 2005. "40 mil podem perder benefício." *O Popular*, June 29.

Rudolph, Thomas J. and Tobin J. Grant. 2002. "An Attributional Model of Economic Voting: Evidence from the 2000 Presidential Election." *Political Research Quarterly* 55 (4): 805–23.

Ruggeri, Silvia. 2012. "En nombre de los derechos: Una mirada a las políticas sociales municipales desde el enfoque de derechos humanos." Tesis de Maestría, Universidad Nacional de Cuyo.

Sager, Fritz, Christian Rüefli, and Eva Thomann. 2014. "Fixing Federal Faults: Complementary Member State Policies in Swiss Health Care Policy." Paper Presented at the 2014 EGPA Conference in Speyer, Germany, September 10–12.

Samuels, David. 2003. *Federalism, Ambition, and Congressional Politics in Brazil.* New York, NY: Cambridge University Press.

2004a. "Presidentialism and Accountability for the Economy in Comparative Perspective." *American Political Science Review* 98 (03): 1–12.

2004b. "The Political Logic of Decentralization in Brazil." In *Decentralization and Democracy in Latin America*, edited by Alfred P. Montero and David Samuels. Notre Dame, IN: University of Notre Dame Press.

Sanzi Souza, Djalmo, Elson Romeu Farias, Angela Gomes Chagas, Ariadne Kerber, Consuelo Lobo D'Avila, Isaurina Dias Dall'Agnol, Juçara Vendrúsculo, Maria Regina Vicentini, Patricia Ligocki Silva, and Rebel Machado. 2003. "O desenvolvimento da Estratégia Saúde da Família no Rio Grande do Sul." *Boletim da Saúde* 17 (2): 9–13.

Sen, Amartya. 1999. *Development as Freedom.* New York: Anchor Books.

Schattschneider, Elmer Eric. 1935. *Politics, Pressures, and the Tariff.* New York: Prentice-Hall.

Schneider, Aaron. 2006. "Responding to Fiscal Stress: Fiscal Institutions and Fiscal Adjustment in Four Brazilian States." *Journal of Development Studies* 42 (3): 402–25.

Schober, Greg. 2015. "Beneficial Policy, Responsibility Attribution, and Electoral Rewards: Evidence from a Randomized Experiment." Accessed February 5, 2016. https://sites .google.com/site/gregorysschober/working-manuscripts.

Seawright, Jason and John Gerring. 2008. "Case Selection Techniques in Case Study Research: a Menu of Qualitative and Quantitative Options." *Political Research Quarterly* 61 (2): 294–308. urn: ISSN:1065–9129.

Shady, Norbert. 2000. "The Political Economy of Expenditures by the Peruvian Social Fund (FONCODES), 1991–95." *The American Political Science Review* 94 (2): 289–304.

Shelly, Bryan. 2008. "Rebels and Their Causes: State Resistance to No Child Left Behind." *Publius: The Journal of Federalism* 38 (3): 444–68.

Silva, Maria José. 2012. "Estado e União unificam programas de assistência." *O Popular*, March 29.

Singh, Prerna. 2015. *How Solidarity Works for Welfare: Subnationalism and Social Development in India.* Cambridge studies in comparative politics. New York: Cambridge University Press.

Skocpol, Theda. 1992. *Protecting Soldiers and Mothers: The Political Origins of Social Policy in the United States.* Boston: Harvard University Press.

Skocpol, Theda and Edwin Amenta. 1986. "States and Social Policies." *Annual Review of Sociology* 12 (1): 131–57.

Skocpol, Theda and Kenneth Finegold. 1982. "State Capacity and Economic Intervention in the Early New Deal." *Political Science Quarterly* 97 (2): 255–78.

Skoufias, Emmanuel and Susan Wendy Parker. 2001. "Conditional Cash Transfers and Their Impact on Child Work and Schooling: Evidence from the PROGRESA Program in Mexico." *Economía* 2 (1): 45–86.

Smulovitz, Catalina and Adriana Clemente. 2004. "Decentralization and Social Expenditure at the Municipal Level in Argentina." In Tulchin and Selee 2004.

Snyder, Richard. 1999. "After the State Withdraws: Neoliberalism and Subnational Authoritarian Regimes in Mexico." In Cornelius, Wayne A., Todd Eisenstadt, and Jane Hindley (Eds.) *Subnational Politics and Democratization in Mexico.* La Jolla: Center for U.S.-Mexican Studies, University of California, San Diego, 295–341.

2006. *Politics After Neoliberalism: Reregulation in Mexico.* New York, NY: Cambridge University Press.

Soares, Sergei. 2012. "Bolsa Família, Its Design, Its Impacts and Possibilities for the Future." International Poverty Center, Working Paper (89).

Soares, Sergei, Rafael Guerreiro Osório, Fábio V. Soares, Marcelo Medeiros, and Eduardo Zepeda. 2009. "Conditional Cash Transfers in Brazil, Chile, and Mexico: Impacts Upon Inequality." *Estudios Económicos número extraordinario*: 207–24.

Soares, Sergei and Natália Sátyro. 2010. "O Programa Bolsa Família: Desenho institucional e possibilidades futuras." In Jorge Abrahão de Castro and Modesto Lúcia (eds). Brasília: Instituto de Pesquisa Econômica Aplicada (IPEA), 27–55.

Soifer, Hillel. 2008. "State Infrastructural Power: Approaches to Conceptualization and Measurement." *Studies in Comparative International Development* 43 (3–4): 231–51.

Soifer, Hillel and Matthias Vom Hau. 2008. "Unpacking the Strength of the State: The Utility of State Infrastructural Power." *Studies in Comparative International Development* 43 (3–4): 219–30.

Souza, Celina. 2015. "Breaking the Boundary: Pro-poor Policies and Electoral Outcomes in Brazilian Sub-national Governments." *Regional & Federal Studies* 25 (4): 347–63.

Sposati, Aldaíza. 2010. "Bolsa Família: Um programa com futuro(s)." In *Bolsa Família 2003–2010: Avanços e desafios*, edited by Jorge Abrahão de Castro and Modesto Lúcia, 275–305 Volume 2. Brasília: Instituto de Pesquisa Econômica Aplicada (IPEA).

Stokes, Susan Carol, Thad Dunning, Marcelo Nazareno, and Valeria Brusco. 2013. *Brokers, Voters, and Clientelism: The Puzzle of Distributive Politics.* New York, NY: Cambridge University Press.

Suarez-Cao, Julieta and Edward L. Gibson. 2010. "Federalized Party Systems and Subnational Party Competition: Theory and an Empirical Application to Argentina." *Comparative Politics* 43 (1): 21–39.

Sugiyama, Natasha Borges. 2007. "Ideology & Social Networks: The Politics of Social Policy Diffusion in Brazil." PhD Dissertation, The University of Texas at Austin.

2011. "Bottom-up Policy Diffusion: National Emulation of a Conditional Cash Transfer Program in Brazil." *Publius: The Journal of Federalism* 42 (1): 25–51.

2013. *Diffusion of Good Government: Social Sector Reforms in Brazil.* Notre Dame, Indiana: University of Notre Dame Press.

Szwarcberg, Mariela Laura. 2015. *Mobilizing Poor Voters: Machine Politics, Clientelism, and Social Networks in Argentina.* New York, NY: Cambridge University Press.

Tendler, Judith. 1997. *Good Government in the Tropics.* Baltimore: Johns Hopkins University Press.

"The Commonwealth Fund Affordable Care Act Tracking Survey, March–May 2015." 2015. News release. 2015. www.commonwealthfund.org/publications/issue-briefs/2015/jun/experiences-marketplace-and-medicaid.

Tiebout, Charles M. 1956. "A Pure Theory of Local Expenditures." *Journal of Political Economy* 64 (5): 416–24.

Tobar, Federico. 2004. "La política de distribución de medicamentos en Argentina: El caso del Remediar." *Banco Interamericano de Desarrollo, nota técnica de discusión de salud 2.*

Tommasi, Mariano. 2002. "Federalism in Argentina and the Reforms of the 1990s." Center for Research on Economic Development and Policy Reform (Stanford University) Documento 69.

Touchton, Michael, Natasha Borges Sugiyama, and Brian Wampler. 2017. "Democracy at Work: Moving Beyond Elections to Improve Well-Being." *American Political Science Review* 111 (1): 68–82.

Tsai, Lily L. 2007. *Accountability without Democracy: Solidary Groups and Public Goods Provision in Rural China.* New York, NY: Cambridge University Press.

Tufte, Edward R. 1978. *Political Control of the Economy.* Princeton: Princeton University Press.

Turner, Edward. 2011. *Political Parties and Public Policy in the German Länder: When Parties Matter.* New York: Palgrave Macmillan.

Tyler, Tom R. 1982. "Personalization in Attributing Responsibility for National Problems to the President." *Political Behavior* 4 (4): 379–99.

U.S. Centers for Medicare and Medicaid Services. "CMS' Program History." Accessed November 2, 2017.www.cms.gov/About-CMS/Agency-information/History/.

Viana, Ana Luiza, Hudson Pacífico da Silva, Maria Fernanda Cardoso de Melo, and Juliana Cajueiro. 2009. "Financiamento e desenpenho da atenção básica no Estado de São Paulo." In Cohn, Amélia (Ed.) (2009) *Saúde da família e SUS. Convergências e dissonâncias.* Rio de Janeiro: Beco do Azougue, 15–65.

Vieira, Hélio. 2005. "Política social num contexto de ajuste estrutural do estado: Goiás no período 1995–2002." Masters Thesis, Faculdade de Ciências Humanas e Filosofia, Universidade Federal de Goiás.

Vieira Ferrarini, Adrane, Cláudia Deitos Giongo, and Sandra Silva Silveira. 2010. *Relatório do Diagnóstico Organizacional dos CRAS Canoas 2010–1.* Canoas: Rio Grande do Sul, Governo de Canoas.

Wampler, Brian. 2015. Activating Democracy in Brazil. Notre Dame: University of Notre Dame Press

Weaver, Kent. 1988. *Automatic Government: The Politics of Indexation*. Washington, DC: Brookings Institution.

Weber, Max. 1978. *Economy and Society*. Guenther Roth and Claus Wittich. Berkeley, California: University of California Press.

Weinberg, Monica. 2003. "Vem aí mais um nome." *O Popular*, October 22.

Weitz-Shapiro, Rebecca. 2014. *Curbing Clientelism in Argentina: Politics, Poverty, and Social Policy*. New York, NY: Cambridge University Press.

Weyland, Kurt. 1996. Democracy Without Equity: Failures of Reform in Brazil. Pittsburgh: University of Pittsburgh Press. http://worldcatlibraries.org/wcpa/oclc/468442787.

1999. "Neoliberal Populism in Latin America and Eastern Europe." *Comparative Politics* 31 (4): 379–401.

Wibbels, Erik. 2005. *Federalism and the Market: Intergovernmental Conflict and Economic Reform in the Developing World*. New York, NY: Cambridge University Press.

Wilson, Alex. 2012. "Multi-level Party Systems in Spain." *Regional & Federal Studies* 22 (2): 123–39.

Wilson, Robert H., Peter M. Ward, Peter K. Spink, and Victoria E. Rodríguez. 2008. *Governance in the Americas: Decentralization, Democracy, and Subnational Government in Brazil, Mexico, and the USA*. Notre Dame, IN: University of Notre Dame Press.

Wolf, Frieder. 2010. "Enlightened Eclecticism or Hazardous Hotchpotch? Mixed Methods and Triangulation Strategies in Comparative Public Policy Research." *Journal of Mixed Methods Research* 4 (2): 144–67.

Woltmann, Eduardo. 2012. "Fundações públicas de direito privado como ferramentas de gestão de serviços municipais de saúde: O caso de município de Porto Alegre." Escola de Administração, Universidade Federal do Rio Grande do Sul.

World Bank. 2006a. "Country Assistance Strategy for the Argentine Republic, 2006–2008: Report 34015-AR." Accessed March 28, 2017. http://siteresources.worldbank.org/INTARGENTINA/Resources/1CASAr.pdf.

2006b. "Project Appraisal Document on a Proposed Loan in the Amount of US$300 Million to the Argentine Government for the Provincial Maternal-Child Health Investment Project in Support of the Second Phase of the Provincial Maternal-Child Health Program: Report 37702-AR." Accessed March 28, 2017. http://documents.worldbank.org/curated/en/658591468003286594/pdf/37702.pdf.

2015. "Poverty and Equity: Latin America and Caribbean." Accessed October 15, 2015. http://povertydata.worldbank.org/poverty/region/LAC.

Ziblatt, Daniel. 2008. "Why Some Cities Provide More Public Goods Than Others: A Subnational Comparison of the Provision of Public Goods in German Cities in 1912." *Studies in Comparative International Development* 43 (3–4): 273–89.

Zucco, Cesar. 2008. "The President's 'New' Constituency: Lula and the Pragmatic Vote in Brazil's 2006 Presidential Elections." *Journal of Latin American Studies* 40 (1): 29–49.

2013. "When Payouts Pay Off: Conditional Cash-Transfers and Voting Behavior in Brazil 2002–2010." *American Journal of Political Science* 47 (3): 810–22.

Interviews

The following list provides the names, position (at the moment of the interview), and date of interview of all interviewees who agreed to disclose their names and positions. The interviewees who did not explicitly consent to have their names and positions disclosed, including all interviewed academics and social policy recipients, are not included here.

Accorsi, Darci. Secretary of Social Development of the Municipality of Goiânia and Former Mayor of the Municipality of Goiânia. Goiânia City, Goiás, Brazil, October 25, 2012.

Aguiló, Juan Carlos. Former PJ-FPV Deputy Candidate for the Province of Mendoza. Mendoza City, Argentina, April 4, 2012.

Alfonso, Dolores. Undersecretary of Social Development of the Province of Mendoza. Mendoza City, Argentina, May 16, 2012.

Algues, Marta. Secretary of Education of the Municipality of Valparaíso de Goiás. Valparaíso de Goiás City, Goiás, Brazil, November 26, 2012.

Alvarenga, Marcela. Sub-Coordinator of Estrategia Saúde da Família at the State of Goiás. Goiânia City, Goiás, Brazil, November 6, 2012.

Alves, Marta. High Official of Primary Healthcare of the East/North-East Region of Porto Alegre. Porto Alegre City, Rio Grande do Sul, Brazil, August 20, 2012.

Amorim, Nicilene. Director of State Program (Jovem Cidadão) of the State of Goiás. Goiânia City, Goiás, Brazil, October 23, 2012.

Antunes, Graciela. Coordinator of Estrategia Saúde da Família at Lomba do Pinheiro. City of Porto Alegre, Rio Grande do Sul, Brazil, September 27, 2012.

Arante, Henrique. Secretary of Social Development of the State of Goiás (SECT). Goiânia City, Goiás, Brazil, October 30, 2012.

Arce, Guido. Director of Health Center (#15) of the Province of San Luis. San Luis City, Argentina, June 19, 2012.

Armiñana, Susana. Coordinator of School Cafeteria Program of the Province of Mendoza. Mendoza City, Argentina, April 12, 2012.

Artiaga, Airmeir. Coordinator of Bolsa Família in the Municipality of Goiânia. Goiânia City, Goiás, Brazil, October 24, 2012.

Assman, Marinês. Justice Promoter of the State of Rio Grande do Sul. Porto Alegre City, Rio Grande do Sul, Brazil, September 11, 2012.

Asso, Jorge. Former Labor Undersecretary of the Province of Mendoza. Mendoza City, Argentina, April 3, 2012.

Baddini Curralero, Cláudia. National Director of Unified Registry (Cadastro Único) of the Ministry of Social Development (MDS). Brasília, Brazil, November 28, 2012.

Balada, Dora. Undersecretary of Labor of the Province of Mendoza. Mendoza City, Argentina, April 10, 2012.

Baltazar, Eva. Food Programs Manager of the Province of Mendoza. Mendoza City, Argentina, April 23, 2012.

Baltazar, Rosane Terezina. Director of Primary Healthcare of the East/North-East Region of Porto Alegre. Porto Alegre City, Rio Grande do Sul, Brazil, August 20, 2012.

Barale, Sebastián. Director of Provincial Program (Viveros y Forestación, Plan de Inclusión Social) of the Province of San Luis. San Luis City, Argentina, June 18, 2012.

Barra de Azevedo, Denise. Coordinator of Bolsa Família in the State of Goiás. Goiânia City, Goiás, Brazil, October 29, 2012.

Barros, Enrique. President of the Health Council of the Municipality of Santa Maria do Herval. Santa Maria do Herval City, Rio Grande do Sul, Brazil, October 3, 2012.

Bartholo, Letícia. National Adjunct Secretary of Social Development (MDS). Brasília, Brazil, December 3, 2012.

Batista, Sandro. Former Coordinator of Estrategia Saúde da Família at the Municipality of Goiânia. Goiânia City, Goiás, Brazil, November 5, 2012.

Bauer, Marcia. Director of State Program (RS Mais Renda Mais Igual) of the State of Rio Grande do Sul. Porto Alegre City, Rio Grande do Sul, Brazil, August 7, 2012.

Bautista, Natalia. Manager of Food Program (Comer Juntos en Familia) of an NGO (Coloba). Godoy Cruz City, Mendoza, Argentina, May 14, 2012.

Baylac, Gladys. Former Secretary of Social Development of the Province of San Luis. San Luis City, Argentina, June 22, 2012.

Becerra, Marcela. Director of Provincial Program (Plan Estratégico de Niñez y Adolescencia) of the Province of San Luis. San Luis City, Argentina, June 15, 2012.

Belem, Patricia. Coordinator of Estrategia Saúde da Família in the Municipality of Goiânia. Goiânia City, Goiás, Brazil, October 31, 2012.

Berrios, Gabriela. Coordinator of a Community Center (CIC-Borbollón) of the Municipality of Las Heras. Las Heras City, Mendoza, Argentina April 24, 2012.

Berti, Yolanda. Coordinator of Anses Mobile Unit of the Municipality of Villa Mercedes. Villa Mercedes City, San Luis, Argentina, June 12, 2012.

Bezerra, Valdi Camarcio. President of PT of the State of Goiás. Goiânia City, Goiás, Brazil, November 1, 2012.

Biffi, César. Former Mayor of the Municipality of Godoy Cruz and Provincial Deputy. Mendoza City, Argentina, May 10, 2012.

Boniatti, Maria Dani. Director of Social Assistance Reference Center (CRAS-Harmonia). Canoas City, Rio Grande do Sul, Brazil, September 24, 2012.

Borges, Danuzi. High Official at Department of Social Development of the Municipality of Porto Alegre (FASC). Porto Alegre City, Rio Grande do Sul, Brazil, September 10, 2012.

Bosio, Marcelo. Secretary of Health of the Municipality of Porto Alegre. Porto Alegre City, Rio Grande do Sul, Brazil, September 4, 2012.

Bragagnolo, María del Rosario. Director of Provincial Program (Programa Desarrollo y Protección Social) of the Province of San Luis. San Luis City, Argentina, June 17, 2012.

Brito, Rosana. Former Director of Social Development of the State of Rio Grande do Sul. Porto Alegre City, Rio Grande do Sul, September 26, 2012.

Britzke, Nadia Simone. Regional Coordinator of Primary Health Care of the State of Rio Grande do Sul. Porto Alegre City, Rio Grande do Sul, Brazil, October 1, 2012.

Calderón, Marcela. Representative of National Social Development Ministry in the Province of San Luis. San Luis City, Argentina, June 19, 2012.

Camara Pinto, Bruno. Advisor of National Ministry of Social Development (MDS). Brasília, Brazil, November 29, 2012.

Camargo, Karen Ramos. High Official at Social Assistance Reference Center (CRAS Extremo Sul). Porto Alegre City, Rio Grande do Sul, Brazil, September 3, 2012.

Capitanio, Carla. Director of Social Development of the State of Rio Grande do Sul. Porto Alegre City, Rio Grande do Sul, Brazil, October 1, 2012.

Cardello, Carlos. First Director of Plan Nacer of the Province of Mendoza and Director of Maternal and Child Health of the Province of Mendoza. Mendoza City, Mendoza, Argentina May 3, 2012.

Cardoso, Rogerio. Councilperson at the Health Council of the Municipality of Santa Maria do Herval. Santa Maria do Herval City, Rio Grande do Sul, Brazil, October 3, 2012.

Carrizo, Susana. Health Agent at Primary Health Center (Llorente Ruiz) of the Province of San Luis. San Luis City, Argentina, June 21, 2012.

Carvalho, Paola. High Official of State Program (RS Mais Renda Mais Igual) of the State of Rio Grande do Sul. Porto Alegre City, Rio Grande do Sul, Brazil, July 30, 2012.

Castagnino, Carlos Oscar. Director of Department of Provinces in the National Ministry of Interior. Buenos Aires, Argentina, October 5, 2011.

Castilhos Gomes, Jeanice. Regional Coordinator of Primary Health Care of the State of Rio Grande do Sul. Porto Alegre City, Rio Grande do Sul, Brazil, October 1, 2012.

Castro Cassiano, Tales. Advisor to PT in Brasília. Goiânia City, Goiás, Brazil, October 21, 2012.

Ceballos, Walter. Former Secretary of Provinces of the National Ministry of Interior and Former Governor Candidate of the Province of San Luis. San Luis City, Argentina, June 19, 2012.

Chaveiro, Mirella. Director of Primary Health Care of the Municipality of Valparaíso de Goiás. Valparaísode Goiás City, Goiás, Brazil, December 5, 2012.

Cobos, Julio. Former Vice-President of Argentina and Former Governor of the Province of Mendoza. Mendoza City, Argentina, May 16, 2012.

Conthe Astorga, Ingrid. Former Coordinator of Plan Jóvenes con Más y Mejor Trabajo of the Municipality of Las Heras. Mendoza City, Argentina, May 10, 2012.

Corengia, Carlos. Former Director of Employment Office of the Municipality of Las Heras. Las Heras City, Mendoza, Argentina, April 26, 2012.

Cornejo, Alfredo. Mayor of the Municipality of Godoy Cruz. Godoy Cruz City, Mendoza, Argentina, May 15, 2012.

Correa de Souza, Bruno. Coordinator of National Program (ProJovem Adolescente) at the Municipality of Valparaíso de Goiás. Valparaíso de Goiás City, Goiás, Brazil, November 26, 2012.

Costa Guadagnin, Simone. National Health Consultant. Brasília, Brazil, December 3, 2012.

Cristina. Neighborhood Leader (Referente Barrial) of Santo Tomás. Las Heras City, Mendoza, Argentina, May 7, 2012.

Da Peña, María Elvira. Manager of Plan Nacer at Hospital (Lentini). Mendoza City, Argentina, April 19, 2012.
Dariva, Maria Veronica. Councilperson of the Social Assistance Council of the Municipality of Porto Alegre. Porto Alegre City, Rio Grande do Sul, Brazil, October 5, 2012.
De Arimateia, Jose. Advisor of Chief of Staff of Municipality of Valparaíso de Goiás. Valparaíso de Goiás City, Goiás, Brazil, November 26, 2012.
De Camargo, Miriam. Director of Primary Health Care of the Municipality of Canoas. Canoas City, Rio Grande do Sul, Brazil, October 2, 2010.
De Farias Nobre, Rudilene. Secretary of Education of the Municipality of Valparaíso de Goiás. Valparaíso de Goiás City, Goiás, Brazil, November 26, 2012.
De Jesus, Maria Joaquina. President of Social Assistance Council of the State of Goiás. Goiânia City, Goiás, Brazil, October 31, 2012.
De Nascimento, Helizangela Alves. Coordinator of Social Assistance Reference Centers in the Municipality of Goiânia. Goiânia City, Goiás, Brazil, October 24, 2012.
De Oliveira. Kácius. Secretary of Labor Department of the Municipality of Goiânia. Goiânia City, Goiás, Brazil, October 29, 2012.
De Ponce, Janjir. Coordinator of Estrategia Saúde da Família at the Municipality of Novo Hamburgo. Novo Hamburgo City, Rio Grande do Sul, Brazil, October 11, 2012.
De Rose, Viviana. Director of Social Development of the Municipality of Villa Mercedes. Villa Mercedes City, San Luis, June 21, 2012.
De Souza Nolasco, Stefania. Councilperson of the Health Council of the Municipality of Goiânia. Goiânia City, Goiás, Brazil, November 8, 2012.
Dhein, Mario Antonio. President of Health Council of the Municipality of Canoas. Canoas City, Rio Grande do Sul, Brazil, October 9, 2012.
Di Chiacchio, Mariela. Press Secretary of Anses of the Municipality of San Luis. San Luis City, Argentina, June 5, 2012.
Di Cristófano, Carlos. Coordinator of Provincial Program (Plan de Inclusión Social) of the Province of San Luis. San Luis City, Argentina, May 29, 2012.
Diva, Cleu. Coordinator of National Program (ProJovem Urbano) at the Municipality of Goiânia. Goiânia City, Goiás, Brazil, November 23, 2012.
Domingues, Vanesa. High Official at the Department of Education of the Municipality of Canoas. Canoas City, Rio Grande do Sul, Brazil, October 10, 2012.
Dornelles, Gilberto. Coordinator of Programs at the Department of Youth of the Municipality of Porto Alegre. Porto Alegre City, Rio Grande do Sul, Brazil, September 14, 2012.
Dos Santos, Alberto Albino. National Coordinator of ProJovem Adolescente. Brasília, Brazil, December 4, 2012.
Dunker, Kelly. High Official of NGO (Centro Cultural James Kulisz, CEJAK). Porto Alegre City, Rio Grande do Sul, Brazil, August 31, 2012.
Dutra, Olivio. President of PT of the State of Rio Grande do Sul, Former Governor of the State of Rio Grande do Sul, and Former Mayor of the Municipality of Porto Alegre. Porto Alegre City, Rio Grande do Sul, October 9, 2012.
Edith. Neighborhood Leader (Referente Barrial) of Algarrobal. Las Heras City, Mendoza, Argentina, May 17, 2012.
Edson. Executive Secretary of the Social Assistance Council of the Municipality of Goiânia. Goiânia City, Goiás, Brazil, November 2, 2012.

Elizalde, Guillermo. Secretary of Social Development of the Province of Mendoza. Mendoza City, Argentina, May 10, 2012.

Espejo, Claudia. Private Secretary of the Department of Social Development of the Municipality of San Luis. San Luis City, Argentina, June 11, 2012.

Espinoza, Miriam. Undersecretary of Employment Office of the Municipality of Godoy Cruz. Godoy Cruz City, Mendoza, Argentina, April 25, 2012.

Fagundes, Sandra Sales. Director of Health of the State of Rio Grande do Sul and Former Secretary of Health of the Municipality of Porto Alegre. Porto Alegre City, Rio Grande do Sul, Brazil, October 4, 2012.

Farjado, Ana. Director of Primary Health Care of the Province of San Luis. San Luis City, Argentina, June 15, 2012.

Febre, Verónica. High Official of Provincial Program (Pasantías, Programa de Inclusión Social) of the Province of San Luis. San Luis City, Argentina, June 21, 2012.

Fernández, Marcela. Secretary of Social Development of the Municipality of Godoy Cruz. Godoy Cruz City, Mendoza, Argentina, May 5, 2012.

Frantz, Vânia Maria. Coordinator of Health Region (Partenon e Lomba do Pinheiro) in the Municipality of Porto Alegre. Porto Alegre City, Rio Grande do Sul, Brazil, September 13, 2012.

García, Claudia. Former Secretary of Health Planning of the Province of Mendoza. Mendoza City, Argentina, April 4, 2012.

García, Paulo. Mayor of the Municipality of Goiânia. Goiânia City, Goiás, Brazil, November 1, 2012.

Godoy, Roberto. Neighborhood Leader (Referente Barrial) of Campo Pappa. Godoy Cruz City, Mendoza, Argentina, May 14, 2012.

Goldar, Rosa. NGO Director (Fundación Ecuménica de Cuyo). Mendoza City, Argentina, March 30, 2012.

Gomes, Darcy. National Coordinator of ProJovem Urbano. Brasília, Brazil, December 7, 2012.

Gómez, Carlos. Founder of Newspaper (El Popular) and Advisor of Councilperson of the Municipality of San Luis. San Luis City, Argentina, June 14, 2012.

Gómez, Juan. Director of Newspaper (El Popular). San Luis City, Argentina, June 20, 2012.

Gómez, Martín. Director of Anses of the Municipality of Las Heras. Las Heras City, Mendoza, Argentina, April 24, 2012.

González, Fabiana. Director of the Ministry of Labor Branch in the Province of San Luis (GECAL). San Luis City, Argentina, May 28, 2012.

González, Germán. Secretary of Youth Department of the Municipality of Las Heras. Las Heras City, Mendoza, Argentina, May 17, 2012.

González, Pablo. Undersecretary of Social Development of the Province of San Luis. San Luis City, Argentina, June 6, 2012.

Guerreiro Osório, Rafael. Director of Social Studies and Policies (Disoc) at the Instituto de Pesquisa Economica Aplicada (IPEA). Brasília, Brazil, December 5, 2012.

Heguiabehere, Diego. Director of Health of Pedernera Region of the Province of San Luis. San Luis City, Argentina, June 12, 2012.

Hernández, José. Pastor (Iglesia Cristiana Evangélica Manantial de Vida) of Eva Perón Neighborhood. San Luis City, Argentina, June 19, 2012.

Janette. High Official at Social Assistance Reference Center (CRAS Leste). Porto Alegre City, Rio Grande do Sul, Brazil, September 6, 2012.

Jorge da Silva, Ademir. Secretary of Social Development of the Municipality of Canoas. Canoas City, Rio Grande do Sul, Brazil, September 24, 2012.

Knorst, Beno. Secretary of Health and Social Development of the Municipality of Santa Maria do Herval. Santa Maria do Herval City, Rio Grande do Sul, Brazil, October 3, 2012.

Kopittke, Alberto. Councilperson of the Municipality of Porto Alegre. Porto Alegre City, Rio Grande do Sul, Brazil, September 2, 2012.

Laborda, Juan José. Former Provincial Deputy (Frente Juntos por San Luis) of the Province of San Luis. San Luis City, Argentina, June 8, 2012.

Lagemann, Eugenio. Advisor of former Governor (Yeda Cursius) of the State of Rio Grande do Sul. Porto Alegre City, Rio Grande do Sul, Brazil, August 8, 2012.

Lecaro, Patricia. Advisor to Department of Social Development of the Province of Mendoza. Mendoza City, Argentina, March 29, 2012.

Lemis de Jesús, Venerando. President of the Health Council of the Municipality of Goiânia. Goiânia City, Goiás, Brazil, November 8, 2012.

Lermen, José Inacio. Director of Monitoring of Health Policies of the State of Rio Grande do Sul. Porto Alegre City, Rio Grande do Sul, Brazil, September 10, 2012.

Leyes, Analía. Coordinator of Health Agents of the Province of San Luis. San Luis City, Argentina, June 15, 2012.

Lewandowski, Telassim. Director of Women's Policies of the Municipality of Canoas. Canoas City, Rio Grande do Sul, Brazil, September 11, 2012.

Liese. High Official of Primary Health Care of the State of Rio Grande do Sul. Porto Alegre City, Rio Grande do Sul, Brazil, September 10, 2012.

Lima, Bernardo. Vice-President of the Health Council of the Municipality of Goiânia. Goiânia City, Goiás, Brazil, November 8, 2012.

Lisángela. High Official of Primary Health Care of the State of Rio Grande do Sul. Porto Alegre City, Rio Grande do Sul, Brazil, September 10, 2012.

Lobo, Christiane Baylão. Manager of Social Development Planning of the State of Goiás (SECT). Goiânia City, Goiás, Brazil, November 6, 2012.

López Conde, José. Advisor of National Senator (Daniel Pérsico). San Luis City, Argentina, June 25, 2012.

Lourdes, Elena. Councilperson at the Regional Council of Social Assistance of the Municipality of Porto Alegre. Porto Alegre City, Rio Grande do Sul, September 26, 2012.

Ludwig, Maria Judite. Councilperson at the Council of Social Assistance of the Municipality of Canoas. Canoas City, Rio Grande do Sul, Brazil, September 25, 2012.

Lumacagno, Gabriela. Coordinator of Provincial Program (Viviendas del Plan de Inclusión Social) of the Province of San Luis. San Luis City, Argentina, June 6, 2012.

Macagno, Luis. Chief of Staff of the Municipality of San Luis. San Luis City, Argentina, June 14, 2012.

Maccio, Carlos. Former Director of Health of the Municipality of Godoy Cruz. Godoy Cruz City, Mendoza, Argentina, May 3, 2012.

Machado, Selma. Coordinator of National Program (ProJovem Trabalhador) at the State of Rio Grande do Sul. Porto Alegre City, Rio Grande do Sul, Brazil, September 17, 2012.

Machado Freitas, Gorete. Coordinator of Bolsa Família at the Municipality of Valparaíso de Goiás. Valparaíso de Goiás City, Goiás, Brazil, November 26, 2012.

Magnaldi, Vanesa. Coordinator of Plan Jóvenes con Más y Mejor Trabajo at the Municipality of Godoy Cruz. Godoy Cruz City, Mendoza, Argentina, April 25, 2012.

Mallmann, Janine. Director of Social Assistance Reference Center (CRAS Leste). Porto Alegre City, Rio Grande do Sul, Brazil, August 23, 2012.

Manoni, Flavia. Director of Non-Contributory pensions of the Province of Mendoza. Mendoza City, Argentina, April 9, 2012.

Mardemattos, Rosi. Director of Basic Social Development of the Municipality of Canoas. Canoas City, Rio Grande do Sul, Brazil, September 19, 2012.

Mariz de Medeiros, Lorena Fonseca. National Coordinator of Integration of CCT Programs. Brasília, Brazil, November 28, 2012.

Martin, Irene. Coordinator of Provincial Food Program (Comer Juntos en Familia) of the Province of Mendoza. Mendoza City, Argentina, April 12, 2012.

Martines, Samy Alves. Coordinator of National Program (ProJovem Adolescente) at the Municipality of Goiânia. Goiânia City, Goiás, Brazil, October 23, 2012.

Martínez, Emilio. General Coordinator of Community Centers of the Municipality of Las Heras. Las Heras City, Mendoza, Argentina, April 24, 2012.

Martins, Paulo. Councilperson of Health Council of the Municipality of Canoas. Canoas City, Rio Grande do Sul, Brazil, October 9, 2012.

Massolo, Noemí. Director of the Right to Food Program (Comer Juntos en Familia) of the Province of Mendoza. Mendoza City, Argentina, April 10, 2012.

Mattar, Arminda. Director of Health of the Pueyrredón Region. San Luis City, June 22, 2012.

Maza, Dante. High Official of Social Development Department of the Municipality of Las Heras. Las Heras City, Mendoza, Argentina, April 23, 2012.

Medaglia, Walter. Director of Anses at the Municipality of Villa Mercedes. Villa Mercedes City, San Luis, Argentina, June 12, 2012.

Medeiros, Marlí. Neighborhood Leader (Dirigente Comunitaria) of Vila Pinto. Porto Alegre City, Rio Grande do Sul, Brazil, August 31, 2012.

Mercado, Mario. Coordinator of Plan Nacer at the Province of San Luis. San Luis City, Argentina, May 31, 2012.

Merlo, Mario Raúl. Mayor of the Municipality of Villa Mercedes. Villa Mercedes City, San Luis, Argentina, June 24, 2012.

Miatello, Ricardo. Director of Health Centers of the Province of Mendoza. Mendoza City, Argentina, May 2, 2012.

Miranda, Daniel. Former Coordinator of Primary Health Care of the Municipality of Godoy Cruz. Mendoza City, Argentina, April 24, 2012.

Miranda, Rubén. Mayor of the Municipality of Las Heras. Las Heras City, Mendoza, Argentina, May 8, 2012.

Morais da Silva, Vanesa. Coordinator of National Program (ProJovem Urbano) at the Municipality of Canoas. Canoas City, Rio Grande do Sul, Brazil, October 10, 2012.

Moyano, Rafael. Undersecretary of Social Development of the Province of Mendoza. Mendoza City, Argentina, May 10, 2012.

Moyano, Ulises. Creator of Provincial Program (Esquinas) of Mendoza. Mendoza City, Argentina, May 14, 2012.

Musotto, Mariano. Coordinator of Plan Nacer of the Province of Mendoza. Mendoza City, Argentina, May 11, 2012.

Musri, Gustavo. Director of Primary Health Care of the Municipality of Las Heras. Las Heras City, Mendoza, Argentina, May 4, 2012.

Natal Cemin, César. Coordinator of National Programs (ProJovem Urbano, Trabalhador) at the Municipality of Canoas. Canoas City, Rio Grande do Sul, Brazil, October 1, 2012.

Netto Fayad, Mauro. Secretary of Science and Technology of the State of Goiás. Goiânia City, Goiás, Brazil, November 8, 2012.

Nichimura, Elso. Technical Secretary of Social Development of the Municipality of Porto Alegre (FASC). Porto Alegre City, Rio Grande do Sul, Brazil, September 10, 2012.

Nieto, Franco. Director of Training Provincial Program (Primer Empleo) of the Province of San Luis. San Luis City, Argentina, May 24, 2012.

Nievas, Patricia. Consultant of Asignación Universal por Hijo in the Municipality of Villa Mercedes. Villa Mercedes City, San Luis, Argentina, June 21, 2012.

Ninov, Daniel. High Official of State Program (RS Mais Renda Mais Igual) of the State of Rio Grande do Sul. Porto Alegre City, Rio Grande do Sul, Brazil, July 30, 2012.

Nunes, Maria Izabel. Former Secretary of Social Development of the State of Rio Grande do Sul. Porto Alegre City, Rio Grande do Sul, October 4, 2012.

Nunes de Freitas, Christiane. Director of Primary Health Care of the Municipality of Porto Alegre. Porto Alegre City, Rio Grande do Sul, Brazil, August 20, 2012.

Nuñez, Fernando. Director of Administration of Plan Nacer at the Province of San Luis. San Luis City, Argentina, May 24, 2012.

Olegário, Assis. High Official of State Program (RS Mais Renda Mais Igual) of the State of Rio Grande do Sul. Porto Alegre City, Rio Grande do Sul, Brazil, August 8, 2012.

Olguín, Jorge. Former Candidate to Vice-Mayor of the Municipality of Villa Mercedes. San Luis City, Argentina, June 13, 2012.

Olmos, Andrea. Director of Plan Nacer in Hospital (Policlinico Regional Juan D. Perón) at the Province of San Luis. San Luis City, Argentina, Villa Mercedes City, San Luis, Argentina, June 12, 2012.

Osch, Zenaite. High Official at the Department of Education of the Municipality of Canoas. Canoas City, Rio Grande do Sul, Brazil, October 10, 2012.

Paulizzi, Anabella. Secretary of Family Agriculture of the Province of San Luis. San Luis City, Argentina, June 1, 2012.

Peralta, Rubén. National Director of Communication with Provinces, Ministry of Social Development. Buenos Aires, Argentina, September 22, 2011.

Pereira, Cassiê. Coordinator of National Policy (Projovem Aldolescente) at the Municipality of Porto Alegre. Porto Alegre City, Rio Grande do Sul, Brazil, September 12, 2012.

Pettignano, Diego. Director of the Ministry of Labor Branch in the Province of Mendoza (GECAL). Mendoza City, Argentina, May 15, 2012.

Pinto, Hêider Aurelio. National Director of Primary Health. Brasília, Brazil, December 3, 2012.

Pinto, Juliana. High Official at the Department of Health of the Municipality of Porto Alegre. Porto Alegre City, Rio Grande do Sul, Brazil, August 17, 2012.

Pisonique, Marli. Former Secretary of Social Development of the Municipality of Canoas. Canoas City, Rio Grande do Sul, Brazil, October 2, 2010.

Ponce, Moira. Director of NGO (Vamos Juntos) and Former Councilperson of the City of San Luis. San Luis City, Argentina, June 14, 2012.

Quintana, Ariel. Territorial Delegate of the Municipality of Las Heras in El Borbollón. Las Heras City, Mendoza, July 5, 2012.

Rabelo, Mercedes. High Official at Statistics Department of the State of Rio Grande do Sul. Porto Alegre City, Rio Grande do Sul, Brazil, September 12, 2012.

Rassi, Elias. Secretary of Health of the Municipality of Goiânia. Goiânia City, Goiás, Brazil, November 5, 2012.

Reales, Adriana. Co-Director of an NGO (Coloba). Godoy Cruz City, Mendoza, Argentina, May 14, 2012.

Regane Alves, Susana. High Official of NGO (Centro Cultural James Kulisz, CEJAK). Porto Alegre City, Rio Grande do Sul, Brazil, August 31, 2012.

Regina de Moraes, Flavia. President of the Municipal Council of Social Assistance of the Municipality of Goiânia. Goiânia City, Goiás, Brazil, November 7, 2012.

Rezende Machado, Iris. Former Governor of the State of Goiás, Former Mayor of the Municipality of Goiânia, Former Federal Senator, and Former National Minister of Agriculture. Goiânia City, Goiás, Brazil, November 1, 2012.

Ribeiro, Carmen. Director of State Program (Bolsa Futuro) of the State of Goiás. Goiânia City, Goiás, Brazil, November 8, 2012.

Ribeiro, Janice. High Official at NGO (Centro Cultural James Kulisz, CEJAK). Porto Alegre City, Rio Grande do Sul, Brazil, August 31, 2012.

Ribeiro Guimarães, Patricia. Director of Social Development (SECT) of the State of Goiás. Goiânia City, Goiás, Brazil, October 23, 2012.

Rodriguez Assaf, Alberto. Former Director of Primary Health Care of the Province of Mendoza. Mendoza City, Argentina, April 12, 2012.

Rodriguez, Inajara. High Official of Estrategia Saúde da Família at the State of Rio Grande do Sul. Porto Alegre City, Rio Grande do Sul, Brazil, September 18, 2012.

Rodríguez Saá, Alberto. Former Governor of the Province of San Luis. San Luis City, Argentina, June 21, 2012.

Rodriguez Vieira, Patricia. Regional Coordinator of National Program (ProJovem Adolescente) at the Municipality of Porto Alegre. Porto Alegre City, Rio Grande do Sul, Brazil, September 14, 2012.

Rosa, Gilmar. President of the Council of Social Assistance of the Municipality of Canoas. Canoas City, Rio Grande do Sul, Brazil, September 25, 2012.

Rousselet de Alencar, Heloisa Helena. High Official of the Health Council of the Municipality of Porto Alegre. Porto Alegre City, Rio Grande do Sul, Brazil, August 15, 2012.

Ruggeri, Silvia. Former Secretary of Social Development of the Province of Mendoza. Mendoza City, Argentina, April 4, 2012.

Russo, Andrés. Director of Information Control in Ministry of Social Inclusion of the Province of San Luis. San Luis City, Argentina, May 29, 2012.

Sabignoso, Martín. National Director of Plan Nacer, Argentina. (Phone Interview) May 30, 2013.

Salcedo, Ivana. Volunteer of Soup Kitchen (Comedor Virgen del Valle). Godoy Cruz City, Mendoza, Argentina, May 14, 2012.

Salomón, Fanny. Planning Manager of the Department of Social Development of the Municipality of Godoy Cruz. Godoy Cruz City, Mendoza, Argentina, May 8, 2012.

Samper, José. Former General Attorney of the Province of San Luis. San Luis City, Argentina, June 26, 2012.

Sandra. High Official of Primary Health Care of the State of Rio Grande do Sul. Porto Alegre City, Rio Grande do Sul, Brazil, September 10, 2012.

Sant'ana de Lima, Ciro. Regional Coordinator of Vigilance in Health of the State of Rio Grande do Sul. Porto Alegre City, Rio Grande do Sul, Brazil, October 1, 2012.

Santos, Carmen. Councilperson at the Regional Council of Social Assistance of the Municipality of Porto Alegre. Porto Alegre City, Rio Grande do Sul, September 26, 2012.

Santos, Fernanda. Coordinator of Estrategia Saúde da Família at the Municipality of Canoas. Canoas City, Rio Grande do Sul, Brazil, September 25, 2012.

Santos, Leandro. Secretary of Health of the Municipality of Canoas. Canoas City, Rio Grande so Sul, Brazil, September 25, 2012.

Santos, Lucrecia. Director of Social Programs of the Municipality of Villa Mercedes. Villa Mercedes City, San Luis, Argentina, June 21, 2012.

Sanzi Souza, Djalmo. Former Manager of Hospital Conglomerate (Grupo Hospitalar Conceição). Porto Alegre City, Rio Grande do Sul, Brazil, October 10, 2012.

Saracco, Sergio. Former Secretary of Health of the Province of Mendoza. Mendoza City, Argentina, April 19, 2012.

Saralago, Liliana. Health Agent of the Municipality of Godoy Cruz. Godoy Cruz City, Mendoza, Argentina, May 3, 2012.

Saravia de Abreú, Mayra Regina. Former Advisor of Social Assistance in the State of Goiás. Goiânia City, Goiás, Brazil, November 2, 2012.

Schiller Thomas, Miriam. Secretary of Social Assistance Council of the Municipality of Porto Alegre. Porto Alegre City, Rio Grande do Sul, October 8, 2012.

Schmidt, Davi Luiz. Director of Citizen Participation of the State of Rio Grande do Sul. Porto Alegre City, Rio Grande do Sul, October 1, 2012.

Seadi, Marco Antonio. Secretary of Social Development of the Municipality of Porto Alegre (FASC). Porto Alegre City, Rio Grande do Sul, Brazil, September 17, 2012.

Serú, Alberto. Secretary of Social Development of the Municipality of Las Heras. Las Heras City, Mendoza, Argentina. May 4, 2012.

Servo, Luciana Mendes Santos. Coordinator of Health at Instituto de Pesquisa Econômica Aplicada (IPEA). Brasília, Brazil, December 4, 2012.

Silva de Paiva, Henrique. National Secretary of Social Development (MDS). Brasília, Brazil, December 3, 2012.

Silva de Souza, Salete. Director of Social Assistance Reference Center (CRAS-Guajuviras). Canoas City, Rio Grande do Sul, Brazil, October 2, 2010.

Soares Tannús, Erika. Manager of Training Activities of the State of Goiás. Goiânia City, Goiás, Brazil, October 26, 2012.

Soria, Arnaldo. Director of Provincial Program (Plan de Forestación) of the Province of San Luis. San Luis City, Argentina, June 6, 2012.

Souza, Lucia Elena. Coordinator of Bolsa Família in the Municipality of Porto Alegre. Porto Alegre City, Rio Grande do Sul, Brazil, September 6, 2012.

Spessatto, Rosane Ines. Director of Social Assistance Reference Center (CRAS Mathias Velho). Canoas City, Rio Grande do Sul, Brazil, September 24, 2012.

Spoliansky, Patricia. NGO Director (Federación de Entidades de Niñez y Adolescencia de Mendoza). Mendoza City, Argentina, April 20, 2012.

Tabosa, Germana. Secretary of Social Development of the Municipality of Valparaíso de Goiás. Valparaíso de Goiás City, Goiás, Gracil, November 26, 2012.

Teixeira, Solange. Advisor of National Ministry of Social Development (MDS). Brasília, Brazil, November 29, 2012.

Teixera Bagattini, Carmen Luisa. Director of Primary Health Care of the State of Rio Grande do Sul. Porto Alegre City, Rio Grande do Sul, Brazil, September 10, 2012.

Témoli, Gastón. Director of Anses at the Municipality of San Luis City. San Luis City, Argentina, June 5, 2012.

Tévez, Jorge. Councilperson of the Municipality of Godoy Cruz and Former Secretary of Social Development of the Municipality of Godoy Cruz. Godoy Cruz City, Mendoza, Argentina, April 27, 2012.

Timmen, Elaine. Director of NGO (Aelca). Porto Alegre City, Rio Grande do Sul, Brazil, September 6, 2012.

Toazza Tura, Lourdes Maria. High Official of the Health Department of the Municipality of Porto Alegre. Porto Alegre City, Rio Grande do Sul, Brazil, August 21, 2012.

Torres Guimarães, Claudia. National Director of Education Policies for Young People. Brasília, Brazil, December 7, 2012.

Torti, Luciana. Director of Education Program at NGO (Vínculos Estratégicos). Las Heras City, Mendoza, Argentina, May 17, 2012.

Traversi, María Fernanda. Consultant of Asignación Universal por Hijo in the Municipality of Villa Mercedes. Villa Mercedes City, San Luis, Argentina, June 21, 2012.

Tula Barale, Federico. Secretary of Social Development of the Province of San Luis. San Luis City, Argentina, June 5, 2012.

Valla, Ana María. Coordinator of NGO (Fundación para el Desarrollo Humano y Regional). San Luis City, Argentina, June 13, 2012.

Varcalcel, Carlos. Secretary of Health of the Municipality of Godoy Cruz. Godoy Cruz City, Mendoza, Argentina, May 3, 2012.

Vecchio, Kizzy. Former Coordinator of National Programs (ProJovem Urbano, Trabalhador) at the Municipality of Porto Alegre. Porto Alegre City, Rio Grande do Sul, October 11, 2012.

Velloso, Marizete. Director of Social Assistance Reference Center (CRAS Extremo Sul). Porto Alegre City, Rio Grande do Sul, Brazil, September 2, 2012.

Vergés, Alfonso. Former Mayor of the Municipality of San Luis. San Luis City, Argentina, June 26, 2012.

Verle, João. Former Mayor of the Municipality of Porto Alegre. Porto Alegre City, Rio Grande do Sul, Brazil, October 13, 2012.

Vilar da Cunha, Heverson. Councilmember of the Health and Participatory Budgeting Councils of the Municipality of Porto Alegre. Porto Alegre City, Rio Grande do Sul, Brazil, August 21, 2012.

Wanize. High Official of Primary Health Care of the East/North-East Region of Porto Alegre. Porto Alegre City, Rio Grande do Sul, Brazil, August 20, 2012.

Zamora, Inés. High Official of the Department of Health of the Municipality of Godoy Cruz. Godoy Cruz City, Mendoza, Argentina, May 3, 2012.

Zlotolow, Alejandro. Director of Employment Office at the Municipality of GodoyCruz. Godoy Cruz City, Mendoza, April 24, 2012.

Index

For EU product safety concerns, contact us at Calle de José Abascal, 56–1°,
28003 Madrid, Spain or eugpsr@cambridge.org.

www.ingramcontent.com/pod-product-compliance
Ingram Content Group UK Ltd.
Pitfield, Milton Keynes, MK11 3LW, UK
UKHW010036140625
459647UK00012BA/1428